"The number one question Christian ʋ _____ the older women?' Singles, wives, and moms want to know God's plan for them and are looking for help with how to live it out. Here, in one priceless volume, is instruction from the Bible and practical guidance from women who know how to make God's teachings a daily reality. From time and life management skills, to building better relationships and much more, every chapter points women toward honoring and pleasing God while blessing others."

Elizabeth George, Jim & Elizabeth George Ministries

"Characterized by distinctive, if not countercultural, ideas for our twenty-first-century world, readers will discover in this new resource a most interesting collection of thoughtful essays on the important subjects of home and hospitality, as well as spiritual and personal health. The contributions found in this volume will be helpful for individuals, groups, and churches. This handbook will be one that many will want to keep on hand."

David and Lanese Dockery, President and First Lady, Union University

"Dr. Dorothy Patterson and Dr. Pat Ennis have performed an invaluable service to the body of Christ by rescuing the word 'homemaker' from liberals who equate the title with 'doormat.' As Dr. Patterson so aptly illustrates, the role of a homemaker is as challenging—and certainly more consequential—than that of any CEO in a Fortune 500 company. The timeless truths found in these pages will motivate every woman to pursue with passion her God-given calling and will encourage every husband to honor his wife as a 'fellow heir of the grace of life.'"

Robert Jeffress, Senior Pastor, First Baptist Church, Dallas, Texas

"Being a wife and mother are some of the greatest and highest forms of Christian servanthood. In this book, a variety of authors help show, in a very positive way, God's grand design. Without casting aspersions upon anyone who chooses to work outside the home, these authors also point to the fact that many women are rediscovering powerful fulfillment by discovering anew God's design for the home. Many women choose to be a part of that group called Christian homemakers. There is no more challenging task. There is no more draining vocation. There is no more important task in all the world. Listen carefully to these wonderful authors and their well thought out words of advice, counsel, and instruction."

Frank S. Page, President & CEO, Executive Committee of the Southern Baptist Convention

"One of the great scandals of the last several decades has been the popular scorn heaped on the home economy, and particularly the homemaker. All the same, even in 2013 and after fifty years of feminist complaints, half of all economic activity in America still occurs in homes—and the most important half by far. In *The Christian Homemaker's Handbook*, Pat Ennis and Dorothy Patterson provide a lively, cogent, and practical guide for women seeking to understand and fulfill their 'God-assigned prioirities.' The authors correctly affirm that God's design for the home, as laid out in Genesis, has not changed and that young women will find the fullest meaning and the greatest happiness in their bonds to husbands and children and in their commitments to home-building. The book also properly emphasizes the importance of hospitality, a welcoming spirit, and a gracious heart to the vital Christian home."

Allan C. Carlson, President, The Howard Center for Family, Religion, & Society; Founder and International Secretary, the World Congress of Families; Distinguished Visiting Professor of History, Hillsdale College

The
CHRISTIAN
HOMEMAKER'S
HANDBOOK

The
CHRISTIAN

homemaker's

HANDBOOK

edited by

Pat Ennis & Dorothy Kelley Patterson

Foreword by W. Mark Lanier

⁞⁞ CROSSWAY

WHEATON, ILLINOIS

The Christian Homemaker's Handbook

Copyright © 2013 by Patricia Ann Ennis and Dorothy Kelley Patterson

Published by Crossway
        1300 Crescent Street
        Wheaton, Illinois 60187

Cover design: Connie Gabbert

Cover image: iStock

Interior design: Kevin Lipp

First printing 2013

Printed in the United States of America

Scripture quotations unless otherwise indicated are from the ESV® Bible (*The Holy Bible, English Standard Version®*), copyright © 2001 by Crossway. 2011 Text Edition. Used by permission. All rights reserved.

Scripture quotations marked KJV are from the *King James Version* of the Bible.

Scripture quotations marked NASB are from *The New American Standard Bible®*. Copyright © The Lockman Foundation 1960, 1962, 1963, 1968, 1971, 1972, 1973, 1975, 1977, 1995. Used by permission.

Scripture references marked NLT are from *The Holy Bible, New Living Translation*, copyright © 1996, 2004. Used by permission of Tyndale House Publishers, Inc., Wheaton, IL, 60189. All rights reserved.

All emphases in Scripture quotations have been added by the authors.

Trade paperback ISBN: 978-1-4335-2838-5
PDF ISBN: 978-1-4335-2839-2
Mobipocket ISBN: 978-1-4335-2840-8
ePub ISBN: 978-1-4335-2841-5

Library of Congress Cataloging-in-Publication Data

The Christian homemaker's handbook / [edited by] Pat
Ennis and Dorothy Kelley Patterson.
    pages   cm
  ISBN 978-1-4335-2838-5 (tp)
  ISBN 978-1-4335-2839-2 (pdf)
  ISBN 978-1-4335-2840-8 (mobipocket)
  ISBN 978-1-4335-2841-5 (epub)
  1. Home economics—Religious aspects—Christianity.
2. Christian women—Conduct of life. 3. Home—Religious
aspects—Christianity. I. Ennis, Pat, editor of compilation.
II. Patterson, Dorothy Kelley, 1943– editor of compilation.
TX295.C485   2013
248.8'43—dc23   2012035469

Crossway is a publishing ministry of Good News Publishers.

This book is dedicated to
Drs. Tim and Beverly LaHaye
Your vision to develop a character-based
home economics curriculum and perpetuate
it made this volume possible.

From Dorothy:
A word of gratitude to my husband, Paige Patterson,
who has allowed and encouraged me to give my
full energies and best creativity to home and
family, and to Armour, Rachel, Mark, Carmen,
Abigail, and Rebekah for giving to me joy beyond
expression as a mother and grandmother.

From Pat:
Special thanks to Carella DeVol, Pat's best
earthly friend. Your moral support, enthusiasm,
and consistent prayer on all aspects of my
ministry are a constant source of blessing.

Contents

Acknowledgments

The creation of *The Christian Homemaker's Handbook* has been a team effort, and we are indebted to many individuals. Across the years some godly administrators cast a vision to develop a character-based home economics curriculum and to perpetuate that program in institutions of higher education. To do so meant to move against the tide of secularism and humanism devaluing the family and especially denigrating the homemaker, who has always been the heart and driving force in managing the family household. We are indebted to **Tim LaHaye**, who challenged Pat Ennis to begin such a program at Christian Heritage College; to **John MacArthur**, who continued that vision at The Master's College; and now to **Paige Patterson** who brought the visions of Pat Ennis and Dorothy Patterson together at Southwestern Baptist Theological Seminary with degrees offered at both baccalaureate and master's levels.

The vision and creativity poured into this unique and timely volume have gone far beyond our dreams and expectations. The **twenty-two contributors** are widespread geographically from coast to coast, generationally from youth to maturity of years, and in lifestyle choices from educators to ministry vocations to marketplace roles; yet these daughters, sisters, wives, mothers, and grandmothers all have a commitment to the importance of homemaking wherever and in whatever season they find themselves.

We are also indebted to the **publication team**. Their commitment to excellence made this partnership in the ministry of the written word a joy. **Jill Carter**, our liaison at Crossway, has extended a myriad of kindnesses to us. **Al Fisher's** enthusiasm for *The Christian Homemaker's Handbook* has been evident from our initial contact to the project's completion. **Laura Talcott's** keen eye for details and editing skills clarified the content and message of *The Christian Homemaker's Handbook*. **Amy Kruis** caught and supported our vision for both the volume and the concept of "The Art of Homemaking: Making Your House a Home" conference.

The students in our classes from the five institutions we have collectively served throughout our professional sojourns have completed their assignments and participated in surveys that contributed to the compilation of this volume. They willingly shared their time and thoughts to add depth, breadth, and critical data to the book. *Tamra Hernandez* and *Shannon McHenry Roelofs* have worked on the details of manuscript preparation, allowing us to present the book to Crossway in a polished format.

A NOTE FROM DOROTHY KELLEY PATTERSON:

My homemaking journey began in my childhood home with the extraordinary example of my mother, *Doris Weisiger Kelley*, who taught me by word and deed unselfish devotion to home care, and the parallel mentoring of *Roberta "Honey" Patterson*, who wanted her son to have a prepared home and accordingly equipped me with many skills and inspired my creativity in the task. My husband, *Paige*, has faithfully provided, protected, and exercised godly servant leadership over half a century of marriage. Our children enriched our home and added to the family circle: *Armour* brought us a daughter-in-love, *Rachel*; *Carmen* gave us a son-in-love, *Mark*. Then came the "grandest touch" with Carmen and Mark's daughters—*Abigail* and *Rebekah*!

A NOTE FROM PAT ENNIS:

My mother, *Mary Ann Ennis*, taught me by example and nurturing to be a "keeper at home" while my seventh grade home economics teacher, *Ellen H. Osborn*, inspired me to teach the younger women (Titus 2:3–5). *Carella DeVol* has provided moral support, enthusiasm, and consistent prayer support for all aspects of our ministry. She is a constant source of blessing to me.

May *our heavenly Father*, who established the foundation for the home in his holy Word and then provided the strength to apply those principles to daily living, accept our love and gratitude and grant to us the privilege of mentoring and inspiring you in your journey to make your home the best ever and a fragrance to him.

Foreword

W. Mark Lanier

For almost three thousand years, wise people have asked the question:

> An excellent wife who can find? (Prov. 31:10)

The Proverbs answer that question in the very next phrase:

> She is far more precious [and rare] than jewels. (v. 10)

If possible, this is even truer today than it was when written. We live in an age where the media informs women what it means to be successful, and rarely is that message congruent with what it means to be an "excellent wife." From the earliest age, girls are taught by what they watch on television, by what they hear on the radio, and by what they read or see on the computer—that success is found in independence, in economics, and in beauty. Yet real independence, real purpose in economics, and true beauty are not often portrayed. The skewed vision is more typically one that makes the girl-turned-woman the center of focus and attention. Independence is valued for the woman who reports to no one and needs nothing. Economics is seen as the drive for consumption and personal satisfaction. Beauty is first and foremost, skin-deep. It is built to a standard made possible only by Photoshop, personal trainers, and the best plastic surgeons.

Unfortunately, the media message is wrong. The real jewels among women are those who rise to the godly level of praise found in Proverbs 31:10–31. The Proverbs passage forms the backbone of this book, even as it forms the character and life of godly women. As a man blessed to live in the midst of Proverbs 31 women, I can testify firsthand to the truth of this message as well as the importance of this book. My marvelous wife Becky exemplifies Proverbs 31, as do my mother, my two sisters, and day by day, our four maturing daughters.

When I first met my wife, she was in middle school, two grades behind me. While she caught my eye early on, it was not simply because she was pretty! Her personality was shown in everything she said and did. Her kindness was apparent to all as she cared about others more than herself, even at the age of fourteen. She was smart, but not showy about it. She was talented, but never flashy. She was popular, but went out of her way to befriend those alone. She knew how to encourage, how to make people laugh, and how to make others feel important. It was no surprise she was always voted "Class Favorite" by the students. The faculty gave her the "I dare you" and "Hall of Fame" awards. By the time she graduated high school, she was voted "Most Likely to Succeed."

She continued on the path to "success" taking her national debate talent from high school, her dexterity in multiple languages, and her high grade point average to college where she ultimately amassed more degrees than a thermometer. She took a bachelor's degree in international trade, a master's degree in Spanish, two law degrees, lived as a rotary fellowship representative in Argentina, and prepared for a "successful" life with great energy and passion. The law firms fought over a chance to have her, and the men lined up outside her door hoping to win her affections! (By my count, she turned down five engagement rings before I cajoled her into accepting mine!)

With this background, and with this talent set, Becky could have done anything in her life she wanted. And she did exactly what she wanted. She settled into a marriage with me where she applied her strong gifts and talents into her truest passion, being the best wife and mother she could possibly be.

My oh my, what a blessing she is to our family. Her days start early, getting in her quiet time before she wakes our two daughters still at home (our son and two of our daughters are already in graduate school). She makes them breakfast, packs their lunches, and typically drives some set of children in some carpool tandem. She stays active as "team mom" in multiple sports and school activities, serves in the Parent Teacher Organization, volunteers her teaching for the school's debate and speech program, and is found serving concessions at volleyball games. In the process, she stays plugged into both my legal work and my ministry efforts. She runs multiple events for the law firm, travels with me as much as possible, and is constantly planning one church event or another. She stays active with our extended family, runs our home, regularly makes costumes for any and all parties or events, strives to ensure that we are all well fed (combining sound nutrition with great flavor), keeps us up to date with doctors and dentists, keeps the pets up to date with all shots and medicines—and somehow keeps her car clean in the process.

In the midst of all this, she constantly amazes me not only for all she does, but for how she does it. She recognizes the importance of sleep. She knows the importance of prioritizing. She knows when too much is too much and when she needs downtime. She gets alone time, not by sacrificing what she does for others, but by careful planning. She thus ensures her batteries are charged so she can do for others. Her greatest joys are achieved when she sees her family happy and successful. She knows that is fruit from labor! Most importantly, she knows that she can achieve nothing, nor is anything she achieves of merit, absent the strength and love of the Lord.

Proverbs 31 is right—such a woman is more precious than jewels and is hard to find. I pray that all young men search for their helpmates and companions by seeking those who are not bent on becoming what they see on television, but rather on what they learn from the Lord. For Proverbs 31 ends instructively:

> Charm is deceitful, and beauty is vain,
>> but a woman who fears the LORD is to be praised.
> Give her of the fruit of her hands,
>> and let her works praise her in the gates. (Prov. 31:30–31)

Introduction

Why Do We Need to Recover Biblical
Patterns for Homemaking?

Dorothy Kelley Patterson

A woman makes choices on what quantity and quality of her time to invest in her home. Her task is overwhelming. She cares for husband and children; she maintains and directs the household with planning and creativity; she coordinates scheduling for the family; she is the catalyst for getting all household tasks done efficiently and effectively; she is on call for emergencies within the extended family, as well as volunteering in the church and community for unpaid tasks that serve society—from the local neighborhood to the international scene. Yet in a sense the homemaker has been sidelined for more than half a century. She is considered a nonperson by many who do not see value in her work. She does not have what others consider a respectable title for her position, and she lacks a clear job description of what is considered worthwhile work. She does not receive a salary for her work. She just does what needs to be done to get the job done!

The modern culture seems to be marked by frantic busyness and "to do" lists in every avenue of life except the home. Even those who choose homemaking sometimes tend to immerse themselves in volunteerism and projects that might lead to recognition and accolades from outsiders, such as the church and community. Other women are looking for a professional pursuit that produces pocketbook rewards. Most believe that the biblical model for a homemaker, who devotes her freshest energies and most of her time to keeping her home, is obsolete. To help your husband and nurture your children has often been rejected in this great age of enlightenment and in the throes of the modern faltering national economy. As maternal nurturing wanes in importance, mothers are eager to cut the apron strings from their babies and get them up and moving self-sufficiently into the world as quickly as possible.

Day care is so interwoven into maternal life that sometimes a child is placed on a waiting list for institutional care from the moment of conception in an attempt to find the best option in light of the tragedies associated with this surrogate care. Institutional care has become the norm from birth onward. Nutrition has evolved into reading labels on prepared food or exchanging drive-through fast food for gourmet-café takeout. In reality, the so-called liberation from feministic ideology has introduced a heavy dose of personal rights and self-fulfillment in modern women, who are drawn more to the right of personal achievement than to the responsibility of family care.

But one must not count God out in this battle for the future of marriage and the family and for the survival of the most precious product—the next generation or those who follow after. From creation God placed in the heart of every woman a maternal drive consisting of a natural nesting instinct, a passion for protecting her child and preparing her offspring for living in the world. However hard the world seeks to invert a woman's God-given priorities, a remnant of those committed to God's plan for the home are pulling for that woman to dig in and seize the opportunity to rear her own children in an earthly shelter she fashions and directs for that very purpose.

Every work has its mundane tasks. To enter the world's marketplace, whatever the prestigious position or lucrative compensation, does not ensure the absence of boredom or the lack of fatigue resulting from hard work. The question is not whether a woman wants the best for her husband and children or even for herself. Rather the matter to consider is this: Is being someone's wife and another's mother really worth the investment of energies, creativity, and a life of sacrifice and hard work? What is necessary to keep a home? Do you need skills? Is it necessary to plan and prepare all along the journey?

Every evangelical woman agrees that Scripture contains timeless and unchanging principles. Such principles form the foundation of living the Christian life and managing a household God's way. However, the problem comes in determining exactly what principles are timeless. Here every woman must continually "test the spirits" against the Word of God (1 John 4:1). What is the ultimate consideration—your own experience, the culture in which you live, or the words written in an ancient book—God's Holy Word?

Every professional pursuit requires training and preparation as well as commitment to the task and dedication to do it well, and this book is our affirmation that homemaking is worthy of this effort as well. The activities are ongoing, and successful advancement is seldom without a cost to be paid in energy, time, and even creativity if you do well. In the modern era, finding anyone who is professionally prepared and motivated to do a job regardless of payment or recognition seems rare. The diversity of opportunities for women in the modern era should not prompt the neglect of God-assigned priorities for their respective responsibilities. If any professional person gives the most productive part of her day to peripheral chores or other commitments, neglecting the use of primary energies and freshest creativity for the most important responsibility, her main job falls victim to mediocrity. Generalities in services rendered and opportunities embraced must be governed and guided by specific purpose and needed preparation.

Homemaking is indeed a career in the sense that it demands a woman's careful diligence in preparation, dedicated commitment to priorities associated with the assignment, freshest energy, and keenest creativity. Most dictionaries define the homemaker as "one who manages a household especially as a wife and mother."[1] Though the homemaker does her job with no expectation of a salary (much less financial bonuses and perks), she cannot duplicate her services for any amount of money (Prov. 31:10). Dorothy Morrison wrote,

> Homemaking is not employment for slothful, unimaginative, incapable women. It has as much challenge and opportunity, success and failure, growth and expansion, perks and incentives, as any corporate career.[2]

Statistics suggest that top priority is assigned to the importance of family life—ranking it even above financial security.[3] Pouring your time and energies into the lives of the people you love most is a rewarding task. Many people are surprised to learn how much time and energy it takes to run a household and care for a family. From my experience, having a marketplace career was far easier than being a homemaker. In the marketplace, I was never called to be on duty twenty-four hours a day, nor have I ever needed the variety of skills and myriad of abilities I have used in managing my household. Laborsaving devices do make my life easier, but the time saved becomes capital to be invested in the lives of my husband and children and in service to others. No professional pursuit so uniquely combines the most menial tasks with the most meaningful opportunities.

When a woman chooses to pursue homemaking with energy, imagination, and skills, she accepts a challenging task. As well as meeting the mundane needs of her family efficiently and completely, she also often finds the time to enrich lives with her tender loving care—encouraging and guiding, counseling or comforting. She is available to divide sorrow or share rejoicing, making the ones most dear to her the first priority in time and the most important work of her life.

---

[1] *Merriam-Webster Online Dictionary* (2010), s.v. "homemaker," March 4, 2010, http://www.merriam-webster.com/dictionary/homemaker.

[2] Dorothy Morrison, "My Turn," *Newsweek*, October 17, 1988, 14.

[3] Dorothy Kelley Patterson, *Where's Mom? The High Calling of Wives and Mothers* (Wheaton, IL: Crossway, 2003), 18.

Why would a woman want to read a book on being a homemaker? After almost half a century of marriage with opportunities to minister to women along the way, here are some goals in my heart for this project:

- A woman can learn the biblical model for the home and family through answers to theological questions like: Why did God design the family at the dawn of creation? Who makes up the family? How do they interface with one another?
- Who should be concerned about establishing a home? Does age, marital status, giftedness, and training have a part?
- What skills are needed to manage a household? How do you acquire those skills?
- Is homemaking to be distinctive when working from a biblical perspective? Are there resources, rituals, and steps to the practical implementation of this kind of homemaking?

Unfortunately, society has suffered some serious blows from the advance of feminism into the heart of the family. The survey done by Pat Ennis, which is described and evaluated in chapter 1, started our thinking and motivated us to move forward in this task. Clearly women want something more.

Preparation for this journey begins with God's design for the home as discussed in Genesis—that is, the creation order. God's principle for marriage as given at creation (Gen. 2:24) and then repeated three times in the New Testament (Matt. 19:4–6; Mark 10:5–9; Eph. 5:31) gives the foundation for a monogamous and permanent union. The paradigm for a homemaker as described in Proverbs 31 will be a pattern to study and embrace. The importance of the extended family is clearly established. These principles established in biblical foundations lift up a banner and call for a standard that is old in its origins but new in its rallying call.

The sanctity of life cannot be separated from the family. The value of a child as well as the discussion of troubling issues faced by women who are making choices concerning birth control and family planning come to the forefront in part 2. The responsibilities of mothers and fathers and even the family's value and care for aging saints and the special needs of the physically and mentally challenged are tough topics that demand wise instruction and careful planning within the family circle. Adoption is also very much a part of any discussion of parenting. Biblical principles on parenting address baby care, preschool education, childhood oversight, adolescent supervision, and young adult influence. Part 3 culminates with a helpful chapter on the building of faith through family worship.

Once the foundations are laid in the first three parts, attention moves to the practical aspects of establishing a household whether here in the United States or overseas. Life-management skills and routines for managing a household as well as addressing technology within the home offer new opportunities for more efficiency and broader horizons. Chapters about establishing a home-based business as well as consumer and financial considerations address money, budgets, and the importance of family resources. Interior design, as well as the selection of furnishings and accessories, is important for the comfort of your family and for the silent witness your home offers to the outside world. The importance of hospitality, woven throughout this volume, includes how to implement a welcoming spirit and gracious manner into your home.

The last two parts are even more specifically addressed to household functions largely ignored in the modern era. Part 5 begins with nutrition and food sanitation, which are essential to family health and meal planning and preparation. The organization of the kitchen and acquisition of equipment is included. Family mealtime and ideas for holiday celebrations provide a springboard for using your kitchen as a ministry.

Part 6 encompasses the making of wise clothing decisions, beginning with the ways your clothes frame your life message as well as your body, and underscores the importance of modesty. A basic understanding of textiles and principles of design lead into clothing selection and care.

The final parts, in addition to specialized and technical information, provide simple and clear instructions on what every homemaker needs to know in order to feed and clothe her family. The emphasis is not on becoming a chef or seamstress but rather on the importance of knowing enough about these subjects to manage your household. The user-friendly indexing and straightforward presentation of facts enables a novice to work her way through the maze of technical information.

Finally, anyone who loves homemaking, as do Pat Ennis and I, knows it is a demanding job, but the fringe benefits are terrific. You keep your attitude right by focusing on the results rather than on the process. Homemaking challenges you to walk the fine line of being able to accommodate others without losing your own identity. A happy homemaker performs even her monotonous duties and routine chores faithfully and patiently. In so doing she serves others and achieves greatness in the process. The Lord expects from every woman the joy of obedient service whatever her assignment, and the service she offers to her family and others is ultimately unto him.

A welcoming home need not be pretentious or ostentatious. Rather than looking down at the world while flaunting her assets and giftedness, a woman can preside graciously and confidently over her humble abode. She can blend into its surroundings and effectively and efficiently meet the needs of its occupants as well as serving those who enter its doors. Behind the scenes a homemaker guides the daily activities and sets the pace for loving care and committed service. She is the angel of the hearth and the heart of the home. May the Lord use this book to revitalize homemaking in the hearts of Christian women. Use the "Attitude Check" that follows to examine your own life (James 1:22).

∼ AN ATTITUDE CHECK ∼
for the Homemaker

- Appreciate God's calling on your life to be a homemaker.
- Visualize the overall purpose of your work.
- Keep yourself at your best in appearance and health.
- Strive without ceasing to keep your interfamily relationships as the most important in your life.
- Learn good homemaking skills and fine-tune them by practice.
- Choose women as friends who affirm your calling and happily encourage you.
- Work diligently as unto the Lord and count your blessings.

Part One

GOD'S DESIGN FOR THE HOME

Chapter One

A Portrait of the Twenty-First-Century Home

Pat Ennis

When I was a very young teacher, one of the key leaders of the National Organization for Women (NOW) was the keynote speaker for my professional association's annual conference. As I listened to her passionate presentation, I realized that NOW claimed to speak for the women of America. Her platform at our conference was to challenge the attendees to cast off the shackles of tradition and become "liberated!" Though at the time I was unfamiliar with the passages of Scripture describing the biblical instructions for male and female roles, I did know that speaker was not accurately representing my beliefs. Regrettably, a large percentage of the professional association's membership did embrace NOW's philosophy; this conference marked the beginning of the association's demise.

Later that summer, Beverly LaHaye, my pastor's wife, approached me after an evening church service and asked, "Pat, would you be interested in joining a group of ladies at my home next week to discuss some issues vital to our roles as Christian women?" Inwardly my mind was racing, thinking, *There isn't anything that I would rather do!* Outwardly, I graciously smiled and responded, "How thoughtful of you to include me—I would be delighted to attend."

The afternoon began with refreshments and the usual ladies' chatter—all the while knowing that a cause greater than "female fellowship" had drawn us together. The room silenced as Mrs. LaHaye rose and began to share with us the purpose of the gathering. She had watched a television interview of Betty Friedan, the founder of NOW, and had drawn the same conclusions as I had at my professional conference. Beverly knew that Friedan was not accurately representing her beliefs and was confident that she was not the only woman who felt that way. A time of discussion, affirmation of Beverly's convictions, and prayer followed.

Subsequently, a meeting led by Mrs. LaHaye to educate and alert Christian women on the Equal Rights Amendment (ERA) was held in San Diego—with more than twelve hundred in attendance. This event served to launch Concerned Women for America (CWA), which became officially incorporated in January of 1979. Today, Concerned Women for America is a vibrant organization with well over five hundred thousand members coming from all fifty states and coordinated by a dynamic staff from its national office in Washington, DC.[1]

TIMELESS PRINCIPLES

The advent of the feminist agenda in the decade of the seventies began the downward spiral for the embracing of traditional roles by evangelicals. Now, some forty years later, the egalitarian view is so widely embraced by the evangelical community that the biblical instructions about male and female roles are no longer aggressively taught in many churches. Numerous individuals who would consider themselves strong Christians believe that the role distinctions described in the Scriptures are archaic and not applicable to the twenty-first century. However, the immutability or unchanging nature of God would be in question if numerous passages of Scripture were not timelessly relevant (Gen. 1:27; 2:15–17, 22, 3:1–7; Prov. 31:10–31; 1 Cor. 11:9–12; Eph. 5:23–29; Col. 3:19–21; 1 Tim. 2:8–15; Titus 2:2–8; and 1 Pet. 3:1–7). If you think that God changed his mind about one passage of Scripture, how can you be sure that he has not changed his mind about others? J. I. Packer, in *Knowing God*, lists six attributes of God that provide a helpful backdrop for analyzing the portrait of the twenty-first-century home:

- God's life does not change.
- God's character does not change.
- God's truth does not change.
- God's ways do not change.
- God's purposes do not change.
- God's Son does not change.[2]

If God does not change, then fellowship with him, trust in his Word, living by faith, and embracing his principles for twenty-first-century believers are the same realities as they were for those living in the eras of the Old and New Testaments. The role distinctions outlined in the Scriptures listed above are not written to suppress or discourage Christians. Rather, they provide a

---

[1] See Concerned Women for America website, accessed April 1, 2010, http://www.cwfa.org/history.asp.
[2] J. I. Packer, *Knowing God* (Downers Grove, IL: InterVarsity, 1973), 68–72.

biblical foundation for the creation of principles by which we, as evangelical Christians, are to live our lives. While the outward historical context has changed, the biblical principles defining character have remained true.

PROTOTYPE OF THE TWENTY-FIRST-CENTURY WOMAN

I am privileged to administrate and teach a character-based home economics curriculum, which I first developed for Christian Heritage College at the request of Tim LaHaye. Each year as I work with new homemaking students, I find that they are increasingly unaware of God's special instructions to women. When I teach Proverbs 31:10–31, the biblical foundation of the curriculum, seemingly the scales drop from the eyes of my students and they understand for the first time that this passage is relevant for their choices today.[3] The majority of the students enrolled in my classes are the products of evangelical homes and churches, so for them to lack a foundational knowledge of the principles that Christian women should embrace is a surprise and disappointment to me. The situation is enhanced when, in their exit class, their understanding of the impact of the feminist movement on the evangelical community is incredibly deficient. Reading and responding to the content of *Recovering Biblical Manhood and Womanhood* is a life-changing experience for them.[4]

My students are asked to discuss the characteristics of the women who have been role models for them. Typically, the woman whose life has been so influential to a student is marked by these characteristics:

- is professionally employed outside the home, even when her family does not need her income to meet the family's basic living expenses
- demands and achieves equal rights with her husband
- prioritizes fulfillment of personal goals
- exhibits an attitude of independence, of wanting to be in control of her circumstances
- frequently does not speak to people in a gracious and kind manner
- fails to respond to God's provision for her with gratitude and contentment
- expects her husband to contribute equally to the maintenance of the home
- places her children in the care of someone else or of a day care center
- may have made ungodly choices, such as divorce or even abortion, to avoid difficult situations or consequences
- leads her family rather than allowing her husband to lead

---

[3] Patricia A. Ennis, "Portraying Christian Femininity," *Journal of Biblical Manhood and Womanhood* 8 (Fall 2003): 47–55. This article provides a snapshot of the content taught.
[4] John Piper and Wayne Grudem, eds., *Recovering Biblical Manhood and Womanhood: A Response to Evangelical Feminism* (Wheaton, IL: Crossway, 1991, 2006).

- has children who are "ministry orphans" (children whose parents prioritize their ministry responsibilities ahead of their parenting roles as outlined in Scripture)

Regrettably, the students' Christian role models have moved a million miles from the teaching found in Proverbs 31:10–31. Apparently the influence of the twenty-first-century culture has slowly infiltrated the evangelical community. Consider the following categories of data collected by the United States Bureau of Labor Statistics and compare them with the demographics of your local congregation:

- the labor force participation rate (the percent of the population working or looking for work) for all mothers with children under eighteen
- the participation rate for married mothers living with their respective spouses
- the labor force participation rate of mothers with children under six years
- the participation rate of mothers with infants under a year old[5]

Consider studying the content presented in the Bureau of Labor Statistics website in light of this question: "If you were free to do either, would you prefer to have a job outside the home, or would you prefer to stay at home and take care of the house and family?"

Research suggests that twenty-first-century society has twisted and blended the male and female roles outlined in Scripture (Genesis 1–3; Prov. 31:10–31; Ephesians 5–6; 1 Tim. 2:1–15; Titus 2:2–6; 1 Pet. 3:1–7). God ordained specific and separate roles for women to fulfill, whether single, married, or with children. Feminism has blended at best, and distorted in many cases, the biblical role distinctions. Have you been impacted? Responding to the "Feminism Quotient" may assist you in identifying whether or not your values have been influenced by the feminist movement.

---

[5] See US Department of Labor, Bureau of Labor Statistics, "Employment Characteristics of Families—2010," last modified March 24, 2011, http://www.bls.gov/news.release/pdf/famee.pdf.

✍ FEMINISM QUOTIENT ✍

What is your perception of the impact of the feminist movement on the twenty-first-century culture and the evangelical community?

Place the number that best reflects your response to the statement in the space provided.

Use the following scale:

1 = Strongly Disagree   **3 = Agree**
2 = Disagree   **4 = Strongly Agree**

1. ____ Roles of men and women are clearly defined in the Bible.
2. ____ God is spoken of in the Scriptures as a male.
3. ____ The tendency today is to stress the equality of men and women by minimizing the unique significance of our maleness or femaleness.
4. ____ God does not intend for women to be squelched.
5. ____ Society, due to the inborn sin nature of each human, automatically rebels against God's rule, resulting in a distorted view of how God originally created men and women.
6. ____ Submission refers to a wife's divine calling to affirm her husband's leadership.
7. ____ Submission refers to a wife's divine calling to follow her husband's leadership through the use of her gifts.
8. ____ Because a husband is given leadership, this means he must make all the decisions.
9. ____ The pattern of male leadership was God's original design before sin affected His creation.
10. ____ Jesus placed a high value on women.
11. ____ Jesus recognized role distinctions for men and women.
12. ____ The Old Testament, Jesus, and Paul all teach the same basic doctrine in relation to role distinctions for men and women.
13. ____ Male leadership in the church was Jesus's intention as displayed by the appointment of all men as apostles.
14. ____ The headship of men over women implies women are inferior.
15. ____ Analogous of Christ and his church, the husband is told to exercise, with love, headship over his wife.
16. ____ Paul's teachings imply that women are not to teach Christian doctrine to men.
17. ____ Paul's teachings imply that women are not to exercise authority directly over men in the church.
18. ____ Submission implies giving up independent thought.
19. ____ Submission is not based on lesser intelligence or competence.

20. ____ The same wisdom and skills necessary for good family management apply also to the management of God's church.
21. ____ The effects of sin have made family relationships difficult to fulfill in a biblical manner.
22. ____ The loss of masculine identity is causing children to become confused about their own identity.
23. ____ Women are valuable not because of any merit of their own but because the Lord has given them value.
24. ____ How women serve in ministry must align with the principle and truth that God has assigned specific roles to specific people and groups of people.
25. ____ The process of cultivating a heart of gratitude allows a woman to place herself humbly under the Word of God and in submission to his commands to fulfill the biblical role of womanhood to which he has called her.

____ **Feminism Quotient Total**

Feminism Quotient Interpretation

Total all the numbers indicating your responses to the statements. Then find the corresponding range of scores listed below:

100–90

A complementarian understanding of the roles of men and women

89–80

A strong understanding of the roles of men and women

79–70

A basic understanding of the roles of men and women

69–60

Further research is needed to acquire a biblical understanding of the roles of men and women.

You may be a part of my study addressing the impact of feminism on the evangelical community by transferring your responses to the identical assessment located at http://www.surveymonkey.com/s/PC7QDKV. An interpretation of the assessment is located at the conclusion of the chapter.

BIBLICAL INTERVENTION FOR THE TWENTY-FIRST-CENTURY WOMAN

The book of Proverbs is a set of teaching guidelines for Jewish families. Proverbs 12:4 and 19:14 commend specific positive qualities of a wife. Proverbs 31 is the final teaching to the son by a godly mother (31:1). In Proverbs 31, verses 1–9 focus on the qualities of a wise king; verses 10–31 deal with the selection of a godly wife. Its content provides the instruction needed to restore the twenty-first-century's woman to a biblical paradigm. The instruction first addresses the character qualities of a godly king including:

- holiness (31:3),
- sobriety (31:4–7), and
- compassion (31:8–9).[6]

The second instruction provides insight on how to select an excellent wife (31:10–31). Six characteristics are emphasized:

- *Her character.* In verses 11–16, "trustworthy" is the word that best defines her. Her husband's care is her primary concern, and he trusts her to manage the home effectively. She is a careful steward of the family assets and helps her husband to profit in his business. Her devotion to him is consistent, freeing him to be all that God means for him to be.

- *Her devotion as a wife and homemaker.* Verses 13–24 suggest that the excellent wife is creative with her hands and works with a positive attitude (v. 13); purchases goods of variety and quality at the best price (v. 14); rises early to meet the needs of her household (v. 15); possesses the ability to make sound financial decisions (v. 16); is utterly unselfish and uses her skills to minister to others (v. 20); plans ahead for unforeseen circumstances rather than living by crisis management (v. 21); is well groomed and appropriately fashionable (v. 22); and contributes to the family income through her home-based industry (v. 24).

- *Her generosity as a neighbor.* Verse 20 reports that the excellent wife both responds to and reaches out to others. Although her family is her first priority, she is not myopic.

- *She is a teacher with influence.* Verses 25–26 describe the impact of the woman on the lives of others. Whether or not a woman is trained professionally, she is a teacher. The excellent woman is confident spiritually. She has gained, through a godly lifestyle, the respect of others who listen to her counsel; she teaches daily in her home and makes a long-term impact on others. Wisdom and loving-kindness characterize her speech.

---

[6] John MacArthur, *The MacArthur Study Bible* (Nashville: Word, 1997), notes for Proverbs 31:2–9.

- *She is an effective mother.* Verses 27–28 record the spontaneous response of those closest to her—her husband and children. Her household is well-managed, and her husband affirms her while her children reverence and honor her.

- *Her reward.* Proverbs 31:30–31 is a reminder that long-term outward beauty has no real value. A woman who loves and fears God is the only truly excellent woman, and only God can produce such a woman. Eventually, if she is willing to embrace God's special instructions to women, she will be privately and publicly rewarded.

The feminist agenda understandably does not define excellence in these terms. Regrettably, our evangelical community frequently fails to define excellence according to biblical standards as the Perceptions of Homemaking Study revealed.

THE PERCEPTIONS OF HOMEMAKING STUDY

The Perceptions of Homemaking Study, which establishes the need for this book, was designed to identify a woman's knowledge of the facts regarding her ability to perform successfully the life skills commonly associated with home management. The respondents overwhelmingly were female. With that general purpose in mind, several research questions were cited:

1. How has feminism impacted the twenty-first-century culture?
2. How has feminism impacted the twenty-first-century evangelical community?
3. What are the homemaking skills many Christian women lack?

These research questions provided the preparation for this study, specifics of which can be found in the appendix.

IMPLICATIONS OF THE STUDY FOR THE TWENTY-FIRST-CENTURY EVANGELICAL COMMUNITY

The enthusiastic response to the survey suggests that a need does exist for the twenty-first-century evangelical community to consider seriously the need for the implementation of the Titus 2:3–5 principle, which challenges women to acquire the facts and life skills needed to manage their homes successfully. Likewise, the devastating effect that feminism continues to exact on its members must be acknowledged, identified, and corrected.

The mean scores of the 1,364 respondents between ages thirty-five and ninety indicated that they possess the majority of the skills and much of the knowledge needed to establish a godly home. However, the same respondents listed the skills, which they had efficiently practiced, as deficient in the younger women. Just as the younger women should embrace a teachable spirit toward acquiring the knowledge base and skills for successful home management, so the older women must heed the Titus 2:3–5 instruction to be willing to teach the younger women.

The Titus 2:3–5 passage states that older women are to be examples of godliness (2:3); they are to teach what is good, and they are to train the younger women in specific skills so that God's Word is not discredited (2:4–5). The résumé of a qualified older woman portrays her as embracing a lifestyle that models the faith she professes. She is circumspect with her speech, self-controlled, and a teacher of things that please God. As

> While not reported in this summary, the e-mails that accompanied the requests for the summary of the survey findings reflected a deep concern that the generation of younger women is frequently theologically sound but practically inept in the godly attitudes and skills required to manage a home that glorifies their heavenly Father. Thus, the admonition offered in Titus 2:5 is coming to fruition—God's Word is being discredited.

a countercultural woman in her commitment to God's special instructions to women, she is willing to thank her heavenly Father for her successes and ask forgiveness of him and others for her failures. She desires to see growth toward Christlikeness in younger women and is willing to invest her most valuable asset—her time—in them.[7] Only when the younger and older women partner together to fulfill this biblical mandate will the Christian home be recovered.

PUTTING THE PRINCIPLES INTO PRACTICE

1. Consider responding to The Perceptions of Homemaking Study and the Feminism Quotient. What did you discern from completing the surveys?
2. How do you perceive feminism has impacted the twenty-first-century culture?
3. How do you perceive feminism has impacted the twenty-first-century evangelical community?
4. How do you perceive feminism has impacted you?
5. Read "Dear Keeper." What is your response to its content? Develop biblical guidelines that will assist you in valuing those things that are "worth keeping."

---

[7] For further elaboration on the Titus 2 principle, see Pat Ennis and Lisa Tatlock, *Becoming a Woman Who Pleases God: A Guide to Developing Your Biblical Potential* (Chicago: Moody Press, 2003), 288–306.

Dear Keeper,

I grew up in the 1950s with practical parents—a mother, God love her, who *washed aluminum foil* so it could be reused, and a father who was happier to get old shoes fixed than buy new ones. Marriage was good [enough] and dreams focused; best friends were barely a wave away; Dad in trousers, T-shirt and a hat; Mom in a house dress, lawn mower in one hand and dish towel in the other. It was a time for fixing things such as curtain rods, the radio, the screen door, or the oven. It was a way of life that drove me crazy sometimes. Waste was affluence. There was always more. And new.

When Mother died, I was struck by the fact there wasn't any "more"— the thing cared about was used up; never more. So while we have it, it's good to love it, care for it, and fix it when broken; heal it when sick.

This is true for marriage, friends, old cars, children with bad report cards, old dogs, and aging parents. We keep them because they are worth it, because we are worth it. Some things are worth keeping, such as best friends, people who are special, and even strangers with whom we share a common human bond.[8]

ABOUT THE AUTHOR

Pat Ennis taught home economics for the San Diego Unified School District while developing the Home Economics Department at Christian Heritage College (now San Diego Christian College). She moved to The Master's College in 1987 to establish the Home Economics-Family and Consumer Science Department. Pat coauthored *Becoming a Woman Who Pleases God: A Guide to Developing Your Biblical Potential, Designing a Lifestyle that Pleases God*, and *Practicing Hospitality: The Joy of Serving Others*. She is a contributing author to *Daily Devotions for Authors, Pearl Girls: Encountering Grit, Experiencing Grace*, and *Think Biblically: Recovering a Christian Worldview. Becoming a Young Woman Who Pleases God*, published by New Hope Publishers, was released fall 2010. Pat relocated to Southwestern Baptist Theological Seminary, fall 2011 to assume the position of Distinguished Professor and Director of Homemaking Programs. Her life's mission is to

- love her Lord with ALL of her heart (Matt. 22:37),
- walk worthy of her calling (Eph. 4:1–3), and
- train the younger women to fulfill the Titus 2 mandate so that God's Word will not be discredited (Titus 2:3–5).

---

[8] This letter with no author attribution has widely circulated on the Internet for some ten years. The Master's College librarian tried to track it down but to no avail.

Chapter Two

Impact of Feminism on the Home and Family

Candi Finch

"If you are a woman sitting in this class and do not consider yourself a feminist, then you are lying to yourself." This statement by my teacher in a communication course during my sophomore year in college had a profound effect on my life for several years. Frankly, I was mad, and I felt as if my teacher had thrown down the proverbial gauntlet in front of me! I was offended by her comment. As a Christian, even though I did not know a lot about feminism, I considered it antithetical to the Christian worldview. My teacher, a self-proclaimed atheist who was also vocal about her lesbian lifestyle, waged a diligent campaign throughout the semester to open the eyes of her female students to the ideology of feminism, though the subject of the class had nothing to do with feminism. Her missionary zeal in trying to convert students to her ideology angered me, and I began to read secular feminist works primarily so I could engage her in class.

However, as I read the feminist literature, the unthinkable occurred. I actually agreed with some of it! Concepts such as equal pay for equal work, protection under the law for women in abusive situations, and access for women to higher education resonated with me. Underneath the angry rhetoric found in these writings stood some ideas that did not seem contrary to Scripture (though I did see much of what they said as going against the Bible). After all, God cared for women just as he cared for men. Both men and women were created in God's image (Gen. 1:27). Some of the things for which early feminists fought were things in which I believed as well. For the rest of my college career, I wrestled with the ideas of secular feminist thought, wondering if I could reconcile what I was reading with my Christian beliefs.

Not until my first semester in seminary did I begin to delve deeper into the underlying message of the feminist movement. Feminism can be defined and understood in two ways:

1. *A movement*—a social, historical movement seeking rights for women; organized activity on behalf of women's rights and interests;
2. *A philosophy or ideology*—the theory of political, economic, and social equality
   of the sexes.

At first glance, this philosophy may not appear to contradict Scripture. However, since this movement defines "equality" as "sameness," there is a problem. God in his wisdom has given distinct roles to men and women. Just as in the Trinity where God the Father, God the Son, and God the Holy Spirit have distinct roles yet are equally God, so, too, within humanity a distinction of roles does not mean that either men or women are any more important or less important in God's design. *Distinctions do not mean inequalities, yet the message of the feminist movement would not allow for this.*

At the heart of this movement is a message that shuns God and exalts humanity, specifically women. The American culture has embraced this message, and to some extent, the church has allowed it to creep within its doors. For any Christian, the essential problem with feminism is that this ideology exalts women and their experience as a source of truth, and in turn women's experience becomes more authoritative than Scripture. For example, if the idea that God may have distinct roles for women in the home or church seems "unfair" to you, then many feminists would advise you to reject what God teaches and go with what you "feel" is right. In their view, each woman is the barometer of her own truth. However, the Bible clearly states that all people—men and women—are sinful (Rom. 3:23). Whenever anyone's experience is seen as trumping Scripture, red flags should immediately flash in your mind.

Speaking of the feminist movement in her book *Radical Womanhood*, Carolyn McCulley states, "Right observation does not always lead to right interpretation."[1] In my journey, I came to realize that although the feminist movement had correctly observed some injustices against women, its "interpretation" of how to solve these problems is incorrect because feminists abandoned God and his plan for humanity. The only lasting answer to the abuse of women is the transformative power of the gospel. Unlike the message of the feminist movement, which points to women for hope, true hope is found only in Christ.

This chapter will examine how the movement and its message have impacted the home and family. Has feminism influenced your ideas about

---

[1] Carolyn McCulley, *Radical Womanhood: Feminine Faith in a Feminist World* (Chicago: Moody Press, 2008), 131. This book is an excellent resource for any woman looking for an expanded discussion on the topic of this chapter.

roles within a marriage, having children, or even the value of a career versus motherhood? Admittedly, the beliefs I held about these things were based more on my cultural conditioning than on God's truth. As Pat Ennis demonstrated through the survey in her chapter "A Portrait of the Twenty-First-Century Home," many women will admit that feminism has impacted the way they think about topics like employment and working outside the home, God's plan for womanhood, what constitutes a family, and abortion. Before beginning to examine the impact of feminism, one must understand a bit about the history and development of this movement.

THE MOVEMENT AND ITS MESSAGE

Feminism as a historical movement is usually broken up into three periods of time, which are often classified as "waves," in order to simplify what is actually a complicated and multifaceted movement.

First Wave (1840–1925): The Fight to Overturn Injustices

The key concern of the first wave of feminism was women's suffrage (from a French word that means "a vote"). However, several other causes were championed by the feminist pioneers:

- abolition (ending slavery)
- temperance
- child labor reform
- education for women
- marriage laws that would give protection to women

The women (and some men) in this movement responded to specific injustices they had experienced, and they fought to bring about change in society. Be honest—their causes were not always bad; in fact, you could argue that the church should have been championing some of these very same issues. As a single, thirty-something woman pursuing her PhD, I am indebted and grateful to feminists who fought for women to have the opportunity to pursue higher education.

One of the best ways to understand the first wave of feminism is to look at a few of its more recognizable proponents:

- *Lucretia Mott* (1793–1880)—a married Quaker minister. She sheltered runaway slaves and formed the Female Anti-Slavery Society.

- *Elizabeth Cady Stanton* (1815–1902)—a staunch abolitionist who was married for more than fifty years and had seven children. In 1848 at the Seneca Falls Convention, she delivered the keynote address, "A Declaration of Sentiments," which was a declaration of independence for women. She viewed the Bible as a tool used to oppress women.

- *Sojourner Truth* (1797–1883)—an African American evangelist and reformer who applied her energies to the abolitionist and women's rights movements. As the daughter of slaves, she was abused by several masters during her childhood.

- *Susan B. Anthony* (1820–1906)—a single woman who began to campaign with Stanton in 1851 for women's education, the right to divorce, women's property rights, careers for women, and the right to vote. She became one of the first major lobbyists in Washington, DC.

- *Margaret Sanger* (1879–1966)—one of eleven children born into a Roman Catholic, working-class, Irish American family. She fought for birth control, contraception, and abortion to be available for women.

These women and others like them played pivotal roles within the formation or development of this first wave. Lucretia Mott and Elizabeth Cady Stanton formed a bond when they were banned from participating in the World Anti-Slavery Convention in London in 1840, an event that they had been invited to attend. Their friendship sparked the movement for women to gain the right to vote. Stanton later wrote speeches for Susan B. Anthony, who gained more notoriety in the suffrage movement because of her public persona.

In Akron, Ohio, in 1851, Sojourner Truth, an African American woman, gave a speech titled "Ain't I a Woman?" highlighting the double oppression that black women faced. Her famous speech illustrated the fact that even at its earliest stages, there was no such thing as a singular feminist movement. Because each woman's experience was different, one is wise to reference "feminisms" and the many facets of the feminist movement. A white woman from a middle-class neighborhood (as many of the feminist leaders were) had a "reality" or "experience" different from that of an African American woman whose parents had been slaves. They had different concerns and battles to fight. Sojourner said in her speech:

That man over there says that women needs to be helped into carriages, and lifted over ditches, and to have the best place everywhere. Nobody ever helps me into carriages or over mud-puddles, or gives me any best place! And ain't I a woman? I have ploughed and planted, and gathered into barns. . . . Ain't I a woman? . . . I have borne thirteen children, and seen most all sold off to slavery, and when I cried out with my mother's grief, none but Jesus heard me! And ain't I a woman? . . . Then that little man in black there, he says women can't have as much rights as men, 'cause Christ wasn't a woman!

Where did your Christ come from? . . . From God and a woman! Man had nothing to do with Him.[2]

Margaret Sanger came on the scene toward the end of the first wave, and her impact is most forcefully felt today. As a nurse working in a poor immigrant neighborhood, she treated women who had undergone back-alley abortions. These experiences galvanized her to fight to make birth control and contraceptives available, and early in the 1900s she began to dream of a "magic pill" that could control pregnancy. She said, "No woman can call herself free until she can choose consciously whether she will or will not be a mother,"[3] and she argued that every child should be a wanted child.[4] She said, "The most merciful thing that a large family does to one of its infant members is to kill it."[5] Sanger's work initiated the idea within the popular American consciousness that, if a woman could not control her own fertility, children would become a burden and not a blessing. Sanger, in 1921, went on to found the American Birth Control League, which in 1942 changed its name to Planned Parenthood Federation of America, Inc.

The key advancements of the first wave included the access for women to higher education, the reform of secondary-school systems for girls, the opening of doors to women for professions like medicine and law, property rights for married women, improvements in child custody rights for women who were divorced or separated from their husbands, and winning the right to vote for women with passage of the Nineteenth Amendment to the United States Constitution in 1920.

Despite some noble causes, at the heart of this movement, the Bible was being attacked. Feminists, even those who claimed some fidelity to Scripture, placed themselves as authorities over Scripture and viewed God's Word as an instrument of oppression. Elizabeth Cady Stanton, in her work *The Woman's Bible*, argued that "all religions on the face of the earth degrade her [woman]; and so long as woman accepts the position that they assign her, her emancipation is impossible."[6] Further she said the Bible "does not exalt and dignify woman."[7]

The message at the heart of the first wave of this movement was that women needed freedom from oppression. Many of the women in this movement felt that sources of this oppression were the church, the institution of

---

[2] Sojourner Truth, "Ain't I a Woman?" [online], accessed August 30, 2011, http://www.fordham.edu/halsall/mod/sojtruth-woman.html.
[3] Margaret Sanger, *Woman and the New Race* (New York: Truth, 1920), 94.
[4] Ibid., 74.
[5] Ibid., 63.
[6] Elizabeth Cady Stanton, *The Woman's Bible: A Classic Feminist Perspective* (Mineola, NY: Dover, 2002), 12.
[7] Ibid.

marriage, and the role of mother. Through the efforts of Margaret Sanger, motherhood began to be viewed as holding women back. *The message of this first wave was that women—not God and certainly not the Bible—should control and determine their own destiny.*

Second Wave (1960–1990):
The Fight to Find Fulfillment Outside of the Home

G. K. Chesterson wrote, "[Feminism] is mixed up with a muddled idea that women are free when they serve their employers but slaves when they help their husbands."[8] He perfectly captured in this statement the approach of the second wave of feminists to marriage and the home. As the first wave of feminism waned in the mid-1920s, the American people focused on greater concerns like the Great Depression in the late 1920s and early 1930s and the Second World War from 1941 to 1945. The 1950s, often characterized as the *Leave It to Beaver* era, were a "golden age" for the home. The television character of June Cleaver was held up as the epitome of womanhood and the "happy housewife." Though she had gone to college and prepared herself for a place in the marketplace, she chose to devote her primary energies to the care of her family.

In the early 1960s, the journalist Betty Friedan became convinced that women were really frustrated and unfulfilled in their roles as wives and mothers. She began to survey her classmates at her fifteen-year college reunion and came to the conclusion, "Each suburban wife struggled with it alone. . . . She was afraid to ask even of herself the silent question—is this all?"[9] The result was the publication of the book *The Feminine Mystique*, which came out in 1963 just in time for the cultural unrest that characterized America in the 1960s. She diagnosed women with the "Happy Housewife Syndrome," arguing that women were just pretending to be happy in their roles when in fact they felt discontented and unfulfilled. Friedan said many women suffered from this "problem with no name" because they were ashamed to admit their dissatisfaction with society's roles for women:

> If I am right, the problem that has no name stirring in the minds of so many American women today is not a matter of loss of femininity or too much education, or the demands of domesticity. It is far more important than anyone recognizes. It is the key to these other new and old problems which have been torturing women and their husbands and children, and puzzling their doctors and educators for years. It may well be the key to our future as a nation

---

[8] G. K. Chesterton, *The Collected Works of G. K. Chesterton* (San Francisco: Ignatius, 1987), 4:440.
[9] Betty Friedan, *The Feminine Mystique* (New York: Dell, 1963), 11.

and a culture. We can no longer ignore that voice within women that says: "I want something more than my husband and my children and my home."[10]

Friedan, and later Gloria Steinem, another leader during this wave, fought for women to have a public voice and find their worth outside the home. Both argued that women needed to find purpose by contributing to the world in a tangible way (i.e., through a profession in the workplace). Being a wife and mother were not considered to be pursuits fulfilling in themselves. In fact, marriage and motherhood were considered limitations or even prisons by some feminists within the second wave.

During this period, the National Organization for Women (NOW) was formed (1966), birth control pills were approved for sale in the United States (1960), and *Roe v. Wade* granted women abortion rights (1973). The fact that the media often portrayed women in the movement as angry men haters is not a fair representation. However, men were seen as the oppressors, and women were seen as saviors. Women became involved in politics, the publishing industry, and higher education administration in order to give a voice to women's experience. Women's own experience became firmly established as the locus of truth, and they claimed the right to define their own roles and reality.

The Bible was dismissed altogether, and marriage firmly came under attack. Gloria Steinem said, "We have to abolish and reform the institution of marriage . . . By the year 2000 we will, I hope, raise our children to believe in human potential, not God."[11] In 1969, a leaflet entitled "Do You Know the Facts about Marriage?" produced to hand out at a protest at the New York Marriage License Bureau, ended with this statement: "We can't destroy the inequities between men and women until we destroy marriage. We must free ourselves. And marriage is the place to begin."[12] *The message at the heart of this wave was that marriage held women back.*

Third Wave (1990–Present): The Fight to Represent All Women

As the twenty-first century dawned, the third wave of secular feminism emerged. By this time, the message of the feminist movement had become firmly entrenched within popular culture. Carolyn McCulley has observed, "Feminism is a given. We breathe it, we think it, watch it, read it. Whenever a concept so thoroughly permeates a culture, it's hard to step back and notice it at work. Feminism has profoundly altered our culture's concept of what it means to

---

[10] Ibid., 27.

[11] Gloria Steinem, Essay, *Saturday Review of Education* (March 1973).

[12] "Do You Know the Facts about Marriage?" in ed. Nathaniel May, Clint Willis, and James W. Loewen, *We Are the People: Voices from the Other Side of American History* (New York: Thunder's Mouth, 2003), 185.

be a woman."[13] Women in this generation of feminist advocates represent different ethnicities, socio-economic statuses, religious backgrounds, and sexual orientations. Rebecca Walker, whose mother Alice Walker wrote *The Color Purple*, coined the term "third wave" in an article in *Ms.* magazine.[14] As a twenty-three-year-old bisexual African American woman from the South, she felt that the second wave of feminism did not represent her reality as a young, nonheterosexual woman of color, suggesting that a "third wave" was beginning.

Unlike the first wave where women rallied together around the right for women to vote and the second wave where women fought for equality in the workforce and supported legislation aimed to protect the "rights" of women, the third wave cannot be characterized by a central cause. Several key distinctions, though, help distinguish this wave from the first two:

- *It is ubiquitous.* As Carolyn McCulley's aforementioned statement illustrates, feminism is a given. Jennifer Baumgardner and Amy Richards put it this way: "For these women, and for anyone born after the early 1960s, the presence of feminism in our lives is taken for granted. For our generation, feminism is like fluoride. We scarcely notice that we have it—it's simply in the water."[15]

- *It is inclusive.* Women in this wave seek to include voices of women who were not represented previously by the movement—women of color, lesbians, bisexuals, transgendered women, low-income women, and women in third-world nations.

- *Men are no longer seen as the enemy.* Unlike second-wave feminists Betty Friedan and Simone de Beauvoir, who felt that motherhood was a trap and that men oppressed women, women in this wave are interested instead in affirming and improving connections between women and men. Intolerance is the greater enemy for the third wave.

- *There are new attitudes toward sexuality.* Today's culture is porn positive; you only have to turn on the TV for a few minutes to see how attitudes toward sexuality have changed. Whereas second-wave feminists protested *Playboy*, third-wave feminists will wear a symbol of the *Playboy* bunny around their necks or on their T-shirts as a sign of empowerment. By embracing and controlling their sexuality, many women feel that they have taken the power from those whom they would want to represent them.[16] The ironic twist is that in doing so, they have become their own oppressors.

---

[13] McCulley, *Radical Womanhood*, 28.
[14] Rebecca Walker, "Becoming the Third Wave," *Ms.* (January/February 1992), 39–41.
[15] Jennifer Baumgardner and Amy Richards, *Manifesta: Young Women, Feminism, and the Future* (New York: Farrar, Straus and Giroux, 2000), 17.
[16] Some feminists dress in seductive clothing and engage in "slut walks" to protest the idea that a woman can be victimized if she is dressed provocatively. See Kirsten Powers, "Feminists' Fallacy," *Dallas Morning News* (March 20, 2011).

In addition to these characteristics, many women in the younger generation simply do not identify with previous generations of feminists. One woman writes,

> I really appreciate what the sixties women's movement did to make my life better, but I can't identify with it. My life is different than my mother's, and so are the issues that matter to me. Mom fought to get a job. I want a job that pays well and lets me advance. Mom worked really hard trying to get better day care for her children. I want to have a marriage and a job that allows me not to have to rely on day care. Her generation fought to make it okay for women not to marry. My generation wants to figure out how to make marriages work better, more fairly. Different generations. Different issues.[17]

Women in this generation live in a society that has been forever altered by feminism both for the good and the bad. As novelist Erica Jong stated in an interview in *Time*, "They don't understand graduating magna cum laude from Harvard and then being told to go to the typing pool."[18] In the same article Claudia Wallis stated,

> Ask a woman under the age of 30 if she is a feminist, and chances are she will shoot back a decisive, and perhaps even a derisive, no. But in the very next breath, the same young woman will allow that while she does not identify with the angry aspects of the movement in the '60s and '70s or with its clamorous leaders, she certainly plans on a career as well as marriage and three kids. She definitely expects her husband—present or future—to do his share of the dusting, the diapering, the dinner and dishes. She would be outraged were she paid less than a male colleague for doing equal work.[19]

The third wave of feminism is my generation. I have never been barred from a job because of my gender. I never questioned whether or not to pursue a college education; and I never thought I might not be allowed to do so because I was a woman. In fact, for most of my educational years, women have outnumbered men in colleges and graduate schools.[20] At various stages of my childhood, I wanted to be a hairstylist, the first female president of the United States, a teacher, a criminal profiler, and a trial attorney. I never questioned

---

[17] Julia T. Wood, *Gendered Lives: Communication, Gender, and Culture,* 8th ed. (Boston: Wadsworth, 2011), 86.
[18] Article by Claudia Wallis, "Onward, Women!" *Time* (June 24, 2001) [online], accessed August 30, 2011, http://www.time.com/time/magazine/article/0,9171,150717,00. html.
[19] Ibid.
[20] See Paul Wiseman reporting on research based on 2008 U. S. Census Bureau data in "Single Women Out-Earn Single Men in Metro Areas," *USA Today* (September 3, 2010), 2A: "'Young women are going to colleges in droves,' Research Advisors reports, 'Nearly three-quarters of girls who graduate from high school head to college, vs. two-thirds of the boys. But they don't stop there. Women are now 1.5 times more likely than men to graduate from college or earn advanced degrees.'"

whether a woman could do any of those professions. However, there have also been times in my life when I have struggled with accepting that God has a different and unique plan for women because I have considered any type of boundary as unfair. In reality, God in his perfect plan (i.e., the creation order) has given boundaries to men and women to enable them to maximize their own potential so that the message of the gospel could be clearly proclaimed through the relationships within the family and church.

FEMINISM'S IMPACT ON THE HOME AND FAMILY

Feminists in each wave have targeted the church and the traditional family and home as oppressive to women. A survey by the Pew Research Center in Washington, DC, found that even the way people define the word "family" is changing:

- 86% say a single parent and child are a family;
- 80% say an unmarried couple living together with a child are a family;
- 63% say a gay or lesbian couple raising a child together are a family.[21]

"Families are more diverse and the structure of them is more in flux," says sociologist Kelly Musick of Cornell University. "One of the things that has happened is people have a lot more leeway to design the families that work for them."[22] Consider the ways feminism has impacted God's design for the home and family. Biblical standards have been replaced with a model developed and set forth by the world.

1. Biblical gender roles have been redefined

Egalitarianism has attacked the male headship of the family and advocated a standard within marriage that is not biblical. This movement has rejected the husband as the provider, and the result has been devastating. Fathers are disappearing from families, and traditional concepts of masculinity are devalued and undermined. Not only are children being denied the right to see biblical masculinity modeled within the home, but also the advent of "employed women" has made institutional day care the replacement for the mother as nurturer.

Unfortunately, the silence from the people in the churches has been deafening. One author stated:

> The feminization of the family has taken place in large measure because the church has mostly been silent. The church has not met the assault of femi-

---

[21] Sharon Jayson, "The Changing Face of the American Family," *USA Today* (November 18, 2010), 4D.
[22] Ibid.

nism head-on with the sword of the word of God. Rather, and shamefully, the church has retreated and actually brought into her bosom many of the alien ideas of feminism. The church has been guilty of teaching such things as egalitarian marriage.[23]

2. Men have been replaced as unnecessary for having children or leading a family

Hollywood is guilty of glamorizing this idea. Television shows aimed at teenagers like *The Secret Life of the American Teenager* on ABC Family and *Sixteen and Pregnant* and *Teen Mom* on MTV show young women who become pregnant, have children, and raise them without fathers. Actress Jennifer Aniston made headlines in August 2010 during press tours for her movie *The Switch* because she confessed that she still wanted to be a mom even if there was no dad in the picture. She said, "Women are realizing . . . they don't have to settle with a man just to have a child."[24] Consider these statistics:

> In 2009, 41% of children born in the USA were born to unmarried mothers (up from 5% a half-century ago). That includes 73% of non-Hispanic black children, 53% of Hispanic children and 29% of non-Hispanic white children. . . . Evidence is overwhelming that children of single mothers—particularly teen mothers—suffer disproportionately high poverty rates, impaired development and low school performance.[25]

3. Homemaking has been disparaged as only valuable if you get paid to do it

Proverbs 31:27 states, "She looks well to the ways of her household." Many women in my generation if asked what they wanted to be when they grew up probably did not say "homemaker" or "wife and mom." In fact, I can remember in high school being surprised that a close friend said that she wanted to be a wife and mom when she graduated. At that time, girls my age, while wanting to be married someday, usually talked first about what college they would attend or what profession they would pursue. How ironic that when I consider the women who have had the most impact on my life for Christ, most of them are homemakers: my paternal grandmother, my youth pastor's wife, my pastor's wife, my college pastor's wife, and now, the wife of the president at the seminary I attend. All these women have poured themselves into my life and shown me by example what the Christian life and God's plan for womanhood is all about.

---

[23] Ibid., 13.
[24] "Jennifer Aniston: Ready for a Baby?" *People* (August 23, 2010), 62.
[25] "Unwed Births Keep Climbing, and the Kids Are Not All Right," *USA Today* (January 25, 2011), 8A.

Nevertheless, the feminist movement has belittled homemaking. Linda Hirshman says, "The real glass ceiling is at home"[26] and explains: "The family—with its repetitious, socially invisible, physical tasks—is a necessary part of life . . . but it allows fewer opportunities for full human flourishing than public spheres."[27] For a woman like Martha Stewart to make millions marketing "homemaking" and teaching skills valuable in keeping a home is okay, but a woman who devotes her primary energies to this task is often denigrated in contemporary society.

The seminary I attend made headlines when it started offering a concentration in homemaking in its college. I was amazed by the amount of criticism the school received, but more surprising was the fact that many Christians were the most vocal opponents of the homemaking curriculum. People seemed to overlook the fact that women in this degree would receive instruction in Old Testament and New Testament, Greek, Latin, history, and other subjects; the protestors criticized the school for offering instruction in cooking, sewing, child rearing, and following a biblical model of the home. One writer in 1916 was prophetic when she stated, "The home of the future is one in which not one stroke of work shall be done except by professional people who are paid by the hour."[28]

4. Motherhood has been belittled as an unworthy investment of a woman's time

The denigration of homemaking is closely tied with the disparagement of motherhood. The feminist movement viewed homemaking and motherhood as holding women back. In articulating this idea, feminists told women that investing in your family is less noble than pursuing a career outside the home. In 2006, *Salary.com* released a report that caused quite a stir by claiming that a stay-at-home mom would earn $134,121 a year "for her contributions as a housekeeper, cook, day care center teacher, janitor, and CEO, among other functions. The stay-at-home mothers' surveys said they logged a total of 92 hours a week performing those jobs."[29] Motherhood and homemaking are often overlooked and thankless responsibilities!

Ann Crittenden said,

---

[26] Linda Hirshman, "America's Stay-at-Home Feminists," *The American Prospect* (November 24, 2005) [online], accessed July 19, 2012, http://www.alternet.org/story/28621/?page=entire.

[27] Linda R. Hirshman, *Get to Work: A Manifesto for Women of the World* (New York: Penguin, 2006), 24.

[28] Charlotte Perkins Gillman, quoted in Lily Rice Foxcroft, "Suffrage a Step Toward Feminism," in *Anti-Suffrage Essays*, ed. Ernest Bernbaum (Boston: The Forum, 1916), 142.

[29] Jeanne Sahadi, "Being a Mom Could Be a 6-Figure Job," *CNNMoney.com* (May 3, 2006) [online], accessed August 30, 2011, http://money.cnn.com/2006/05/03/pf/mothers_work/.

The job of making a home for a child and developing his or her capabilities is often equated with "doing nothing." Thus the disdainful question frequently asked about mothers at home: "What do they *do* all day?". . . A mother's work is not just invisible; it can become a handicap. Raising children may be the most important job in the world, but you can't put it on a résumé.[30]

Theodore Roosevelt once said, "The good mother, the wise mother . . . is more important to the community than even the ablest man; her career is more worthy of honor and is more useful to the community than the career of any man, no matter how successful."[31]

Consider Titus 2:3–5:

Older women likewise are to be reverent in behavior, not slanderers or slaves to much wine. They are to teach what is good, and so train the young women to love their husbands and children, to be self-controlled, pure, working at home, kind, and submissive to their own husbands, that the word of God may not be reviled.

God instructed older women to teach younger women to love their husbands and children *so that the Word of God may not be reviled.*

5. Children have been devalued and considered a burden rather than a blessing

Abortion, family planning, birth control, the delaying of fertility—all are symptomatic of a larger issue. The idea that children are a blessing of the Lord is almost extinct in today's society. Careers are established before having a family is considered. In a letter to James Dobson of Focus on the Family, one woman writes:

Do you recall the story of the "Emperor's New Clothes"? The story tells of an emperor so vain he buys clothes that only those who are fit for his position can see. So he walks about naked for none wanted to be thought unfit or a fool. It is a child who points out the truth and the foolishness of the adults around him. Today people conduct themselves based on the "political correctness" of what the world says this particular day. Are not the children of today by their actions pointing a finger at our foolishness? The feminist movement devalued children by legalizing abortion, then it further devalued the children by

---

[30] Ann Crittenden, *The Price of Motherhood: Why the Most Important Job in the World Is Still the Least Valued* (New York: Henry Holt and Company, 2001), 2–3.

[31] Quoted in Robin Gerber, *Leadership the Eleanor Roosevelt Way: Timeless Strategies from the First Lady of Courage* (New York: Prentice Hall, 2001), 51.

causing women to believe that childbearing was not as important as a career or a money making job.[32]

God says, "Behold, children are a heritage from the LORD, the fruit of the womb a reward. Like arrows in the hand of a warrior are the children of one's youth. Blessed is the man who fills his quiver with them! He shall not be put to shame when he speaks with his enemies in the gate" (Ps. 127:3–5).

6. Sexual intimacy has been cheapened to become casual without commitment

A few years ago a new book made headlines for its shocking discussion of the sexual lives of teenage girls. *Oral Sex Is the New Goodnight Kiss* argued that girls are taught to feel empowered when they are the center of sexual attention, and the culture has sexualized young girls and teenagers:

> Advertising and media feed off each other, generating a proliferation of images that are sexually suggestive or blatantly pornographic. These ads, music videos, video games, television shows, internet sites, and teen fiction then become guidelines for acceptable teenage social behavior. Sexual imagery is such a normal part of teens' daily lives that, regardless of family pressures, disapproving peers, or religious taboos, very young girls are influenced into dressing provocatively, acting sexy, and becoming sexually active.
>
> Drunk, underage girls bare their breasts in *Girls Gone Wild* videos. T-shirts for girls read "Porn Star," "The Rumors Are True," and "I Know What Boys Want" across the chest. Sweat pants have "juicy," "yummy," and "sweet" emblazoned on the backside. The current brand identity for girls is clear: "I am something to be consumed."[33]

This book illustrates what anyone with an ounce of discernment already knows: Sex is no longer sacred. Instead of portraying a sign of commitment between a husband and wife, it parades the idea of "no strings attached."

7. Marriage has been dismissed and is not permanent or even necessary

An article in *USA Today* proclaimed, "Marriage is increasingly optional and could be on its way to obsolescence."[34] Although the majority of Americans value marriage, the article stated, "People rightly recognize that marriage is no

---

[32] "The Infiltration of Feminism in the Church" [online], accessed March 20, 2003, http://www.jeremiah project.com/prophecy/feminist3.html.
[33] Sharlene Azam, *Oral Sex Is the New Goodnight Kiss* (Los Angeles: Bollywood Filmed Entertainment Inc., 2009), 32.
[34] Sharon Jayson, "We're Just Not That into Marriage," *USA Today* (November 18, 2010), 1A.

longer essential."[35] Despite the fact that the Bible presents marriage as a divine and sacred institution, in today's world getting out of a marriage is almost easier than getting into this sacred union. Margaret Sanger said, "The marriage bed is the most degenerating influence in the social order."[36] God's view on the matter is quite the opposite: "Let marriage be held in honor among all, and let the marriage bed be undefiled, for God will judge the sexually immoral and adulterous" (Heb. 13:4).

Table 2.1

⟨⟩ FEMINISM'S IMPACT ⟨⟩
on the Home and Family

The Bible Says	The Culture Says
Men are to be heads of their families (Ephesians 5; Colossians 3).	There should not be any distinction of roles within a marriage.
Keeping a home is a valuable pursuit for women (Proverbs 31; Titus 2).	Homemaking is not a worthy task for women; it is menial and demeaning.
Children are a blessing of the Lord (Ps. 127:3–5).	Children are a burden if you have too many of them. If you get pregnant and do not want the child, it is okay to abort your baby.
Marriage is a covenant between one man and one woman with the Creator God (Gen. 2:18–24).	Marriage is not necessary, not permanent, and not just between a man and woman. It can also be between two men or two women.

The rise in cohabitation, cheating, and divorce shows a growing disrespect of marriage. A news story in 2011 stated, "The number of Americans with children who live together without marrying has increased twelvefold since 1970. . . . The report states that children now are more likely to have unmarried parents than divorced ones. . . . Cohabiting parents are more than twice as likely to break up as parents who are married."[37] Another story noted, "Cohabitation has nearly doubled since 1990."[38] Hollywood has popularized the disdaining of marriage. Consider actress Kate Hudson, who made headlines in April 2011 when she announced she was pregnant: "First comes baby,

---

[35] Ibid.
[36] Sanger, *Woman and the New Race*, 23.
[37] Sabrina Tavernise, "More Unwed Parents Live Together, Report Finds," *The New York Times* (August 17, 2011), A13.
[38] Jayson, "We're Just Not That into Marriage."

then comes marriage."[39] Marriage is no longer considered a prerequisite to having children, living together, or engaging in sexual relations.

CAN THE TIDE BE TURNED?

Christian women must rediscover God's plan for men and women, children, and the home. While women are free in Christ, they are bound by the Scriptures to be faithful in applying biblical truth to their lives. In both the Old and New Testaments, the home is considered the central place in God's design for rearing and nurturing children, practicing hospitality, experiencing community, and engaging in ministry. The home has become simply a place to store our many belongings and sleep at night. Scripture calls us to recover the idea of the home as a haven; it must be the place for discipling the next generation. "To live according to biblical principles today requires women to be bold enough to stand against philosophies and strongholds that seek to undermine God's Word and His authority."[40]

Christians have reason to hope that the tide can be turned. Something curious began to happen in the 1990s. There was a backlash against feminism from non-Christian women. Women had achieved everything for which the movement had worked, yet they were not fulfilled. Secular author Danielle Crittenden, in her book *What Our Mothers Didn't Tell Us: Why Happiness Eludes the Modern Woman*, illustrates the sentiment of many of these women:

> For all the ripping down of barriers that has taken place over a generation, we may have inadvertently also smashed the foundations necessary for our happiness. Pretending that we are the same as men—with similar needs and desires—has only led many of us to find out, brutally, how different we really are.[41]

> American women have achieved the most egalitarian marriages in the history of the world. And yet they actually feel *more* oppressed in their marriages than their grandmothers did. How is this possible?[42]

> In a way, the situation women wake up in today is more dire than . . . when Friedan first sat down to write about the gnawing "problem with no name." For unlike the problem about which Friedan spoke—which afflicted educated sub-

[39] "First Comes Baby, Then Comes Marriage," under "Lifeline: 'Idol' Wrap and More," *USA Today* (April 28, 2011), 1D [online], accessed September 14, 2011, http://www.usatoday.com/LIFE/usaedition/2011-04-28-lline28_ST_U.htm.
[40] McCulley, *Radical Womanhood*, 29.
[41] Danielle Crittenden, *What Our Mothers Didn't Tell Us: Why Happiness Eludes the Modern Woman* (New York: Simon and Schuster, 1999), 25.
[42] Ibid., 80.

urban wives trapped and unfulfilled in their well-upholstered ranch homes—this new problem with no name affects the female executive high atop the city in her glass office as much as the single mother struggling to lift a stroller onto a bus thirty stories below. Despite sweeping government programs, tens of billions of dollars in social spending, and massive social upheaval in the name of sexual equality, you only have to glance through a newspaper or switch on the news to be subject to a litany of gloomy statistics about today's women: We are more likely to be junkies or drunks or to die in poverty. We are more likely to have an abortion or to catch a sexually transmitted disease. If we are mothers, even of infants and very small children, we are more likely to work at full-time jobs and still shoulder the bulk of housework as well.[43]

In *Newsweek*, Kay Ebeling wrote an article entitled "The Failure of Feminism":

To me, feminism has backfired against women. . . . I see feminism as the Great Experiment that Failed, and women in my generation, its perpetrators, are the casualties. Many of us, myself included, are saddled with raising children alone. . . . Feminism freed men, not women. . . . What's worse, we asked for it. Many women decided: you don't need a family structure to raise your children. We packed them off to day-care centers where they could get their nurturing from professionals. Then we put on our suits and ties, packed our briefcases and took off on the Great Experiment, convinced that there was no difference between ourselves and the guys in the other offices. . . . The reality of feminism is a lot of frenzied and overworked women dropping kids off at day-care centers.[44]

The cover story for the October 29, 2009 issue of *Time* magazine was a special report on "The State of American Women: A New Poll Shows Why They Are More Powerful but Less Happy." The *Newsweek* and *Time* articles illustrate the growing dissatisfaction many women have with the feminist movement. Women have gotten all they asked for and then realized maybe what they wanted all along would not fulfill them. Christians must be vocal in pointing women to the source of true fulfillment. As women start to realize that the "problem with no name" is actually their own sinfulness, believers must show them that hope is found in Christ. Christ said, "The thief comes only to steal and kill and destroy. I came that they may have life and have it abundantly" (John 10:10). May the women in this modern era realize that the message of feminism is a thief that will rob them of the abundant life found in Christ!

---

[43] Ibid., 22.
[44] Kay Ebeling, "The Failure of Feminism," *Newsweek* (November 19, 1990), 9.

PUTTING THE PRINCIPLES INTO PRACTICE

1. Consider the different waves of the feminist movement; what are some of the positive and negative outcomes of each wave?
2. Do you hold any ideas concerning the home that are more culturally conditioned than biblically grounded?
3. What biblical texts form the foundation for your understanding of God's unique plan for womanhood?
4. Have you ever looked down upon homemaking as unworthy of your investment of time and energy? Why do many people think you must "get paid" in order for your work to be considered valuable or meaningful?
5. Look over the list of how feminism has impacted the home and family. Do you hold any of those same views or attitudes?

ABOUT THE AUTHOR

Candi Finch earned her undergraduate degree in communication from the University of South Florida in Tampa, Florida, and her Master of Divinity degree in Women's Studies from Southwestern Baptist Theological Seminary in Fort Worth, Texas. She is currently working on her dissertation with a major in systematic theology and a minor in church history at Southwestern, where as adjunctive faculty she also teaches such classes as Feminist Theology and Introduction to Women's Studies in the Women's Studies program within the School of Theology. She provided research assistance for Mary Kassian's book *The Feminist Mistake* and has written a chapter on the wives of Adoniram Judson in *Adoniram Judson: A Bicentennial Appreciation of the Pioneer American Missionary* recently released by B&H Publishing Group. She has also written sections in *The Women's Evangelical Commentary on the Old Testament, The Women's Evangelical Commentary on the New Testament,* and *The Impact Bible.* She is currently serving as a section editor for the forthcoming *The Study Bible for Women.*

Chapter Three

Home: A Prepared Place

Dorothy Kelley Patterson

The family unit, as God's foundational institution for human society, preceded civil government, communities, and assemblies of worship. In fact, other institutions have been built around the family. In the family, one finds beginnings for the institutions of society: as the first synagogue or church—spiritual truths are embedded; as the first school—wisdom and life skills are taught; as the first state—a civilization is born in which law and order bring productivity and usefulness where families are gathered under the legal umbrella. The family was God's idea and not a phenomenon that evolved from human ingenuity or cultural invention.

God created the man and the woman and brought them together to forge a unique union that would enable them to accomplish his creative purposes in continuing the generations and in exercising dominion over the world he had created. He chose the family and the relationships therein to be his primary classroom and the most comprehensive object lesson for teaching women and men about himself and for challenging them to pursue the holy life he demands so that they can reveal him more effectively. The strength of the family should surpass all other human liaisons. The divinely appointed exclusive commitment within its circle calls for the ultimate design to meet physical, emotional, intellectual, and spiritual needs of women and men in every season of life through selfless, loving service of each to all!

At the beginning of creation God described the family shelter as a "garden," which he named Eden (probably from a Persian root word meaning "delight"), suggesting a place covered or hedged around—perhaps even hidden in the sense of its privacy for those within the family circle. Everything needed for sustenance, comfort, and even happiness—food, water, beauty, and fellowship—were obviously in this first home (Gen. 2:8–10, 15–18). Consider the gardens you have visited. Doubtless they have certain common characteristics:

- set-apart areas with boundaries, whether visible or invisible, with the security that comes within those boundaries

- living plants, whether merely greenery or sometimes beautiful and fragrant blooming flowers
- vegetation that provides food for the table
- often an atmosphere of solitude or quietness that pulls you to rest and even to spiritual meditation

My husband and I have been blessed by some gardens in our life experience. At Magnolia Hill, our home in Wake Forest, North Carolina, we had a small, gated prayer garden just outside our bedroom. My granddaughters would go into the garden, where from my desk in the bedroom, I could watch them happily playing. Because the garden was enclosed, they could enjoy their outdoor pleasures without danger. On the other hand, our dog Noche considered this garden as an extension to our home. When I was alone late at night, it was more convenient for me to let Noche go into the garden. Yet he refused to "soil" the garden, which in his canine mind was a "room" of the house. He insisted on the more challenging second-floor exit via the deck. Then he would make his way down the steps and into the wooded area behind the house without any hesitation. The garden to Noche was a special part of our "home" and was to be treated as such!

Beauty, utility, and sheer joy can easily come in many garden settings, but the difficulty is in the planning, preparation, and ongoing care of this lovely setting. Thus, the metaphor fits well as a reference to the place where you and your family live, learn, play, pray—and even make messes! Not only should your home welcome you and every member of your family, but it should also be an oasis for all whom the Lord may send through your doors—not as a residential hotel with the most luxurious comforts and latest conveniences and a big mortgage, not as a short-order restaurant serving up individual meals according to whim and demand, not a hideout for each family member to escape from the world and even from his family. Your home should be a sanctuary to which you can retreat when the outside world is crazy and in chaos. Your home should be a place to settle in and stay, creating memories through the seasons of life, a place for unconditional love and unending encouragement. Your surroundings affect you and your activities, how you view life as well as your spiritual, mental, and physical health. Your presence should send a fragrance through the house. In fact, your dwelling is home *because* you are there—not as a boarder or visitor but as a resident—familiar with every room and even the cozy corners!

CREATING A SANCTUARY

The greatest compliment anyone can give you on your home is wrapped up in these words: "It looks like you!" Your home should express your personality, your values, and your heart. Surround yourself with people and things you love, and you will always feel at home. When you begin to express yourself, you can quickly find joy in making a home! You can recycle, reuse, reinvent with energies and creativity that refresh and inspire. Often people use "house" and "home" within the same conversation or article as if these two words were interchangeable. I do not believe they are. A "house" is the building or structure in which people live. A "home" is much more—the place that is uniquely prepared for you. You put down roots, weave values, and make memories. You rear your children; your children's children come to visit! You receive family and friends and extend your unique welcome and hospitality. In your home you will always find *lagniappe*, as they say in New Orleans—just a little something extra!

Begin building your "nest" by appraising the priorities of you and your family, the lifestyle you want to follow, even your personal tastes in color and furnishings and overall décor. Respectfully consider each member of the family in your choices, or someone could feel *homeless* in his own home. Anybody is going to be more comfortable and thus happier with familiar furnishings and items that awaken personal treasured memories. You should determine to express your uniqueness as a family. George MacDonald said: "God's fingers can touch nothing but to mold it into loveliness!"

The homemaker is an artist who paints into existence her family's set-apart place or haven, which becomes like heaven in the sense of ultimate rest. The house or apartment, as well as the area surrounding it—whether concrete or garden—together become a canvas upon which the homemaker can create the perfect shelter for those whom she loves most in the world. She is seeking to combine comfort with a style that fits her family. Much of creating this prepared place lies in the art and accessories to be used. These items usually are not newly purchased *en masse* but rather are gathered over a lifetime, expressing who you are and what you like, a distinctive place in your own world and one in which every family member can see himself.

When my children were able to have their own rooms, one of my priorities was to lead each child through the process of organizing furnishings and accessories in a way that expressed his own respective interests. For example, my daughter was quite impressed with the British designer Laura Ashley, who created some wonderful textiles. I could not afford to purchase the fabric in Dallas where we lived, but when traveling in England, I found the factory and with great effort went to the outskirts of London via train to secure a bolt of fabric—enough to do bed linens and accessories for Carmen's room. It was a sacrificial purchase and quite a challenge to get the fabric back to Dallas, but what joy I experienced in making my daughter's room special. On the other hand, my son had a number of public figures whom he admired—some still living. I took the time to track down a few of these, and together with a collage from the life of his much-loved grandfather's military service, I created the art for his room with photographs, autographs, and other memorabilia. My husband has been an admirer and student of great preachers. I gathered handwritten sermons and photographs—even back to the eighteenth century—and over the years had each framed. These framed treasures were a part of his office décor for many years and now have been gifted to Southwestern Seminary. My desire was to create personal space for each member of the family.

Another important step in this process is the development of a sanctuary within the shelter of home, providing comfort for hearts as well as a context for living. You will not make the sacrifice to spend time together as a family unless you plan how to do it! The poet-philosopher Edgar Guest said, "It takes a heap o' livin' in a house t' make it home."[1]

◦⌒ TIPS ON CREATING YOUR ⌒◦ OWN COZY CORNER

- Find a space—even the tiniest alcove.
- Carve out a small area within a larger room.
- If your private place is within a public area of your home, coordinate its decoration with the larger room.
- Personalize the space with things that inspire and comfort you—photographs, keepsakes, collections.
- Indulge in a few good pieces of furniture or art to make it special.
- Keep it neat since clutter hinders creativity.
- Limit the access of others to your special space.

Within your home, you, as I, should find a more intimate space for withdrawing. Our friends Howard and Roberta Ahmanson have a beautiful and spacious home, and they offer gracious hospitality continually in the midst of beauty and orderliness; but what I love most about their home is what they call "the withdrawing room." It is small in size but more important is its warmth and comfort, which draw even a guest into meditation and rest! I promptly came home to try to establish some "withdrawing rooms" here at Southwestern Seminary and Pecan Manor!

---

[1] Edgar Guest, "Home" in *A Heap o' Livin'* (Chicago: The Reilly & Lee Co., 1916), 28.

Franklin Roosevelt's mother had a small sitting room she called the "snuggery." I visited the room when I toured Roosevelt's presidential library and homeplace, and indeed it was prepared for snuggling! Here at Pecan Manor, I find my most intimate setting in front of the fireplace in our library—no telephone or television—with two recliners facing each other and tables for a cup of tea, Kleenex tissues, pens; excellent lighting; a lap blanket to cover my feet—and all within easy reach! Or in our bedroom I have a "grandmother's chair" that will hold me and my granddaughters with its own hassock and lap blankets and tables on either side.

My husband and I have lived in a public house for several decades and experienced a fishbowl of ministry throughout our marriage. Carving out a place for intimate family fellowship and private time has been quite a challenge. It does not just appear; I must work to make it happen. Once our children had left home and my husband and I were in a public house—the center for hospitality on large seminary campuses, first in North Carolina and now in Texas—we needed to cordon off an apartment or suite in which we could find privacy. The apartment in North Carolina was sealed behind a hidden door with full kitchen and a small living/dining area, a large bedroom, a walk-in closet, laundry facilities, and a covered deck where we could escape interruptions during our mealtime even from the telephone and visitors. In Texas, we have a large suite with a small dining area in the bedroom, a morning kitchen, individual offices, a bathroom with laundry facilities, and a medium-sized closet. We are grateful for this bit of privacy, but the absence of a full-service kitchen and the juggling of visiting with family and eating in the room where we sleep do have a downside! However, we continue to work at ways to make this area meet our family needs. When our granddaughters come, the four of us have found a way to gather around our small table for a family meal. And I reserve the right to use all the public rooms of the house, especially during the holiday seasons, as needed for family gatherings. The hospitality staff at Pecan Manor work hard to help me protect family times even in the midst of our heavy institutional schedule. Living in a large, hospitable home does not make finding family time easy. Whatever the challenges, a homemaker must create what is needed for her family and add her own flourishes.

A. W. Tozer said it beautifully

First, He created for utility and purpose and then added decoration and beauty. There probably is a sense in which we could get along without decoration, but it is better to have it. There is that which is in the mind of God that desires to be pleased—not only satisfied. Order and usefulness and purpose bring satisfaction, but God desired that there should be beauty in His work.[2]

A MODEL OF ORDERLINESS

For some women, household management and orderliness is second nature. Everything has a place, and everything is in its place. For years, I have clipped or photocopied helpful hints on organization, cleaning, and managing a household. Hundreds of volumes in my personal library are related in some way to the challenging task of managing a household—interior design, food preparation, gardening, floral arrangements, hospitality, tablescapes, and even napkin folding.

A clean and orderly household acts as a balm to soothe my spirit and allow my body to relax in genuine rest. I take delight in the tasks of home. Although I am not physically able to do some of the chores important to me, I find that technology and helpers enable me to continue to maintain the standards that are important to me and that are associated with the responsibility of a public house.

Despite the fact that American homes have been rapidly expanding in square footage, surveys show that housework, or doing the tasks of home, has greatly declined in the amount of time spent and resources used. What is involved in running even an ordinary household: meal preparation and cleanup, household maintenance, cleaning and repairs, laundry and ironing, gardening and yard work, animal care, financial planning and accounting, the nurturing of children, the supervision of health plans, and the coordination of schedules for all family members—all these are basic to the overall management of a household. However, more and more shortcuts and time-saving devices are not tools to get a job done in the best way, but devices that shortchange the family in the quality and even the realization of goals. For example, cooking is often exchanged for a stop at the deli counter in grocery markets where you can select an assortment of entrées for your family members—perhaps a different one for each person. You arrive home and unload to the table, eat on whatever schedule you desire and wherever suits you, and then dump all the remains in the trash!

Many consider the tasks of the home to be dull and boring. However, perhaps this misconception has come because we have removed the creativity and excellence from the tasks. Note our chapter on family mealtime for some ideas on how to revive this ritual in your home (see chapter 33). There is no better tool

---

[2] A. W. Tozer, *Who Put Jesus on the Cross?* in *The Best of A. W. Tozer,* comp. Warren W. Wiersbe (Camp Hill, PA: Christian, 1980), 2:237.

for building your family's *esprit de corps*. Table conversation in a creatively prepared mealtime experience has benefits beyond the mere physical sustenance of the family. Spending some time as well as energy and creativity can provide rich dividends for your family.

Every time our family has moved I have spent many hours organizing and reorganizing cabinets, closets, and pantries and planning how to make my household run more smoothly. Developing an efficient inventory seems a lifetime challenge, but my goal is a worthy one—to reach a point where anyone can immediately find whatever is needed by simply accessing the master inventory. Unfortunately, I seem to be less efficient now than as a novice of household management in my early years. Of course, the inventory has greatly expanded! Within this volume you will find chapters on food preparation (see chapter 30), routines for cleaning (see chapter 23), hints for interior design (see chapter 27), and life management skills (see chapter 20). The overwhelming task of making a home is a lifelong learning experience. This volume offers you the basics for beginning your journey.

REMINDERS
for a Homemaker

- Everyone in the family should have responsibilities.
- Everything in the home should have a place.
- Every household task should have a routine system for its execution.
- The tasks you cannot find time to do should be thoughtfully delegated.
- Instead of being stressed over meals, plan your menus in advance.

A TREASURY FOR MEMORIES

Family traditions and rituals give personality and character to a home. In my experience a family tradition has often boosted spirits when I was down and hurting, reminding me that life is worth the effort even in the midst of difficulties and sorrows. My father died in December several weeks before Christmas. Although we could rejoice in his freedom from pain and suffering and his being ushered into the presence of the Lord, we as a family acutely felt the loss of our patriarch. Nevertheless, as we gathered for Christmas, we found comfort and strength in our reunion and in continuing the traditions from our childhood—reading the Christmas story, reciting Christmas poems, singing carols, each child contributing something to the Christmas program, the same menus our father loved. These rituals brought the happy memories of Christmases past—humorous, poignant, and treasured remembrances of what it meant to be part of the extended Kelley family guided by my father. Seemingly we created a living family album remembering the past and our roots and celebrating

Christmas with joy even in the midst of our sorrow. We were also recharging our lives to move forward into future challenges even without Daddy's presence. It was much easier to accomplish that feat with the solidarity of family (Ps. 68:6).

Some words of wisdom lodged in my heart many years ago: focus on the given rather than the not given. Instead of coveting what you do not have, spend your energies on managing carefully what you do have. Again, create your own special family traditions or inspire a friend to embrace a new holiday ritual. Many years ago our family had a Christmas tablecloth to which we affixed our names. It has disappeared or is buried in some unknown corner. I saw an article recently in a ladies' magazine about a mother who not only started this tradition for her family but continued it over a lifetime. I loved it and was inspired anew. When I began to plan the recognition of our provost and his wife for their ten years of faithful service to the seminary, I thought of this special ritual. With the help of our homemaking department, the tablecloth was accented with the provost's monogram in the center, and then more than 120 faculty members and administrators affixed their names to the cloth. All who participated were pleased to honor this special legacy.

CONCLUSION

Caring for your home and meeting the needs of your family are ministries. If you have chosen to marry, God has given you a special assignment. That choice is followed by God-given requirements. Keeping a home not only requires time, energy, and creativity, but it also calls for skills and experience. I believe homemaking is an art, and to pursue the development of any piece of art demands time and talent. Your expenditure of time and effort does not always bring rewards in the sense of instant gratification. You may experience challenging trials and difficulties or even despair and discouragement. Yet you must not be deterred from the great work God has given you to do. An anonymous poet penned these words:

> The beauty of the house is order;
> The blessing of the house is contentment;
> The glory of the house is hospitality;
> The crown of the house is godliness.

Homemakers often complain that they are not appreciated and receive no gratitude for their selfless investment in the family. One of the most inspiring sites for me over my years of travel around the world is the magnificent

Taj Mahal in Agra, India. In the late 1970s, my husband and I had a ministry assignment in India. Although we were on a very limited budget and had little time, my husband did take me to see this monument. I was overwhelmed with its exquisite beauty but even more impressed that it took twenty-one years to complete its construction! I do not know of any structure a woman has built to honor herself, including Hatshepsut's temple in Upper Egypt, that is equal to this magnificent edifice. The lesson to be learned is this: if you build your own monument, you may fail miserably, but if you serve your husband and family and the Lord, in the process they are helping you build your mansion in heaven. And, believe me, it will surpass the gem-studded marble Taj Mahal built by a husband for his wife, whom he affectionately called the "Pride of the Palace."

A homemaker is prepared from creation to provide comfort, order, relaxation, peace, and restoration in an atmosphere especially planned for her own family to provide a loving center to which everyone in the family will be drawn. Truly, there should be no place like home. Single women are not without the DNA from the Creator to create a prepared and welcoming place. Even without husband or children, a woman needs home to satisfy her nesting and nurturing instincts. A single woman, too, should prepare a place of comfort, solace, and one in which to recharge her energies. As you create your home, you not only meet your personal needs, but you also can receive those whom God sends to you for ministry.

PUTTING THE PRINCIPLES INTO PRACTICE

1. How does your home echo your greeting of welcome?
2. Do your children like to bring friends home with them? Why?
3. How does your home meet the unique needs of your family?
4. In what ways does your home glorify God?

ABOUT THE AUTHOR

Dorothy Kelley Patterson, wife of Paige Patterson, president of Southwestern Baptist Theological Seminary in Fort Worth, Texas, and a former president of the Southern Baptist Convention, describes herself as first and foremost a homemaker, an assignment that has commanded her priority in time, energies, and creativity. The Pattersons are proud of their children: Son Armour and his wife Rachel are living in Arizona; daughter Carmen and her husband Mark Howell reside in Florida with their daughters, Abigail Leigh and Rebekah Elizabeth.

Patterson serves as Professor of Theology in Women's Studies at Southwestern and is a widely used freelance writer and speaker. She has been teaching women for more than four decades in the church as well as in baccalaureate, graduate, and postgraduate degree programs.

Patterson is the author of numerous books. She is also the general editor for the *Women's Evangelical Commentary*—New Testament and Old Testament Volumes—published by Broadman & Holman, of *The Woman's Study Bible* published by Thomas Nelson, and of *The Study Bible for Women*, forthcoming from B&H Publishing Group. She regularly contributes chapters and articles to books, journals, and periodicals.

ADDITIONAL RESOURCES BY DOROTHY KELLEY PATTERSON

Patterson, Dorothy Kelley. *The Family: Unchanging Principles for Changing Times.* Nashville: Broadman, 2002.

————. *A Handbook for Ministers' Wives: Sharing the Blessing of Your Marriage, Family, and Home.* Nashville: Broadman, 2002.

————. *BeAttitudes for Women: Wisdom from Heaven for Life on Earth.* Eugene, OR: Wipf and Stock, 2008.

————. "Nurturing Mothers." In *Biblical Womanhood in the Home*, edited by Nancy Leigh DeMoss, 161–70. Wheaton, IL: Crossway, 2002.

————. *Touched by Greatness: Women in the Life of Moses.* Ross-Shire, Scotland: Christian Focus, 2011.

————. *Where's Mom? The High Calling of Wives and Mothers.* Wheaton, IL: Crossway, 2003.

————. *A Woman Seeking God: Discover God in the Places of Your Life.* Nashville: Broadman, 1992.

Patterson, Dorothy Kelley, and Armour Patterson. *A Handbook for Parents in Ministry: Training Up a Child While Answering the Call.* Nashville: Broadman, 2004.

Chapter Four

God's Plan for Marriage

Dorothy Kelley Patterson

Marriage is not merely a flexible contract; it is a covenant commitment to the permanent union of one man and one woman, and the most important witness to this covenant is the Lord himself. God's plan for marriage (Gen. 2:24; Matt. 19:5; Eph. 5:31) includes these purposes:

- intimate companionship (Gen. 2:18–23; Eccles. 4:9–12)
- sexual fulfillment (1 Cor. 7:3–5; Heb. 13:4)
- responsible parenthood (Gen. 1:28; Psalms 127, 128)
- family unity (Deut. 6:4–25; Ps. 68:6)
- spiritual teaching (Eph. 5:18–33)

God designed the differences between the man and woman so they would complement and complete each other. Their mutuality as a couple does not exclude either from any particular contribution to the family, nor does it call for them to do the same tasks. Their goal should be to work together as a team in fulfilling the divine mandate to have dominion over the earth and to prepare the next generation (Gen. 1:28). This is an unselfish union in which the emphasis is not on personal interests and goals but on commitment to each other and to the divinely assigned task.

The woman was created from and for the man (1 Cor. 11:8–9; see also Gen. 2:18). A wife is to help, assist, and undergird her own husband in whatever assignment God gives to him. Because this "helper" (Hb. *'ēzer kenegdo*, literally "a help like or corresponding to him") was an inspired ideal before her creation, the words used to describe her had to express God's own purpose (Gen. 2:18).

Although in the modern era the term *helper* suggests a menial position, careful examination of the word's biblical usage does not indicate a servile role. In fact, the word is often associated with divine assistance (Ps. 30:10; 54:4). A wife may well be described as the "universal spare part." She is often called upon to reverse gears and shift directions according to need. The responsibility is demanding but rewarding.

The woman is also identified as one "comparable to him [the man]" (Hb. *kenegdo*, used only in Gen. 2:18, 20). In other words, the woman is like and equal to the man in her person (both are "in the image of God," Gen. 1:27). However, *identical* is not a synonym for *equal*, and you do not achieve equality by mimicking someone else or by doing the same thing as another. It is through the differences and unique functions that husbands and wives reach their full potential and greatest productivity. Their commonality was just as clear as their distinct role assignments. Both were created in the image of God, and each was to participate in having dominion over the earth and continuing the generations.

God created the man with a need for the woman—mentally, he desires a counterpart; emotionally, he needs a companion; spiritually, he seeks a co-laborer; physically, he craves a lover. For any wife there is no more important task or more sacred duty than to devote your energy and creativity to meeting these needs of your husband. For every aspect of life and intimacy to reach its greatest satisfaction a spiritual dimension must be included.

Outward acts of affection will only strengthen inner feelings of loving devotion. No greeting or departure, no awakening or retiring ought to be experienced without tender kisses and hugs. Both husband and wife need communication at the deepest level and companionship as well as affirming compliments and loving encouragement. Both need the enrichment of a continuing exclusive courtship that is fun, romantic, intimate, and even a bit adventuresome. Just as a plant denied water and sunlight will eventually die, affection without loving touches and tender words will wither and fade. In other words, the sharing of affection must be a habit never to be broken.

In the biblical creation narrative, God's boundaries for marriage are clear. The man and woman are created and then united by God himself (Gen. 2:24). The New Testament reaffirms these same boundaries (Matt. 19:4–5; Mark 10:6–9; Eph. 5:31). Complete consistency is found throughout Scripture without any contradiction of God's plan for marriage.

GOD'S PLAN FOR MARRIAGE

This biblical formula contains three parts. First, *leaving father and mother* refers to the movement of the couple beyond former ties, that is, the flesh-and-blood, birth relationship with father and mother. Of course, the parents who have given you life and selflessly nurtured you to adulthood are not to be cast aside or forgotten. A baby is linked to his mother with an umbilical cord that serves as the lifeline throughout the baby's sojourn in the womb. Yet, when the baby is delivered, the cord must be cut—not because the baby no longer needs his mother but because the baby now has a new relationship to his mother. The mother is still a *lifeline* but in a different way. She is to feed and nurture the baby; she is to comfort the infant and oversee his care. Their bonding should continue as their lives are uniquely intertwined. In the same way, a husband and wife are to establish a new *first* loyalty to each other in the monogamous union of one man and one woman. Their parents should remain an important part of their lives. They are to be honored and respected. They deserve an investment of time and fellowship, but they no longer have the first place.

Second, *the husband and wife are to cling to each other.* In this exclusive fellowship between the husband and wife, they are to focus on each other— sharing dreams and goals and nurturing an exclusive companionship. Their love for each other is to increase while their covenant commitment to each other remains as the strong and immovable foundation for their union. In the same way that plants require water and fertilizer to grow and flourish, couples must realize that *growing* a marriage does not just happen. It demands an investment of time and effort— not for a week or month or year but for a lifetime.

GOD'S PLAN

- *Leave father and mother*—the public commitment or wedding ceremony
- *Cling to each other*—the personal journey of doing the acts of loving devotion
- *Become one flesh*—the physical and most intimate union of body and spirit

Our children are adults with their own families, but my husband and I still have a lifestyle ministry that invades the whole of our lives with duties to family. We must work at finding times to be alone and uninterrupted. We may take a day or two in the midst of our travel schedule throughout the year. Occasionally we set aside time to spend in a remote place where we can relax without obligations. We do not plan excursions and entertainment; we just enjoy each other in a quiet and peaceful setting. I recommend the getaway from work and even children to concentrate on nourishing your marriage and cherishing your spouse.

Finally, the biblical plan calls for *a "one flesh" relationship.* The Creator's special gift of physical intimacy is God's seal on the marriage. God created the woman from the man and presented her to the man. The two God made out of one become one again in this unique union. Such a high and holy intimacy is not designed for casual personal gratification. In some surveys, married couples actually report more frequent sexual activity and higher levels of sexual satisfaction than couples engaged in sexual activity outside of marriage. Exclusive commitment gives them the edge in many ways.[1]

For both husband and wife sexual intimacy is important, but wives also have deep needs for emotional intimacy. Any husband does well to remember that his wife is designed by the Creator to be a responder. Tender love and affection must be included—not just with sexual intimacy but in the daily course of life—because she is precious to him.

⟡ PROTECTIVE ⟡ BOUNDARIES

- Exclusive monogamy
- Nurturing fellowship and loyal love
- Physical affection and warm intimacy

A more stable and enduring relationship creates the environment in which ultimate expressions of love flow naturally. Both husband and wife are to meet the needs of the other instead of their own (1 Cor. 7:3–5). This physical intimacy provides the channel for the next generation, but its purpose goes beyond procreation. Rather, it is a means of meeting mutual needs for ultimate knowledge about each other, for uniquely satisfying comfort, for personal relaxation and play, and for mutual resistance to temptation. In fact, a husband is commanded to find satisfaction and joy in his wife, and he is admonished to find ways to meet her personal needs (Prov. 5:19; Eccles. 9:9; see also Deut. 24:5; 1 Pet. 3:7). A wife, on the other hand, is to be available, to prepare and plan for times of intimacy, and to be sensitive to the unique needs of her husband (1 Cor. 7:3–5; Song 4:9, 16; 5:2; see also Gen. 24:67).

Such an intimate relationship provides the exclusive union into which others dare not intrude. Physical nakedness holds no shame for a husband and wife. In fact, total transparency and openness with each other in every aspect of life is to characterize this highest level of intimacy.

These boundaries protect the marriage from outsiders who attempt to intrude and steal away affections and loyalties. They also wrap the couple in a tender cocoon of loving affection for each other so that the needs of each will be met by the other (1 Cor. 7:3–5). Finally, the protective seal of ultimate physical intimacy is an exclusive union in which no one else shares. It is a language of love that does not require words.

Marriage is a lifelong, permanent, and binding commitment. The con-

---

[1] Glenn T. Stanton, "Sexual Satisfaction in Marriage," *Focus on the Family: Today's Spotlight*, January 23, 2012 [online], accessed July 19, 2012, http://www3.focusonthefamily.com/broadcast/todays-spotlight/articles/male%20sexual%20satisfaction%20and%20marital%20longevity.aspx#; and Elizabeth Bernstein, "What Couples Want to Know But Are Too Shy to Ask," *Wall Street Journal*, May 29, 2012, D1 [online], accessed July 19, 2012, http://online.wsj.com/article/SB10001424052702304840904577426600963764604.html.

sequences of breaking this holy covenant reach far beyond the couple and extend throughout the generations of family and even to friends. The hurt extends even to the community and affects not only emotions but even mundane matters like the economy. Most important is the hurt to the kingdom of Christ. To break the covenant of marriage is to destroy the metaphor God chose to reveal the kind of commitment he has with his children and his church. With this in mind one can understand the prophet's strong language: God hates divorce and does not choose dissolution of a marriage (Mal. 2:16; Matt. 19:4–6). Nevertheless, sin entered the world, bringing with it the chaos and tragedy that have permeated all human relationships. When divorce happens, God works redemptively so that anyone who seeks his forgiveness will be reconciled to him.

Marriage requires the unconditional love of husband and wife, one for the other. You cannot have this kind of love without being willing to accept each other and without making a commitment to do what is necessary to make your marriage work. Do things together—engage in play or relaxation, read to one another, attend the theater, have coffee or tea, talk together, or go for walks. Develop outside activities that provide pleasure and relaxation. Encourage your husband to have hobbies and to carve out time to enjoy them. You, too, should do the same.

WIVES WHO SUBMIT TO THEIR OWN HUSBANDS

In marriage, a wife is to be submissive to her own husband (Eph. 5:21–24; Col. 3:18; Titus 2:5; 1 Pet. 3:1). She is designed to be a responder. Her submission encourages her husband to assume responsibility and develop leadership. Submission is not "obedience" in the sense of forced compliance but rather an attitude of yielding her own rights.

Submission is more than specific acts you do; it is an attitude of the will that willingly bends, seeking ways to obey in everything. There is not stubbornness. Although submission begins with an attitude of the will within, it works itself outward with purpose so that you put all of yourself—your energies, knowledge, feelings—at the disposal of the person in authority over you. Most important—submission is a choice and must be freely given; a husband cannot require or demand it. Nor does a husband dare to abuse his wife by using submission as a demand to achieve his own selfish purposes.

The Lord is clear concerning his protection of a wife from an unreasonable husband who would harm her in any way (Col. 3:19; 1 Pet. 3:7). A wife should also turn to her church family and civil authorities for shelter and support.

Every wife can consider her home as a classroom for learning the ultimate submission, that is, to God himself. Biblical submission is not coercive compliance but deliberately chosen acquiescence by one to the will of another. Submission should not be based on what kind of husband a wife has but on what kind of God she serves. Submission acknowledges an awesome, capable God and expresses confidence in his plan.

⌒ WHAT DOES A ⌒ HUSBAND NEED
from His Wife?

- He needs a gentle and quiet spirit and submission to his leadership (1 Pet. 3:1–4).
- He needs to have her respect and honor in the home and in every venue of life (Eph. 5:22–24, 33).

Submission does not suggest that a wife cannot have her own opinions, the prerogative to disagree with her husband, or the freedom to change her personal convictions. A wife can be strong and even outspoken yet remain submissive in her attitude if she respects and is content for her husband to make the final decision when there is a difference of opinion that cannot be resolved. In this case, she responds with an attitude of cooperation knowing that the Lord established these guidelines and will use her obedience to his plan as a means of glorifying him.

Submission is not coerced slavery or cowering fear but is the reflection of a free and joyous yet refining and strengthening determination to humble oneself and line up under the guidelines of the one leading. This spirit of humility in no way puts a husband in the place of Christ, yet a wife's responsiveness to her husband is rooted in her reverence for Christ.

In addition to honoring her husband with submission, a wife is admonished to respect her husband in the sense of admiring him, meeting his needs, and managing the household efficiently and effectively (Eph. 5:33). This command mirrors and prepares wives for how they are to relate to Christ.

A wife should be attentive to what her husband says, giving him her full attention. She should listen not only to what he says but also to the unspoken needs he has. A wife should never betray a confidence her husband has shared with her. Little things not only count, but they also can enhance even the most stagnant marriage.

When your husband hits the winds of difficulty and trials, you should encourage him. You and your husband are one; whatever may come, you are together for better or worse. You will never push your husband to success, but you can inspire him to realize his dreams by praising his successes and expressing gratitude for the qualities he has that will help him succeed. By your appropriate words, you help him visualize his goals and potential. Sincere praise and appreciation will drive him to give his best efforts to the task before him. A wife's obvious confidence in her husband goes a long way toward making him look good to others.

HUSBANDS WHO LOVE LIKE CHRIST

Husbands are commanded to love their wives as Christ loved the church (Eph. 5:25). This *agape* love is protective, nurturing, serving, and edifying. It is accompanied by—but not overshadowed or replaced with—servant headship in which a husband cares lovingly and responsibly for his wife's spiritual, emotional, and physical needs.

The husband's headship was established before the fall and is part of the creation order (Gen. 2:15–17). It is also affirmed in the New Testament (1 Cor. 11:3). The unique understanding of biblical headship parallels the paradox found in biblical submission. To lead, a husband must be humble enough to serve those over whom his authority and guidance extends. As he meets their needs, they look eagerly for his leadership. To submit, a wife must choose to line up under the husband's authority, and in turn this gracious action on her part awakens in him the desire to serve her and meet her needs. There is a balance between leadership and servanthood, which is perfectly modeled in Jesus. Just as Jesus models selfless submission for wives, he is the perfect example of servant leadership for husbands. The mutuality comes as the husband humbles himself to meet his wife's needs for loving care, and the wife submits herself to her husband's leadership to receive his care and correspondingly to meet his needs.

The apostle Paul clearly lays out the immense responsibility of the husband in the divinely appointed plan for marriage (Eph. 5:25–33). He emphasizes self-sacrifice and service due a wife from her husband. The husband is the primary initiator. The love (Gk. *agapaō*) described is one in which the husband is willing to give up his own best interest so that his wife's needs are advanced. Even the care a husband would bestow on his own body should be equally bestowed on his wife (Eph. 5:28–29). Her well-being is indissolubly bound up with his own (Eph. 5:31–33; 1 Tim. 3:2).

Creating a good and lasting marriage takes hard work and sacrifices by both husband and wife. A husband's wife and children must be his priority right behind the time he spends sustaining his personal relationship to the Lord. A husband is to pursue a personalized understanding of his wife—of her needs and even her desires (1 Pet. 3:7). His role modeling is also important to his children and others as well. A husband does well to show his respect and esteem for his wife. In fact, if he fails to treat his wife respectfully, he not only damages his relationship with his wife but also hinders his relationship with God (1 Pet. 3:7). A wife must understand that part of her husband's family commitment is his primary responsibility for providing support for the family. With husbands and fathers, "the sweat of your brow" goes with the territory (Gen. 2:15; 3:19 NLT). Time and energy are necessary to fulfill his responsibilities in the workplace from which he receives his livelihood, and the family must be understanding of the need for him to do his work in order to support them.

ᐸᔕ **WHAT DOES A** ᔕᐳ **WIFE NEED** from Her Husband?

- She needs to be tenderly loved and cared for (Eph. 5:25-33).
- She needs to be protected and guided through his servant leadership (Eph. 5:22-24).

Headship is a responsibility to embrace with humility and not a right to assume autocratic rule. Headship does not suggest the right to grasp in order to rule and control; rather it is the responsibility to love like Christ and to execute the same servant leadership characteristic of his life. Human headship must guard against abuses. It is a high and holy calling for a husband to assume the primary responsibility for Christlike servant leadership, protection, and provision in the home. Biblical headship calls for the husband to exercise servant leadership (Eph. 5:23–29). In turn, this godly leadership awakens a response from his wife to honor and affirm that leadership (Eph. 5:22–24, 33; 1 Pet. 3:1–4). Headship is not merely a plan of action; rather it is a way to accomplish family goals in an efficient and edifying way.

Headship and submission as defined biblically are intertwined. You cannot have one without the other. The husband must step up to his assigned leadership role with loving concern and full responsibility; a wife must respond with an inclination to say yes to her husband's leadership. Neither assignment is based on giftedness, intellect, or experience; both are arbitrarily assigned by the Creator himself as part of his creation order.

Mutual submission (Eph. 5:21) does not rule out hierarchy and distinctive roles. The analogy includes Christ and the church. Christ does not submit to the church as the church is to submit to him. But Christ did submit to the church through his servant leadership and eventually by laying down his life (Phil. 2:5–8). In a different way, the church submits to Christ by affirming and honoring Christ's leadership and yielding to him in obedience to his commands. Thus mutual submission for a husband and his wife does not mean that each submits to the other in the same way. A husband must put aside his own self-interest for the best interests of his wife, not in the sense of transferring his decision-making to her but in making his decisions based on what is best for her. As a husband leads his wife in a God-glorifying partnership through loving headship, he is humbling himself to meet her needs—loving, nourishing, and cherishing her as a treasure (Eph. 5:25–29; 1 Pet. 3:7). A wife guides the household and manages the care of the family day by day, but her household management does not overshadow her husband's overall leadership of the family.

CONCLUSION

God's plan for marriage is marked by a holy reciprocity in which the husband's loving headship awakens in his wife a responsive submission just as a wife's submissive cooperation draws from her husband servant leadership. With a loving spirit, equal personhood in the image of God, and complementary roles within marriage, a husband and wife can glorify God and reveal him in unique ways by the metaphor he himself designed. Nowhere is the image of God more poignantly reflected. Fortunately, God's plan does not depend on perfect people or perfect circumstances because it is a perfect plan. Truths recorded in holy Scripture will stand forever as the standard by which men and women created by God in his image are to live. In studying how best to make a marriage work, the closer you come to following the instructions of the Creator, the more successful you will be.

PUTTING THE PRINCIPLES INTO PRACTICE

1. What do you see as the most challenging part of a wife's assignment?
2. What specific steps can a wife take to revitalize her marriage?
3. In what ways can a godly marriage impact the church and the kingdom?

ADDITIONAL RESOURCES BY DOROTHY KELLEY PATTERSON

Patterson, Dorothy Kelley. *A Handbook for Ministers' Wives: Sharing the Blessing of Your Marriage, Family, and Home.* Nashville: Broadman, 2002.

———. *The Family: Unchanging Principles for Changing Times.* Nashville: Broadman, 2002.

———. "The High Calling of Wife and Mother in Biblical Perspective." In *Recovering Biblical Manhood and Womanhood: A Response to Evangelical Feminism,* edited by John Piper and Wayne Grudem, 364–77. Wheaton, IL: Crossway, 1991, 2006.

Chapter Five

The Role of the Wife

Glenda Hotton

And the rib that the LORD God had taken from the man he
made into a woman and brought her to the man.

GENESIS 2:22

These words set the stage for the creation of the woman. Woman was not taken
from man's head that she should rule over him or from his foot that she should
be trampled upon, but from a place close to his heart that he should love and
cherish her.[1]

In my many years of counseling wives, I have noticed a common thread
woven into their stories as they share hurts and discontentment in their marriages. It may be the ill-prepared young bride who is adjusting to her role or
the wife experiencing the "letting go" phase as the children prepare to leave
home. Sometimes an older wife is hearing of her husband's dreams of adven-
ture for the first time during their retirement years. She has focused her life on
raising children and on their needs and activities. She begins to wonder about
this strange man to whom she has been married all these years. These are not
uncommon scenarios. When a wife does not understand her role, she lives her
life according to her natural inclination. "There is a way that seems right to a
man, but its end is the way to death" (Prov. 14:12). God understands the heart
of a woman, and he has given clear instructions for her role.

Our contemporary American society is breeding an entitlement generation
with a mind-set to "do my own thing" and "have it my way." This entitlement
thinking encouraging a woman to abandon her role as a wife is propagated
through magazines, books, and electronic media. This false teaching says a
woman can be a superwoman—have a career, a home, a marriage, and a family.
She becomes stretched in every direction except the one that is revealed to her
in God's Word. It is a relief for her to know that Superwoman does not really
exist except on television.

---

[1] Matthew Henry, *Commentary on the Whole Bible*, vol. 1 [online], accessed December 5, 2012, www.ccel.org/
ccel/henry/mhc1.Gen.iii.html.

Commonly a woman marries with the expectation that this man to whom she has given her all is going to meet her needs, satisfy her desires, comfort her emotions, and treat her like "his queen." As the days, weeks, months, and years pass, her expectations crumble, and she is left feeling alone and unloved. What happened? Ruth Bell Graham offers sound advice:

> It is a foolish woman who expects her husband to be to her that which only Jesus Christ Himself can be. Always ready to forgive, totally understanding, unendingly patient, invariably tender and loving, unfailing in every area, anticipating every need, and making more than adequate provision. Such expectations put a man under an impossible strain.[2]

A woman may overlook a man's little irritations before marriage because her expectations are that after marriage she will change him. Thus, she develops a carefully crafted plan to effect the change that often begins the day she says, "I do." However, such a response is contrary to the creation order, which describes her role as a helper to her husband (Gen. 2:18). Thus, she has the God-given assignment to make herself ready to do just that—help her husband. The humorous piece "How to Cook a Husband" describes it well:

> A good many husbands are entirely spoiled by mismanagement in cooking, and so are not tender and good. Some women keep them too constantly in hot water; others freeze them; others put them in a stew; others keep them constantly in a pickle. It cannot be supposed that any husband will be good and tender if managed in this way, but they are truly delicious if properly treated. Don't keep him in the kettle by force, as he will stay there himself if proper care is taken; if he should sputter and fizz, don't be anxious—some husbands do this. Add a little sugar, the variety that confectioners call "kisses," but on no account add vinegar or pepper. A little spice improves him, but it must be used with judgment. Do not try him with something sharp to see if he is becoming tender. Stir him gently lest he lie too long in the kettle and become flat and tasteless. If you follow those directions, you will find him very digestible, agreeing nicely with you and he will keep as long as you want to have him.[3]

The role of a wife does not include "cooking" a husband. She does not rule over him, and her focus is not on changing him.

---

[2] Ruth Bell Graham, *It's My Turn* (Minneapolis: Grason, 1982), 74.
[3] "How to Cook a Husband Circa 1934," posted at *GroupRecipes 2.0* website with the attribution: "This is from *Good Housekeeping* magazine 1983. Credited to 'Mrs. A. Hutchings Frith, from Bermuda's Best Recipes, Warwick Cookbook Fund'", accessed March 5, 2012, http://www.grouprecipes.com/57798/how-to-cook-a-husband-circa-1934.html.

GOD HAS DESIGNED SPECIALIZED ROLES FOR WIVES

As a wife, she gets to know God and trust that his ways are perfect; she begins to relax and enjoy her newfound security in each phase of her marriage. Marriage is for life. The wife's role is very important for a marriage to be "joy unspeakable and full of glory."

God never leaves his children ill-equipped for a role he designed. It behooves wives to seek his instruction, diligently search for it, and apply it generously.

As a young bride, I did not have a clue what it meant to be a wife. When my husband issued his ultimatum to me—either "shape up or ship out," I asked the Lord to teach me from his Word how to be a godly wife. I was amazed at the change that happened in my marriage as I chose to be obedient to God's instructions. There is an axiom of life that says we cannot change other people; we can only change ourselves. Similarly we cannot control other people; we can only control ourselves. As I began to change, God chose to "restore . . . the years that the swarming locust has eaten" (Joel 2:25).

God's plan for a wife is that she first and foremost love the Lord with all her mind, soul, and spirit. A woman must first cultivate a close relationship with Christ: "And he [Jesus] said . . . 'You shall love the Lord your God with all your heart and with all your soul and with all your mind'" (Matt. 22:37).

When a wife cultivates a close relationship with Christ first, she then can focus on the earthly priority, which is that she adapt to her own husband's ways. The dictionary defines one who is *fit* as one who is "adapted to an end or design: suitable by nature or by art" or "adapted to the environment so as to be capable of surviving."[4] Although Scripture does not define the word *fit* for us, this definition affirms the wife's responsibility to submit to and/or be subject to her own husband. The wife is called to *fit* into her own husband's way.

> For this is how the holy women who hoped in God used to adorn themselves, by submitting to their own husbands, as Sarah obeyed Abraham, calling him lord. And you are her children, if you do good and do not fear anything that is frightening. (1 Pet. 3:5–6)

> To be self-controlled, pure, working at home, kind, and submissive to their own husbands, that the word of God may not be reviled. (Titus 2:5)

> Wives, submit to your husbands, as is fitting in the Lord. (Col. 3:18)

---

[4] *Merriam-Webster's Collegiate Dictionary*, 11th ed., s.v. "fit."

> Wives, submit to your own husbands, as to the Lord. . . . Now as the church sub-
> mits to Christ, so also wives should submit in everything to their husbands. . . .
> However, . . . let the wife see that she respects her husband. (Eph. 5:22, 24, 33)

Interestingly a woman is not required to submit to any or all men; a wife is to submit or be subject to her own husband. That is a relief. When a wife knows innately that she is fulfilling her natural God-given role, there is a true sense of peace and joy in her heart.

Endeavoring to Be a Companion

A wife is to *fit* into her husband's ways by becoming his companion, his friend. This is evident in the creation story. "Then the LORD God said, 'It is not good that the man should be alone; I will make him a helper fit for him'" (Gen. 2:18).

- A companion is someone with whom you enjoy spending time. If a wife has developed behaviors that embarrass him, including loud speech, coarse words, or sloppy dress, her husband may not relish her company.

- A companion is someone with whom you should be comfortable. Since men are visual beings, a wife should also strive to keep herself attractive.

- A companion is someone with whom you enjoy discussing things. A wife will attempt to keep up on world events and her husband's interests, keeping her brain alert and stimulated.

- A companion is someone with whom you enjoy going places. She should strive to be available to go along.

Helper by Design

A wife also *fits* into her husband's ways by being his helper. A helper will respect and protect his dignity. A loving wife will never repeat to anyone else the things her husband shares with her in private. Although some women consider female confidants important, a wife needs to be extremely careful that she protects her husband's confidences. People can be fickle. Friends move away. Careful consideration should be given as to what friends may remember a wife saying about her husband the next time they see him.

Intentionally Affirming and Praising

A wife demonstrates her *fitting* into her husband's ways by looking for ways to affirm and praise him. She can become a good student of her husband by devel-oping a list of his good qualities. If she finds it difficult to think of anything good about him, if the memories are distant, she can remind herself about the qualities that initially drew her attention to him. Consider your husband's good qualities that others admire. Observe him carefully and strategically to identify his strengths.

Look for ways regularly to affirm good things, but only what is true, about him. Never make up things—he will see fake praise as manipulation. Frequently review the list of good qualities. When you observe one of his good qualities, express your appreciation to him. If one of his qualities is that he is faithful, say, "One of the things I appreciate about you is your faithfulness." If he has good work habits and/or helps with the children's schoolwork, say a simple thank you. If he has completed a task worthy of recognition, let him hear your recognition and affirmation.

Consistently Communicating

A wife *fits* into her husband's ways by learning to communicate with him. Men are different. When a wife says to her husband, "Let's sit on the couch and talk," he needs a subject. How long is it going to take, and will he need to resolve a problem?

When a husband does talk about things that are important to him, he wants his wife's total and enthusiastic attention, listening with interest. He wants her undivided attention; he does not want to compete with the laundry or the TV. It is important not to interrupt, jump to conclusions, or make assumptions.

⮞ GOOD COMMUNICATION ⮜

- Develop shared interests.
- Develop friendships with other like-minded couples.
- Plan time together.
- Speak the truth in love and with grace. Be careful; wives tend to nag.
- Introduce negative subjects tactfully. Learn to bring to the discussion facts, information, thoughts, ideas, intuitions, and opinions. Many times women talk through their feelings. He may not have a clue what this means to or for him.

Creating a Comfortable Home

When a wife *fits* into her husband's ways, she will learn to keep their home comfortable for him. She will make it a restful place to which he can retreat.

If it is important to her husband that the house is clean and tidy and she finds this difficult, she will work hard to learn efficient time management techniques and housekeeping skills. If he thinks the home is too perfect, she will try to learn ways to make the home environment more relaxed for him; for example, let the newspaper stay on the coffee table more than an hour. Each person is different. Some become overwhelmed when their surroundings are a mess; some feel tense when surroundings are too perfect. The home needs to be tidy enough and comfortable enough for each person residing in it.

Attending Social Events

Fitting in is also manifested by attending social events with your husband. A wife should be willing to accompany her husband as appropriate to business and other social functions.

As a very shy wife of an outgoing, vivacious, successful salesman, I would say to my husband on the way to a function, "Please don't leave me when we get there." But in the course of an evening, he would inevitably become distracted. His attendance and the contacts there were part of his work. In an effort to fit into his ways, I frequented the library. There I collected phrases and questions of interest from books, wrote them carefully on pieces of paper, and tucked them into my pockets so I would be prepared at the next social event. When placed in an uncomfortable position, I would excuse myself to the powder room, peek at the phrase in my pocket, and return to the function with something to use in conversation with strangers. This tool was just one of many I discovered to teach me how to be an asset to my husband at any event.

A wife should cheerfully include her husband's family in social events. She should not speak badly of them. He may; she may not. She may need to make sacrifices to be in harmony with them. She never wants to cause her husband to choose between her and his family. Equally important is accepting his friends graciously. She should be willing to entertain or show hospitality to them.

Enjoying Physical Intimacy

A wife's *fitting* into her husband's ways includes meeting his needs sexually (Gen. 2:24–25). God created this one-flesh experience between husband and wife—to be the most intense height of physical intimacy and the most profound depth of spiritual oneness.

Men are stimulated by visual image, by touch, and by thought. They are spontaneous. A married man needs regular release and fulfillment, and God included sexual intimacy in his plan for marriage. Just as in every other area of marriage, sexual intimacy is a learning and growing experience.

There may be times when a wife is ill or for some other legitimate reason cannot be available at a given time. But, to neglect this responsibility and opportunity out of selfishness is a sin (1 Cor. 7:3–5). This passage teaches that marriage is God's only provision for sexual fulfillment. A loving wife will not deprive her husband sexually.

A wife may wish to ask herself:

- Have I misused the sexual relationship in the past?
- Have I used sex as a tool of manipulation or as a weapon against my husband?
- Have I rejected him on a whim?
- Have I withheld physical intimacy to get even with him?
- Have I been dishonest with him, playing games?
- Have I battered his sexuality through hostility or criticism or ridicule?

Ed Wheat in his book *Love Life for Every Married Couple* addresses wives:

> You should realize that your husband is psychologically vulnerable to injury in the area of sex just as he is physically vulnerable to injury. If you have damaged his sense of manhood and participated in producing an attitude of failure within him, you will have to start all over again and build him up by your tenderness, your sensitivity, your respect and your responsiveness.[5]

A couple needs to talk about the sexual aspect of their marriage and be willing to let the past go and begin anew. If there are areas in which forgiveness is needed, purpose to do that.

"Be kind to one another, tenderhearted, forgiving one another, as God in Christ forgave you" (Eph. 4:32). This wonderful exhortation begins in the home, in the marriage relationship. God created the sexual union and blessed it. He endorses marital love as wholesome and pure. Rejoice and enjoy!

Praying Together

One of the most important ways to show love as your husband's helper is to pray for him. Become his prayer warrior. Pray that he will be "filled with the knowledge of [God's] will in all spiritual wisdom and understanding" (Col. 1:9).

A wife asks friends and loved ones, "How can I pray for you today?" It is more important that she asks her husband before he leaves home every morning, "How can I pray specifically for you today?" He needs to know she is praying for him. It is a reminder of accountability.

While picking up her husband's dirty clothes, instead of harboring anger

---

[5] Ed Wheat and Gloria Okes Perkings, *Love Life for Every Married Couple* (Grand Rapids, MI: Zondervan, 1980), 96.

that he left them on the floor, she can lift up a prayer for his safety, his health, his spiritual growth. She can pray for his protection physically as well as for his protection from the evil forces that would seek to pull him away from the Lord.

Recording a prayer list is a great way to remember his needs. A wife is the one who knows best what makes her husband happy or angry. Because she knows what makes him sad, she is the one who really knows how to pray for him.

Not only does a wife pray for her husband, but she prays about him. There may be times of challenge in the marriage. A wife needs to take her "talk" upward to God in prayer, not outward to a friend. By bringing all to the Lord, she does not allow a root of bitterness, which can ultimately destroy her and her ability to show her love by submitting to its growth in her heart (Heb. 12:15).

Parables in Luke 11 and 18 can teach a wife to continue with her godly request until she receives the answer. A wife is wise to be quiet in a couples' prayer meeting, showing respect for her husband and allowing him to function as the spiritual leader of their home. Sometimes a man hesitates to pray in public because he feels embarrassed that he does not pray as beautifully as his wife. Her lengthy and eloquent prayers may make her husband look unspiritual, causing other men to look down on him.

Living Godly

Ultimately, a wife can live in the manner described above only as she becomes the woman God created her to be and commits herself to doing all to glorify and honor him. "Whatever you do, work heartily, as for the Lord," do it "in the name of the Lord Jesus" (Col. 3:23, 17), and "do all to the glory of God" (1 Cor. 10:31). A Christian wife is a vessel housing the living God (1 Cor. 6:19). When she gave her life to Christ, the Lord moved in. Now her first command is to love him. Second, she is to love her neighbor (and her husband is her closest neighbor) as herself (Matt. 22:36–39). The ability to obey God's commands is a direct reflection of a wife's personal walk with him. Who she is as a vessel of Christ, not what kind of man her husband is, will determine how she shows love to her husband.

Character is a woman's moral foundation—who she is in the closets of her life where no one else can see. But she does not live in a closet. She lives in a community of people, and what is on the inside comes out in relationships. With and by God's grace, the godly woman has complete control of her character, which includes her ethics, values, beliefs, and commitments.

If a wife allows anger, bitterness, unforgiveness, disappointments, jealousy, or hurts to fester, she will become an angry, hard, mean woman whose influence is certainly not Christlike. A biblical example is Moses's wife Zipporah, who seemingly had an explosive temper. Their home was less than congenial. She appears far from being an inspiring wife, helper, or woman of godly character (Ex. 2:15–22; 4:25–26). On the other hand, Abigail is an example of a godly wife. She was a woman of good understanding and beautiful countenance, winsome and wise. She had beauty but did not lack in intellectual assets. Her influence was one of kindness, love, and compassion (1 Samuel 25).

A wife cannot effectively fit into her husband's ways unless she is holding tightly to the right hand of God who created her to be her husband's helper. God will sustain her and has equipped her to submit to her husband (Phil. 4:13). God has promised that he will never leave or forsake those who trust him (Heb. 13:5). He blesses the step of obedience (Ps. 18:20). Contrast this to Eve's disobedience and rebellion. Eve's trouble began when she did not believe God knew what was good and desirable for her. She feared that he did not have her best interest at heart (Genesis 3). A wife who has the Holy Spirit living within no longer needs to fear (1 John 4:18).

A wife who shows godly love by *fitting in* with her husband brings glory and honor to God and does not discredit his Word. She can trust God who created her and established a perfect plan for marriage. Fearlessly, a wife can willingly accept her husband's leadership, not because he is deserving or because of her feelings but because God has commanded her obedience to his plan. Her obedience becomes a good example for the Christian faith.

A godly wife will love her husband, learn to become his helper, and live with him by fitting into his ways, thus contributing her part to a God-glorifying marriage. She then will experience in her marriage indescribable joy.

PUTTING THE PRINCIPLES INTO PRACTICE

1. What new concept about marriage was presented to you in this chapter?
2. Are you willing to create a list of your husband's good qualities and affirm him often using the examples from that list?
3. Is there something for which you need to ask forgiveness from your husband? Are you willing to change?
4. Do you know a Titus 2 woman whose experience and witness you respect? Are you willing to ask her to teach you?

ABOUT THE AUTHOR

The concept of "The Role of the Woman" is very dear to Glenda Hotton's heart. She and her high school sweetheart have been married over fifty years. They reared four daughters who married godly men and gave them ten grand-children. It is her passion to encourage wives to learn to "fit into their own husband's ways." Although she has several degrees, including a master's in marriage and family counseling, the degree she treasures the most is her "Mrs. degree." The first thirty-five years of her marriage, she had the distinct privilege of being a full-time homemaker and rearing her daughters. In the year 2000, as a Titus 2 older woman she joined the faculty in Home Economics-Family and Consumer Science Department at The Master's College and has the privilege of teaching the courses Dynamics of Family Living, Principles of Parenting, and Childhood Education.

Chapter Six

God's Paradigm for the Homemaker

Dorothy Kelley Patterson

A career is a profession for which you train and an endeavor that you undertake as a calling worthy of the commitment of a life. It demands full-speed or intense exercise of activity and the pursuit of consecutive progressive achievement. A career requires training and preparation, commitment and loyalty, energy and time, excellence and creativity—all of which result in achievement. Harriet Beecher Stowe and her sister Catharine expressed the hope to "elevate [homemaking] to a 'profession offering influence, respectability and independence.'"[1]

How often do you find an individual who is professionally adequate in many and varied careers simultaneously? Would you want your postman or policeman also to be your family doctor? Why not? Because you want these community servants to specialize and sharpen their respective expertise in the career each aspires to pursue. Especially that is true of your family physician, whom you expect to have expertise in the field of medicine including preparation of clinical practicums and hands-on experience. Yet what doctor does not dictate letters to his colleagues, prepare reports on his patients, and sit down with a troubled patient as a counselor-advisor? In other words, within most careers there is a diversity of opportunity but a priority of responsibility. You do not want your doctor to make his report preparation or counseling sessions more important than updating his professional skills and performing his medical services to you in the most efficient and effective way.

IS *HOMEMAKING* A CAREER?

The dictionary defines the homemaker as "one who manages a household, especially a wife and mother." Why, if indeed homemaking is a career, is it important to demand your foremost commitment, full energies, and greatest creativity? Domestic incompetence has arisen not only because of the conscious rejection

---

[1] Catharine Esther Beecher and Harriet Beecher Stowe, *The American Woman's Home* (New York: J. B. Ford and Co., 1869).

of household tasks by some women, but work in the home has also been abandoned because of the convenience and consumerism that characterize this age, offering substitutions for the homemaker's tasks in her home workplace.

Keeping the home is an assignment to the wife from God himself (Titus 2:3–5) through the apostle Paul who outlines the curriculum for women in the church: "Be reverent in behavior, not slanderers or slaves to much wine. . . . Teach what is good, and so train the younger women to love their husbands and children, to be self-controlled, pure, working at home, kind, and submissive to their own husbands, that the word of God may not be reviled." From the introduction of the creation order, the woman's purpose is clear. She is to be her husband's helper (Gen. 2:18–22), and she is the mother of all living (Gen. 3:20). In Proverbs 31, the scope and magnitude of the homemaker's task is vividly portrayed. Women are still viewed overwhelmingly as the guardians of the family hearth, including the health and happiness of the family. Many are surprised to discover how much time is required to oversee a household and care for a family.

Cleanliness, also indispensable to health, must be studied in regards to person and house. Frugality and economy have virtues without which no household can prosper. The Beecher sisters in their 1869 volume decided to take their cue from the Bible and define domestic wisdom accordingly. Horace Bushnell, a famous Protestant theologian, said,

> Home and religion are kindred words: names both of love and reverence; home because it is the seat of religion; religion because it is the sacred element of home. . . . The home, having a domestic spirit of grace dwelling in it, should become the church of childhood, the table and hearth a holy rite, and life an element of saving power.[2]

The home has long been the locus of moral authority, and the women who preside over homes in many ways provide the necessary cohesion for the entire society. A good society and a good home are inextricably intertwined. You cannot have one without the other.

Home is still a workplace—not as in the preindustrial world where all worthwhile production took place on site (just as with the woman of strength in Proverbs 31 who used her cottage industries and bartering to increase the resources of her family) but rather as a haven from the difficulties and discouragement of the relentless demands of the marketplace. Home becomes a refuge from the public workplace.

The management of a household is demanding in time and energy. In

---

[2] Horace Bushnell, *Christian Nurture* (New Haven, CT: Yale University Press, 1916), 350.

addition to cleaning routines and meal service, the homemaker must keep order in the home, moving through each day with a myriad of tasks. Even with laborsaving devices, the time required remains relatively constant; any time saving in food preparation and cleanup is quickly replaced with marketing, errands, and added activities away from home. Homemakers must also realize the importance of time and attention to the mealtime itself. Guests at the table are not the only reason for preparing an attractive setting for the meal and giving attention to the menu (see chapter 33, "Family Mealtime").

Being a helper to her husband is a wife's God-given assignment. This public role for the wives of ministers, politicians, administrators, and high-level businessmen is especially challenging because they are expected to maintain an orderly and attractive home, keep themselves well-groomed, become a part of volunteer activities in church and community, host hospitality events on a regular basis, and serve as mentors and role models for other women. These are high expectations. Selfless service and sacrifices are required. But there is also the opportunity for great satisfaction and even rewards.

Rearing the next generation is an awesome task. Is a maternity sabbatical allowing only a few weeks for delivering a child and finding child care enough? Is it even absurd to hand over parenthood and the rearing of your child, which indeed is the production of our nation's greatest resource, to people who are often at the lowest level of compensation and who have had the least motivation for acquiring qualifications and doing professional preparation? Motherhood should encompass a lifetime investment. For this task a woman must cultivate a good temperament and high degree of patience. Done properly, being a wife and mother demands more time and effort than any full-time job in the working world. The greatest challenge to a mother is to be *all* there, focusing on a child, recognizing his weaknesses and strengths in order to support, guide, listen to, love, and encourage the child in developing into a worthy and contributing citizen of the world.

Standing in the gap for the family and the neighborhood brings its own satisfaction, especially in view of the desperate need for volunteer forces in every venue of life, including your own family's emergencies and crises. There is scarcely any income so small but that something can be spared from it—perhaps a "widow's mite." Sharing household knowledge in a pleasant and unobtrusive manner (cleanliness, cookery, good household management) is in itself a ministry best done by the homemaker herself through a natural mentoring process.

THE NOBLE PURSUIT OF HOMEMAKING

Homemaking, in my view and understanding, is not something you fit into the leftovers of life as you would serve up the remnants of a meal; it is not barely getting by as in maintaining a home base; it is not skimping on time with family to splurge on spending for possessions; it is not giving up the beautiful, comfortable, and memorable; it is not the abandonment of pleasures or amusements that bring delight to you. Homemaking begins with feeding, clothing, and sheltering the family (the absence of which would put the ones you most love as hungry, threadbare, and in need of home and affection—the very problems all the governments and activists of the world want to solve); but by no means is that all there is in this noble pursuit, which reaches to include the most interesting and worthwhile endeavors known to woman or man.

The homemaker, as in the case of military commanders, educational administrators, or corporate executives, will accomplish her goals because of her positive spirit and attitude and with the help of her household in proportion to how she performs her duties—intelligently, thoroughly, and joyfully. The well-being of her entire family is dependent on her own joyful spirit, comfort, and commitment to her task.

The genuine Christian homemaker is going to lead in overflowing the boundaries of the home walls and extending its ministries and her influence to the entire world. You will be amazed how the world will come to your front door. The Old Testament has a clear pattern for hospitality from the home, and the New Testament follows with more reminders of its importance (Matt. 25:34–40) and examples of its outworking.

Setting up a household and maintaining its smooth operation, though involving a myriad of mundane and, in the eyes of some, mindless tasks, is essential wherever you live. Yes, its tasks are repetitive and thus readily learned, but they are varied enough that no one seems equally adept at doing them all well, and certainly no one is expected to enjoy all equally. For example, I have always enjoyed ironing—not just to produce a garment in mint condition and ready to wear, not just because it spreads my love to all the family in a morning's work, but primarily because this job can be easily multitasked—iron and supervise children who are at play, doing schoolwork, or pursuing art projects; listen to audiobooks or music; watch a movie; or my favorite, link the task with personal prayer time.

As a Christian woman, I especially love the tasks of home because I am literally working for those whom I love most—whether family members in the home or those whom I have invited to enjoy my hospitality. I am preparing "holy" or "sacred" space in the sense that I have the opportunity to create in the midst of the desert of life an oasis for me as well as for those whom I love. I can carve out my own idea of heaven on earth, and I have done that in a three-room garage apartment enhanced with curtains made from my wedding aisle runner and a bit of trim but also infested with rats (our first dwelling place—where my husband started his hunting); then in a broken-down, two-story parsonage that had been a fire station with many windows (each a different size), which we furnished with what no one else wanted, such as an old door hung from the wall to make a buffet table; then a small two-room seminary apartment in which I again used secondhand, very meager furnishings and metal bookcases to separate sections for our living area and our foldaway efficiency kitchen with two burners and small oven (our first seminary apartment had no stove or drawers).

But in these and many other dwellings, I have always found a way to prepare a place of shelter to which we always longed to return even after a visit to what to us seemed to be a palatial retreat! In no way could I have envisioned and done this in my own strength. As I look back, I believe God, according to his creation order, equipped me as a woman with the creativity and nurturing instinct to nest into whatever place I would find myself and there with comfort and contentment prepare a shelter for me and for my family! After all, being a Christian is not just doing certain things but doing everything a certain way, as my friend Mary Crowley used to say. As I build into my life the disciplines prescribed by Christ, I find that there are unique tools I have at my disposal *because* I am a Christian. I have chosen to follow Christ and to try to walk in his steps, to take on myself the disciplines of life he prescribes. Wipe from your mind the suggestion that homemaking is a Neanderthal idea, a waste of time and effort, or simply one hobby a woman can choose. Keeping a house—in the sense of locking and unlocking doors, preparing for bed and breakfast, and cleaning—is not all that is involved in making a home.

DEBUNKING THE MYTHS

Myth 1: Housework is not really "work" but merely low-status activity.

Germaine Greer said that housewives "represent the most oppressed class of life—contracted unpaid workers, for whom slaves is not too melodramatic a description."[3]

Response. God uses images of the homemaker as being one who clothes and is clothed and one who feeds people and animals in order to describe his

---

[3] Germaine Greer, *The Female Eunuch* (New York: HarperCollins, 1991), 369.

own activities. The psalmist portrays God as a great housekeeper, pitching a tent, clothing himself with light and the earth with water as with garments, ordering boundaries, making homes for animals, giving them food, sustaining all life, and creating and re-creating through the Spirit (Ps. 104:1–2, 5–6, 10–11, 27–28, 30).

Before this at the dawn of creation, God set the man and the woman in a garden, the home he had prepared for them (Gen. 2:9). Even when they were expelled from the garden for their sin, God clothed them (Gen. 3:21). God provided all the necessities of shelter and sustenance during their wandering in the wilderness (Ex. 16:4); he used miraculous means to preserve even their clothing (Deut. 8:4).

One of the most beautiful pictures God provides concerning how he relates to his children is presented through his presence in dwelling places and home activities. He visited Abraham at his tent near the Oaks of Mamre through the appearance of three strangers (Genesis 18). He notes specifically the work required in the tent of meeting during the wilderness wanderings (Num. 4:4–14). He meticulously notes the work required in ongoing priestly service in the temple Solomon built (1 Kings 8:27–28).

Jesus continues this pattern of showing himself quite familiar with the details of housekeeping in his parables (Luke 15:8–10) and describes himself as the recipient of hospitality throughout his journeys (Luke 10:38–42). And he does not fail to note the mundane needs of those in the household such as the little girl he healed—"Give her something to eat" (Mark 5:43).

Myth 2: Housework does not really have to be done. Everyone can and should fend for himself for any necessities.

Response. Jesus puts the homemaking tasks, as all other responsibilities, in perspective in the gospel account of the lives of his friends Mary and Martha (Luke 10:38–42), an incident as notable for what Jesus does not say as for what he does say. Perhaps most important is Jesus's clear statement that these services in the home are tantamount to performing these same tasks for him personally (Matt. 25:40). It matters that your family and hurting people who come to you have a place to which they can come home and receive rest, food, and comfort in the midst of orderliness.

Myth 3: Take-out food is necessary in the modern culture.

HMR (home meal replacement) truly answers the consumers' demand for instant gratification with "simulated home-cooked meals" when almost-made is not quick enough—potatoes are sold already mashed. Your choice is ready-to-cook, ready-to-heat, ready-to-eat. Overriding everything, including nutrition, is convenience. One mother says, "I would love to spend time making a meal in the kitchen, chatting with my kids, but when you are really busy, something gives. . . . I recognize I am making choices."

Response. Perhaps women want to do their work out of the home and maybe kids say they do not care about their mothers being home with them because the households have become so unstructured and unorganized and have been so long without care—much less loving attention—that people would rather be anywhere (even at work long hours) than at home. After all, codes require that the workplace be relatively clean and orderly; they usually have a break room with vending machines and even people for fellowship; they can accomplish something in a structured fashion; assigned responsibilities demand that messes be cleaned up, etc. Maybe people are just looking for someone to take care of them, to show concern about what happens to them, or to meet their individual needs.

Myth 4: Housewives are parasites on society—comparable to the blind, retarded, and disabled.

Response. Homemaking is not an effortless and mindless job. It is sometimes frustrating, especially when you never finish certain tasks and seldom achieve your standard of perfection. Tragically, statistics show that the amount of time women spend doing housework has fallen nearly by half (and the input of men in this arena has not risen in a comparable way). That means we have lower standards of cleanliness and hygiene in our homes. Is it any surprise that staph infections are on the rise as are other bacterial assaults? We are eating at home (or at least preparing food at home) far less frequently. Is it any surprise that obesity is on the rise more than ever? We are caring less and less about how we appear in public or private. In Atlanta, Georgia, there was an attempt to institute and enforce a dress code forbidding the showing of underwear in public. Are we surprised that such a drastic measure would even be considered? The denigration of a woman who invests her primary energies and creativity in the home is definitely a factor in the physical and moral decline of society.

Myth 5: Unpaid menial activity is not only a waste of time but taking something for nothing—freeloading.

Response. A homemaker's work is never done—a room will not stay "picked up" even if you are the only one in your household; a meal will disappear after being cooked and served, and anyone imbibing in the feast will eventually be hungry again—even on Thanksgiving; the clothes and linens you wash and iron today, the towels you pick up and run through the washer—all will be in the hamper again via the cycle of use—never will you have everything pristine clean and perfect even for a day. Yet a home must be tended if it is to be productive and make a meaningful contribution to its residents. Faithfulness to whatever assignment is yours is essential in all physical work—whatever the venue—and for spiritual growth. Especially this is true in the home.

Your work does produce results—varied because this world is fallen so that as much as you work for the good the Devil and his demons are working for evil. But look around you for the products of tender, loving care in the home; consider how the most prized properties in the hospitality industry and many of the most sought-after restaurants are trying to duplicate home living and home cooking—because it can be the highest level of service and efficiency and because it is desired above all when done right.

Your work does matter to those who enjoy its fruits. Note the marketing appeal of advertising that uses the family kitchen and a mother's loving care and delightful interaction with her children. Household management provides a pattern of rituals for everyday life. Homemakers of the past enriched their family's life with personal touches. They gave time and attention to seasonal celebrations building unity within a family. Together in fun and play they turned casual routines into treasured rituals through a bit of flourish or ceremony (lighting candles for family dinner, cutting sandwiches into special shapes for a school lunch, spending time as a family scrapbooking or planning a special party, creating holiday crafts to use as gifts for others). It is not hard to enhance the mundane so that the ordinary becomes extraordinary and creativity pays dividends. Home should be the happiest place on earth.

Your work is one way to remind you and your family, and all who experience your hospitality, to remember the heavenly home God has promised for those who accept him. In Judaism the Sabbath has a central role: a family looks back to the previous week's celebration of the Sabbath with warmhearted gratitude; they experience the Sabbath in process with delight and joy at focusing on the Lord and his blessings; they look forward and anticipate the coming Sabbath as yet another opportunity for rest and spiritual renewal.

God is the creator of all work—including work in the home. That work should be creative, imitating God's own work in creation. He started with chaos—as indeed most women begin the structuring of their household—and ended with a unique, orderly, and beautiful world. Adding flourishes with a loving touch is a way to glorify God and express your love even in the most modest home. When you work in your home, you are constantly bringing beauty and order out of emptiness and chaos (dirty laundry on the floor becomes fresh clothing in the closets and drawers; within the clutter of papers and possessions are tools for work and play organized in their own assigned spaces; a box of recipes and bulging pantry can become delicious and attractively presented family meals; a blaring television or booming CD can become family conversation about the day with soothing music as a backdrop).

Nowhere but heaven will supply full satisfaction to the longing you have for home. Yet here on earth you dare not neglect to remind those whom you love of the ultimate hope in Christ to be in his blessed presence. That eschatological expectation must be nourished by existential details and hard work because the deepest longing for home is part of God's gift to human hearts. For this reason, women do want to know more about doing the tasks of home more efficiently and more creatively.

BIBLICAL PICTURES OF HOME

Biblical pictures of home provide encouraging vignettes for every Christian homemaker:

- Mary and Joseph sought refuge at an inn (Luke 2:7), as did the man rescued by the Good Samaritan (Luke 10:34–35). Travelers in the biblical era found lodging and a basic meal in their inns. Many traveling in undeveloped countries even today look for Christian families, believing they will find secure and gracious shelter among God's people.

- Homes bind together into communities in which families with common goals and commitments can link their resources and enjoy their fellowship.

- Homes are compared to the dwelling place or sanctuary of God—places set apart for the kind of environment in which you meet God, an enlarged area within which the joys of the sanctuary of your heart find an outworking (John 14:2; 1 Tim. 3:15). You are not looking for isolation, but you do need solitude and quietness to renew your energies and fuel your spiritual growth so that you have a launching pad for reaching out with the gospel and with the Savior's loving touch.

- God's dwelling places—tabernacle and temple—are clearly prepared in such a way to include far more than the necessary elements for meeting God. Rather the requirements for furnishing these special dwelling places include what is beautiful and artistic (Num. 4:1–15; 1 Kings 7). In a God-glorifying way, Christian homemakers should give attention to creating beauty and symmetry within their homes, and they ought also to include "stones of help" (1 Sam. 7:12) to make memories and continue to bring these memories to mind and heart. The saying, "The beauty is in the details," is a good one.

CONCLUSION

What action am I suggesting? After examining again the priorities you have been given in Scripture, you must determine that they will govern your life choices, trumping the culture and the opinions of others as well as any personal ambition. Your domestic tasks should not be merely mindless duty but also a responsible choice. Home can indeed be the launching pad for self-expression and self-improvement. Individual talents and giftedness are often ignored or overshadowed or even belittled in the secular workplace, but at home you can unveil creativity and imagination to blossom into individualized expressions, which ultimately may become valuable far beyond the borders of home. Never should a committed homemaker quench creative pursuits. Rather she should work beyond the mundane basics in the home. Home should be a seedbed for creativity.

If you are married, talk with your husband about the choices and decide together as a couple the best course of action for your family—whether you devote full energies and creativity to managing your household or seek employment in the workplace. If your decision is that you should be in the workplace—not merely because of your personal happiness or desire for career advancement but because of what is best for your family—seek the Lord's help for keeping priorities and making the best out of a very challenging dual career responsibility. If your decision is that you should devote full energies and time to managing your household, then attack this assignment with all your creativity and giftedness. Truly make this assignment a career to which you give your best to your family and to extending your family's ministry to everyone God brings to your home. Balance is not so much fitting everything into your life but rather the understanding of priorities to govern what goes into your life.

If you are single, make your dwelling place—room, apartment, or house—a prepared place over which you determine to preside with excellence and commitment. Create a place of comfort for personal retreat, and be alert to the opportunities God brings to you for hospitality. Never be ashamed of your nesting instinct. Do not feel guilty over spending your time and resources to furnish and accessorize your dwelling in a useful *and* beautiful way. Invite those God sends your way to experience your personal hospitality. Honor the Lord by presiding graciously over your household—however small.

PUTTING THE PRINCIPLES INTO PRACTICE

1. What are your personal goals to make your dwelling a prepared place for your family?
2. What are your personal priorities? Where does managing your household fall in that list of goals?
3. What is your favorite memory of home? Why?

ADDITIONAL RESOURCES BY DOROTHY KELLEY PATTERSON

Patterson, Dorothy Kelley. *The Family: Unchanging Principles for Changing Times*. Nashville: Broadman, 2002.

———. *A Handbook for Ministers' Wives: Sharing the Blessing of Your Marriage, Family, and Home*. Nashville: Broadman, 2002.

———. "Nurturing Mothers." In *Biblical Womanhood in the Home*, edited by Nancy Leigh DeMoss, 161–70. Wheaton, IL: Crossway, 2002.

———. *Where's Mom? The High Calling of Wives and Mothers*. Wheaton, IL: Crossway, 2003.

Patterson, Dorothy Kelley, and Armour Patterson. *A Handbook for Parents in Ministry: Training Up a Child While Answering the Call*. Nashville: Broadman, 2004.

Chapter Seven

God's View of the Extended Family

Rhonda Harrington Kelley

Christmastime had come, and I looked around my crowded dining room table to see the faces of the ones I love. My husband and I were hosting our families for the holidays. We were joined by both our mothers, my father, two sisters, a brother-in-law, four nephews, and a niece. Tears filled my eyes at that special moment, realizing our abundant blessing of extended family.

God did not want Adam to be alone, so he gave him a wife and a family. God does not want us to be alone, so he places each of his children in a biological family as well as a spiritual family to nurture and encourage us. Though my husband and I were not able to have children of our own, God has more than blessed us with our extended families and many spiritual children.

An extended family is a group of relatives often living in close proximity. While an immediate family typically includes husband–wife–children, an extended family may include parents–grandparents–siblings–aunts/uncles–nieces/nephews–cousins. Most members of the extended family are related by blood or adoption, though other close relatives and friends are sometimes included. Extended families range from small to very large and may extend to different cultures.

The word "family" comes from the Latin word *familiare*. In most societies, the family is the principal institution for socialization and security. The extended family creates a sense of belonging for its members and provides role models for behavior as well as support systems during crises. The bond of family holds strong across the ages, the miles, the differences, and the years.

The Bible teaches about the importance of family. This chapter will discuss God's view of the extended family, examining the biblical basis and Christian mandate for the family as well as dynamics within the family. Attention will be given to the need for human support and individual responsibility within extended families. Finally, this chapter will explore how to reconcile differences within the family and leave a lasting spiritual legacy.

BIBLICAL BASIS

The Bible is one of the earliest documents to discuss the family. In *The Family: Unchanging Principles for Changing Times*, Dorothy Patterson presents this time-tested biblical definition of the family: "God defined family as the foundational institution of human society."[1] Adam and Eve were God's basis for family in the garden of Eden. Since that time, all other institutions have been built around the family. The family unit was the first community, first church, and first school. It was God's perfect plan for his children, not an invention of the human mind. Throughout the Bible, the family is presented as God's plan to fulfill all human needs.

God's purpose for the family is introduced in the Old Testament and reinforced in the New Testament. In the beginning, God's pattern for marriage was presented—the husband is to care for his wife, and she is to help her husband (Gen. 2:15–23). The Ten Commandments include several specific guidelines for family: "Honor your father and your mother" and "You shall not commit adultery" (Ex. 20:12, 14). The Old Testament includes parental instruction, family directives, and relationship principles. Scripture calls for family members to care for each other and live in harmony. *Honor* is the biblical basis for the family.

Exodus 20:12 says, "*Honor* your father and your mother, that your days may be long in the land that the LORD your God is giving you." This commandment is a biblical promise with a condition—*if* you honor your father and mother, *then* your days will be long. Honor is a verb that means "to show respect for," "to hold in esteem," or "to confer distinction on."[2] The Hebrew word translated "honor" actually means "treat with respect." Throughout the Old Testament, God's children were commanded to honor others. While honor may be initially directed toward parents, it is to include other people—relatives, superiors, friends, and even strangers. Though the world does not demonstrate respect for authority, the Bible clearly teaches about honor and respect, especially within families (Deut. 27:16; Matt. 15:4; 19:19; Eph. 6:1–3). Those who love the Lord should honor others in everything (1 Cor. 12:24–26).

My parents taught me to obey them and honor others. Respect for self and other people was practiced in our home. I have always sought to honor my parents, though it was difficult when my dad left the Lord. While I did not approve of his ungodly lifestyle, I respected his role as my father. I tried to love him back to the Lord through cards, letters, gifts, and visits. God blessed my

---

[1] Dorothy Kelley Patterson, *The Family: Unchanging Principles for Changing Times* (Nashville: Broadman & Holman, 2002), 19–22.
[2] *Merriam-Webster's Collegiate Dictionary*, 11th ed., s.v. "honor."

obedience, and Dad returned to the Lord. Honor is not always easy, but it is always right.

The New Testament also teaches about the family. In the Gospels, Jesus taught about family in words and actions. He loved his mother, blessed the children, and affirmed the home (Matt. 19:13–15; Luke 2:51–52; John 19:26). The book of Acts established the home as well as the synagogue as a place of worship (Acts 2:46; 12:12), and Paul often discussed relationships within the family (1 Cor. 11:1–16; Eph. 5:21–6:4; Col. 3:18–21). Parents are to love their children, and children are to obey their parents (Eph. 6:1–4).

The basis of love in the family is found in the Great Commandment. Jesus said, "Love the Lord your God with all your heart and with all your soul and with all your mind. . . . And a second is like it: You shall love your neighbor as yourself" (Matt. 22:37–40). Christians are to love their families as they love the Lord and themselves. Love is the Great Commandment. Love for family should be patterned after Christ's love—unselfish, unending, and unconditional.

CHRISTIAN MANDATE

Christians have a biblical mandate to love and care for their families. The Bible teaches family members to honor their parents and strengthen God's special institution. In addition, Christian practices through the years have supported the family. Though many families in the Bible and many families in Christian life have struggled, the goal for all families should always be God's perfect plan.

From Bible times and throughout Christian history, families have lived together and gathered together as a group or unit. Joshua 7:13–18 presents the family as an important part of society. Tribes and clans were composed of individuals and families. Families became the human units of society and the basis for property laws. The family context was the focus of biblical teaching and Christian conduct (Deut. 6:4–9). While the immediate family included parents and children, the "family" in ancient Israel included the entire extended family, which could have totaled fifty to a hundred people. All family members were to love and support as well as teach the Scriptures to one another.

Families in the Bible often passed down professions as well as faith. Customarily sons followed the vocations of their fathers. Sons became priests or kings or farmers or warriors like their fathers (1 Sam. 1:3; 8:1). The family structure often set the path for the future. Positions and possessions were passed from one generation to another. Families tended the land of their ancestors and left the land as an inheritance to their children.

The Bible assigned responsibility of headship to the men (Eph. 5:23).

Husbands are the head of the wife and the head of the family. With headship, fathers had spiritual authority and legal responsibility for the family. Fathers were and are to teach their families about God and explain to them about God's work in history. The extended family became the means for proclaiming biblical truth and teaching godly virtues from one generation to the next. The extended family gave each member its sense of spiritual identity.

The home has also been a place of worship. Families taught about God and gathered together to worship him. In the home, families often celebrated Sabbath and the feasts as they read the Scripture and sang psalms. Tenets of the faith were learned and discussed during family devotions. Similarly Christian homes today should be places of worship and biblical instruction.

In the Old and New Testaments, the family was God's conduit to teach ethical practices. The Old Testament consistently relates ethical ideals to the family and connects morality with kinship relationships. The New Testament teaches moral values as well as Christian virtues. Specific guidelines were given for family relationships to be healthy and family members to help one another. Jesus confronted cultural abuses within the family and ignited sociological change in the society.[3]

Paul in his second epistle to young Timothy reminded him of his godly heritage. He acknowledged the influence of Timothy's grandmother Lois as well as his mother, Eunice, in sharing their faith and teaching the Scriptures (2 Tim. 1:3–7). All Christian families today have that same mandate to pass along their personal faith to family members in words and actions.

FAMILY DYNAMICS

The culture has redefined the family. Single parents, same-sex parents, unmarried couples, and literally any combination of people are identified as family to some people today. Christians and churches are impacted by the changing nature of the family. Most sociologists agree that there is no universal definition of the family. The family does influence its individual members as well as public policies, economic development, and health-care delivery. This section will explore the dynamics in the extended family from a Christian perspective.

Though the family structure has changed through the years, the family unit has remained important to society. Whether related by blood, marriage, or adoption, the family is the foundational institution of human society. The nuclear family typically includes a father and mother as well as sons and/or

---

[3] Richard S. Hess and M. Daniel Carroll R., eds., *Family in the Bible: Exploring Customs, Culture, and Context* (Grand Rapids, MI: Baker Academic, 2003), 111, 145.

daughters. The extended family goes beyond the immediate household to include grandparents, great-grandparents, uncles/aunts, cousins, nephews/nieces, and brothers-/sisters-in-law. Dynamics differ among families and vary, depending on size and culture as well as locations and personalities. Christian faith should positively affect family dynamics.

The term "family dynamics" describes the way families communicate and exist together. Relationships between and among family members may be challenging, but the bond of family necessitates cooperation. Family ties connect loved ones across the years and the miles and provide stability in an ever-changing world. In order to strengthen family, effective communication must be maintained.

Communication is one of the most unique and challenging dynamics of human relationships. While on one level, communication is simply the exchange of ideas and information, it is complicated by the nature of its interactive process. Family relationships can be strengthened or weakened by effective or ineffective communication.

In *Raising Moms: Daughters Caring for Mothers in Their Later Years*, I suggest Ten Commandments to strengthen mother-daughter communication.[4] These guidelines can be extended to all interactions among extended family members.

◌◈ TEN COMMANDMENTS ◈◌
for Mother-Daughter Conversation

1. Thou shalt set a regular time for conversation.
2. Thou shalt think from the other person's perspective when communicating ideas.
3. Thou shalt not take comments personally.
4. Thou shalt not be in a hurry when talking.
5. Thou shalt consider the emotions when talking.
6. Thou shalt listen with interest before giving advice.
7. Thou shalt clarify concerns with some concrete evidence.
8. Thou shalt write things down to remember them later.
9. Thou shalt anticipate concerns and questions.
10. Thou shalt involve others for conversation when you are unavailable.

For all members of the family to keep talking and developing their personal communication skills is important. Communication is one part of family dynamics. *Coexistence* is the other. Some extended family members live

---

[4] Rhonda H. Kelley, *Raising Moms: Daughters Caring for Mothers in Their Later Years* (Birmingham, AL: New Hope, 2006), 97–101.

together permanently, while all are together at times. Therefore, each must learn to understand and respect the other so each can get along in harmony. Family interactions are influenced by individual personalities, backgrounds, and roles.

The family unit is the first small group to which a person ever belongs. In the family you learn to relate to relatives and also to other people. Healthy family dynamics can strengthen other interpersonal relationships. Individuals learn to negotiate differences as they work to get along with family members.

Human Support

Members of an extended family can provide needed support for one another. Everyone needs the help and support of others at times. The extended family is a natural support system and should rally to assist at times of crisis. As family members support each other in practical ways, the bonds of love and respect grow.

Not all members of the family will offer help or assistance willingly. Some family members have positive attitudes and are cooperative. Others are negative and passive. Though each extended family member should have some interaction and provide some support, to expect each person to offer the same type of support is unrealistic. People are different, thus human support will differ.

Family support can be provided in many different ways. Before a time of crisis, families can build strong relationships as they spend time together and develop family traditions. Rituals and traditions connect individuals within the family circle establishing support and encouraging a sense of belonging. When a need arises, the extended family can work together to provide necessary support. Crises are tangible opportunities to demonstrate love and concern.

As family members work to support one another, they will learn how to reach out beyond themselves to others. Small children must be taught to be helpful and fulfill responsibilities. Modeling supportive behavior will encourage other family members to be helpful. Human support should be offered throughout the life span but becomes even more essential as family members grow older.

In this season of our lives my sister and I are both supporting our parents. She lives in the same town as our dad and helps him in specific ways with his daily care and financial concerns. I offer more general support and advice because of my geographical distance. On the other hand, I offer more practical support to our mother since we live in the same city. My sister and I take joy in being the support systems for our parents who have supported us for so many years. We are learning more about their needs each day and praying that we are models of good caregiving for others. Family members can become more supportive as they work together and learn from each other.

Reconciling Differences

Every member of an extended family is marked by unique temperaments and personal opinions. Geographical distance, busy schedules, and challenging circumstances cause confusion. Therefore, it is not a surprise for conflict to arise. Misunderstandings develop and miscommunication occurs, often resulting in tension among relatives. Christian and non-Christian families alike encounter family conflicts. The problems must be acknowledged in order to resolve them.

Most family feuds develop from disagreements, distrust, divorce, and distance. These four factors often lead to dysfunction among family members. *Disagreements* occur when individuals have different perspectives, priorities, and personalities. *Distrust* develops when promises are broken, confidences are betrayed, or lies are believed. *Divorce*, which now impacts most families, often causes division and dissension. *Distance* in geography can lead to distance in relationships. These factors among many others may hurt family members deeply. However, relationships can be restored through forgiveness and love.

Personal effort and the work of the Holy Spirit can change enmity to friendship. Jesus Christ provided reconciliation between God and sinful human beings through his death on the cross (2 Cor. 5:18). Jesus Christ can also help his children reconcile with one another. Hurts can be forgiven and relationships can be restored.

In *Raising Moms*, I suggest ten practical principles for rebuilding family relationships. Families who work toward reconciliation can experience closeness and harmony again when they do these things.[5]

TEN PRINCIPLES
for Rebuilding Family Relationships

- Communicate clearly.
- Clarify the situation.
- Understand other opinions.
- Try not to judge.
- Forgive and forget.
- Look for common ground.
- Create boundaries and set limits.
- Compromise for the good.
- Seek third-party input to help work out differences.
- Work hard on the relationship.

---

[5] Ibid., 123–135.

God's Word can encourage and instruct families in turmoil as they confront differences in love (Matt. 18:15) and wait patiently for response (Eph. 4:1–3). Christians are to love each other unconditionally (Col. 3:12–14) and forgive willingly (Matt. 6:14). Restoration of broken relationships brings joy, peace, and love to the family (Ps. 133:1; John 16:33). Most important, God is glorified when family unity resumes.

SPIRITUAL LEGACY

A legacy is something that is handed down from generation to generation. Each person and every family leaves a legacy, good or bad. Christian individuals and families should seek to leave a godly spiritual legacy. Families often pass down important ideas and beliefs. A spiritual legacy is the Christian faith of ancestors passed along to the next generation.

Lydia made a profound spiritual impact on her whole household. Acts 16:11–15 records her personal testimony. Lydia was a busy working woman when she accepted Jesus Christ as her Savior. She shared Christ with the members of her household, including family members and servants, and they were also saved. Together Lydia and her household were baptized (Acts 16:15). Later a church was started in her home. Lydia's spiritual legacy impacted her life, her family, her household, and the church across the ages. She left a lasting spiritual legacy.

I have been blessed personally with a spiritual legacy. Both my grandmothers taught me about Scripture from an early age. My mother and my mother-in-love have taught me the importance of the Bible as a guide for living. My dad has taught me how to be a bold witness of my faith to others. Though I do not have children of my own, I still have a responsibility to my family to leave a spiritual legacy. My spiritual legacy can also influence others.

In *The Mother-Daughter Legacy: How a Mother's Love Shapes a Daughter's Life*, Carole Lewis and her granddaughter Cara discuss a family's legacies. They suggest that a spiritual legacy provides guidance and belonging to the generations that follow. They identified some specific legacies to pass down:

- a legacy of *care*
- a legacy of *connection*
- a legacy of *character*
- a legacy of *contribution*
- a legacy of *concern*[6]

---

[6] Carole Lewis and Cara Symank, *The Mother-Daughter Legacy: How a Mother's Love Shapes a Daughter's Life* (Ventura, CA: Regal Books, 2004).

Families are to teach their children about God and his Word. They are to teach the Christian virtues by word and deed. While children must accept a personal faith in Christ and then develop godliness in their own lives, they can be greatly influenced by the legacy of their faithful relatives and friends. Within the context of family, the next generation can learn how to care for others, connect in love, build character, and contribute to society. Individuals and families can leave a godly spiritual legacy when they follow the Bible's principles about family.

CONCLUSION

The family today is changing and being attacked by the culture. However, God's perfect plan for the family remains the same. God desires that the family be the spiritual and moral center of society. Christians are to follow biblical principles in their extended families, teaching timeless truths to their children. They are to live together in harmony and support each other in times of need. They are to leave a spiritual legacy for families to follow. Then family members will experience God's promise of long life and abundant blessings.

PUTTING THE PRINCIPLES INTO PRACTICE

1. What do you understand the Bible to teach about the role of family? Describe how you are following God's viewpoint in your own extended family.
2. How is your home a place of worship and biblical instruction? List some spiritual traditions that you practice and prayerfully plan to leave as a spiritual legacy.
3. Consider the members of your immediate and extended families. How well do you communicate and coexist? Identify several steps you can take to relate to each other in a more healthy way.
4. Do you consider your family members to be your greatest support system? Describe how you support them and how they support you.
5. Have differences developed between you and any member of your family? Consider how to reconcile your differences and restore your relationship.

ABOUT THE AUTHOR

Rhonda Harrington Kelley is professor of women's ministry at New Orleans Baptist Theological Seminary. Formerly the director of speech pathology at Ochsner Medical Center, Dr. Kelley completed advanced degrees at Baylor University and the University of New Orleans. She lives in New Orleans, Louisiana, with her husband, Chuck, president of New Orleans Baptist Theological Seminary. An author and speaker, she is the director of women's ministry at First Baptist Church New Orleans.

ADDITIONAL RESOURCES

Hess, Richard S., and M. Daniel Carroll R., eds. *Family in the Bible: Exploring Customs, Culture, and Context.* Grand Rapids, MI: Baker Academic, 2003.

Kelley, Rhonda H. *Raising Moms: Daughters Caring for Mothers in Their Later Years.* Birmingham, AL: New Hope, 2006.

Lewis, Carole, and Cara Symank. *The Mother-Daughter Legacy: How a Mother's Love Shapes a Daughter's Life.* Ventura, CA: Regal, 2004.

Osiek, Carolyn, and David L. Balch. *Families in the New Testament World: Households and House Churches.* Louisville: Westminster , 1997.

Patterson, Dorothy Kelley. *The Family: Unchanging Principles for Changing Times.* Nashville: Broadman, 2002.

Perdue, Leo G., Joseph Blenkinsopp, John J. Collins, and Carol Meyers. *Families in Ancient Israel.* Louisville: Westminster, 1997.

Part Two

GOD'S VIEW OF THE SANCTITY OF LIFE

Chapter Eight

The Value of a Child

Dorothy Kelley Patterson

The family is God's first institution, as recorded in Genesis, the book of begin-nings. For whatever reasons, God chose to reveal himself through the meta-phor of the family and the relationships therein. He identifies himself as Father, you as his child, heaven as home, Jesus as the Bridegroom, the church as the bride. No one who studies the Bible can doubt that children are signifi-cant. The psalmist puts into perspective the high value of a child in the divine economy (Ps. 127:3).

WHO IS WATCHING THE KIDS?

How often do parents forget what blessings their children bring! Although studies of time use in America show that, since 1985, the time parents have been spending with their children has been increasing,[1] the percentage of children (younger than eighteen) living apart from at least one of their parents has increased dramatically over the past several decades.[2] A culture filled with fractured families is confronted at every turn with the devastating loss of posi-tive parental leadership in the home, resulting in more depression, homicide, suicide, drug usage, and an out-of-wedlock pregnancy rate twice that of any other developed nation.[3]

Children increasingly are spending more time with a surrogate parent. Researchers study, evaluate, and argue about the effect of substantial non-parental care on a child. In 2001, 61 percent of preschoolers regularly received some form of nonparental care. For children between kindergarten and eighth grade, 51–52 percent received some measure of nonparental care. Older chil-dren are expected to care for themselves. Youth beyond eighth grade are not even included in the survey since they are presumably looking after them-

[1] D'Vera Cohn, "Do Parents Spend Enough Time with Their Children?" *Population Reference Bureau* [online], accessed July 26, 2012, http://www.prb.org/articles/2007/doparentsspendenoughtimewiththeirchildren.aspx.
[2] Gretchen Livingston, "A Tale of Two Fathers: More Are Active, But More Are Absent," Pew Research Center Publications, June 15, 2011 [online], accessed July 24, 2012, www.pewsocialtrends.org/files/2011/06/fathers-FINAL-report.pdf.
[3] Sylvia Ann Hewlett and Cornel West, *The War Against Parents* (New York: Houghton Mifflin, 1998), 250.

selves.[4] The simple observation of dangers to which these young people are regularly exposed should nullify this tragic oversight. Some use their church's day care or after-school care for oversight of their children, forgetting that even the best church program is institutional care.

Some parents tend to push their children into the background to be retrieved for leisure enjoyment or to be relegated to optional responsibilities. These parents never learn God's purpose in parenting, nor do they accept the demanding task of understanding a child's role in the divine economy. To assume the primary responsibility of modeling the life of a helpless baby into a godly, courageous, confident, creative, one-of-a-kind person is truly an awesome task. Every child should be a symbol of hope for the future.

Some modern parents reject the opportunity to continue the generations with the mind set that their high professional and financial goals preclude the distraction children bring to life. Although most pursue parenthood with enthusiasm, even godly parents, busy with other important matters, are sometimes too eager to push their children into a world of responsibility to function on their own in order to free their parents to follow their own goals.

Christian parents may assume that living in a godly home will pass to their children godly character traits and equip them with a working knowledge of values. Parents often do not have the energy or the patience needed to pour out tender loving care, not to mention patient instruction in biblical principles and meticulous training in living God's way, to their offspring. In short, they can be overwhelmed with the unimportant because wrong ideas coming from the influence of a worldly culture inevitably overtake the right ideas found in heavenly principles.

The marketplace of ideas offers two mutually exclusive worldviews—living according to the absolute truth found in God's Word, that is, the Bible, on one hand, and, on the other hand, imbibing the postmodern choice of establishing your own truth base, that is, "situation ethics," or deciding what is right and wrong according to personal experience.

Commitment to the task of rearing children in the nurture of the Lord, preparing them for the world where they will encounter an assault upon their faith and spiritual foundations, is a demanding challenge.

Our first and primary mission field is our children. God values our children. Jesus became indignant when the disciples didn't embrace the worth of children in God's expanding kingdom (Mark 10:13–16). God tells us that children

---

[4] Federal Interagency Forum on Child and Family Statistics, *America's Children: Key National Indicators of Well-Being, 2002* (Washington, DC: U.S. Government Printing Office, 2002), 10–11.

are his blessing to us (Ps. 127:3). And he places great importance on our teaching our children to love and serve him (Deut. 6:7–9).[5]

As young apologists, children must be equipped to stand against the wiles of the Devil—however winsome, logical, and relevant these enticements might be—and must be determined to measure every temptation against the pure and true Word of God. C. S. Lewis perceptively noted that Christians are the best arguments for *and against* Christianity.[6] Nothing hurts your vulnerable child any more than shallow or pseudo-Christianity. Knowing this danger should help you encourage your children to put their focus where it needs to be—not on Christians but on *Christ*!

CHILDREN DEMAND TIME

Would any believing Christian woman dare question the value of a child? Most want children themselves and would grieve if an infertile womb were to make that impossible. However, too few understand that with blessings and opportunities come responsibilities and accountability. What costs you nothing is worth just that.

During the conservative resurgence in the Southern Baptist Convention, my husband—and our family—experienced some dark hours. Friends refused to speak to us in public; we were excluded from certain gatherings; my husband's integrity was questioned; his motives were judged; his reputation was maligned. Most of these personal attacks came from Christians—even from leaders in our denomination. Some who believed as we did quietly encouraged our stand behind the scenes, but they did not want to be seen with us publicly. During this decade of great hurt in our lives the single most important human escape for us was the personal friendship, genuine love, and sensitive ministries of our children. Armour and Carmen, aged ten and eight when the movement began, not only sensed our hurt and discouragement and responded with tender loving care on every level—physical, emotional, social, and spiritual; they also caught a vision of our mission. Without our verbal invitation, and certainly without any coercion, they decided to join us! They attended conventions; they fielded telephone calls and located people; they ran errands and planned meals. But more important than any of these tasks, they distracted us from pressure and made us laugh, hugged and held us when we were hurting, stood with us when we felt alone.

---

[5] Jani Ortlund, "Missional Mothering," *The Resurgence* [online], accessed February 11, 2011, http://theresurgence.com/2010/10/22/missional-mothering.
[6] See C. S. Lewis, *Mere Christianity* (San Francisco: HarperCollins, 1952, 1980), 216–17.

Children demand both quantity and quality time. That time has its dividends. However bad a day, whatever burdens are on your shoulders, you can escape for just a moment when your child greets you with a welcoming hug and words of love.

God absolutely forbids the child sacrifices of pagan nations (Deut. 12:31–32). He also forbids sacrificing your children, even in a figurative sense, on the altar of your own ambition or dreams (Isa. 23:4; Jer. 9:21; Lam. 2:11; 4:10).

In Scripture childlessness was always looked upon as an affliction. Sarah laughed at her childlessness, but she despised it. She was full of sorrow and experienced much heartache over her barren womb. Rebekah grieved greatly over her difficulty in having a child. Rachel was very bitter as again and again she watched Leah bear children while she remained barren. The brokenhearted Hannah pleaded with the Lord to give her a son, promising to return him to the Lord, which she did.

Even the repetitive and seemingly endless tasks of motherhood should bring unspeakable joy to the maternal spirit fashioned by the Lord. One woman describes her life under the shadow of a "golfing, blackjack-playing, martini-drinking" mother who rejected cooking, sewing, or crafts. Thanksgiving dinner was at the golf course, which was the gathering place for the few family occasions she remembered. When her mother died, she scattered her mother's ashes on the golf course. She went out to establish her home in a very different way, attempting to compensate for her own mother's lack of interest in home and family.

Children are more than the by-product of a biological function. The Lord placed tremendous importance upon teaching children about himself and training them to walk in joyful obedience to his way (Deut. 6:7–9). Jesus said that a person would be better off dead than to bring harm to a child (Mark 9:42), and he affirmed that your investment in a child is service to him (Matt. 10:42).

The Hebrews pictured rearing children as a building process (Hb. *banah*, "build," the root word from which comes *ben*, "son," and *bat*, "daughter"). Parents lay a foundation of faith, upon which they build character and inspire service to God and others. Finally, they polish their children through fervent prayer and diligent nurturing and lay them as crowns at Jesus's feet (see Psalm 128, often called "The Builder's Psalm"). The cycle continues as their children select godly mates, establish Christ-honoring homes, and build their own sons and daughters. Children indeed are the most valuable fruit from the family's work. In their young years, they are usually sensitive to receiving the gospel and then full of energy to offer the Lord years of service.

The psalmist uses word pictures to express the building of a house, which could be a metaphor for the rearing of a family. Children are obviously a blessing from the Lord (Ps. 127:3). In fact, they are described as "a heritage from the LORD," or a gift that extends through the generations. They are also "a reward" in the sense of a benefit received for time and work invested.

PASSING YOUR FAITH

A deeply rooted faith will insulate your child from the tentacles of a secular society without isolating him from the world. Genuine faith will fortify him with answers and magnify the biblical standard without nullifying his identity, stifling his questions, or belittling his struggle. Passing faith to your children demands far more than attending church, listening to family devotions, and following pious platitudes.

Children are observant. Actions are more effective than words. The Lord seized upon lifestyle instruction when he gave the Israelites his law. He did not assume that they would know how to pass along this vital information about him and his kingdom. Through his spokesman Moses, the Lord instructed parents to use every conceivable time, position, and occasion to teach his commandments to their children (Deut. 6:7–8). The demonstration of a lifestyle of faith must be integrated into every facet of life, so that God's truth is not merely taught in purposeful encounters but also caught as you move through the daily events of life. Lifestyle teaching will fill in the gaps beyond years of sermons and formal instruction. Creativity is essential to weave these truths into all the mundane chores of life. The children's spiritual education is ultimately the responsibility of the parents.

Three words are used to give understanding to this important task (Deut. 6:1 KJV):

- *Commandment* (Hb. *mitzvah*), which is a reference to the sum and substance of the law or the Ten Commandments or perhaps all the Torah
- *Statutes* (Hb. *chuqqim*), which may be a reference to the ceremonial laws about how to approach God
- *Judgments* (Hb. *mishpatim*), which could allude to narrative passages describing what happens when you keep or violate the law

Nothing was more important for my children than developing a time of personal intimacy with the Lord beyond corporate worship and family devotional time. How delightful to observe during their teen years well-marked Bibles at church, at home, and even on family vacations! How did they develop this habit? Not through lectures and assignments, but by watching this discipline at work in the lives of parents and grandparents! My children will not remember the words of wisdom I have passed along over the years, nor will yours remember the good advice you have given. However, etched in their minds and planted in their hearts is a permanent picture of who you are and how you have lived before them. Even if a child strays far from the faith carefully taught to him in his childhood and youth, God may use the picture of godly parents to bring him home—not just to parents but to the heavenly Father as well.

The life you live before your children is not in vain. They should see you read the Bible, pray, worship with God's people, and live so that spiritual disciplines obviously make a difference in your life. Every parent has some regrets—careless words, inappropriate actions, ungodly moments, costly mistakes. These inconsistencies come and go but are seldom erased from memory. Your children will note flaws in your character. However, if you acknowledge mistakes, seek forgiveness, and renew your commitments, these mistakes and resulting consequences can be another classroom for your child. Intuitively a child knows and his experience confirms that you are not perfect. What he needs is consistency. He needs a pattern for what to do when you mess up. When you fail, if you ask God's forgiveness, begin anew, and refuse to abandon seeking the Lord with your whole heart, your child will have a marvelous, tested-and-proven-faithful blueprint for his own pilgrimage of faith. Whatever his detours, he has the best map for finding his way back.

Parents must prayerfully define boundaries and set goals for their children. They must live in practical ways to show that their faith works. Family time must include devotionals with the family in worship together, meaningful rituals unique to the household, regular mealtimes, and special seasonal celebrations as well as recognitions of special events. Into all you must interject fun and fellowship—laughing and talking with one another. The family circle should be the place of greatest joy. Parents must be clear and specific in communicating expectations. They can be firm while still showing respect for their child. Even a parent's voice and demeanor should exude confidence so that the child will listen and obey. To admonish a child "to be good" is too vague and nebulous to send a meaningful message. Ridicule and sarcasm have no place in rebuking your child, nor should disciplinary action be preceded by an escalating degree of threats, suggesting that your child need not listen until your voice reaches the pitch indicating action is imminent. Praise and respect must be part of governing your child and preparing him to be confident as well as effective as he makes his own place in life.

Biblical instruction is not to be confined to a home classroom. Moses made clear that this instruction was not only to be woven into daily life but also to be incorporated into times of rest. In fact, he describes the process as including *repetition integrated* into life every day so that a child sees God as central to his family, to his relationships with others, and to his work and play whatever the circumstances might be—happiness or sadness, blessing or tragedy, feast or famine. A child sees the integration of faith as applying to the whole of life—not merely regularly scheduled meetings within the four walls of the church. Parents are to provide a living *demonstration* of how biblical principles work in daily life. *Repetition* and *integration*, together with *demonstration*, become a living *validation* for a faith that works because it is woven into the tapestry of life (see Deut. 6:6–9).

NURTURING CHILDREN

What are some practical ways parents can nurture their children?

- Take time to play with your child. Even allow your child to choose the game or make up one that pleases him.
- Plan plenty of sleep for your child. Starting in infancy, schedule regular sleeping periods and allow your child to learn the discipline of relaxing and going to sleep.
- Take seriously your responsibility to set limits for your child, and exercise control by guiding his choices appropriately.
- Keep mealtime as a family priority. Eat at least one meal together as a family daily, and make it special.
- Develop a sense of responsibility in your child. You want to guide him into the responsibilities necessary for ordering his life.
- Even babies love to hear the comforting sound of a parent's voice. Read books to your children from infancy onward.
- Watch over the health of your child. Keep a medical history of vaccinations and other general information.

A common denominator in all these practical suggestions is the fact that parents must invest time in their children. Quality time demands quantity hours; happy and memorable experiences call for time spent planning and investing creativity.

CONCLUSION

Children are a family treasure—not just a community trust. The family is at the center of life; wives and mothers, according to Solomon, should be more precious than jewels (Prov. 31:10), and children ought to be treasured (Psalm 127). The family has been the cornerstone on which civilization rests, and yet modern society now seems intent on hastening the disintegration of the family. Children are being removed from the governance of their parents and relegated to the rule of "community experts," who are supposedly better able to prepare them for the complexities of life.

Some years ago a prominent American woman began to tout an old African proverb, "It takes a whole village to raise a child." No child should be reared in isolation from the larger community and world, but families gather to make a village! The village works to protect and nurture the next generation through common goals and projects. However, the physical, emotional, and spiritual security must be inherent in the family circle in order to ensure your children have satisfying and productive lives.

Some say, "It takes a church to raise a child." The church made a unique contribution to my life and to the lives of my children. My granddaughters Abigail and Rebekah love their church. When as young teens they moved from Texas to Florida, the loving church family who welcomed them made their transition so much easier. Churches are important team members for spiritual nurturing that begins in the home. Ultimately, mother and father stand accountable to God for rearing their children in godliness. Someone has to get the child to church.

Freedom to be yourself does not mean liberty to thumb your nose at others. Within the family you learn to relate to others. You conform to life in community, but you also make personal contributions. As you learn to interact with other family members, you are better equipped to take your place in your "village" and ultimately in the world.

God *started* civilization with a family—not a village or a religious institution. One man and one woman were created by God for the purpose of linking their lives in an exclusive monogamous relationship with one another. Together they were commissioned by God to have dominion over the world and to extend the generations (Gen. 1:27–28).

As the descendants of this first family multiplied, families extended to clans; communities developed; nations came into being. But in the founding document of civilization—holy Scripture, revered by Jews and Christians—there is no evidence that the nurturing of children was primarily a community responsibility. Rather, mother and father together reared their own children unto the Lord (Deut. 6:1–9; Prov. 1:8–9) and guided them into becoming contributing members of an ongoing society (Prov. 22:6). Committed parents—not merely a good "village" or a willing congregation—rear a child. Families then band together to establish a healthy society.

No schoolroom, government program, or system of religion is in a position to lay spiritual and moral foundations for the family. The family acts as a watchman on the wall to protect the community from alien values and untested changes. Parenthood is a lifetime investment. God chose parenthood as a metaphor for his loving care for all who believe and trust him. Believers become his children, and to all who call him Lord he is Father with tender affection and firm discipline through a program of discipleship that never ends. In the words of the reformer Martin Luther, parents must look at the very ordinary tasks required in nurturing a child and realize that the ordinary deserves to be sanctified.

> What then does Christian faith say to this? It opens its eyes, looks upon all these insignificant, distasteful, and despised duties in the Spirit, and is aware that they are all adorned with divine approval as with the costliest gold and jewels. It says, O God, because I am certain that thou has created me as a man and hast from my body begotten this child, I also know for a certainty that it meets with thy perfect pleasure. I confess to thee that I am not worthy to rock the little babe or wash its diapers, or to be entrusted with the care of the child and its mother. How is it that I, without any merit, have come to this distinction of being certain that I am serving thy creature and thy most precious will? O how gladly will I do so, though the duties should be even more insignificant and despised. Neither frost nor heat, neither drudgery nor labor, will distress or dissuade me, for I am certain that it is thus pleasing in thy sight. . . . God, with all his angels and creatures is smiling—not because the father is washing diapers, but because he is doing so in Christian faith.[7]

There is no greater mission field than children. God values every child as his creation and the object of his love. He describes children as a blessing (Ps. 127:3). The Lord instructs parents to invest the whole of their lives in teaching their children to love and honor him (Deut. 6:7–9). Jesus took the opportunity to affirm the worth of every child when he expressed disgust over the indifference of his disciples toward the children (Mark 10:13–16).

---

[7] Martin Luther, "The Estate of Marriage, 1522," in *Luther's Works*, trans. Walther I. Brandt, ed. Jaroslav Pelikan and Helmut T. Lehmann, American Edition (Philadelphia: Muehlenberg and Fortress, 1955), 45:39–40.

PUTTING THE PRINCIPLES INTO PRACTICE

1. Do you consider your child an appendage to your life or an afterthought and sometimes an inconvenience to your plans? How do you show your child that he is special to you?

2. Is your child the apple of your eye—a precious treasure entrusted to your care by God himself? How do you prepare your child to take his place in the world?

Chapter Nine

Biblical Insights on Birth Control and "Family Planning"

Dorothy Kelley Patterson

Complex issues go beyond superficial questions, making the task of accepting or rejecting parenthood a challenge. Fundamental confusion exists between "finding a solution" and "eliminating a problem." The topic of contraception is indeed "pregnant" with possibilities for positive discussion and vehement disagreement. Although no specific biblical text will settle the birth control issue, for me as a theologian who happens also to be a woman, moral imperatives and timeless principles are readily apparent in Scripture. From these you can then make specific applications to contemporary decisions and situations. God did not restrict his revelation only to cultural problems of the past. The Bible is adequate *and* relevant to every generation.

God started civilization with a family—not a village or community or even a religious institution. According to the order of creation, the family is God's first institution. The details of his creativity are recorded in Genesis, the book of beginnings. The family is the cornerstone upon which communities and even nations rest. Children are not only a family treasure but also a community trust. Because the family is a natural institution established by God, who created human beings endowed with certain inalienable rights that cannot be denied by government, these human beings do not exist to serve the state, nor is the state assigned to rule the family. Government then should recognize and respect the natural family just as surely as they should recognize and respect basic human rights.

One man and one woman were created by God for the purpose of linking their lives in an exclusive, monogamous relationship. The opening chapter of Genesis contains a mandate for the first man and woman to "be fruitful and multiply and fill the earth" (Gen. 1:28). If the human race ceases to be fruitful and to multiply, the race will disappear in a generation.

LIFE IN THE WOMB

Life is a continuous tapestry, beginning in utero and ending in death. Within those bounds are designations such as zygote, embryo, fetus, infant, child, adolescent, and adult. Modern embryological knowledge seems to push creationist theologians more and more toward an understanding that the soul is given by God at conception, at which time the DNA molecular pattern fixing the new individual's identity occurs:

> One can hardly look for the origin-point of personhood anywhere other than at the moment when all potentialities necessary for its functioning enter the picture: namely, at conception.[1]

Subsequent human acts do not create personhood but simply illustrate the unique identity that was already begun at conception. The baby in the womb is alive, or he would not be growing. The Bible regards personal identity as beginning with conception (Ps. 139:13–16).

There are many "authorities" (physicians, scientists, theologians, judges, and of course, the self-appointed authorities—the bearers of rights) who are quick to address any matter with absolute certitude. However, their answers concerning conception range from no life to potential life to some life to developing life to full personhood. The discussion on who ultimately controls that life is just as broad. Theology addresses the nature of the human soul, medical science studies the nature of the "fetus," philosophy debates the nature of personhood, and ultimately ethics examines the moral and societal problem concerning whether or not abortion in any form—early or late—ought to be allowed. These issues all come to the table in discussions of life and death.

CONCEPTION AS FERTILIZATION, NOT IMPLANTATION

Because conception and fertilization have been understood as being virtually synonymous, both words are used interchangeably to refer to the beginning of human life. A contraceptive (i.e., a device to contradict conception) prevents fertilization. Before 1976, a contraceptive was understood as that which prevented the union of a man's sperm and woman's ovum. However, a new politi-

---

[1] John Warwick Montgomery, "The Christian View of the Fetus," in *Birth Control and the Christian*, ed. Walter Spitzer and Carlyle Saylor (Wheaton, IL: Tyndale House, 1969), 81.

cal agenda calls for revising this definition to mean anything that prevents implantation of the blastocyst, which occurs six or seven days after fertilization. Conception then becomes "the onset of pregnancy marked by implantation of the blastocyst," blurring the distinction between what would prevent fertilization and what would abort an **already fashioned** week-old embryo. In this chapter, I will return to the classical definition of *conception* as a synonym for fertilization and as the point at which the new human life begins. Contraceptives are then chemicals or devices that prevent conception or fertilization. Although a birth control method may function as a contraceptive some or most of the time, the moment whatever the contraceptive may be kills an already conceived human being or embryo, that device is then an abortifacient. In other words, some forms of contraception not only prevent conception but also prevent implantation of an already fertilized ovum, resulting in what is actually an early abortion.

BIBLICAL PERSPECTIVES ON LIFE AND FAMILY

Beware of hearing words that are welcome and excluding teachings that are unwelcome. Birth control affects a complex network of human relationships. Hot issues include the question of life and how life manifests itself in various stages of human development as well as how physical actions hold spiritual meaning. The extent to which a biblical worldview should direct a non-Christian world and how human endeavor should relate to divine will are also important. The prevalence of sexual immorality in the modern world does not relieve a woman from her responsibility for honoring Old Testament principles and New Testament practice. A strong emphasis upon the family and procreation within marriage as the divine means for extending the generations and producing godly seed is found throughout Scripture. Fruitfulness of the womb remains a sign of great blessing. However great biological and genetic advances are, creation and control over life and death have not been passed from the Creator God to the scientific and impersonal means of those who have been created. Being free from religious legalism does not mean calling for the removal of biblical boundaries in all of life.

Replacing the natural with the artificial through modern medicine and science has a history of consequences that are anything but beneficial—monstrosities, deformities, deficiencies; yet the world shows an unwillingness to learn from the past.[2] To suggest that any woman (or man) is master of her own destiny is alien to a biblical worldview. Every individual is responsible;

---

[2] Philip Edgcumbe Hughes, "Control of Human Life," in *Birth Control and the Christian*, 127.

cause and effect do enter the sphere of human conduct. Despite sowing what you reap, you are not the center of the universe. God alone is sovereign in creation. He exercises his providence and judgment according to his own will and redeems his creation according to his plan. Knowing that God is ultimately in control assures his creation that the future rests with him.

To be God centered is to be family sensitive and other conscious. The desperation and tragedy that characterize modern families is not limited to a certain ethnic background, particular geographical region, select economic bracket, or common religious commitment. The problems that exist are not stereotyped to exclude or pinpoint a particular set of circumstances. The breakdown continues unabated and seemingly worldwide, and all must work together to seek solutions.

Totalitarian governments have entered the bedroom demanding birth control policies, which without compliance are then followed by abortion and even infanticide. Schools have become managers of child rearing and education. Teachers and educational administrators have assumed a position of dictating to parents how a child's life is to be molded, including the kind of home environment he is to have. Health requirements, mealtime nutrition, and moral standards are all set by educators, who demand more money from parents to pay for their mandates. Some employers (even some religious agencies) have been bold enough to dictate to employees how many children they can have and when those children are *convenient* to company plans.

Both mothers and fathers have been drawn away from the family and into the workplace. A woman no longer devotes herself exclusively to family, that is, to nurturing and supervising children and maintaining the home. In fact, no one is charged with rearing the children and keeping the home. Is it any wonder that parents want to use virtually any means to limit the size of their families and thus lessen responsibilities at home?

God's reasons for marriage certainly go beyond procreation (Gen. 1:28; Ps. 127:3–5) to include companionship and mutual fellowship (Gen. 2:18), to create unity (Gen. 2:24), to bring pleasure and satisfaction and enjoyment (Eccles. 9:9), as well as to produce godly seed. Sexual union is the means for continuously uniting husband and wife in the most exclusive way, through which they are uniquely "known" to each other in the fullest expression of mutual love.

THE PRIVILEGE AND RESPONSIBILITY OF MATERNITY

Profound and persistent biological differences exist between the sexes, and these differences mandate different and unique responsibilities. How can a woman be free from her own nature of maternity and still be herself? For many, contraception would seem to be uniquely a woman's issue. The central position of the woman in her own family and in all of civilized society is derived from her necessary and exclusive role in procreation and from her most primary and inviolable human tie, which is to her own offspring. To refuse to accept life in the womb is to violate God's purpose for the womb, which is receiving, nourishing, and protecting fetal life.

The basic moral question is not whether or not a baby is *wanted* but whether or not the baby was *willed*. By divine fiat, the choice or consent to have intercourse is the implicit consent to bear children, which is God's way of continuing the generations. The woman is not a baby-making machine, but she has by nature a baby-making body. Only one woman can bear a particular child, and her tie to that child is personal and her bonding virtually unbreakable. In the rearing of that child, she has the opportunity to impart within the privacy of her family circle her own values to the child. To refuse that procreative role and to throw upon society that nurturing responsibility is to abdicate her highest calling and greatest usefulness to the Creator and to his created order.

Women are called upon to make sacrifices; they are challenged to live selflessly. These sacrifices and a selfless life are essential for the continuation of the generations. Women cannot shun this greatest responsibility of maternity without endangering all of civilization.

Unfortunately, individualism has driven parents to seek only personal goals and to be manipulated by selfish whims. Materialism has captured their hearts so that things are more important than children. This self-centered ideology allows many socially approved and legitimate ways of doing things, as if the right way is to be determined by personal choice or community consensus.

BARRENNESS IN SCRIPTURE

In Scripture, godly women were not concerned with whether they would receive discrimination in the marketplace but rather whether their wombs were barren. Childlessness was considered an affliction, an indication of worthlessness and insignificance (Gen. 29:32; 30:1). Women were not pining away, pleading with the Almighty that they might be priests or prophets. They were praying for the privilege to bear a child. In Israel every Jewish mother hoped to become the mother of the Messiah, whose coming had been promised to Eve, the first mother (Gen. 3:15). Children were considered a direct gift from God (Gen. 4:1; 16:2; 17:19; 29:31; 30:22; Ruth 4:13). God has always been actively involved in fashioning the child in the womb (Ps. 139:13–16).

Hannah was brokenhearted over her childlessness (1 Sam. 1:1–2:1). Feeling forsaken of God, her maternal instinct prompted agonizing prayer for a child, and her heart's burning intent was to give the boy back to God. Hannah deemed nurturing a child the highest service. This motivation was not borne out of slavery to procreative responsibility. Hannah was a brilliant and spiritually sensitive woman, as is shown in her poetic psalm (1 Sam. 2:1–10). In conversations with her husband and Eli the priest, she was treated as an equal (1 Sam. 1:21–23). The decision of when to go to Shiloh was left entirely with Hannah, and she was given the privilege of naming her son. Hannah was her own woman, but for her this meant committing herself to the purposes of God, and she knew no higher purpose than being a wife and mother.

Hannah went from brokenhearted barrenness to extraordinarily privileged maternity. Although Hannah's psalm of thanksgiving with spiritual lyrics equal to any psalm and full of a theological truth marked her as a poetess and prophetess and although her words became the basis for Mary's Magnificat (Luke 1:46–55), Hannah did not reckon her literary acclaim as more important than the task of nurturing her child. Her greatest reward was not the birth of a son but rather the joy she experienced through giving her son back to God (1 Sam. 1:27—28; 3:19–20). For mothers, moments of unequaled joy are coupled with difficulty and time-consuming work. Children are not things to be acquired, used according to your own time and schedule, showcased for your personal satisfaction, and then put aside to facilitate personal convenience and personal ambition. That a woman who bears and nurses a baby should care for the young life and for the dwelling in which the child lives is both consistent with the creation order and practical for the basic qualities that nature has given the female.

Limiting families was not a theme of the Old Testament. A married man and woman in the Old Testament world could limit their reproductive capacity. Abortion, sterilization, and infanticide were strictly forbidden (Lev. 18:21; 20:2). Continence (self-restraint from yielding to desire or sexual intercourse) and contraception by withdrawal (*coitus interruptus*) are mentioned.[3] The Old Testament forbade infanticide (Lev. 18:21; 20:2). Continence was appropriate during ritual uncleanness that came with menstruation (Lev. 15:19–28; 18:19; 20:18) and childbirth (Lev. 12:1–8). Whether or not this ceremonial law contributed in some way to the spacing of children is a subject that calls for more research.

---

[3] Bruce K. Waltke, "Old Testament Texts Bearing on the Problem of the Control of Human Reproduction," in *Birth Control and the Christian*, 9.

The emergence of inexpensive, effective birth control measures, not to mention widespread abortion, has cut the average size of families. Women have always been expected to carry the primary responsibility for childbearing and rearing or for human reproduction. Some feel that this role has been thrust on women not only because of their biological makeup but also because of cultural conditioning.

Women in this generation are giving less of their time to the bearing and rearing of children; marriage is being delayed to allow for career preparation and pursuit. Motherhood has become as mechanical and insignificant as other household tasks and is just as quickly farmed out to others—even the carrying of the child may be assigned to a surrogate womb through in vitro fertilization. Some women consider an embryo in the womb as personal property to be accepted or rejected according to personal preference. Women who insist on personal sexual freedom also want to choose whether or not they assume the responsibility of motherhood.

THE ISSUE OF FERTILITY

Women are infertile most of the time during the reproductive years of their lives. Conception can occur only during a few days of the menstrual cycle. Natural Family Planning (NFP) is a general phrase referring to a thoughtful and scientific approach based on the fact that during each menstrual cycle a woman becomes fertile and then naturally infertile and that there are physical signs to indicate these fertile and infertile times. It is not a reference to the old calendar-based "rhythm" method, where decisions were made according to biological averages.

Various methods have been developed to help women and men determine in a highly accurate and reliable way the fertile and infertile times of a woman's menstrual cycle. This information can be used to achieve or avoid pregnancy. A woman learns to work with her body, its natural ebbs and flows of fertility and infertility. Then a man and woman learn to appreciate their fertility as a gift from God to them as a couple. NFP is safe and healthy. No foreign substances are introduced into the body. A couple must increase their communication with one another and learn to better understand their own bodies. In the process they develop greater intimacy, sharing, and spiritual bonding in their relationship. Although 40 percent of the couples practicing NFP, through teaching and charting the body's flow, achieve pregnancy within one year, evidence also shows that NFP, when correctly understood and applied, is 97–98 percent effective in avoiding pregnancy if that is a couple's choice.

Couples who have used NFP effectively express satisfaction in their marriages. One couple describing their experience included the following comments in their two-part article titled "What NFP Taught Me."[4] The first quote is from the wife's part; the second is from the husband's:

> NFP has always kept our relationship focused on God. It reminds us that God is ultimately the center of our relationship and we are to trust Him. It wasn't always easy trusting God when it came to our intimacy, especially in the beginning of our marriage.

> I have learned that in times of abstinence, I have removed my own selfishness and have come to appreciate my wife more and love her deeper.

The latter testimony is a reminder of the creativity often lost or ignored by a couple in developing their intimacy during a woman's period of fertility. Dr. Marc Pecha, a physician in San Antonio, Texas, notes that the discipline required to make NFP effective can improve "every aspect of life . . . the depth of married love flourishes; and into that flourishing of marital love comes the fruit: a new soul reflecting the love of the Maker."[5]

Research published in 2007 in the medical journal *Human Reproduction* demonstrated that when used correctly, NFP methods are as effective as the contraceptive pill for avoiding unplanned pregnancies.[6] Experts are clear that fertility awareness, without chemicals or devices, works as a contraceptive only if a wife chooses either to postpone intercourse or use a barrier method, both of which have a failure rate during her fertile phase. Statistically, the use of fertility awareness is most effective if a couple chooses to abstain during the fertile phase. Fertility is dependent upon the viability of both sperm and egg. A wife is fertile for longer than twenty-four to forty-eight hours only because the husband's sperm can live up to five days. The length of a wife's fertility is totally dependent on the husband's fertility, which emphasizes again that this process is a couple's journey. When fertility awareness is used for birth control, typically abstinence or a barrier method of contraception is required for nine to ten days, which includes a significant safety margin both before and after the wife's fertile phase.[7]

---

[4] Fernando and Jackie Buitrago, "What NFP Taught Me: He Said, She Said" (blog), July 26, 2012, accessed August 7, 2012, http://livinginfaithtogether.wordpress.com/tag/natural-family-planning.

[5] Tom Hoopes, "The Truth about Natural Family Planning: Beyond the Myths to the Mystery of Married Love," *Columbia Magazine*, July 2012, 18.

[6] P. Frank-Herrmann et al., "The Effectiveness of a Fertility Awareness Based Method to Avoid Pregnancy in Relation to a Couple's Sexual Behaviour During the Fertile Time: A Prospective Longitudinal Study," *Human Reproduction* 22 (2007): 1310–1319.

[7] Toni Weschler, *Taking Charge of Your Fertility: The Definitive Guide to Natural Birth Control and Pregnancy Achievement* (New York: HarperCollins, 1995), 111.

The success of sexual intimacy should not be based on sexual performance but on the quality of genuine affection that permeates the union. Relieving oneself of responsibility for sexual behavior pushes this beautiful intimacy to mere self-gratification and destroys the pleasure for which coitus was designed. There is most decidedly more to marriage than sex, and there is more to sex than procreation and personal pleasure. True intimacy cannot be achieved by an individual on his own. By definition, intimacy depends on the interaction of one with the other. Any time of jointly appointed abstinence by husband and wife presupposes mutual love and trust of, as well as confidence in, one another. Nowhere is a couple challenged as much to look beyond themselves, rising above personal desires, to consider another and ultimately to be faithful to the Creator's design and mandate (Gen. 1:28). Husband and wife should be wrapped up in one another rather than respectively self-absorbed.

Natural methods of birth control demand good communication and require the willingness of both the husband and wife to accept responsibility mutually. Natural Family Planning methods are successful only for couples who are married and in the God-ordained, committed relationship of marriage. Sharing the responsibility and coping with abstinence together helps each partner to be other oriented. Maturity and stability are essential on the part of both. Wives and husbands must have a capacity to postpone gratification and to delay the satisfaction of impulses. Yet it is also important to note that more affection, not less, is needed during abstinence. Certainly some of the finest qualities of character are introduced—self-restraint, discipline, and a sense of responsibility.

ARTIFICIAL BIRTH CONTROL

Some shortsighted mothers and fathers decide that the family, baby, or the world would be better if conception or birth does not occur. They refuse the grace God offers to fulfill his challenges and validate his promises (Mark 10:27). Can a couple be blessed through an unplanned child? Is an unplanned child an "accident" or a "precious gift from God"? If a child is unplanned by parents, does that mean the child is not part of God's plan? Although husbands and wives may think they "have accidents" or "make mistakes," God does not make a mistake. God's gifts are not always timed according to your preferences and convenience. Not only does God create a new human being by design, but he offers to parents the opportunity to love selflessly and to live in obedience to him by accepting their procreative responsibilities.

The contraceptive method of withdrawal is mentioned in the Bible, as in the case of Onan (Gen. 38:8–10). The context clearly indicates that Onan sinned because he refused to honor his levirate duty to provide for his brother's widow and more important to preserve the name of his deceased and childless brother (Deut. 25:5–10). The emission of semen apart from coitus was not regarded in itself as a sinful act. Although the Old Testament prohibits infanticide and sterilization as the means of avoiding pregnancy, the example of Onan would suggest that contraception, or withdrawal, is not absolutely prohibited. The condemnation of Onan was based on the attitude of his heart rather than the act itself. Nevertheless, nowhere in the Old Testament does God regard children with contempt or treat the bearing of children as a common thing; nor is contraception mandated or encouraged.

Birth control pills (BCPs) use synthetic hormones to fool a woman's body into thinking everything is normal. Then a normal menstrual period is produced by withdrawing those hormones at just the right time but without producing an egg. However, if by chance an egg develops, even though it may be fertilized, there are not enough hormones present to prepare the uterus for the egg's implantation. Implantation always involves an already conceived human being, and thus a contraceptive that prevents implantation is by definition an abortifacient. Essentially manufacturers of BCPs in various forms ultimately admit that although the primary mechanism of the oral contraceptive is to inhibit ovulation. If that does not happen for whatever reasons, other alterations have been introduced, including changes in the cervical mucus. The latter action increases the difficulty of sperm entry into the uterus and thus produces "changes in the endometrium which reduce the likelihood of implantation."[8]

Of the three mechanisms of birth control (inhibiting ovulation, thickening the cervical mucus to make it more difficult for sperm to travel to the egg, and shriveling the lining of the uterus so that it is unable or at least less able to facilitate the implantation of a fertilized egg), the first two are preventive and the third is abortive. In the latter case, BCPs prevent a woman's body from creating the most hospitable environment for a child since the endometrium is deficient in both food (or glycogen) and oxygen, which means the new life may die because the child lacks nutrition and oxygen. If implantation is unsuccessful, the child is flushed out of the womb in a miscarriage.

The consumer advice from the manufacturers of BCPs does caution that pregnancy should be avoided in the first three months after stopping the use

---

[8] Medical Economics Staff, *The Physician's Desk Reference*, 49th ed. (Montvale, NJ: 1995), 1775.

of oral contraceptives because the prolonged effect on the endometrium and the cervix can make a woman more susceptible to miscarriage. Her womb may need time to return to normal. Nearly all birth control devices, except the diaphragm and condom, operate between the time of conception and implantation. No evidence is forthcoming that would link the diaphragm and condom to abortion, although a woman should certainly investigate possible side-effects of anything she puts into her body.[9]

Undoubtedly there has been a conspiracy of silence on the part of the manufacturers of the oral contraceptive about its abortive effect. Christian physicians certainly do not want to believe that this simple-to-use and convenient contraceptive causes early abortions, and they may therefore resist the evidence. Instant gratification will often blind eyes to eternal consequences. A physician who refuses to prescribe BCPs may lose patients to other doctors. Oral contraceptives are a multi-billion-dollar worldwide industry. Evidence must be examined; rather than reading your position into the evidence, you must allow the evidence to determine your position, especially when that evidence is the Word of God.

Unfortunately, often political ideology is given greater importance than the health and safety of women. For example, the United States Food and Drug Administration in December of 2003 recommended allowing "emergency contraceptives," which could be used within seventy-two hours after sexual intercourse, to be sold over the counter without physician oversight or prescription. These pills would contain higher doses than what is prescribed for a woman on a long-term basis after a medical exam and under the supervision of a physician. Even smaller doses have risks: blurred vision, cramping, irregular menstrual bleeding, heart attack, stroke, high blood pressure, increased incidence of blood clots, pelvic inflammatory disease, ectopic pregnancy, infertility, and even breast and cervical cancer. As is true with other oral contraceptives, this drug can cause an abortion once fertilization has occurred.[10]

The hormones usually "trick" a woman's body in the sense that her body functions as if she is pregnant. Thus the expected side effects associated with the BCP come. However, if ovulation occurs despite this defensive action, secondary post-fertilization mechanisms then determine that the changed lining

---

[9] See information on nonabortive contraceptives: Healthwise Staff for WebMD Medical Reference, "Barrier Methods of Contraception" (Healthwise, Inc., 1995–2011) [online], accessed January 17, 2012, http://www.webmd.com/sex/birth-control/barrier-methods-of-birth-control-19059.

[10] United States Food & Drug Administration, "Plan B: Questions and Answers – August 24, 2006; updated December 14, 2006" [online], accessed January 18, 2012, http://www.fda.gov/Drugs/DrugSafety/Postmarket DrugSafetyInformationforPatientsandProviders/ucm109783.htm.

of the uterus will prevent the egg from being implanted and thus prevent clinically recognized pregnancy by inducing early "miscarriage" or abortion. This task is accomplished by simply thinning the uterine lining.

A Student's Story

"A teacher by her pupils will be taught" is a word of wisdom. One of my pupils brought this issue to my attention. Before their marriage in 1999, this student and her husband studied and discussed the issue of birth control in general and prayed about what their personal practice should be. They became convinced that birth control was appropriate under two circumstances: (1) when a married couple believe God is leading them to wait to have children (for medical reasons or other) and if there is on their part an attitude of openness and gratitude, should God choose to send children despite the use of birth control; and (2) when the method in no way acts as an abortifacient.

This couple read about different forms of birth control, including oral contraceptives (OCs), also known as "the Pill," noting its two types: progesterone-only and progesterone/estrogen. They determined that the progesterone-only pill primarily functions as an abortifacient but that the dual-hormone pill worked only to prevent conception. During her prewedding gynecological visit, the student requested a dual-hormone pill because of her belief in the sanctity of human life. Her doctor declared with confidence that this variation of BCPs would not endanger the baby, if pregnancy should occur unexpectedly.

During theological graduate studies, an ethics professor mentioned that all birth control pills functioned as abortifacients. Although not agreeing with the professor's argument concerning contraception in general, this couple was concerned that the professor could be right about BCPs. They carefully studied all of the fine print regarding its medicinal functions on the packaging. The Pill's function was explained completely in terms of preventing conception and even stated that it would not cause harm to fetal life. They trusted the information.

Six months later, an information sheet unexpectedly arrived with the oral contraceptives from the mail-order pharmaceutical distributor. The sheet explained that the BCPs work to prevent pregnancy in three ways:

1. the prevention of ovulation;
2. the thickening of cervical mucus to create a barrier to sperm; and
3. **the thinning of the endometrium (uterine lining) to prevent implantation should conception occur.**

This third function had not been mentioned in any of the literature provided by the manufacturer. This function implied that the BCPs worked not only to prevent conception but also to terminate any conception that might have occurred.

This wife, though skeptical at first, began researching. She studiously avoided information sources that seemed fanatical or lacking in medical basis. However, after research on the Internet, in pharmaceutical textbooks (drug functions/indications), and elsewhere, she confirmed that the information provided by pharmaceutical distributors was correct. While progesterone-only pills *primarily* function to prevent implantation after conception, the dual-hormone pills *secondarily* function this way.

Are Oral Contraceptives Abortifacients?

There seems to be little question, medically, about whether or not oral contraceptives cause a thinning of the endometrium or uterine lining. Most women who use BCPs notice the visible results of this as their menstrual period lessens in volume, shortens in length, or disappears altogether. Few physicians would question that a thinned or absent endometrium would discourage or prevent the implantation of a fertilized egg since hormonal changes taking place immediately after conception do cause the endometrium to thicken. However, regardless of postconception changes, the condition of the endometrium before conception will affect implantation, which is why a thinned uterine lining is considered to be a "contraceptive" benefit of the birth control pill.

Dual-hormone oral contraceptives *primarily* function to prevent conception. *Secondarily*, however, they do work to prevent the implantation of any fertilized egg breaking through during ovulation. Birth control pills are considered to be 99 percent effective, including the prevention of ovulation, the prevention of fertilization, and the prevention of the implantation of a fertilized egg. Little research has been done to determine what percentage of the time ovulation and conception are prevented and what percentage of time implantation is prevented. Even women who are consistent and regular in their pill taking ovulate only a small percentage of the time. A woman who uses dual-hormone oral contraceptives very consistently could experience a "medically induced miscarriage" or abortion at least once every two to three years.

While taking an oral contraceptive is certainly not equal to purposely getting an abortion, the ethical considerations are similar. One function of oral contraceptives is to help prevent the implantation of a fertilized egg. If life begins at conception, this function of BCPs is not contraceptive but abortive.

Although the percentage of times BCPs actually function this way may be comparatively low (less than 10 percent), it *is* one of the designed functions. Many women who take oral contraceptives do not desire to have an abortion, but use of BCPs does introduce this possibility.

NEED FOR INFORMED DECISION MAKING

Information concerning the postconception function of birth control pills is often not provided to women by their doctors or by the manufacturers/distributors of the BCPs. This issue has also been largely overlooked by the mainstream Christian community and popular Christian ethicists. Although the reasons for this disinformation cannot be known, certainly each woman should have the right to be fully informed concerning any medication she is advised to take, especially those involving ethical considerations. If a woman chooses to use oral contraceptives, she should have full knowledge of each medical function of BCPs.

For a Christian woman, any decision concerning the sanctity of human life should be well informed. Is the use of oral contraceptives truly compatible with a pro-life stance? To hide this information from a woman suggests a disrespect for her intelligence, indicates a disregard for her moral convictions, and inhibits her ability to weigh the evidence and make her own choice. A woman dare not excuse what is comfortable, convenient, natural, or widely accepted by simply expressing her "sense of peace." Every woman must accept responsibility before God for her own choices, and she would be wise to weigh carefully her decisions against the backdrop of Scripture, depending upon the Holy Spirit to guide her in light of what God has objectively said in his written Word rather than merely what she subjectively feels. Medical decisions are often difficult, and human life may be jeopardized no matter what the choice. However, the decision of whether or not to use BCPs usually revolves around the issue of convenience. Is mere convenience a good enough reason to take a drug that may terminate human life, no matter how low the risk?

My student and her husband decided to discontinue use of the Pill. Although they had originally tried to make an informed decision and did not consciously choose to take a medication that might harm unborn life, the wife had struggled with guilt concerning using BCPs for three years. She also felt resentment toward the doctors, the pharmaceutical companies, and even leading Christian ethicists who did not make this information available.

My responsibility *is not* to convince people not to use BCPs. However, I *do* want to provide women with the tools necessary to make an informed decision rather than one based on disinformation or ignorance. The moral issues surrounding use of BCPs are difficult and noticeably more "gray" than many issues concerning the sanctity of human life. In matters of conscience, one must allow others grace to make their own decisions before God.

How does one reconcile liberty and license? Is genuine liberty merely doing what you want to do and not doing what you do not want to do? Some seem to think so. However, God has a completely different idea. His challenge is for you to do what you ought to do—what he meant for you to do. Although I am created in God's image, I am not God! His liberty is predicated upon my obedience; my freedom in his order must be sanctified by my discipline according to his boundaries. There has never been any question about the power to choose—even to choose to disobey. Every woman is capable of doing many things that she is not supposed to do. Yet clearly the ability to do a thing is not a command or even a permission to do it.

At the heart of the whole issue of liberty is the matter of personal choice. You always have choices, and the right choice is not always the easy choice or the painless choice, but it should be the faithful choice. To go, do, see, and have what you want and to reject what you do not want; to determine the timing of God's blessings and the kind of blessings you would accept; to demand individual rights—selfishness rather than selflessness—the price of this freedom is too great. The woman who chooses faithfully believes in a God who not only controls the big things but the little things as well.

CONCLUSION: A POINT OF PERSONAL PRIVILEGE

When I was twenty years of age, I came face-to-face with the importance of life within the womb and more specifically with my own maternity. My husband and I had been married a year, and we were ready to begin our senior year at the university. Our lives were planned. We intended to have a family—after our educations were complete.

Despite careful planning and calculated precautions (including an oral contraceptive taken exactly as directed), I became pregnant as I began my senior year. I was frustrated and even annoyed at the inconvenience and the complications that would come from this unexpected pregnancy, but abortion never entered my mind. I may have viewed my unwanted condition as my entry to martyrdom, but the taking or rejecting of a life in the womb was never an option. Within several months, I began miscarrying. Suddenly, the unwanted life became a very-much-wanted baby. I willingly confined myself to bed, understanding that I could lose my studies in Greek and jeopardize my grade point average. Several weeks passed, and one day while at home alone, in great pain, I lost my baby—not a *zygote*, embryo, or fetus—but **my** baby—in the earliest stage of development but already bonded to my heart. That was my first lesson in the sanctity of life. In bitterness of soul, I vowed never again to reject—even in my thoughts—life offered by God.

More months passed, and graduation came. We prepared to move to New Orleans to attend seminary. In a checkup before moving, my doctor discovered a tumor in my reproductive organs. Because of my youth, he decided to wait a few months before performing surgery. On the eve of the surgery, I signed a paper giving up my fertility—again with bitterness of soul and great repentance for ever rejecting what once God had so graciously offered. The tumor was benign, but its location required the doctor to remove a portion of both ovaries. He indicated that there was little chance I would ever conceive a child. My second lesson in the sanctity of life was complete.

The years passed, and I poured myself into the lives of young people in our church, especially one whom I took into our home to rear during her teen years. Finally, after I had given up the hope of having children of my own, I unexpectedly became pregnant, beginning another joyous lesson in the sanctity of life. I was quite ill during those months and distraught because of an insensitive doctor. I made every effort to change physicians but to no avail. The time for delivery came; I went through a hard and lengthy labor. My doctor left the hospital briefly. When he returned and checked me, the baby had jerked his umbilical cord loose, was without oxygen, and in a breech position. The doctor suggested to my husband that the baby was probably dead and at the very least brain damaged. He suggested that they cautiously prep me for surgery and remove the baby, giving greater consideration for my life. Fortunately, my husband quickly told the doctor to make every effort to save the baby. The doctor administered the spinal himself and in fourteen minutes delivered our son alive and normal and a miracle of life—completing my third lesson on the sanctity of life.

Several years later I again unexpectedly became pregnant, conceiving shortly after I stopped breastfeeding my son. This was an easy pregnancy with a carefully planned delivery date via C-section. All went well, my parents returned home, and my husband went to our apartment to get some sleep. Before he could get back to the hospital the next morning, a nurse informed me that my baby was dying, having developed hyaline membrane disease during the hours following her delivery. Again the bitterness of soul came, and I anguished for some hours before releasing to the heavenly Father the fate of my tiny daughter. On a Sunday evening with people praying all across the country, suddenly our baby daughter turned from the path of death to the way of life. This was my fourth lesson in the sanctity of life. I needed no other.

God had given me two children and, in a sense, miraculously given each of them twice. I have never had nor ever will have a greater privilege than linking hands with the Creator God to create new life and then to nurture that life in the womb and to rear up a son and a daughter, who have become another generation. And to think that I could have lost it all. The interruption to education, the uncertainty of financial burden, the willful desire to control my own body, lifestyle, and timing—all these factors weighed upon me as I sought to set my own timetable for conception.

The habits and practices of society or culture are often based on convenience, personal whim, whatever is currently popular, or even the best rationale of natural man. None of these is adequate for providing a secure foundation for ethical choices. The Bible records the beginning of the family; history has traced its pivotal role in society. God grant that in this enlightened age you and I do not "drop the ball" but rather hold to the ageless pattern of leaving life and death in the worthy hands of the Creator God.

PUTTING THE PRINCIPLES INTO PRACTICE
1. In what way is contraception uniquely a woman's issue?
2. Contrast infertility in Scripture with barrenness in the modern era.
3. How should a couple deal with family planning according to biblical principles?

Chapter Ten

A Life Full of Days: Caring for the Aged

Terri Stovall

Do not cast me off in the time of old age;
Forsake me not when my strength is spent.

PSALM 71:9

Roscoe and Louise were in their seventies when their only child and son, Joe, moved them from the west Texas city where they had lived most of their adult lives to Corpus Christi, Texas, where he now lived. Roscoe and Louise lived comfortably in an apartment complex that First Baptist Church of Corpus Christi had built for its older members. After fifteen years of this semi-independent living, clearly Roscoe and Louise needed to live under a little closer supervision, and Joe moved them out of the church-owned apartment into a home next door to him.

Dementia began to ravage Louise's mind, and Roscoe, approaching his ninety-eighth birthday, began to have significant health issues. Joe faced difficult decisions involving where and how to best care for his parents. One fall day Roscoe was hospitalized with heart failure, and Joe took this opportunity to move Louise into a nursing facility that had a secure wing for patients experiencing dementia.

Finding comfort that his mother was being well cared for, Joe turned his attention to his father. The same nursing facility had a hospice wing, and there Joe and the doctors found the best place for Roscoe to live out his remaining days.

As Joe drove his father to the nursing home, Roscoe turned to his son and asked, "Is your mother in one of those homes now?" Joe, taking a deep breath because he was not sure how his father would respond, replied yes.

Roscoe then asked, "Is it a good one? Will she be okay there?" Joe assured his dad that she was being well cared for.

After a long pause, Roscoe turned his head away from his son, looked out the passenger window and said quietly, "That's good. I guess I am going there too. But I don't think I will be there very long."

This scene is not uncommon. The people change and the circumstances may be slightly different, but adult children are making decisions every day about the care of their aging parents. Some are making this difficult decision with comfort and assurance that they are providing the best care possible. Others are doing so with guilt that they cannot do more. Still others are avoiding these difficult decisions altogether because they are just too painful.

The purpose of this chapter is to understand the current trends of the aging population, which will balloon over the next fifty years, making this a critical issue for today and tomorrow. We will also examine what Scripture says to seniors and their families and offer some practical ways to allow a senior adult to live a life full of days.

TRENDS RELATED TO THE AGING POPULATION

Before looking at Scripture and how best to care for the aged, first consider the critical need for this care and how it is impacting modern society. If a family or a community has yet to feel the effects of caring for an elderly loved one, they soon will, as we will see.

Demographics

One can simply look around or read the news briefs and see that people are staying active longer and living longer. The proportion of the population over sixty-five years of age is growing. The federal Administration on Aging reports on global statistics, "Rapidly expanding numbers of very old people represent a social phenomenon without historical precedent. In 2000 the number of persons aged sixty years or older was estimated at 605 million. That number is projected to grow to almost 2 billion by 2050, when the population of older persons will be larger than the population of children (0–14 years) for the first time in history."[1]

In the United States, it is estimated that by the year 2030, 20 percent of the US population will be over the age of sixty. That means that 71 million Americans will be senior adults. Of these seniors, the numbers who are over eighty-five years will almost double as life expectancy continues to increase.[2] Currently, women outnumber men with 20 million senior women to 15 mil-

---

[1] Administration on Aging, *Challenges of Global Aging Fact Sheet* (Washington, DC: United States Department of Health and Human Services, 2003), 1.

[2] United States Centers for Disease Control and Prevention, *The State of Aging and Health in America* (Washington, DC: United States Department of Health and Human Services, 2007), iii.

lion senior men. This trend is expected to continue. Interestingly, the typical senior man will be married while half of all older women are widowed or unmarried and are more likely to live alone.[3]

Life Expectancy and Health Issues

Life expectancy, having reached 78 years of age for both men and women, is at its highest point in history.[4] Statistics indicate a slight difference between men and women. If a man reaches age sixty-five, he is expected to live an additional seventeen years while a sixty-five-year-old woman is expected to live an additional twenty years.[5]

The death rate of older adults is decreasing slightly with heart disease and cancer being the top causes of death among older adults. Incidences of both of these are dropping, but deaths caused by hypertension and accidental falls are climbing:[6]

> Falls are the leading cause of injury deaths and the most common cause of injuries and hospital admissions for trauma among adults aged sixty-five and older. Fall-related injuries cause significant mortality, disability, loss of independence and early admission to nursing homes. Many falls can be prevented by addressing personal risk and environmental factors.[7]

The increase in life expectancy has created issues surrounding health care of senior adults. Health care costs are almost three times higher for those sixty-five and older than for those younger, and thus the top financial concern of seniors is providing for health and welfare. "Forty-two percent of the population 65 and over reported some type of long-lasting condition or a disability in 2000. Thirty-two percent of people 65–74 reported at least one disability, in contrast with 72% of people 85 and over."[8] Some of the most commonly diagnosed conditions include hypertension, heart disease, cancer, arthritis, and diabetes.

Caregivers

The growing aging population is affecting those who are responsible for the primary care of these aging adults. The typical caregiver will be a woman car-

---

[3] Administration on Aging, *A Statistical Profile of Older Americans Aged 65+* (Washington, DC: United States Department of Health and Human Services, 2006), 1–2.

[4] United States Centers for Disease Control and Prevention and National Center for Health Statistics, *Health of the United States* (Washington, DC: United States Department of Health and Human Services, 2006), ii.

[5] Federal International Forum on Aging, *Older Americans Update* (Washington, DC: National Center for Health Statistics, 2006), 8.

[6] Ibid.

[7] United States Centers for Disease Control and Prevention, *The State of Aging and Health in America*, v.

[8] "Even Wealthy Seniors Concerned About Health Care Costs, Medicare," *Senior Journal*, January 23, 2006, accessed September 10, 2007, http://seniorjournal.com/NEWS/Medicare/6-01-23-EvenWealthySeniors.html.

ing for a family member or friend, though 44 percent of parent caregivers are men. Often, the caregiver is the spouse of the one needing care. That may mean that the caregiver is also a senior adult with health concerns.

Most caregivers will also hold a job outside the home and give eighteen hours per week of care on average. Twenty percent of caregivers will provide forty or more hours per week of primary care for an older adult. It is estimated that one-fourth of the adult population has been in the role of primary care-giver for a senior adult (family or friend) and that many adult caregivers will care for a senior adult longer than they cared for their own children.[9]

One concern of many is the health and well-being of the caregiver. Researchers are beginning to see that the stress of family caregiving is impacting mortality rates, resulting in higher incidences of chronic illnesses and symptoms of depression or anxiety.[10] Many caregivers realize that they need help but do not know how or where to find it. This includes respite, relief from isolation, and skills in navigating available medical and care resources. Caregivers also struggle in communicating with aging parents, especially when trying to determine a parent's wishes at the end of life. It has been found that

> Satisfaction with parents' future plans significantly reduces adult children's worry over their parents' well-being and this underscores the importance of parents making and discussing future plans with their children. Ironically, worries about being a burden on their children and difficulty coping with the unknowns of dying or end of life care cause many parents to avoid making plans or having discussions of plans with children.[11]

The situation is often a catch-22. Adult children would be put to ease if the parents would discuss future plans, yet parents often hesitate for fear of worrying their children or putting undue stress upon them.

Recognizing that the general population is growing older, families must not ignore the inevitable but be prepared to respond on a personal basis. The struggle arises when a family of believers tries to understand what the Bible says about families caring for family members and how to follow those biblical principles to offer the best care possible for their aging loved ones.

[9] Dennis R. Myers, "Transformational Parent Care Ministry: A Resource Guide for Congregations," *Journal of Family Ministry* 17, no. 4 (Winter 2003): 13.

[10] National Family Caregivers Association, "Statistics on Family Caregivers and Family Caregiving," 2006, accessed September 10, 2007, http://www.nfcacares.org/who_are_family_caregivers/care_giving_statistics.cfm.

[11] Michael Parker et al, "Parent Care and Religion: A Faith-Based Intervention Model for Caregiving Readiness of Congregational Members," *Journal of Family Ministry* 17, no. 4 (Winter 2003): 54–55.

THE BIBLE SPEAKS ON AGING

God established families when he created the man and the woman. Families are close to his heart, and he has not left us wondering how to care for one another. Looking at God's plan for the family and the guidelines he put in place is important. The Bible speaks to those who are growing older and to their families, especially the children.

Full of Days

The Bible is clear that growing old is a gift from God that should be held with honor and esteem. Scripture speaks of Abraham, Isaac, Job, David, and others as dying old and full of days or full of years (Gen. 25:8; 35:29; 1 Chron. 29:26–28; Job 42:16–17; 2 Chron. 24:15). The term *full of days* or *full of years* refers to the termination of life on earth. This biblical term is not used to describe everyone but may refer to one's lifetime being satiate with the days of life, especially a life ended without reluctance. It is almost as if the person dying knows that he has done what he came to do and it is time to go home. These patriarchs of the faith did make mistakes, and they did not lead painless lives. But, at the end of life, they lived under the grace of a merciful God.

Living a life full of days brings with it benefits and responsibility. Proverbs 16:31 declares that "gray hair is a crown of glory; it is gained in a righteous life." The man who finds wisdom and understanding will hold riches and honor in one hand and long life in the other (Prov. 3:13–16). Fearing the Lord brings wisdom, knowledge, and understanding, which will add years to life (Prov. 9:10–11). While these passages are not a guarantee of long life, we still live in a fallen world; clearly the one who fears the Lord seeks his wisdom and understanding. A life full of days ends satiated and with expectation regardless of biological age. One of the primary gifts you can give your senior loved ones is to help them end their lives feeling content that they have done all that God has intended for them, so they can leave this world without twinges of emptiness or regret but with a satisfying fullness:

> My son, do not forget my teaching,
>   but let your heart keep my commandments,
>   for length of days and years of life
>   and peace they will add to you. (Prov. 3:1–2)

The Ministry of the Older Adult

Too often we focus on what we can do for the senior adult when we should be helping that senior adult remain active in the lives of others. The aging adult who has gained wisdom and understanding has the responsibility to pass this on to the next generation. Through the natural development of life, children will become more independent of their parents, but this is not a complete separation. It is a growing interdependence. The loving bond between parent and child is not to be broken as the child reaches adulthood, moves out of the home, and marries. Rather a commitment between the parent and child to be responsive to each other begins at birth and remains until death.

The ministry of the senior adult, mentioned in Scripture, involves declaring the works of God to the next generations (Ps. 71:17–18; Joel 1:2–3), prayer (1 Tim. 5:5), and passing along life skills to the younger generation (Titus 2). The senior adult should still be practicing the spiritual disciplines (Deut. 5:32–33) and continuing to grow in his faith. There is no age too old for God to use in ministry. While you still have breath, your life still has a purpose and value. God promises in Isaiah:

> Even to your old age I am he,
>   and to gray hairs I will carry you.
> I have made, and I will bear;
>   I will carry and will save. (Isa. 46:4)

Honor Your Father and Your Mother

When God gave his children the Ten Commandments, he addressed their relationship with him and their relationships with one another. The fifth commandment is to "honor your father and your mother" with the promise "that your days may be long" (Ex. 20:12). This command is repeated in Ephesians 6:1–3 where Paul addresses family relationships and again when writing to the church at Colossae (Col. 3:20). The command to honor father and mother does not have an age limit or a time of expiration. Some may think the command to honor father and mother applies primarily to minor children still living at home, but that is not the case. Rather, as a child continues to honor his father and mother into adulthood and to the end of his parents' lives, he is promised long, prosperous days.

The act of honoring, or showing respect to parents, will look different at various stages of life. Sometimes, especially for a young child, honoring is simply obeying parents. As the child becomes an adult and the parent moves into the last season of life, it may be expressed by physically caring for a parent and/or loving, encouraging, and staying connected to a parent. Even when a parent may make decisions that are not ideal, a child is still to honor his parent; an adult child is not asked to approve of sinful behavior but to "listen to your father who gave you life, and do not despise your mother when she is old" (Prov. 23:22). Many times, God will use this constant respect and honor to love a parent back to Jesus. "Knowing how to honor comes first from making a commitment to God. You show your honor by choosing to be present with your elder, emotionally, if not physically, and treating her with tenderness and good will."[12]

Caring for Older Adults

In Scripture and in biblical history, God's plan is that the children and family be the source of care for an aging adult. The plan is straightforward and efficient: parents are to care for their children until they reach adulthood, then children reciprocate by caring for their parents as they age. This is a natural outflow of honoring father and mother. Jesus took this responsibility so seriously that while on the cross, in the midst of his pain and suffering, he made sure his mother would be cared for as his time on earth was coming to an end:

> When Jesus saw his mother and the disciple whom he loved standing nearby, he said to his mother, "Woman, behold your son!" Then he said to the disciple, "Behold, your mother!" And from that hour the disciple took her to his own home. (John 19:26–27)

When Paul wrote to Timothy regarding the care of widows, he was clear that the first place to turn for their care was to the family and children (1 Tim. 5:4). Jesus held the Pharisees accountable for not caring for their parents with the excuse of doing ministry (Mark 7:10–13). Scripture really gives no excuse for a child or family not to be the primary person responsible for the care of an aging parent.

One of the challenges faced today in caring for parents involves distance and travel. In biblical times, multiple generations of families lived together or very close to each other. This provided a natural setting to transition from parental care for children to children's care for parents. The fact that families no longer live together does not negate the plan set forth in Scripture. Adult children will simply need to be more intentional and creative in how care is provided.

A PRACTICAL RESPONSE TO THE NEEDS OF THE AGED

How do you put together the trends related to the aging population with what Scripture has to say regarding the care of those growing older? How does what

---

[12] Focus on the Family, *Complete Guide to Caring for Aging Loved Ones* (Carol Stream, IL: Tyndale House, 2002): 20–21.

the Bible says about caring for your aging loved ones blend with the realities of the twenty-first century?

To say that if one does X, Y, and Z his aging parent will have the best care is futile. There is no magic plan for every situation. There are so many variables—from the needs and resources of the senior adult to the needs and resources of the extended family and even to the culture in which a senior is living. One must remember you are not *curing* senior adults; you are *caring* for senior adults. But there are some things to keep in mind as families seek to care for their loved one.

RESPONDING TO THE NEEDS OF THE AGED

How should you respond to the needs of those who are in their senior years? We will build upon the three biblical principles of finishing life full of days, staying involved in ministry, and following the command to honor father and mother.

Help Seniors End Life Full of Days

- *Introduce them to Jesus.* Most of tomorrow's senior adults are classified as "baby boomers." Born between 1946 and 1964, the boomer generation grew up with the Vietnam War, Kent State, Watergate, and a 50 percent divorce rate. However, many did not grow up learning about Jesus and are approaching the end of life still not knowing him. Unfortunately, many people as they age move away from religion instead of turning to God for hope. Do not be afraid to have conversations with senior adults to confirm their belief in Christ or to introduce them to him.

- *Help seniors continue growing in their faith.* Providing opportunities for seniors to stay involved in even the rituals or ordinances of religion (regular worship, the Lord's Supper) provides a sense of meaning, significance, and celebration while sharing in community. Pastoral care affirms that God continues to care for the senior adult.[13] "Being a part of the Body of Christ gives one a sense of connectedness and roots, as persons desire to belong to and be a part of something larger than self."[14] Keep in mind that in the darker evenings of the winter months, many seniors are uneasy about driving to church. Volunteer to drive them to and from church.

Help Seniors Stay Involved in Ministry

- *Encourage them to tell their stories.* Senior adults can impact the lives of generations to come by telling their stories. Some senior adults may wish to write down stories about their childhood or what it was like during the war. For

---

[13] Patricia Gleason-Wynn, "Enhancing the Quality of Life for Older Persons," *Journal of Family Ministry* 17, no. 4 (Winter 2003): 40.
[14] Derrel Watkins, *Practical Theology for Aging* (Binghamton, NY: Haworth Pastoral Press, 2003), 132.

those who do not care to write often, you could offer to record their stories. It can be as simple as saying, "Grandma, I am getting married next week. Tell me about your wedding." Even those with some dementia may have difficulty remembering yesterday, but the memories of long ago are held hard and fast.

- *Involve them in ministry and missions.* Senior adults can stay involved in ministry by volunteering for short-term missions. Those who are retired from a vocation now have time to invest in kingdom work. If they are not physically able to go on mission trips, enlist them as your prayer support. Some of the best prayer warriors are senior adults.

There are many other ways to help a senior adult to retire to something, not to retire from something, by involving them in volunteer opportunities or mentoring situations. Use them as advisers who can speak wisdom out of their experiences.

Senior adults, like all humans, want to experience purpose in life. In Scripture, Anna and Simeon both played active roles in ministry, as did Lois and the unnamed widow who gave her mite. Seniors who continue to grow in their faith and remain involved in ministry approach the end of their time on earth with more satisfaction and with less reluctance. They truly end their lives full of days.

Give Seniors Honor and Respect

- *Help them come to a place of contentment.* Paul writes in his letter to the church at Philippi, "Not that I am speaking of being in need, for I have learned in whatever situation I am to be content" (Phil. 4:11). Most discontent arises from uncertainty and fear. Assure your loved one that he will be safe, well cared for, and not alone.

- *Walk with them to the end.* As a senior adult approaches the end of life, he may notice that your natural response is to distance yourself from him. However, this is the time to walk with him to the end, in the sense of giving your loved one permission to go home. It has been shown that some will linger because they sense the family is not okay or there is unfinished business. Assure him that everything is okay and that it is fine for him to rest. Let him have a strong finish of his life, but in God's timing.

- *Help them talk about their final wishes.* As we mentioned earlier, adult children experience less worry and anxiety as their parents approach the end of life if they know what their parents really want. Although it may be difficult, talk to your parents about any medical directives they have in place and their wishes regarding medical intervention. Also talk to them about the kind of funeral they would like to have, even going into detail regarding arrangements, music, those who will speak, and where their final resting place will be.

A PRACTICAL RESPONSE TO THE NEEDS OF THE CAREGIVERS

Caregivers have their own needs. Especially when a family member is caring for a senior adult loved one, the caregiver will experience a roller coaster of emotions, along with physical and spiritual needs.

Help caregivers know how to honor their fathers and mothers

Caregivers often struggle with honoring their parents if past issues have not been resolved or forgiven. As roles shift from the parent's caring for the child to the child's caring for the parent, the adult child often gains new insight and perspective regarding his parent and past actions. Regardless of the parent's response, now is the time to lay aside the past and forgive or honor. Additionally, the caregiver must give herself permission to make difficult decisions.

- *Realize that honoring father and mother does not mean that you do it all yourself.* God has charged the family with the primary care of the aging loved one, but this does not mean the family has to do it all. You must recognize that accepting the help of others is not a sign of weakness. The family can still be very involved in care and care decisions, but delegate, so to speak, the hands-on, day-to-day care to trained professionals. This may even mean placing a loved one in a care facility to provide the best care possible.

- *Limiting independence can be an act of love.* The most difficult emotions often surface when the adult child or caregiver must limit the independence of her loved one. For example, it may be necessary for the adult child to take possession of a vehicle or its keys to ensure that the parent does not drive; it is often in the best interest of the safety of the parent and the public. Losing the ability to drive is often the last point of independence to which a senior adult will cling tenaciously. For his son or daughter not to allow him to drive may elicit an angry response. In such a case, you may have to remind yourself that limiting independence can be an act of love.

Help caregivers care for themselves

Providing care for an aging loved one can be all consuming and extremely demanding twenty-four hours a day, seven days a week. Many caregivers find themselves physically exhausted, mentally spent, and spiritually drained. In the midst of caring for her loved one, the caregiver must also care for herself. My sister-in-love, who was once a flight attendant, uses the illustration that when the safety demonstration is made, the flight attendants instruct you first to put on your own oxygen mask and then help those around you. You must take care of yourself if you are going to take care of your loved one in the best way.

- *Spiritual Needs.* Find a Bible study, small group fellowship, or accountability partner who can help you maintain your own spiritual health. Even if it is not possible physically to join a Bible study group, there are many online Bible studies. Accountability does not always have to be face to face, but can be by telephone or e-mail.

- *Physical Needs.* Find resources that can offer respite care. For those caring for a loved one with Alzheimer's, this is especially important as many people with Alzheimer's are physically healthy but simply cannot be left alone. The constant watch can be more exhausting than sitting in a hospital waiting room.

- *Emotional Needs.* Caregivers need someone to talk to, "vent" to, and find assurance from. A caregiver who is a spouse or an adult child is often providing care while dealing with personal grief over the changing relationship. Many times, in a sense, you are saying good-bye while the loved one is still living. When the caregiver is also a senior adult, this can be especially difficult, as the oldest generation tends to be more private. Holding in emotion is not always the best response. Look for ways to find emotional support, even if you are simply keeping a journal as an emotional outlet.

A CHURCH'S PRACTICAL RESPONSE

What is the best thing that a church can do to benefit both seniors and the family caring for them? In short, to strengthen the families. Overwhelming increases in the number of senior adult Americans needing assistance and care come just as the family has been weakened by ideological, cultural, economic, and social forces. You can talk about ways to care for seniors and give rest to the caregivers, but the bottom line is strengthening families and giving them the foundation that will carry them through the difficult times. Caring for an aging parent is never easy. There are physical demands. The emotional toll is sometimes even more dramatic as an adult child has to make the hard decisions for the love of his parent. Caring for these seniors allows you to give as well as to gain the gift of life. George Washington Carver reminds us, "How far you can go in life depends on your being tender with the young, compassionate with the aged, sympathetic with the striving, and tolerant of the weak and the strong. Because some day in life you will have been all of these."[15]

CONCLUSION: THE REST OF THE STORY

There is more to the story of Roscoe and Louise. God had a few gifts left to give.

Roscoe had just come to terms that he would not be going back to the house where he and his wife had lived. Joe and Roscoe continued driving to

---

[15] George Washington Carver quoted in Clara Villarosa, *The Words of African-American Heroes* (New York: HarperCollins, 2011).

the nursing home in silence. While stopped at a traffic light, a motorcyclist rode by on a beautiful touring bike. Roscoe turned to his son and said, "I sure would like to get one of those. Would you ride with me?" As the two laughed, Joe answered, "Anytime, Dad."

Soon Joe was settling Roscoe into the nursing home. On the other side of the facility's campus, Louise suddenly became agitated, insisting that her husband was there and she needed to be at his side. The nurse, not knowing Roscoe had just been admitted, assured Louise that he was being cared for at the hospital. But Louise's increased agitation led them to check anyway, more to placate her than anything else. When the nurses learned Roscoe had indeed been admitted, they immediately wheeled Louise to his room. For the next thirty-six hours, God gave Louise a lucidity not seen in some months, and she and her husband were able to share memories, laugh together, cry together, and say their good-byes before God called Roscoe home two days later.

I tell the story of Roscoe and Louise because they were better known to me as Pappaw and Mammaw. Joe is my father. I watched my dad honor his father and mother through all stages of life. Even when the frustration of aging and the influence of dementia resulted in harsh words and uncharacteristic behavior from his parents, God gave my dad the grace and wisdom to continue to love and honor them. In the end, Dad still recounted one of the last laughs he and his dad had as that motorcyclist rode by.

> Do not cast me off in the time of old age;
>> forsake me not when my strength is spent. (Ps. 71:9)

Rather,

> Honor your father and your mother, that your days may be long in the land that the LORD your God is giving you. (Ex. 20:12)

PUTTING THE PRINCIPLES INTO PRACTICE

1. What are some practical ways that you can help the oldest adults stay involved in the lives of others or stay involved in ministry?

2. What does a life *full of days* look like today? What are some specific things you can do to help someone live a life full of days?

3. List some of the specific spiritual, emotional, and physical needs a caregiver might have. How can these needs be met?

ABOUT THE AUTHOR

Terri Stovall serves as dean of women's programs at Southwestern Baptist Theological Seminary in Fort Worth, Texas. She oversees the academic programs and organizations for women at Southwestern. Terri has served churches in the area of educational and women's ministry. Her passion is to equip women to impact the lives of women and families for Christ. She and her husband Jay are members of Fielder Road Baptist Church in Arlington, Texas.

ADDITIONAL RESOURCES

Focus on the Family. *Complete Guide to Caring for Aging Loved Ones.* Carol Stream, IL: Tyndale House, 2002.

Kelley, Rhonda H. *Raising Moms.* Birmingham, AL: New Hope, 2006.

McIntosh, Gary L. *One Church, Four Generations.* Grand Rapids, MI: Baker, 2002.

Watkins, Derrel. *Practical Theology for Aging.* Binghamton, NY: Haworth Pastoral Press, 2003.

Chapter Eleven

The Impact of a Handicapped Individual on a Family

Rhonda Harrington Kelley

Handicaps occur more often than one realizes. Most people today have been impacted directly or indirectly by a handicapped loved one. A disability can happen to you personally or to one of your family members. Disability knows no boundaries from educational background, social status, or financial level.

Disabilities affect all ages of the population. The 2010 United States Census Bureau reports that:

- Nearly 19 percent of the United States population experiences some degree of disability.
- Over 12 percent experience a disability requiring assistance from a person or device. Over 4 percent of children ages six to fifteen have a "severe disability" requiring assistance.[1]

In addition, "Census 2000 counted a total of 72.3 million families and found that nearly 28.9 percent of them (about 2 in every 7 families) reported having at least one member with a disability."[2]

Disabilities are serious because of the impact on individuals, families, and even the church. This chapter will briefly discuss the nature of handicapping conditions and the biblical principles that address God's viewpoint. The responsibility of the church will be described as well as the challenges facing the individual and the family. Suggestions for family support will be summarized as well as family blessings. While disabilities can negatively

---

[1] "Table 1: Prevalence of Disability for Selected Age Groups: 2005 and 2010," United States Census Bureau, http://www.census.gov/people/disability/publications/disab10/table_1.pdf; and "Figure 2. Disability Prevalence and the Need for Assistance by Age: 2010," United States Census Bureau, Survey of Income and Program Participation, May–August 2010, http://www.census.gov/people/disability/publications/disab10/figure_2.pdf.
[2] Qi Wang, "Disability and American Families: 2000" (CENSR-23), Census 2000 Special Reports (United States Census Bureau, July 2005), 3.

impact the individual and family, many positive contributions are also experienced.

HANDICAPPING CONDITIONS

Disabilities come in many varieties, and all influence the family. Some disabilities are mild; others are severe in nature. Some disabilities are physical while others are mental or emotional. There are many different handicaps within any given spectrum, and handicaps are as unique as each individual who possesses a handicap. Before discussing types of disabilities, consider what is meant by the term "disability."

A "disability" is not a person or an object. It is a process that characterizes some people. Several terms are used to describe the special needs of individuals—*impairment*, *disability*, and *handicap*. Although different, they are related. Here is a simple definition of each:

- *Impairment*—an abnormality or loss of physiological form or function
- *Disability*—consequences of the impairment
- *Handicap*—the disadvantage that results from an impairment or disability[3]

In the United States, the term "disability" is most often used in education and in the legal system to protect the rights of people with disabilities.

Impairments which lead to disability or handicap may be present at birth or acquired later in life through injury or illness. Physical impairments are usually more visible and may include cerebral palsy, spina bifida, spinal cord injury, stroke, or hearing loss. Cognitive impairments substantially limit intellectual function and may include developmental disabilities, mental retardation, learning disabilities, or autism. Emotional impairments are often more difficult to identify and may involve a wide spectrum of psychological and psychiatric disorders. No matter the type of impairment, every handicap impacts the individual personally and the family. Accurate diagnosis and appropriate treatment often take years and may never be completely effective.

For eighteen years, I pursued a professional career as a speech-language pathologist in a medical setting. I was a member of a multidisciplinary diagnostic team as well as clinical director of a craniofacial team. Our task was to diagnose infants and children with congenital abnormalities, developmental disabilities, or acquired impairment. No matter how mild or severe, handicapping conditions greatly impacted the child and family. The personal impact also led to an impact on the church, the Christian's spiritual family.

---

[3] Deborah Beth Creamer, *Disability and Christian Theology* (New York: Oxford University Press, 2009), 13–14.

BIBLICAL PRINCIPLES

Throughout history, Christians have expressed different viewpoints about handicapping conditions. Some believe that handicaps, like all trials and tribulations, are inevitably a part of life. Others have the conviction that handicaps result as a consequence of sin or bad choices. Most accept God's creation, even though imperfect, and respond in love.

Many times Christians do not know how to respond to people with handicaps. An individual with disabilities wrote personally of responses from religious people to his disability. In his opinion, well-meaning Christians often said the wrong thing:

- "You are special in God's eyes; that's why he gave you this disability."
- "Don't worry about your pain and suffering on earth—in heaven you will be made whole."
- "God gave you this disability to develop your character."
- "If you have enough faith, you will be healed of your disability."
- "If you are not healed, you must have hidden sins."[4]

While these statements may or may not be true, they are hurtful to the handicapped person.

Christians must learn to respond appropriately to handicapped individuals from God's perspective. Three biblical principles should guide Christians in caring for those with physical or mental impairments: (1) God views with profound grace those who face disabilities and calls his children to do the same; (2) Jesus reached out to the broken and disabled with compassion and healing; and (3) the body of Christ (the church) is to reach out to all who seek him in faith and extend compassion.

The Old Testament records biblical responses to those who faced disabilities. King David showed kindness to Jonathan's son Mephibosheth who was "crippled in his feet" (2 Sam. 9:3–11). Despite his physical impairment, Mephibosheth ate at David's table and received his rightful inheritance. The suffering servant Job asked for mercy in his affliction and received it from God and others (Job 19:21–27).

The New Testament includes examples of Jesus's example and Paul's teaching about the care of the disabled. A centurion sought Jesus to heal his paralyzed servant (Matt. 8:5–13), and friends of a paralyzed man brought him to Jesus to be healed (Matt. 9:1–8). Paul taught Christians to have the same love

---

[4] Nancy L. Eiesland and Don E. Saliers, eds., *Human Disability and the Service of God* (Nashville: Abingdon, 1998), 218.

and mercy toward all people (Phil. 2:1–4) and to take the gospel to all people, including those with handicaps (1 Cor. 1:26–31).

God's Word can provide comfort and strength to individuals who must live with handicapping conditions. Family members can be encouraged by Scripture as they care for their disabled loved ones. All Christians can respond to handicapped people as Christ did, with love, care, and compassion.

CHURCH MANDATE

The church family must be aware of the needs of the special-needs family in order to minister to them effectively. Church buildings are now required by law to be accessible to all handicapped individuals. Many churches should be able to provide Bible studies for those with special needs as well as support for the caregiving family.

Numerous Christian ministries provide information and instructional material for those with handicaps. LifeWay Christian Resources of the Southern Baptist Convention offers a Special Needs Ministry. Other ministries to the disabled include:

- Joni and Friends (www.JoniandFriends.org)
- Christ for People with Developmental Disabilities (www.christforpeople.com)
- Friendship Ministries (www.friendship.org)
- Christians with Disabilities Fund (www.heavensfamily.org)

Individual Christians and the body of Christ would do well to gain understanding of the nature of handicapping conditions as they reach out in love with the gospel. Handicapped individuals are important parts of the body of Christ. They can be used by God to reveal needs and present opportunities for service. Often spiritually sensitive, the disabled person can model for others simple faith in God. Well-known theologian and itinerant Bible teacher R. C. Sproul said of his disabled daughter: "She is my spiritual better." What a great reminder not to neglect the souls of the disabled.

When I was a teenager, the Lord placed special-needs children on my heart. I began working during Sunday school in the special department at our church. An older couple, longtime members of our church, noticed the many handicapped children and younger adults in our congregation. The special class provided appropriate Bible teaching for these youth and allowed their parents to attend their own classes. Evangelistic outreach focused on residential facilities for the disabled in our area. It was a privilege for me to be a part of this special department. God used that type of ministry to clarify my professional calling to special education and speech pathology. It is a joy for me to see two of the people from that special class still in our church today. Link and Jimmy radiate their love for the Lord and their love for all God's children.

No Christian has done more to focus the church on the needs of the disabled than Joni Eareckson Tada. As a teenager, she was paralyzed from the neck down in a diving accident. Her belief that no wheelchair can confine the soul has motivated her ministry called Joni and Friends. Through her writing, speaking, and painting, Joni has encouraged disabled individuals, families, and churches to minister in Christ's name to those with special needs.

Joni wrote these beautiful words after visiting with her heroine in the faith, Corrie ten Boom, who had recently experienced a debilitating stroke:

> Paralyzed people can walk with the Lord.
> Speechless people can talk with the Almighty.
> Sightless people can see Jesus.
> Deaf people can hear the Word of God.
> And those like Tante Corrie, their minds shadowy and obscure,
>   can have the very mind of Christ.[5]

Joni's insightful lines challenge Christians and churches to minister to handicapped individuals and their families.

INDIVIDUAL CHALLENGES

While each individual is different, handicapped people do face some similar challenges. Though disabilities vary greatly in type and severity, every disabled individual encounters personal problems. Less severe disabilities require less adjustment. More severe disabilities demand constant adjustment. Some disabilities are so severe they will never be overcome. With the strength of the Lord and the support of family, handicapped individuals can learn to cope with the inevitable challenges.

Handicapped individuals face many different challenges. The first challenge is attempting to understand and accept the nature of the handicap. They must try not to blame themselves or others for the condition. They must seek to develop a strong self-esteem despite handicapping conditions.

Those with disabilities may often be considered a victim or the helpless object of pity. They may be marginalized, discriminated against, or treated as second-class citizens. Some handicapped individuals report verbal or physical abuse as well as patronizing behavior. At best, they are babied and at worst they

---

[5] Joan Winmill Brown, ed., *My Heart Sings: A Book of Encouragement* (Waco, TX: Word, 1987), 155–56.

are ignored. Christians must see the disabled through God's eyes—created by him and of great value.

Many handicapped individuals face inaccurate stereotypes. Uneducated or insensitive people treat all disabilities alike. Some people talk loudly to every person with a disability, thinking they are hard of hearing. Others talk down to them, assuming they are mentally retarded. Some regard the handicapped as villains, deserving the challenges they face due to evil or depravity. Others laud them as heroes who have overcome great obstacles. Christians must avoid stereotyping those with handicaps, looking beyond the handicap to see the heart.

Evangelist David Ring has overcome many challenges of his handicapping disability. Born with cerebral palsy, he has not let his physical limitations define him. He finished school, got married, and parented children. He leads what would be considered a normal adult life. Through his dynamic preaching, many people have come to faith in Christ. Through his ministry Christians have become more aware of the challenges of handicapping conditions. David Ring has definitely helped others accept those with disabilities and acknowledge their abilities for Christian service. Though the challenges are great, many handicapped individuals can live productive and fulfilling lives.

FAMILY CHALLENGES

The families of handicapped individuals also face challenges. While each individual is unique and every family responds differently, there are some common problems the family of a handicapped individual encounters. Faith in God and support from God's family can help the family thrive, not just survive, a handicapping condition.

Shock, anger, and fear are initially experienced by families when a disability is diagnosed. Embarrassment, loneliness, and disillusionment may follow. However, fatigue, financial problems, and marital conflict are the most significant challenges of the handicapped individual's family.

Families of those with disabilities often experience crises during four periods of time.

- *When the handicap is first detected.* Initial responses include anxiety, helplessness, inadequacy, bereavement, and/or guilt.

- *When a child reaches five years of age.* Developmental concerns present a greater challenge when a child enters school. Accurate diagnosis and a comprehensive treatment plan should help with the educational process.

- *When school enrollment ends.* Independent living and employment options may be limited for a handicapped individual. Again, the family must acknowledge unfulfilled dreams for their loved one.

- *When the parents become older.* As caregiving parents age, other living arrangements must be considered. Siblings or other family members may need to provide care.

A handicapped child's siblings often suffer from the focus on the special child. Siblings can feel neglected by parents, jealous of the handicapped sibling, or burdened by their extra responsibilities. Brothers and sisters of handicapped children may be embarrassed by their sibling's differences or feel guilty because of their own normal abilities and activities. However, most scientific studies have found no major problems in the siblings of handicapped children. In fact, the siblings often show greater emotional maturity and unselfish behavior.

In a *Parade* magazine article, the parents of an autistic child asked the question, "Who will care for Dana?" The challenges of the family of a handicapped individual continue throughout the individual's lifetime. An adult with a handicapping condition presents the family with as many challenges as when the diagnosis was first made. How will he be cared for? Where are jobs? What financial support is available? While resources for the disabled have increased across the years, these challenges are real for their families.[6]

FAMILY SUPPORT

Christians and churches can provide great support for families of handicapped individuals. The process begins with awareness of handicapping conditions. Prayer, patience, and perseverance are essential responses to the individual needs of family members. Marriage support can help a couple cope with the stresses of a handicapping condition. Honest communication and complete trust must be encouraged.

The church—the people of God—needs to help integrate the handicapped and their families into the family of the church. As much as possible, a disabled person should be allowed to worship and fellowship with nondisabled church members. Acceptance and friendship should be promoted. The handicapped individual, like everyone else, needs to hear the gospel of salvation and be nurtured in the faith. Evangelism and discipleship programs are essential ministries to special families. The goal would be for handicapped individuals and families to be involved in church ministry if possible.

A young couple at my church has four children, including a daughter with seizures. Their constant need is child care for this special child and siblings. The family of a young boy with spina bifida worries about his safety as he

---

[6] Joanne Chen, "Who Will Care for Dana?" *Parade*, April 3, 2011, 9–11.

walks around the church on crutches. Physical barriers are this family's greatest concern. Faithful church members who are parents of an adult child with mental retardation are unable to attend Sunday school if there is no special education class. Volunteer help, building adjustments, and dedicated teachers provide invaluable support to families of handicapped individuals.

⤜ SUGGESTIONS ⤛
for Providing Support to Special
Needs Individuals and Families

- Be sensitive to the needs of those with handicaps and their families.
- Get to know individuals with handicapping conditions and their families.
- Become an advocate for those with handicaps.
- Provide help or assistance to the disabled person and family.
- Encourage them with positive statements or kind words.
- Share helpful resources in the church and community.
- Provide respite care for parents/caregivers when possible.
- Pray regularly for the handicapped individual and family.

FAMILY BLESSINGS

Though many challenges face the family of a handicapped individual, there are many blessings as well. Love, acceptance, loyalty, and determination are generally experienced by the handicapped individual and family. Christians should extend unconditional love to all people including special-needs individuals. In return, they receive undeserved love.

Christian families who have a handicapped member are often blessed by the support of a family of faith. While personal faith provides strength, extra encouragement is provided when the body of Christ prays for, helps, and loves the individual and family. Christian friends are a source of true blessing.

One of the greatest blessings to the family of a handicapped individual is witnessing progress and improvement. Because disabled individuals must work much harder than their "normal" peers, even the smallest gains or improvements give reason to rejoice. Realistic expectations are often met with the help of the Lord, therapeutic intervention, and supportive family members and friends.

A handicapped individual usually has a network of professionals to assist in diagnosis and treatment. Early intervention has become standard for developmentally delayed children. These trained workers become an important part of the family's life. Though special services may be very costly, the benefit of resources and personnel are great. Medical doctors, rehabilitation therapists, and other parents/families can provide real comfort and mutual understanding. Support groups are organized for many handicapping conditions, offering education and empathy. And, many resources are now available online and in books to help an individual or family receive the best care possible.

Siblings of handicapped individuals receive blessings as well. Though the disabled one must receive more attention and time, siblings are not negatively impacted. In fact, as previously noted, siblings most often show greater emotional maturity and compassion. Responsibility and patience are learned through helping a handicapped brother or sister. From my observation, siblings often achieve better in school and perform better in their work.

Another blessing to the family is witnessing spiritual growth in a handicapped individual. Young disabled children can usually understand about God and trust him by faith. Adults who become disabled later in life often depend on the faith of their childhood. As our parents have aged and experienced some physical limitations and cognitive losses, their strong faith has been such a powerful testimony. When asked how he is doing, my dad always responds, "I'm happy in the Lord." His positive attitude as he faces physical challenges blesses all of us. Papa Kelley's faith was such a blessing even as his dementia progressed. He recalled familiar Scriptures and hymns even when unable to carry on a conversation. He blessed all those around him with his sweet spirit and words of truth. Family members are truly blessed by the faith, hope, and love of their handicapped loved ones.

CONCLUSION

A handicapped individual definitely has an impact on the entire family. Since handicapping conditions are fairly common, many families will experience the challenges and blessings. Christians should be guided by biblical principles as they support their disabled loved ones. The church as a whole should minister to the handicapped individual and the family. The challenges faced by the individual and family can often be overcome with the help of the Holy Spirit, appropriate resources, and supportive friends.

Special families can grow emotionally and spiritually as they care for the handicapped individual. As Winston Churchill said, "We draw from the heart of the suffering itself the means of inspiration and survival." Christians with handicaps can be godly role models.

God himself strengthens those who experience handicaps, their parents, their siblings, and their children. But God requires his children, the church, to minister to the unique needs of the special family. In ministering to the families of the disabled, the church itself is blessed—blessed by obedience to the Father and care for the family.

PUTTING THE PRINCIPLES INTO PRACTICE

1. Do you know anyone personally who has a handicapped family member? How is her family impacted by the handicapping condition? Pray about ways you can support that family.
2. What types of ministry or support does your church offer for individuals with handicapping conditions and their families? If you do not know, investigate these programs with your ministry staff.
3. What is your personal understanding about disabilities? If you are not very informed, research information from the websites and resources listed in this chapter. Try to become informed as a Christian advocate.
4. How do you think your own family would be impacted by a disability? How would you want to respond initially and over time?
5. How do you think handicapped individuals bless their loved ones? Give specific examples from personal experience when possible.

ADDITIONAL RESOURCES

Colsten, Lowell G. *Pastoral Care with Handicapped Persons*. Philadelphia: Fortress, 1978.

Creamer, Deborah Beth. *Disability and Christian Theology*. New York: Oxford University Press, 2009.

Eiesland, Nancy L., and Don E. Saliero, eds. *Human Disability and the Service of God*. Nashville: Abingdon, 1998.

Gillibrand, John. *Disabled Church—Disabled Society: The Implications of Autism for Philosophy, Theology, and Politics*. Philadelphia: Jessica Kingsley, 2010.

Kelley, Rhonda. "Writer Calls on Churches to Minister to Families of Handicapped Children," *Baptist Message*, February 28, 1991.

Reinders, Hans S. *Receiving the Gift of Friendship: Profound Disability, Theological Anthropology, and Ethics*. Grand Rapids, MI: Eerdmans, 2008.

Waters, Larry J., and Roy B. Zuck, eds. *Why, O God? Suffering and Disability in the Bible and the Church*. Wheaton, IL: Crossway, 2011.

Webb-Mitchell, Brett. *Unexpected Guests at God's Banquet: Welcoming People with Disabilities into the Church*. New York: Crossroad, 1994.

Chapter Twelve

Placing the Solitary in Families

Pat Ennis

A blond-headed, blue-eyed daughter, I looked like the perfect blend of my mother and father. As others commented on the likeness, my parents smiled inwardly, knowing that it was their heavenly Father who had chosen the custom matching of their adopted daughter as he had made "a home for the lonely" (NASB) or, as the King James Version notes, had set "the solitary in families" (Ps. 68:6). Older when they commenced the adoption process, Oliver and Mary Ennis were willing to commit to nurturing a child. Eventually they welcomed to their home an abandoned child with pneumonia. She had lain so long on her back that the back of her head was bald. As you may have surmised, I was that abandoned child.

Many children spend numerous years with one or both parents. My older-than-average parents, not knowing how many years they would enjoy with me, maximized each to its fullest.

Celebrations were important in the Ennis home. I recall well when I arrived home on January 31st and found the dining room table set with Mom's best linen and china. Lying across my bed was a new "fancy" dress, and my favorite black patent leather shoes were awaiting my feet. I was ten. Without giving me extensive details—my parents explained many things to me but did not feel obligated to try to make a child understand all adult decisions—I was helped to dress for dinner. Dad arrived, stayed in his best suit, and a special dinner was served. He then explained the celebration—January 31st was the day that they had brought me home from the hospital, six months after my birth. I was not their birth child but very special because they had chosen me. That evening we were celebrating the day that I joined the Ennis family. His explanation made the subsequent transition to salvation smooth. Salvation was like being adopted into God's family. How could I not desire heavenly adoption when my earthly adoption was so wonderful?

THEOLOGY OF ADOPTION

The biblical basis for adoption is concisely stated in James 1:27, "Religion that is pure and undefiled before God the Father is this: to visit orphans and widows in their affliction, and to keep oneself unstained from the world." John MacArthur writes,

> James picks two synonymous adjectives to define the most spotless kind of religious faith—that which is measured by compassionate love (cf. John 13:35), orphans and widows. Those without parents or husbands were and are an especially needy segment of the church. Since they are usually unable to reciprocate in any way, caring for them clearly demonstrates true, sacrificial, Christian love.[1]

To adopt, by definition, means to "to take by choice into a relationship," especially "to take voluntarily (a child of other parents) as one's own child."[2] Since Christians, through God's grace, are accepted into his family without limitation or restriction and enjoy all of the rights and privileges bestowed upon his children, they should readily grasp the concept of adoption. Ephesians 1:5 clearly states that God the Father "predestined us for adoption as sons through Jesus Christ, according to the purpose of his will." The theological basis of adoption can help the believer in comprehending that the goal of adoption exhibits the glory of God's grace.

Adoption imagery is infused throughout the New Testament. John 1:12–13 affirms, "But to all who did receive him, who believed in his name, he gave the right to become children of God, who were born, not of blood nor of the will of the flesh nor of the will of man, but of God." Writing to the Romans, Paul states:

> For you did not receive the spirit of slavery to fall back into fear, but you have received the Spirit of adoption as sons, by whom we cry, "Abba! Father!" The Spirit himself bears witness with our spirit that we are children of God, and if children, then heirs—heirs of God and fellow heirs with Christ, provided we suffer with him in order that we may also be glorified with him. (Rom. 8:15–17)

Examples of adoption, or circumstances comparable to such commitment, are woven throughout Scripture:

- Moses was essentially adopted by Pharaoh's daughter (Ex. 2:1–10).
- Samuel was left in the care of Eli the high priest rather than being nurtured by his biological mother, Hannah (1 Sam. 1:1–2:21).

---

[1] John MacArthur, *The MacArthur Study Bible* (Nashville: Word, 2000), notes for James 1:27: orphans and widows.
[2] *Merriam-Webster's Collegiate Dictionary*, 10th ed., s.v. "adopt."

- Esther was adopted as a child by her adult cousin, Mordecai (Est. 2:7).
- Jesus was nurtured by his stepfather, Joseph of Nazareth (Luke 2:4, 41–50).
- All believers are adopted into God's eternal family (Gal. 4:3–7).

The placement of these solitary individuals into families was a part of God's sovereign plan. A journey through the Scriptures teaches us:

- There is significant financial and emotional expense associated with human adoption. However, those expenses are insignificant when compared with the costliness of a believer's adoption into God's eternal family (Gal. 3:13; 4:4–5).

- The process of legal adoption requires careful planning and execution of a myriad of legal formalities. This detailed process is a reminder that the heavenly Father planned far in advance for our adoption—he predestined us for adoption before the creation of the world (Eph. 1:4–6).

- Most children available for adoption need to be rescued from precarious situations. Often they are difficult to deal with. Such was our state when God adopted you and me. Adoption is a reminder that by nature we are *children of wrath* (Eph. 2:3). Though the distance between who God is and what we are is great, he still chooses to adopt us into his family.

- Legally adopted children have the privilege of receiving full rights of inheritance from their parents. This legal privilege prompts believers to recall that as children of God we become his heirs (Gal. 4:6–7). God appointed his Son to be heir of all things (Heb. 1:2). Every child adopted into God's family is a joint heir with Christ (Rom. 8:16–17).

Placing the solitary in families may be viewed through two different lenses—the choices the adopted child makes and the parenting strategies of the father and mother.

ADOPTED CHILDREN'S CHOICES

Do you recall the movie or stage play *Annie*? This spunky child with auburn curls built a fantasy about her parents and the life she would experience once they returned to the orphanage to claim her. Even when Daddy Warbucks expressed a desire to adopt her, she steadfastly refused because she was confident that nothing could be better than life with her birth parents. The truth of her abandonment, when eventually revealed, was far from the fantasy she had created.

Such is the case with scores of children who have lovingly been adopted—their discontentment in their God-ordained family casts a cloud of gloom over the entire family. The apostle Paul provides advice in Philippians 2:14–16 and

4:11 to those experiencing discontent: Refuse to complain and learn to be content in the situation where God has placed you.

I conducted a database search to see what advice might be available to adopted children. My search yielded seventy pages and 6,640,000 results. While a plethora of information was available to adoptive parents, not one resource in my personal search surfaced for the adopted child. Understandably, adopted children experience challenges unique to their heritage. Concurrently they make choices that will either enrich or encumber their lives. Placed within the framework of the word *adopted*, the following principles offer *all* of God's adopted children guidelines to make choices that will produce a God-honoring lifestyle (Col. 3:17).

A—Acknowledge

Choose to acknowledge what your heavenly Father thinks of you as his adopted child.

- Your heavenly Father provides provision and protection (Ps. 84:11).

- While you were in your worst, sinful condition, God gave his dearest treasure, Christ, out of his unfathomable heart of love for you (Rom. 5:6–11; 8:32).

- You were indwelt by Christ at the moment of salvation (Rom. 8:9; 1 Cor. 12:13; Eph. 3:14–19).

- Nothing can separate you from God's love (Rom. 8:31–39).

- Although God knows *everything* about you (Psalm 139), you are accepted totally and unconditionally by him because of Christ's substitutionary death (Eph. 1:6 KJV).

- You are a person in process, not fully like him but becoming more like him daily as you yield to his ways. He does not expect perfection (Eph. 2:10; Phil. 1:6), but he does expect that you will ask him for the strength to become conformed to his image (Phil. 4:13).

- Regardless of life's circumstances, God's love remains unchanged (1 John 4:7–16).

D—Delight

Choose to do those things that delight your heavenly Father (Ps. 37:4); then apply this spiritual principle to pleasing your earthly parents. Honoring your parents (Ex. 20:12; Eph. 6:2) brings delight to their hearts and to the heart of your heavenly Father.

O—Obey

Choose to obey your parents in all things (Eph. 6:1–3; Col. 3:20). The only limit on a child's obedience is when parents demand an action that is contrary to God's Word. First Samuel 15:22 reminds God's children that he desires a heart of obedience.

P—Pray

Choose to pray for your parents. The command to pray is repeated throughout the Scriptures (Luke 12:12; 18:1; Eph. 6:18; 1 Thess. 5:17; 2 Thess. 1:11; James 5:13–16). Prayer will most assuredly improve your relationship with your heavenly Father and will more than likely mellow any negative attitude toward your parents.

T—Thank

Choose to cultivate a thankful spirit. Did you know that true gratitude enriches your life? Consider implementing this "Gratitude Cycle":

- The more thankful you are, the more you are aware of your many blessings.
- If you offer praise and thanksgiving only when things go your way, you develop tunnel vision.
- If you are grateful for *all* that your heavenly Father brings into your life, then your horizons expand.
- When your horizons expand, your ability to offer praise sincerely, regardless of the circumstances, increases.

✑ REMEMBER ✒

- Giving thanks is generated from the will.
- Being thankful is generated from the emotions.
- The Psalms are written to activate the will, not the emotions. (Read the book of Psalms, underlining every use of the phrase "I will." What is your final count?)
- If you are unwilling to extend gratitude to those whom you can see, you are unlikely to thank your heavenly Father whom you cannot see.

E—Eliminate the "Elijah Effect"

Choose to eliminate the "Elijah Effect." Consider the account of Elijah as recorded in 1 Kings 18:18–19:14. He emerged from his experience at Mount

Carmel a victor—the 450 false prophets of Baal were destroyed, and the calamity of drought and famine brought about by idol worship ended. Regrettably, Queen Jezebel did not share his enthusiasm over the victory—in fact, she was *very* angry. Instead of surrendering, as Elijah expected, she issued an ultimatum to him, "So may the gods do to me and more also, if I do not make your life as the life of one of them by this time tomorrow" (1 Kings 19:2). Elijah's response is similar to that of many Christians—they observe God performing repeated miracles in their lives, then a bit of minor turbulence occurs, and the downward spiral of the Elijah Effect sets in (see 1 Kings 19):

- The cycle of fear of others or specific circumstances begins (vv. 1–2).
- The logical reaction is to run from the problem (challenge) rather than facing it head-on (v. 3).
- Rather than meditating on God's faithfulness, faulty negative thinking begins (v. 4).
- The faulty negative thinking is fanned by emotional and physical fatigue, which frequently produces discouragement (vv. 5–9).
- Further faulty negative thinking yields false expectations and unrealistic attitudes regarding God's sovereign plan (v. 10).
- These false expectations and unrealistic attitudes can lead to the cultivation of self-pity (v. 14).

An intervention strategy for the Elijah Effect must be applied to reverse the process. In Elijah's case, as in ours, the intervention cycle to renew his spirit involved using the Word of God as a sword to fight the source of discouragement, Satan (Eph. 6:17). Acquiring God's truth and promises during times of refreshment enables you to engage confidently in battle; for example, Psalms 33, 42, 43, and 71 teach the hope you are to have in God. Lamentations 3:21–23 describes the downcast man who nevertheless relies on the steadfast love of the Lord. First Peter 1:13–21 challenges you to proclaim the faith and hope you can have in God through Jesus Christ, while Romans 8:18–39 reminds you that nothing can separate you from God's love. Choosing to embrace this intervention strategy will ensure that you will emerge as a victor rather than a victim when challenges confront you.

D—Develop a Heart of Forgiveness

Choose to embrace a spirit of forgiveness. Much like the legendary Spanish water torture where victims were strapped down so they could not move, and cold water was dripped slowly onto a small area of the body until they were gradually driven frantic, so for one who has been adopted the choice not to forgive your birth parents destroys family unity slowly but effectively. The antidote? Follow the Lord's example (1 Pet. 2:21–23) and develop a *forgiving spirit.*

Forgiveness is essential for building relationships. Though the actions of others will at times disappoint you, you are to forgive them unconditionally. To realize that relationships fracture when forgiveness is rejected is a sobering thought.

There is no getting around it, the actions of others will at times disappoint you. Disappointment can lead to anger. Anger breeds an unforgiving spirit and damages relationships. To avoid that heartache, Ephesians 4:26 calls you to deal with broken relationships before you lay your head on the pillow at night.

Ephesians 4:32 teaches that to forgive is the most Christlike action possible. God by nature is a forgiving God. You reflect his character when you choose to forgive (1 John 1:9).

Peter generously offered to forgive seven times. Jesus corrected his faulty reasoning by suggesting that he was to forgive at least 490 times! Matthew 18:21–35 clearly teaches that those forgiven the greater sins are to forgive the lesser sins. You practice this truth when you offer to others the same mercy that God daily extends to you. Holding a grudge is an unrighteous act. Eventually it will produce a bitter spirit. How many times are you to forgive others? The same number of times you expect to be forgiven—a number that far exceeds 490.

All the injuries and injustices that others commit against you are the trials God uses to perfect you. Realigning your reactions to them and viewing them as tools by which the heavenly Father makes you more like Christ are the responses that please him (James 1:2; 1 Pet. 5:10; 2 Cor. 12:7). When you respond to trials biblically, your spiritual stamina increases because God's strength is perfected in *your* weakness. Consider these thoughts in relationship to any responses you may have as an adopted child:

- Choose to control your thought life (2 Cor. 10:5; Phil. 4:8–9).
- Use discretion in attempting to locate your birth parents (Phil. 3:13–14).
- Bask in the truth of God's sovereignty. A. W. Pink suggests that embracing the concept of God's sovereignty is the fundamental difference between the person of faith and the person of unbelief:

The unbeliever is "of the world," judges everything by worldly standards, views life from the standpoint of time and sense, and weighs everything in the balances of his own carnal understanding. But the man of faith *brings in God*, looks at everything from *His* standpoint, estimates values by spiritual standards, and views life in the light of eternity. Doing this, he receives whatever comes as from the hand of God. Doing this, his heart is calm in the midst of storm. Doing this, he rejoices in hope of the glory of God.[3]

Will you ever understand all of the circumstances that God allows to enter your life? Scripture answers this question directly by stating that God's judgments are "unsearchable" and "how inscrutable his ways" (Rom. 11:33). You will never fully comprehend God's ways, plans, or purposes. You must walk by faith, trusting in the fact that God is accomplishing his perfect, sovereign plan. Peter Enns summarizes this concept by stating, "God's wisdom and knowledge cannot be comprehended. God has consulted no one and no one has advised Him. But because God knows all things He controls and guides all events for His honor and for our good (Ps. 104:24; Prov. 3:19)."[4]

Pointers for Adoptive Parents

A couple hoping to adopt must consider and discuss openly many issues before a decision can be made. It is a lifelong commitment. The adopting family gives its name to the adopted child. There is no turning back. The child is legally in line for the same inheritance as biological children. Psychological components that affect the marriage relationship must be considered. When the wife is more eager to adopt than the husband, he can hear nagging in her frequent introduction of the topic. When the husband is the one who desires to adopt, the wife can feel that he is increasing her responsibilities. The husband and wife must have a strong relationship. Children bring a challenge that can destroy the marriage. Spouses must put each other first and acknowledge that a child is a welcomed member of the family but not its center. As the family size increases, so does the dynamic of the family. Each child represents the family and is to be taught to respect the home and family name. Teaching this principle extracts time from both Dad and Mom. When additional children are integrated into the family, the parents must be willing to adjust their commitments, allowing them to invest the time and effort to "train up [each] child in the way he should go" (Prov. 22:6). Consider the following pointers from Glenda Hotton:[5]

---

[3] A. W. Pink, *The Sovereignty of God* (London: The Banner of Truth Trust, 1978), 18–19.

[4] Peter Enns, *The Moody Handbook of Theology* (Chicago: Moody Press, 1989), 204.

[5] Glenda Hotton is a licensed marriage and family counselor, as well as the mother of an adopted child. Additionally, she is a professor in the family life strand of the Home Economics–Family and Consumer Sciences Department at The Master's College. She graciously provided the "Pointers for Adoptive Parents" that are based upon her professional and personal experiences.

- When weighing the decision to integrate children into the family structure, whether biologically or through adoption, remember that parenting demands mature people. Parenting is not for the fainthearted!

- The husband and wife must be united on the decision to adopt. If there are hardships with the child, the one who was talked into adopting can retreat and become challenging to live with; sometimes the "convinced spouse" cultivates a spirit of resentment and in extreme cases abandons the home. A couple must remember that their relationship is of first and foremost importance. The child will grow up and leave, as do biological children, and the couple must build toward the empty-nest years.

- Seek counsel from a trusted pastor or a peer family who have adopted. Try not to allow emotions to dictate the decision to adopt. A woman has an innate nurturing instinct, and she can be overtaken with emotions. A baby is a heart-stopper. Most women are emotionally drawn to babies.

- Evaluate the age of the adopted child and how that fits into the existing family structure of siblings. The oldest child in the family may desire to retain that status. The youngest may also have a strong opinion, depending on his age. Many times the youngest enjoys the idea of having a baby in the family. The oldest may see it as a source of more work and responsibility for him.

- Adopting older children can be an enormous challenge as they often have a difficult time adjusting to "normal" family living, which can bring much unwanted stress on the family. I have seldom seen a successful adoption of an older child. They come with so much history. Of course, God is a miracle worker, and he can work in the heart of an adopted child (Gen. 18:13). As well, there are exceptions when the parents die and a family member chooses to raise the children.

- Consider if drugs or alcohol are a part of the child's health history. Seriously contemplate the choice to adopt a special-needs child. In either case, pray for an extended period of time and seek godly counsel before making the decision to adopt a child with additional medical constraints. Remember that adoption is for a lifetime, and there is no turning back. Once a child is adopted, the child is no different than if born into the family biologically.

- Remember that an adopted child makes irrational choices, not because he is adopted but rather because of his sin nature (Rom. 3:23). Often there is a greater tendency to take personally the disobedience of an adopted child. When our adopted daughter began to show her sinful heart and ultimately run away from home, my reflex response was to blame myself. The ifs are huge at this time. I then recalled how each child (I have four children) had brought me to my knees at one time or another. By meditating on this truth, I was able to concentrate on the reality that she chose to sin. I was then freed to pray and anticipate with open arms her return. I chose to model my behavior after the biblical story of the prodigal son (Luke 15:11–32), watching and waiting rather than pursuing her and forcing her home against her will. Failure to embrace this type of response can create a breach between the husband and wife.

- The same mandate to train up a child is for all of the children the parents are raising (Prov. 22:6). The identical issues are found in the sinful heart of a child, whether biological or adopted. *Shepherding a Child's Heart* by Tedd Tripp is an excellent resource for parents with biological or adopted children.

- Talk about the child being adopted in a natural way that does not cause the child to feel odd but rather comfortable in knowing he was adopted or chosen. Helping the child acclimate to the word "adopted" may remove the awkwardness of his place in the family. When our little girl was new in our home, I would rock her at night, sing songs to her, and use the words, "You are our little adopted angel." We decorated her bedroom with a yellow porch swing, hanging from the ceiling. It became a place of storytelling and chatting for us. Many times she would take my finger and pull me to her room. Climbing up on the swing, she would motion for me to sit down and say, "Tell me my story." She felt loved as I explained that God used another woman to birth her. The woman could not care for her, so that woman, because of her love for her little girl, wanted us to care for her daughter as our own. Somehow it gave the child reassurance that she was loved. After the recounting, she would hop down and go on her way.

Hotton concludes her pointers for adoptive parents by sharing,

> As an adopting parent, I forget that my fourth daughter is adopted. She is as much mine as my other three girls. Truly this is how it should be. The adopted child must know she is loved and will be treated equally. *Adoption* should be as natural to their ears as "Mom" and "Dad." If adoption is not something talked about often, the child may feel odd. A family is a family. There are responsibilities and considerations from each side.

ADOPTION IMPLICATIONS FOR THE TWENTY-FIRST-CENTURY EVANGELICAL COMMUNITY

Adoption is an issue that is on the heart of God. Reflecting again on James 1:27, you are reminded that "Religion that is pure and undefiled before God, the Father, is this: to visit orphans and widows in their affliction." Practically speaking, this means reaching down to the abandoned person who is helpless and may die without physical care and spiritual nurturing.

Orphans teach you about the love of God, call you to sacrifice, and challenge you to value Christlikeness above your comfort. Not every family is called to adopt, but within the Christian community there are probably more families who should consider it. Are you willing to ask your heavenly Father, "What do you have for me in relation to adoption?" His response might just change the course of your life.

PUTTING THE PRINCIPLES INTO PRACTICE

1. Meditate upon the miracle of your adoption into God's family. Review the Scriptures presented in the section called "Theology of Adoption," conduct additional research, and then write about your adoption experience.

2. Petition your heavenly Father to create a tender spirit toward adoption and then become practically involved by the following:

   - Identify orphans in your church or community. Make a concentrated effort to meet their emotional and physical needs.

   - November is National Adoption Month, a month set aside each year to raise awareness about the adoption of children and youth from foster care. Visit www.childwelfare.gov/adoption to garner ideas for involving your Christian community in the month's activities.

   - Consider supporting financially the ministry of adoption.

   - Prayerfully contemplate adopting children into your family as an overflow of the inheritance that you have in Christ from God your Father.

   - Record your experiences at the conclusion of your adoption experience.

3. Complete the "Gratitude Gauge" located at the conclusion of this chapter. Interpret your score by using the Gratitude Gauge Scale. What is your reaction to your score? Use the verses that follow to develop principles for increasing your "Gratitude Gauge" score. I provided an example for you.

   - Psalm 18:49—*I will choose to give thanks to God and sing praises to his name.*

   - Psalm 103:3–5

- Romans 1:21

- 1 Corinthians 15:57

- 1 Thessalonians 5:18

- 1 Timothy 4:4

4. Proverbs 23:7 states that as you think, so you are. Write on cards each of the verses contained in the "Adopted Children's Choices" section of this chapter. Choose to memorize and meditate upon what your heavenly Father thinks of you as his adopted child. Record on the back of the card specific times God has demonstrated his love to you; include these events in your meditation thoughts.
5. Create your own ADOPTION acrostic following the model in the "Adopted Children's Choices" section.

☙ GRATITUDE GAUGE ❧

Place the number that best reflects your response to the statement in the space provided.

Use the following scale:

5 = regularly	2 = seldom
4 = usually	1 = very seldom
3 = sometimes	0 = never

1. _____ I quickly acknowledge that expressing gratitude is a biblical instruction.
2. _____ I recognize that a complaining spirit is symptomatic of the fact that I lack a grateful heart.
3. _____ I understand that cultivating a grateful heart is a lifelong process.
4. _____ I believe that the condition of my spiritual heart determines my spiritual health.
5. _____ I am increasing in my knowledge of the Word.
6. _____ I thank my heavenly Father for my spiritual blessings.
7. _____ I thank my heavenly Father for my material blessings.
8. _____ I thank my heavenly Father for my joyful experiences.
9. _____ I thank my heavenly Father for my difficult experiences.
10. _____ I offer thanks to others when they extend kindness to me.
11. _____ I seek to speak encouraging words to others.
12. _____ I quickly acknowledge that sincere gratitude enriches my life.
13. _____ I am looking for ways to serve others.
14. _____ I maintain contact with missionaries and seek to share some of their burdens.
15. _____ I understand that giving thanks is generated from my will.
16. _____ I am aware that being thankful is generated from my emotions.
17. _____ I "pause for praise" throughout the day.
18. _____ Others affirm my grateful spirit.
19. _____ I acknowledge that how I respond to the biblical instruction about expressing gratitude affects my spiritual health.
20. _____ I am like the one leper who returned to thank the Lord for healing him (Luke 17:15–16).

_____ **Gratitude Gauge Total**

Gratitude Gauge Scale

Total all the numbers indicating your responses to the statements. Then find the corresponding range of scores listed below:

100–90
A maturing attitude of gratitude

89–80
A commitment to an attitude of gratitude

79–70
An understanding of what constitutes an attitude of gratitude

69–60
A minimal commitment to an attitude of gratitude

59–0
An attitude adjustment is needed

Part Three

FOUNDATIONS FOR PARENTING

Chapter Thirteen

Biblical Foundations
for Parenting

Dorothy Kelley Patterson

The Hebrew word for parents is *horim* from a root meaning "teacher." Ultimately to be a parent is to teach—instruct the next generation in every way possible to prepare them to step into their own responsibilities. The psalmist declared, "God settles the solitary in a home" (Ps. 68:6). Building this unity demands time and work as well as teaching. An atmosphere of love, understanding, appreciation, respect, patience, and kindness must be painstakingly created. Spontaneity is good, but it must not replace planning. Family life must include interesting activities for each member and some special times for all to join together in productivity or simply fellowship. Within the home or in other venues such as museums or theaters, outside in the family yard and garden or in public sites like a zoo or sporting events, nearby or far away, with the family alone or with neighbors and friends—every family must create its own memories and history to be passed as a legacy to the next generation and to be nourished as Samuel described the "stone of help" (Hb. *'eben 'ēzer*; 1 Sam. 7:12) for each generation.

MOTHERS

Being a mother is often considered a thankless and joyless, as well as over-whelming, task. Many view rearing children as a hardship tour in the mundane duties of life—burdens and sacrifices, self-denial and boredom, an interruption and inconvenience. Yet perception does not always present *accurate* information but rather has the tendency to frame that information while distorting reality in the process.

Every woman, married or single, with or without children, has a maternal instinct given to her by God himself. Some women try to bury this maternity in pursuit of professional goals; others try to extract and discard this nurturing sensitivity under the guise of true freedom; still others seek to minimize their feminine natures by reversing priorities and roles so that maternal nurture is merely a job to be assigned to anyone willing to take it.

The biblical model—based on the creation order found in Genesis 1, the book of beginnings—has been honored throughout the generations. Husbands and wives have worked together to build their families; wives have labored faithfully to keep their homes and manage their households; and mothers have nurtured their own children. However, some are suggesting that this model is now obsolete.

Women have been brainwashed to believe that the absence of a titled, payroll occupation condemns a woman to failure, boredom, and even imprisonment within the confines of the home. Although feminism speaks of liberation, self-fulfillment, personal rights, and breaking down barriers, in reality these phrases inevitably have produced the opposite. In fact, a salaried job and titled position can inhibit a woman's natural nesting instinct and maternity by inverting her priorities so that she almost inevitably experiences failures in her life in the arena that should be most important, that is, in the fashioning of an earthly shelter for those whom she loves most and in the rearing of her own children.

In the quest to be *all* you are meant to be, you must not forget *who* you are meant to be and *what* you are meant to do! The mundane accompanies every task, however high-paying or prestigious the job, and escaping boredom is not inevitable just because the workplace is located away from home. Whether or not a woman wants the best for her husband and children and even for herself is not the question. Rather the real question is this: Is being someone's wife and another's mother worth the investment of a life? Are the preparation of skills, the concentration of energies, and the commitment of your primary focus valuable to keeping a home? The secular presuppositions of the present age, as well as your own assumptions and priorities, must continually be tested against inherent values and priorities from the pages of holy Scripture.

Perhaps the modern challenge is not so much the sacrifices a mother is challenged to make for her children as much as it is the overwhelming peer pressure a mother feels to do everything—work a professional job, render community service, and pursue her own dreams while simultaneously helping her husband, caring for her children, preparing family meals, maintaining her own household, and guarding her own health. Her life becomes all work, and she is overwhelmed with the pressures of mundane tasks. She has no time for relaxation or play and no opportunity to enjoy the fruit of her labor. Maternity should be viewed as being intellectually respectable and emotionally reward-ing as well as a worthy profession in the marketplace.

Motherhood is indeed an earthly work with eternal consequences. Rearing up godly children through teaching them God's Word and praying for them and *never, never* giving up on them is an overwhelmingly important task. Thousands of mothers around the country pray for their children with serious and specific intercession not only for their children but also for those who are in positions to influence them. As such, they are a formidable force in the courts of heaven.

◌⊱ **MOTHERS NEED TIME** ⊰◌
to *renew* their energies, *revive* their
spirits, and *revitalize* their bodies

- *Daily diversions*—an hour to spend in spiritual meditation or quiet relaxation without interruption
- *Weekly withdrawal*—a trip to the beauty salon or a neighbor-hood Bible study
- *Annual abandonment*—getting away for several days or even a week to evaluate the past year, look at current happenings, project future goals and plans, or enjoy something for sheer pleasure and joy

---

Women cannot shun the responsibility of maternity without endangering all of civilization. The demands of motherhood include the following com-mitments:

- *Unconditional love.* Genuine love without bounds is not merely an emotional reaction but rather is fashioned by determination—the unselfish outpouring of your life into the life of another; doing what is best for your child even at your own personal sacrifice.

- *Never-ending nurture.* Physically, emotionally, intellectually, and spiritually—you are responsible for helping your child navigate the pitfalls and challenges of life, moving from dependence on you, to maturity for himself, to embrac-ing a partnership with community and society. This whole-of-life instruction fashions your child's worldview, shapes his character, and instructs him in an intentional way, including the guiding discipline that sets boundaries and protects.

- *Ever-present welcoming and comforting home.* A mother guides the household well with a primary responsibility for maintaining the setting and place in which love and nurture will operate effectively and for providing the child a model for marriage and an example of parenting. Show-and-tell instruction is much more effective than teaching on the run.

◦✍ RESPONSIBILITIES ✎◦
OF THE MOTHER

• Offering solace and comfort—caretaker of the shelter
• Nurturing and teaching
• Developing right attitudes
• Developing femininity in daughters
• Developing masculinity in sons
• Following the father's spiritual leadership

FATHERS

Fathers have moved from the center to the fringe of family life. Masculinity has been redefined with more emphasis on personal ambition and achievement and less importance on effective fatherhood. Genuine manliness is marked by courage, duty, chivalry, and saturated with virtues that inhibit inappropriate aggression. The father's role in the family has been devalued and stripped of any authoritative position, which breeds delinquency, violence, sexual promiscuity, pregnancy out of wedlock, drug abuse, and suicide.

A study reported in the *Journal of Marriage and Family* concluded that conservative evangelical fathers are more likely to read with their children, eat dinner with them, and engage in outside activities together. Although some greet this phenomenon with surprise, genuine evangelicals understand that a father's commitment to invest in a significant way in the lives of his children is the natural result of his commitment to the biblical paradigm for the family. On the other hand, some estimate that 88 percent of the teens attending evangelical churches will forsake their churches, and perhaps even their faith, by the time they reach the age of eighteen.[1]

Mothers spend more time with their children, teaching them the lessons of life and training them to be citizens of the world, but fathers must be involved in this process as well. Fathers tend to play with their children in a different way than do mothers. Young children need adventurous play and roughhousing from their fathers just as they need reading and games with their moth-

[1] W. Bradford Wilcox, "Religion, Convention, and Paternal Involvement," *Journal of Marriage and Family* 64: 780–792. For key points see the following news release from the University of Virginia, where Wilcox is Associate Professor of Sociology and Director of the National Marriage Project: "Good Dads: Faith Makes a Difference," *University of Virginia News* [online], accessed March 1, 2012, http://www.virginia.edu/topnews /releases2002/faith-aug-1-2002.html.

ers. Fathers are important to boys as a role model and are equally important to their daughters, teaching them how to relate to men and how to develop confidence in themselves and in their femininity. Fathers model behavior for responsible and godly masculinity, and they help their daughters identify a godly man when they see one.

A father's presence in the home is essential to the rearing of children. They have the privilege and duty of sharing in their children's lives. My husband has always been a wonderful playmate for our children and grandchildren. He realizes that play is important to children as a part of their physical, mental, and even spiritual development.

Children need both parents—emotionally as well as economically. Boys need fathers to learn how to be men, and girls need fathers to learn how to relate to men. In most cases a girl's first love is her father. The development of a daughter's relationship to her father prepares her to appreciate her femininity and to expect that same affection and respect from other men in her life. Fathers need to model responsible manhood for their daughters as well as for their sons.

Parents are responsible for supervising their own children in their study of the Bible, memorizing Scripture, telling them the stories of the Bible, and drawing moral lessons from those stories.

A career and its accompanying economic benefits should never be more important to a father than his children. However, his responsibility in the biblical model is to *provide* the necessities of food, shelter, and clothing for his family (Gen. 2:15–17; 1 Tim. 5:8). He defeats the value of that provision if he does not take into account his other responsibilities to *protect* (not just physically but also mentally, emotionally, and spiritually) as well as to *lead* the members of his family entrusted to his care. Love is balanced with discipline; one-on-one attention given to each child is balanced with time together with the family; development of mind, body, and spirit must be apportioned appropriately; study, play, and work must all be considered.

Fathers are entrusted with spiritual leadership in their families (Eph. 6:1–4). The Puritans treated their families as their own "little church" with hymns and prayers as well as reading and discussing Scripture. They are to instruct their children in righteousness and train them to follow God's way in all venues of life. They must rebuke and correct when appropriate. In this safety net of shelter, security, and adequate life preparation provided by fathers and mothers, a child will find freedom to develop in the midst of wholesome and protective boundaries.

Training a child to honor his father and mother is his prelude to a lifetime of honoring and glorifying God with his obedience. A child who enjoys the loving care of his father and learns how to respond in obedience to his father will more easily relate to his heavenly Father, to whom he has been introduced in Scripture through anthropomorphic language. When an earthly father is distant and uninvolved, his child will have more difficulty relating to his heavenly Father.

✑ RESPONSIBILITIES ✑ OF THE FATHER

- Providing
- Protecting
- Disciplining
- Developing masculinity in sons
- Developing femininity in daughters
- Spending quality time with children
- Assuming spiritual leadership

PRINCIPLE 1: DEMONSTRATE TO YOUR CHILDREN A PATTERN FOR CHRISTIAN MARRIAGE

1 Timothy 2-3; Titus 2:1-5

Marriage, the uniting of one man and one woman in a lifelong, exclusive, monogamous relationship, is the beginning of a family. Within this union, love can and should reach its highest human expectation. The up-close observation of this marital love is important for children as well as for husbands and wives.

Parents must provide good models of what Christian marriage ought to be. Husbands and wives must be committed to a growing, healthy relationship with one another. They ought to exhibit a strong, loving relationship in which they complement each other and show unconditional and loyal love one to the other. As their children's most effective teachers, the parents have the best chance to pass along to the next generation a biblical pattern for marriage and to give to their children the ultimate security. The most loving thing a mother and father can do for a child is to let him see that they love one another. Being a good husband or wife, just as being a good parent, takes time and effort. If you are too busy to invest energies and creativity in couple time as well as in family time, you are busier than God wants you to be.

Mothers are increasingly moving their primary energies out of the home and into the labor force, and America is facing a generation of children who have spent more time in institutional care than under parental supervision. Statisticians are reporting the marriage rate as being at an unprecedented low and the divorce rate at an all-time high. The absence of character in modern society is underscored by the prominence of scandals uncovered in the workplace. A poor work ethic is accompanied by low productivity. Today's children, as tomorrow's workers, should be the most important national product for any nation.

Although secular experts in psychology, sociology, and other disciplines, as well as religious leaders, continue to note that the family is the central and most important unit of society, they seem impotent when it comes to acknowledging the importance of maintaining order in the community and shaping the next generation. No other force is so effective in shaping the physical, emotional, mental, and moral aspects of behavior for a human being than the family that gives birth, nurtures, and molds the character of those within its circle and those under its influence.

Families then have a choice of either awakening the best and restraining the worst or unleashing the worst and sabotaging the best in those who are a part of the family. There is no better setting for building camaraderie, achieving cooperation, inspiring selflessness and sacrifice, and finding unity of purpose than within the family circle.

Fathers and mothers are challenged to work together to form the most effective teaching team for their children. They must prepare their children to take their own places in the world, forming their own families as the next generation. Whatever the family now is, the society evolving from its presence will become. Parents must faithfully *show* their children what they ought to do and how they ought to live rather than settling for merely *telling* them or *making* them do certain things.

Expressing love to your child is not unimportant. Nevertheless, for your child to see your consistent expression of love for your spouse is more important than to see expressions of your love for him. A child needs to see that his father and mother love one another. A wife whose husband has become busy with his professional pursuits becomes lonely, and she may be neglected. The message of indifference she receives is also transmitted to the child.

One of the most important lessons to be taught by parents is the responsibility and reward of an exclusive sexual relationship. Too often contemporary sexual views suggest that any sexual encounter is merely a personal decision and that monogamy is just a lifestyle choice in which consequences and risks are to be borne by the individual alone. The fallacy of that position is reflected in the rampant epidemic of AIDS and other sexually transmitted diseases with documented fallout that spills over to innocent victims, such as a baby in the womb. The risk to immediate and extended family and society at large is clear. The innocent often pay with their own lives for the choices of others, which is especially reprehensible when the *others* should be their life-givers and protectors.

Promiscuity has not only instigated moral anarchy, but it has so preoccupied today's society that America is coming dangerously close to depopulating its own citizenry. When sexuality is considered pleasure alone, children soon become an inconvenience or obstacle to pleasure. Not only does the birth rate drop, as it has in the past two decades, but also abortion and sterilization become by-products and tools to propagate a libertarian attitude. In addition to turning away from bearing and rearing children, couples experience a lessening of parental instinct. They are willing to settle for custodial care of their children while giving greater attention to pursuing personal careers and social pleasures.

Putting before your children a pattern for monogamy within marriage is important. The pattern for Christian marriage and the framework of a godly family life can provide a protective cocoon in which you can rear your children with some protection from unwholesome influences. Yet they should see how you respond and react to adversities, challenges, and difficulties as well as to successes.

PRINCIPLE 2: TEACH YOUR CHILDREN SPIRITUAL TRUTHS
Deut. 6:4–9; Ps. 78:1–8; 2 Tim. 1:4–5; Eph. 6:4

Parents have a multifaceted task. They are to shepherd their children to an understanding of themselves and how they fit into God's world, and they are to teach their children obedience to authorities in their lives. Children are not to be robots controlled in thought and action by someone else, nor are they to be automatons obsessed with their own autonomy. Parents must not mold their children to a personal agenda or allow them to take the slippery slope of convenience that leads to being squeezed into the mold of the world. Rather, they are to act as agents of the Lord in guiding their children along the pathway God has placed before them. Parents are to guide their children to understand themselves and the world in which they live.

Parents should never *assume* that their children will adopt only their commitments in standards of speech, dress, and lifestyle. They must be proactive in setting a standard and making an *apology* or defense for the standard. Just saying *no* is not enough. Children and teens need to be given well-reasoned explanations for what you expect of them in daily living. These standards must be taught as well as caught! When I was a teenager, I will never forget my father's lessons concerning total abstinence from the use of alcoholic beverages. Daddy had an ambulance service as well as a mortuary; so he worked in the midst of suffering and death, of crisis and sorrow. One evening he returned home particularly crestfallen. He told me about a tragic accident in which a drunken driver had hit a car carrying some of my high school friends who had been attending a youth event at a nearby church. They were all killed, but the intoxicated driver walked away. To this day, I have never been tempted to take even a sip of an alcoholic beverage.

The parent is his child's teacher in every sense of the word. Parents nurture the child's academic capabilities and facilitate his learning experience. Instead of encouraging meaningless activities with the child's peers, parents must be committed to providing their offspring with productive time together as a family. First and foremost must be the teaching of values, which ought to be determined by parents after a careful study of Scripture. Parents develop the character of their children by teaching them guidelines for living a godly life and boundaries for healthy relationships.

Teaching involves giving instruction and showing a child how to do a particular task. Children learn everything best through observing and imitating. A child will be shaped from his birth by the way his parents live before him. Sometimes the child's proficiency is imparted by teaching or drilling. Parents may certainly choose to involve others from the public or private sector in the educational process, but they may also elect to deliver the education themselves through the venue of homeschooling.

Parents cannot depend on the church, Christian school, or any parachurch organizations to provide spiritual nurture. They should enlist the help of all these entities, but only parents can take the responsibility to ensure that nothing is missing. God's Word should set the standards they adopt for their children.

A child's spiritual formation must begin with teaching him the Bible. Its stories, its truths, its applications—all must be incorporated into the learning experience. Parents are in the prime position to guide this teaching. As the revelation of an all-knowing God, the Bible provides absolute truth. Neither taking your child to church nor placing him in a Christian school for his general education is enough. The knowledge transmitted must permeate the child's entire life, and he must have the opportunity under the careful supervision of his parents to apply the facts he has learned in everyday life experiences. All you need to know about the parenting task and rearing and nurturing your children in the Lord—information about children, family life, values, training, discipline—is found in Scripture. Yet you must use every resource to learn the principles and understand their application to your own parenting task.

In preparing a new generation to enter the Promised Land, Moses emphasized the importance of the home in teaching truth and obedience. He assigned two primary responsibilities to God-fearing parents:

- Parents were instructed first to *hear* with a view to obeying and applying that Word to their own lives (Deut. 6:4–6). Without a personal relationship with God, a parent could not communicate effectively the truths of God's Word to his children. To pass on something effectively, you must first possess it yourself.

- Parents are to incorporate these spiritual truths within the family circle. If the truths are central in the hearts of the parents, they will mold the home as well. Moses offered two ways of communicating these truths to children: specific teaching and general talking. The most effective teaching requires some planned, formal instruction—an assigned time, an appointed place, and a developed curriculum. No one can teach without first being taught. Parents themselves must determine to study and learn God's Word.

Specific teaching within the home is usually done in family worship—set-apart times for the family to come together and hear God's Word read and explained. Since my husband is a born teacher, our times of family worship included instruction in one form or another. My husband would ask the children questions to be used as a springboard for teaching truth, but he did so in an entertaining way. Frequently, he would direct his light inquisition to a visiting student or friend, fully intending his instruction to be primarily for our children. The children, delighted to see some enterprising young theologue stumped by a question, would then receive the answer more eagerly. Also, they saw they were not the only ones to need their father's instruction.

Specific teaching (planned times for instruction) is not enough. Spontaneous instruction (unexpected moments for reinforcing virtues and values) also should occur as part of everyday living. Parents must maximize every means of communication, even common interchange and ordinary conversation. Many experiences in family life lend themselves to teaching spiritual truths. Some of the most valuable lessons come in the natural course of events and provide a way to flesh out biblical principles. Moses describes this lifestyle teaching clearly—as you walk, stand, sit, or lie down (Deut. 6:7). Through both specific and spontaneous teaching, parents make the Word of God so powerful that it influences a child's thoughts and actions throughout life, including private moments and public actions.

Deuteronomy also describes the way parents were to place God's Word in their homes. Phylacteries were to be worn on the hand and arm as a symbol of reaching to the heart, and frontlets were to be placed between the eyes as a symbol of controlling thought life. The *mezuzah*, the small piece hung on doorposts, reminded the family that God's Word should govern even the most intimate areas of family life. Both the phylacteries (small leather boxes) and mezuzah (small, decorative cylinders of metal, pottery, or porcelain) contained a portion of Scripture to remind everyone of the pervasive influence of God's Word. These same tools are effectively used in Jewish families even in this generation. In fact, I use the mezuzah on doorposts throughout my own home.

The "God-shaped vacuum" in every child is not filled by instinctive faith. Therefore, parents have a God-given responsibility to introduce their children to God in carefully planned ways. Your child should be sharp and wellfashioned because he is destined to be an arrow of the Lord on the spiritual battlefield, commissioned to pass on a godly heritage to the next generation just as you have entrusted it to him (Ps. 127:3–5). The apostle Paul commended the mother and grandmother of Timothy, his own protégé, because of the importance they assigned to Timothy's childhood education. Paul had made an investment in Timothy, but the young man's spiritual moorings were built on the foundation of the truths he learned in his childhood home (2 Tim. 1:5). Timothy's godly home prepared him to live in an ungodly world. Once a child learns the truths found in Scripture, he is ready to move toward commitment to those truths (2 Tim. 3:15). Parents must diligently and lovingly build boundaries of protection around their children—the most priceless treasure God gives.

One of the greatest barriers to family worship is overcommitment. It takes time to build relationships with one another, and it takes time for a family to build a relationship with God. If a time of family gathering is geared to the convenience of when it feels right and when it fits into everyone's schedule, the occasion will lose its value. The events of any given day, important at the time, may not even be remembered the next day, the following week, or in a year's time. Nevertheless, spiritual nurture will take root and become a part of the foundations of life.

PRINCIPLE 3: LEAD YOUR CHILDREN TO GO GOD'S WAY VIA PARENTAL DISCIPLINE

Prov. 13:24; 19:18; 20:30; 22:6, 15; Heb. 12:5–8, 11

Parents must assume the primary responsibility for the important task of disciplining the child. Too often discipline is seen as being confined to prescribed punishment. However, in truth, discipline is the training of a child, molding his character, and helping him learn to live in the world. *Training involves molding what is given, correcting what is wrong, strengthening what is right, and perfecting what is in process until the task is complete.* Parents must make disciples out of their children. Underlying such a program is the necessity of spending time with your child, earning the child's respect and trust, and then modeling in your own life what you want to teach the child.

This third biblical principle for rearing children—leading them to go God's way via consistent discipline—may be the most challenging of all. It requires unconditional love, unending patience, relentless determination, consistent follow-through, and individualized creativity. The goal for parents is to lead their children to go God's way by equipping them with character qualities and virtues coming from the teachings found in the Bible. They must use a combination of lifestyle training and discipline in order to help children, by whatever persuasive means are required, to be obedient.

The book of Proverbs expresses parental responsibility in this way: "Train up a child in the way he should go; even when he is old he will not depart from it" (Prov. 22:6). "Train" (Hb. *chanak*) suggests "putting something into the mouth." The word referred to the Hebrew practice of opening the throat of a newborn.

The midwife, after delivering a baby, would dip her fingers into crushed dates and then massage the baby's gums so that the sweet taste on her fingers would stimulate his sucking. This prelude prepared the way for the infant's taking nourishment at his mother's breast. The same word was used to describe breaking a wild horse by means of a rope in his mouth. This message admonishes parents to be committed to breaking the willfulness of their child in order to prepare that child to seek God's way instead of following his own path. To fail in breaking the child's willfulness is to lay a foundation for self-willed living from which the child will not depart.

A child's training must begin long before formal teaching. Many people are deceived into believing that the child must first be taught with facts and information, which later would become the foundation for trained behavior. Actually the opposite is true. Training begins at birth as a program of discipleship in which parents move a child through learning *parent-controlled* behavior to adopting *self-controlled* or independent behavior.

The goal is not to change the nature or personality of the child but rather to govern how he expresses his nature. In fact, for parents committed to the Judeo-Christian worldview, the final step is to move your child to a *God-controlled* lifestyle in which the child learns to make wise, God-honoring decisions. No longer is the child governed by his own willfulness and determined to go his own way. Rather he is committed to God's way (Heb. 12:10–11).

Some child-rearing experts suggest that a parent must break the child's *will*. To call for such action is to misunderstand the purpose of the will. No one accomplishes anything without a will to do so. The will is the seat of choice and motivation. You cannot decide between two courses of action without using the will. At the heart of fulfilling every duty is the will to move forward with a particular task. To crush the will is to make the child a useless and thoughtless entity with no purpose in life. On the other hand, a parent does have the responsibility to break a child's willful determination to go *his own way* and miss God's best in life.

Selfish willfulness is a tragic path for the child. The Bible repeatedly warns against allowing a child to go his own way or seek his own fancies (Prov. 1:28–31; 3:5–7). My own understanding of the Proverbs 22:6 admonition to parents is clear in my personal translation or paraphrase from the Hebrew text: "Train up a child to go his own way, and when he is old he will not depart or abandon going his own way." A child who grows accustomed to having his own way may well show promise in the ability to make good choices early on—so much so that his parents are lulled into letting him consistently do as he pleases. Though slow in coming, the tragedy will come as the child or youth begins to make wrong choices with ease and confidence because he is convinced that his way is best.

Solomon received the greatest gift of wisdom ever bestowed on a mortal man, but it was not enough. He completely messed up his life, and, as a result, he set in motion the end of the united kingdom of Israel, which he had inherited from his father, David. He received wisdom, but he was not faithful to use *discernment* in appropriating that wisdom.

The parent's task is never to be taken lightly as he must use every means at his disposal to set apart and direct the child's will toward holy and wholesome objectives. The parent cannot permit the child to do only what he wants to do. A battle naturally ensues between the will of the parent and the will of the child because genuine obedience demands the cooperation of the will. The child must learn to do what he ought to do when he is told to do it whatever his personal feelings may be. This life lesson has ramifications that follow the child throughout life.

Consequences for disobedience must be clear, but before reaching this ultimate contest, a parent must lovingly and patiently guide the child into the right way, helping him to obey. This action takes a tremendous investment of time and energy.

Children learn to obey the commands of their parents while they develop sensitivity to the guidelines presented to them by their parents. They are then under *parent control*. The next step is *self-control*, a phase of development during which children reach the plateau of no longer needing continual parental supervision because their spirits and wills have been molded into such self-control and discipline that they make appropriate choices and decisions on their own. However, the process should not end with self-control. Ultimately a child should be prepared to order his life according to God's way and to govern his actions according to biblical principles. The child has then reached the highest plateau, which is *God control*. Battles will most certainly come en route to this goal, for the world is obsessed with the importance of making a child feel good about himself. In fact, this ideology of elevating self-image or self-esteem above all else permeates everything a parent does. It elevates personal rights in the child and tears down personal discipline and self-control. The goal becomes achieving personal desires and goals in lieu of giving oneself in service to God and others.

One of the most challenging aspects of this lifestyle training is the control that must be present in the life of the one who is administering the training. A child will never respect what his parents have to say if they fail to emulate those teachings in their own lives. *To stand for what is right is one thing; to order your own life according to what is right is something else.* Any inconsistency in the life pattern of parents not only will be noted but also will usually be magnified in the lives of their children.

The Bible is full of examples in which a parent's sin shows up in the life of his child: David, whose son Absalom tried to become king by killing his own father; Solomon, whose polygamy and pagan marriages made it impossible to produce godly seed for the throne and inevitably ensured that the kingdom would be divided; Eli, whose personal commitment and position as a prophet and priest of Israel were not enough to prevent the deaths of his own sons in shame and ignomiy before the Lord because of their spiritual disobedience. Eli further dishonored the Lord when he allowed his sons to sin openly without any effective effort to correct them (1 Sam. 2:29).

- Discipline is not primarily an assessment of penalty for wrong; it is more an unveiling of God's care for his children.

- God chastises (understood in modern language as *spanks* or *corrects*) those whom he loves. God uses discipline to remind you that you are his child (Heb. 12:7–8). In contrast to correction alone, the word *discipline* provides the total picture—correction as well as gentle guidance. Parental discipline should be an inclusive program of discipleship that also prepares a child for obedience to God's authority (Heb. 12:9–10).

- Spiritual formation is the most important fruit to come from godly discipline.

The world's view of authority vacillates between anarchy and tyranny. God's pattern for authority is loving service and committed responsibility. A parent is wise to lead a child to submit to discipline that molds life and character even if a child may despise it, chafe under it, or faint because of it (Heb. 12:11–13). Scripture never wavers on the sanctity of life and value of the child, yet its message concerning appropriate discipline is also clear.

Parents should not pretend they have never made mistakes. If they make mistakes, they need to be accountable and seek forgiveness even from a child. A parent cannot fool his child. Whether or not you as a parent have a genuine commitment to the Lord, whether spiritual things are important to you, whatever really takes first place in your life—these choices will be evident to your children (Prov. 23:26). The problem in achieving discipline that moves the child toward God control begins with the kind of training administered. *An inadequate kind of training, ineffective ways of doing the training, an insincere administrator of the training, and ineffectual examples for the trainees all contribute to inferior and incomplete training.*

Behavior that produces desirable results tends to recur, while behavior that brings undesirable consequences for the child is not as likely to happen again. Behavior that is not rewarded is far less likely to become ingrained and often completely disappears.

Unfortunately, many parents who show concern for the physical and social development of their children ignore their spiritual needs. They assume that regular attendance in church, participation in youth activities, enrollment in a Christian school, prayer at mealtimes, and sometimes even a form of family devotions will give their child the spiritual foundation necessary to have a productive life.

Parents must learn to hold their children close with supervision and interaction in all of life, but a day comes when they must let them go. If the foundation has been laid correctly, careful training in the early years will give children the confidence they need to move out of that supervision to their own reconnaissance and will give parents the peace to allow them to do that.

Dealing with strong-willed children requires godly wisdom and wise strategy. A strong-willed child is often willing to die for the right to do things his way. Much of your discipleship of such a child comes as you inspire him to do the right thing, but inevitably corrective measures are also necessary.

In order to counteract the weaknesses found in a strong-willed child, consider these strategies:

- Make the child feel unique and special.
- Use *let's* or add *okay?* instead of simply issuing direct orders.
- Choose your battles since you cannot die on every hill.
- Never give up helping the child learn to obey, but lighten up heavy-handed communication.
- Reaffirm to the child that he is loved unconditionally.

Parents must pull and push using every ounce of creativity and energy to get their children to go God's way. Parents move children into their own decision-making process by holding them in a pattern of obedience. Children must never lose sight of the ultimate authority in their lives. They must move from *parent-controlled* to *self-controlled* to *God-controlled* behavior, and parents are responsible for not letting them loiter along the way. Parents are warned not to direct their children toward the wrath of God but instead to guide them through nurturing and admonishing them in the Lord (Eph. 6:4).

ENRICH THE FAMILY CIRCLE

Take Advantage of Regular Routines

Building up the family should center in the warp and woof of life so that special threads are woven together effectively and beautifully to produce a tapestry that reflects the unique family circle. There are some natural ways to approach this task:

- *Family mealtime* can be a joyous occasion and not merely a dull necessity. Plan a relaxed and cheerful atmosphere rather than bringing tension, preoccupation, weariness, or grouchiness to the family mealtime. Conversation around the table—sharing interesting things that happened during the day, introducing important current events, giving updates on extended family and friends—is stimulating. Mealtime is not the time or place for reprimands and scolding. In fact, perhaps the unwritten rule should be that table talk will be happy or at least an opportunity to place any sorrowful events that are introduced within the assuring promise of God's providential care.

- *Bedtime* is especially important for young children. Even if the child is cross and tired, parents must overcome their own fatigue and anxieties to provide comfort and stability for the child. The process of going to bed should start early enough to allow for laughter and even a bit of foolishness. It should have a definite pattern and should be the highlight of the day.

- *Work at home*—the chores necessary to keep the family household functioning—can be fun if approached in the right spirit. From earliest years, your child should be taught the joy of being a helper. He should see tasks at home as important and fun, and he should see these tasks as uniting the family in joint goals for the good of the whole.

- *Free time* is not all delegated to individual pursuits. The family should anticipate having unexpected time together as a bonus for enjoying one another's company. Special outings should be planned for whatever time is available. Hobbies and crafts should be developed for the family's interaction. This time should not always be designated as spectator time—whether television or sports!

Maximize Times of Worship

The Lord's Day should be the high point of every week. Christians have devoted Sunday to God for worship, which should include rest or re-creating in the highest sense. Other activities should not be allowed to distract the family from full participation in corporate worship. The Lord's Day is not merely a day of rest from work or a day for pursuing one's favorite entertainment. The family should seek privacy, tranquility, and even seclusion from the rest of the world to worship, relax, and enjoy fellowship with one another. The Jews love and cherish the weekly Sabbath. They anticipate its coming and then look back upon its memories. The day begins at sundown and is formally welcomed by the family in their best clothing, the mother's lighting of the candles, the recitation of prayers, the reciting of Proverbs 31:10–31 by the father or a child in honor of the mother, and then a festive family meal. Sunday should be the best day of the Christian family's week. Wearing special clothing, eating favorite foods, enjoying unique family rituals, indulging in extra relaxation and rest, and perhaps playing with special toys should be tempered with a slower pace.

Daily worship within the family is important and is a means of glorifying God and extending the virtues of his kingdom first to your children and even beyond your family circle (see chapter 19). Select and protect time so that nothing interferes with its practice. Pray and set aside time to wait for a word from the Lord in quietness and openness. Praise and thank the Lord; read and discuss his Word.

Capitalize on Special Occasions

- *Birthday celebrations* do not have to be elaborate to be memorable, but nothing should keep the family from commemorating birthdays for each family member—and with a bit of fanfare just to make each family member feel special at least one day a year.

- *Seasons* bring other options for celebration (entering the New Year, Valentine's Day, Easter, Mother's Day, Father's Day, patriotic emphasis on July 4, Harvest Festival, Thanksgiving, Christmas).

- *Hosting special guests*—my husband and I also use our home as a gathering place for friends from around the world so that our children, and now our grandchildren, can experience fellowship and friendship with people from a variety of ethnic backgrounds and cultures. We like to serve ethnic foods and talk about the different cultures and customs. This international hospitality is coupled with a determination for our children to visit other countries through their senses and immerse themselves in cultures unlike their own.

Capture Some Time in the Summer for More Extended and Carefree Family Fun

- Special trips or local outings, visits to relatives or seeing new places—each outing has its own potential for family fun and enrichment.

- The kind of family fun, which is characterized by a lack of structure, is dictated by the season and offers a quantity of time spent with parents. Not only can a child enjoy more undivided attention, but there is also the possibility of serving others in unique ways.

Watch for Ways to Honor Those within Your Family Circle for Special Achievements

- Graduations and recitals are inevitable in the course of life's journey.

- Unexpected challenges such as an illness or extended time away from the family offer opportunities for a special homecoming.

- Honors and recognitions for achievement in academics, sports, and the arts are deserving of special notice by the family.

Every Family Should Be Diligent to Develop Traditions

A customary or special way in which a family performs a routine and a family's unique way of celebrating special occasions—the best and longest lasting rituals and traditions—are attached to the everyday routines of family life. They do not demand extravagance or even elaborate details. Rather these family distinctives take an event out of the mediocrity of routine and make it a special occasion—even if it happens regularly. They create memories that help to build a pride in ancestry and gratitude for heritage (Isa. 51:1). Such traditions give a child a sense of security that always accompanies the familiar. They also give a child a strong sense of identity with his family and even help him to affirm his own self-identity. For that reason these traditions should be thoroughly integrated with faith.

PUTTING THE PRINCIPLES INTO PRACTICE

1. What is the ultimate goal for a parent in rearing a child?
2. How do you blend home and church and even school and community in preparing a child for life?
3. How can family spiritual formation be creatively and firmly included in the life of a family?

ADDITIONAL RESOURCES BY DOROTHY KELLEY PATTERSON

Patterson, Dorothy Kelley. *A Handbook for Ministers' Wives: Sharing the Blessing of Your Marriage, Family, and Home.* Nashville: Broadman, 2002.

———. *The Family: Unchanging Principles for Changing Times.* Nashville: Broadman, 2002.

———. "Nurturing Mothers." In *Biblical Womanhood in the Home*, edited by Nancy Leigh DeMoss, 161–70. Wheaton, IL: Crossway, 2002.

———. *Where's Mom? The High Calling of Wives and Mothers.* Wheaton, IL: Crossway, 2003.

Patterson, Dorothy Kelley, and Armour Patterson. *A Handbook for Parents in Ministry: Training Up a Child While Answering the Call.* Nashville: Broadman, 2004.

Chapter Fourteen

God's Design for Nurturing Motherhood

Glenda A. Eitel

Mary and Joe were urban professionals in their mid-thirties, expecting their first baby. They asked many questions in childbirth class. Mary delivered a healthy baby boy. The nurse assisting Mary with breastfeeding reminded her to burp the baby and move him to the other breast, as she had been shown in class. Mary proceeded to put her hands on each side of the baby's face and lift the baby. Visualize a newborn baby dangling loosely while being held by his head with no support to the back, neck, or body. Hands were quickly placed under the baby's arms and body, and he was eased to safety.

What the birthing class instructor sensed was coming true. This couple had no clue about parenting. It was alarming to think that in less than twenty-four hours Joe and Mary would be on their way home with a new baby, without the basic skills needed to parent. They did not know how to change a diaper, swaddle, burp, bathe, calm, or quiet their little one. The nurses spent extra time with them, but Mary was still very insecure. The morning of discharge, Mary cried, saying, "I am so afraid to go home where I have no one to help me, I do not know if I can do it." This mother had head knowledge without any real understanding of the practical side of parenting a newborn.

This true story illustrates why mentoring and education are important. How can a mother prepare for the birthing experience and avoid the frustrations that Mary felt? What does Scripture have to say about mothering? What is the significance of bonding and nurturing? Is breastfeeding really the best way to feed my newborn? Does culture influence parenting? This chapter will answer these important questions.

PREPARING FOR PARENTHOOD

Every new mother will have some feelings of inadequacy before giving birth. I remember when a friend of mine came home in tears, distraught after a visit with her obstetrician. Fearing she had received bad news, I asked her what was wrong. She replied, "I am going to have to have this baby." The reality of the labor and delivery process became real to her for the first time. My friend had to discover that the birthing process is normal, natural, and God given. One should not approach it with fear but with excitement. The first step to a gratifying birthing experience is making sure you are prepared. Utilizing local resources, including friends, family, birthing classes, and a breastfeeding support group, will enhance your learning process. Friends and family members with young children should provide good answers to your questions. Since spouses seldom have prolonged time off work, the new mommy and baby are often left alone at home. Plan ahead and line up some relatives or friends to help out for the first few days.

Although planning ahead for the logistics of the birth is recognized as important, parents-to-be often wonder if childbirth classes are really necessary. Many say, "I am going to have an epidural with the first pain, so why go to a class?" However, childbirth classes prepare you for much more than pain relief. Fear is a powerful force that can escalate the perception of pain. It can quickly overwhelm anyone. Couples who have attended classes and practiced the techniques they learned have better coping skills during the labor process. If complications arise, they have some idea of what to expect, and this preparation lessens their anxiety.

Ask for recommendations for good childbirth educators. Make sure the childbirth instructor is up to date on the standards of practice in the local area, so you can understand what options are available to you. A good instructor should address the following issues in a childbirth class:

- the final stages of pregnancy
- the potential complications of labor
- the signs of beginning labor and when to call the doctor
- breathing and relaxation techniques, including practice
- the induction of labor, C-sections, episiotomy
- pain control methods, IV pain medication, epidural
- the stages of labor, pushing, and actual delivery
- APGAR score (a test—based on **A**ppearance, **P**ulse, **G**rimace, **A**ctivity, and **R**espiration—given newborns one minute and five minutes after birth to evaluate the baby's physical condition and determine any immediate medical needs)
- basic newborn care
- breastfeeding techniques (a separate class for breastfeeding would be better)

Choosing the right doctor is important. Interview doctors and find a facility that will support your desired birthing needs. There are many birthing options for you: hospital births, freestanding birth centers with midwives, and home births with a midwife. If you choose to use a midwife, make sure she is certified and has been recommended by someone you trust. A midwife must have a doctor and hospital that cover patients in case of an emergency. While medical providers have your best interest in mind, remember that you always have the final say in your care. You have the right to ask questions and get answers. Your spouse needs to be your advocate, prepared to run interference with medical staff and even family if necessary.

Finding a facility that allows rooming-in is preferred. Rooming-in allows the newborn to remain at the bedside with the parents rather than being in the nursery with strangers. Couples that room with their babies are much more comfortable rendering care when they go home. A new mother is tired whether she rooms-in or not. A mother should try to sleep when the baby sleeps; short naps will get you through. Having your newborn with you results in the baby's bonding with parents rather than with the hospital staff. Take advantage of the time when facility staff is available to answer questions. Becoming familiar with basic skills such as nursing, diapering, swaddling, changing clothes, calming, and quieting makes the first few days at home enjoyable. Head knowledge alone will not adequately prepare parents for childbirth. Looking at God's design and how it applies to your life will enhance this journey to godly parenting.

GOD'S PLAN FOR PARENTING

The way one *chooses* to pursue mothering greatly influences the emotional, physical, and spiritual development of children. Parenting choices you make today will affect you for life. What a huge responsibility the Creator has given women. God chose the mother—a woman—to conceive, give birth, nurse, and protect her gift of new life by giving her baby the best possible beginning to life. The loving heavenly Father created women with the innate ability to love, bond, and nurture their offspring. The godly woman must understand how best to utilize this special, God-given gift.

Having children is part of your loving Father's original design as seen in Genesis 1:28: "And God blessed them. And God said to them, 'Be fruitful and multiply and fill the earth.'" The heavenly Father loves children and refers to a man who has children as "blessed," describing the children as a heritage from the Lord (Ps. 127:3–5). What a privilege to know that the Lord can use your womb to bless your husband. One would conclude that parenting is truly one of the Lord's greatest gifts.

The role of mothering fulfills God's plan for the family and must be taken seriously. It should be a priority. Investing in the lives of your children and grandchildren is never a waste of time or energy. One cannot change how she was mothered, but one *can* choose to parent from a godly perspective. No one can be 100 percent prepared for all aspects of mothering. However, starting from the birth of your child, the Lord gives you an intense connection to your baby, which will bind your family together.

BONDING WITH YOUR NEWBORN

The baby, although tiny and helpless, is intricately created to survive. The first hour after birth is very important for the bonding process. Most babies are in a quiet alert state for about forty-five minutes to an hour after delivery, so take advantage of this special time together. A newborn already knows his mother's voice and sees her face clearly when held close to her face. Interestingly the newborn's visual range happens to be the very distance from the mother's breast to her face, clear evidence of God's design. As both parents explore every inch of the newborn's tiny body, they are moved to love in a way never imagined possible. A wonderful relationship begins between parents and baby.

The baby has arrived and is placed onto your tummy, and it is time to cut the umbilical cord. If feasible, encourage your husband to cut the umbilical cord. It is a simple procedure, and the doctor will tell him what to do. It is a dramatic moment—severing what has been the lifeline from the mother to the baby in the womb and allowing the baby to begin life outside the womb. Playing this role helps the husband become directly engaged in the birthing process and enhances his own bonding process. Make sure the camera is ready for a picture.

Developing trust between mother and baby is important for the baby's overall emotional health. As a mother nurtures and responds quickly to the cries of her baby, trust develops. Leaving a new baby to "cry it out" can cause stress, leading to lack of trust. Prolonged crying results in elevated blood pressure and rapid heart rate, leading to increased pressure in the brain. Crying is your baby's way to communicate. An infant has no understanding of the world outside the womb—the other responsibilities you have or why Mommy would be busy with anything other than his needs. Responding quickly to an infant's cries will offer comfort and cause trust to develop. Eventually the baby will be able to wait longer for his needs to be met because he is confident that help will come. This lesson will help the infant as he matures to be patient with others. The baby's emotional needs are real and should be met. A strong bond and attachment to his mother results in a well-adjusted child down the road.

While responding appropriately to the baby's emotional needs is essential, you can lay your newborn down. Do not think you are a bad parent if you cannot hold your baby all the time. From the beginning, once the baby has been changed, fed, swaddled, and calmed, lay him down in the bassinet. Place a reassuring hand on him and speak calmly or sing to him. Most of the time, these comforting techniques will be all that is needed. Babies will learn habits quickly. If you hold him all the time, he will come to expect constant attention. The priority is to build trust and a sense of safety for the infant.

The Lord knows that mothers need an internal push to connect and bond. He gave new mothers the hormones that go to work at just the appropriate time to enhance bonding. The hormone oxytocin is released with breastfeeding. This creates a sense of calmness, relaxation, and sleepiness, often described as a warm "fuzzy" feeling. This is a perk experienced only by nursing mothers. Bonding will occur with mothers who cannot or choose not to breastfeed, but it takes more effort. Oxytocin has more than a calming effect and will be discussed further with breastfeeding.

IS BREASTFEEDING REALLY THE BEST WAY TO FEED MY BABY?

God made nursing a uniquely cherished experience. God shows the bond between a mother and child to be so strong that he repeatedly used the example of a nursing mother and her baby to demonstrate his tender compassionate love for us. What a beautiful analogy the Lord gives in his Word (see Isa. 66:11–13). Psalm 22:9 says, "Yet you are he who took me from the womb; you made me trust you at my mother's breasts." The heavenly Father gave a mother the perfect milk for her baby, and unless there is a medical contraindication, she should give the benefits of breastfeeding to her baby. There are many benefits of breastfeeding for mother and baby.

⮞ BREASTFEEDING ⮜ BENEFITS FOR BABY

- Bonding and closeness
- Immunities: antibacterial and antiviral
- Higher IQ (9 points on average)
- Fewer cases of leukemia, diarrhea, and SIDS
- Fewer ear infections and sick visits to doctor
- Colostrum (laxative effect that decreases jaundice)
- Stronger teeth (fewer cavities)
- Less need for orthodontic procedures later in life

◌⟩ BREASTFEEDING ⟨◌
BENEFITS FOR MOTHER

- Bonding and closeness (leading to better mothering)
- Convenience
- Aid in maternal pregnancy weight loss
- Monetary savings (average cost of formula is $1,000 to $1,500 a year)
- Decreases in mother's risk of breast cancer (if you nurse for at least six months)
- Decrease in postpartum bleeding (by the release of oxytocin)
- Return of uterus to normal size more quickly
- Decrease in ovarian cancer (prior to menopause)
- Natural child spacing due to delayed ovulation if nursing regularly

When is the best time to initiate breastfeeding? A newborn will usually be quiet and alert about an hour immediately after delivery. Keep the room calm and quiet without bright lights. God designed mothers with an automatic thermostat that warms the newborn naturally and efficiently when the baby is placed skin to skin on the mother's chest. Now that the baby is warm and cozy, breastfeeding can begin. When a newborn is breastfed within the first hour after birth, he generally responds more efficiently to subsequent feedings.

The area around the nipples has Montgomery glands that secrete a substance that lubricates, decreases bacteria growth, and attracts baby to the breast. Because of this, a mother should not wash her breast just prior to a feeding. Allow the nurse to assist with the attachment process. Proper positioning is important for a successful connection. Once the baby is sucking well, and without pain, mother and baby should be relaxed. Every time the baby nurses the hormone oxytocin is released. But immediately after birth, the hormone has a special function. Oxytocin triggers a milk ejection reflex (letdown), which moves the colostrum (first milk) from the breast to the baby. This hormone also provides the mother a sense of calmness, relaxation, and sleepiness while nursing:

> The first milk from your breast, which is called colostrum, is low in fat and carbohydrates, and high in protein. It is exceptionally easy to digest, and it contains many living cells that defend the newborn against a number of potentially harmful agents. The immunoglobulins and other substances in colostrum take over from the placenta and continue the job of protecting the baby.[1]

---

[1] La Leche League International, *The Womanly Art of Breastfeeding*, 6th rev. ed. (New York: Plume, 1997), 348.

There is *no* artificial formula that has the special qualities found in colostrum, which is all your baby needs until the mature milk comes immediately after birth. Your baby at birth is overhydrated and does not need water or formula. You doctor will tell you if or when to give supplements. Colostrum is very thick and concentrated, and a little goes a long way. Keep in mind your baby's stomach is the size of a small walnut at birth and only holds about one to two teaspoons, just the amount of colostrum awaiting the baby at delivery. The way God intricately designed your body is amazing.

In three to five days mature milk will come in. Getting your baby to the breast early and often will establish your milk supply as quickly as possible. Prolactin, the milk-producing hormone, is excreted once the placenta separates, sending a message for your body to make milk. Prolactin is present for about two weeks and is essential for initiating and increasing milk supply. It works by supply and demand. As the breast is emptied, more milk is produced. Emptying the breast often and well is critical in order to obtain optimum milk supply. Avoid a pacifier until the baby has mastered breastfeeding. Placing a clean finger in the baby's mouth often will quiet him until you can nurse him.

When your milk comes in, your breasts become fuller and heavier. Your baby will swallow more frequently while nursing. He may be overwhelmed and gulp and may even choke as he adjusts to the increased milk flow. Since you may experience some milk leaking from your breasts, have breast pads available in your supplies gathered prior to delivery. If using cloth pads, you should change and wash the pads often. Feeding the baby frequently during this time will decrease the possibility of breast engorgement. Cold compresses may be used to decrease any inflammation or swelling of the breast. This possible side effect usually lasts no more than a couple of days.

Remember that poor positioning and/or attachment are the most frequent causes of breast soreness. Express a little colostrum and rub onto the nipple area to promote healing and prevent infection. A thin layer of pure lanolin ointment also helps. If breasts or nipples become painful while at the hospital, tell your nurse, who will assess and help correct the situation as soon as possible to prevent further discomfort. If the baby latches incorrectly, the milk will not transfer from the breast to the baby. For the baby, it is like chewing on the end of a straw; if nothing comes out there is resultant damage to the tip of the straw (or, in this case, the mother's nipple).

When considering how often to nurse your baby, keep in mind that the more you put the baby to the breast in the first few days, the less weight the baby will lose and the faster your mature milk supply will come in.

Flexibility is the key to survival. Nurse your baby at least eight to twelve times per twenty-four hours, until the baby is back to birth weight and gaining weight well. Do not let your baby go longer than three hours without a feeding during the daytime, though you may allow for one four-hour stretch at night. Some babies will cluster feed, nursing every one to two hours for several hours, and then sleep for a longer stretch (but still needing eight to twelve feedings per day).

The normal length of the feedings will vary. Attempt to keep the baby at the breast for at least fifteen to twenty minutes per feeding; then burp him and offer the other breast. Not all babies will nurse on both sides with each feeding, which is acceptable once a mother's milk is fully in and as long as the baby has nursed actively enough to soften fully at least one breast. As your baby nurses, milk is removed in phases. The largest volume of milk is removed in the first seven to ten minutes, but it is skim milk. Then it transitions to whole milk and finally to cream. The baby will be satisfied longer between feedings and will gain weight faster if he gets to the final stage of rich fatty cream.

Observe your baby to determine if he is getting enough to eat. A satisfied baby will be calm and relaxed after the feeding. Look for a softened breast at the end of the feeding. The baby will have at least *six to eight soaked and three to four dirty diapers per twenty-four hours by day five.* Stools should be yellow/green in color and seedy (like fine cottage cheese curds). Record all feedings and diaper changes until the baby is again at birth weight.

If your baby seems hungry all the time, it could be a growth spurt. These usually occur around one to two weeks and between the third and sixth months. Nature's way is to increase milk supply as your baby grows. Feed as often as needed to satisfy your baby; it may be every one to two hours for a couple of days until the supply increases. Remember, your supply will meet your baby's demand. The American Pediatric Association recommends breastfeeding for the first year. Your doctor will tell you when to begin solids. Breastmilk is all your baby needs for the first five to six months of life.

DOES CULTURE PLAY A ROLE IN HOW WE PARENT?

A materialistic world has instilled the expectation of instant gratification. But what does that have to do with baby care? Obviously, much of this influence appears before the baby is born. How many baby products were purchased or given to you to make your life easier? "Mother substitutes" abound in the modern culture. Acquiring all these extras is the norm and expensive. Examples of mother substitutes include:

- pacifiers, instead of breastfeeding or cuddling;
- expensive toys and gadgets to entertain the baby;
- stuffed animals with "heartbeats" to replicate human contact for the baby's crib;
- bottles to be placed into the baby's mouth (long before baby is able to hold a bottle) while in car seat, crib, or grocery cart to replace parental cuddling and nurturing.

All of these *things* pacify and entertain the baby so Mom can do other things. These things are not wrong in moderation, but consider the lessons you are teaching your children. As they continue to grow, they will likely be playing video games for hours on end, blocking out communication with family and friends, and promoting an unhealthy isolationism.

Much can be learned from other cultures. My children, Angela and Paul, were born while we were living in West Africa. The Africans taught us how to be content with less. I learned that the saying "less is more" holds true. I saw that the local women and their babies were content and happy. Mothers kept their babies close to them all the time. They would nurse them wherever they were. The mothers taught me how to carry my child on my back with a cotton cloth about the size of a beach towel, allowing me to do normal chores hands free. I used this simple carrier all the time.

While cooking dinner one evening, for a split second a panic came over me as I wondered where Angela was. About ten months old and becoming more active, she was on my back, safe, secure, and sound asleep. I had become so comfortable with carrying her on my back that I forgot she was there. She loved being on my back, where she could snuggle and hear my voice and heartbeat. She would play for a while and then fall asleep. Life was simple and family was everything. Carrying your baby in a sling or Snugli will be similar, but this practice must be started early so the baby acclimates to it.

One afternoon, as I was sitting with a group of African women, a toddler came running up to her mother crying because she had bumped her head. The mother pulled her breast out and tapped her nipple onto the bump. I asked, "What are you doing?" She replied, "This will make it better." They really believe the breast has healing power, and maybe they are right.

Your children yearn for your attention and touch, not expensive toys or gadgets. When you supply them with an abundance of expensive things as infants, they become bored easily, resulting in spending more money on bigger and better toys and offering less personal time for building character and relationships.

PREPARING FOR HOME

Take advantage of every opportunity to practice newborn care prior to going home. Give your baby a sponge bath the day of discharge with your nurse observing to offer you pointers. Make sure you change as many diapers as possible prior to discharge. Practice swaddling or wrapping your baby. Planning ahead will ease tensions on the day of discharge. Make sure your home is ready for your return. Have all the supplies needed for basic care—diapers, wipes, receiving blankets, and clothing. Have extra baby clothes with you. Make sure Dad is familiar with how to operate the car seat, which you must bring to the hospital for use en route home. Do not leave the hospital with a hungry baby.

Once home, make sure you change diapers frequently. This helps your baby to avoid diaper rash. Due to sensitive skin, newborns should be bathed every other day. Take extra care to wash the hair thoroughly to prevent cradle cap. Lotions are not recommended for newborns. The oils can block pores, leading to skin irritation. Save lotions until the baby is older.

Emotions are fragile during the early postpartum period. There are many hormone changes occurring. Getting adequate sleep by sleeping when your baby sleeps will allow you to cope better. Soon you will be adjusted to parenthood, and you will become a good mentor for others.

PUTTING THE PRINCIPLES INTO PRACTICE

1. Review the Scriptures cited in this chapter (Gen. 1:28; Ps. 22:9; 127:3–5; Isa. 66:11–13). What does the Bible say about mothering?
2. Make a list of priorities for choosing a childbirth class and a birthing facility.
3. In what ways can a new mother promote maternal-infant bonding?
4. Review breastfeeding and list several positive reasons that encourage young mothers to breastfeed their infants.
5. What role does culture play in the development of the family?

ABOUT THE AUTHOR

Glenda Eitel has been a nurse since 1974. Beginning as a LVN, she graduated with the RN degree in 1987. She has a Registered Nurse Certified (RNC) status, issued by the National Certification Corporation, with a specialty in inpatient obstetrics since 1996. Additionally, she earned a Certified Lactation Consultant status. She worked with mothers and babies for six years as a missionary nurse in Cameroon, West Africa. She spent most of her career as a hospital labor and delivery nurse. She established the lactation program at Duke Raleigh Childbirth Center in North Carolina, including responsibility for the birthing center's staff lactation education. She continues to teach childbirth and breast-feeding classes under the auspices of the campus clinic at Southwestern Baptist Theological Seminary in Fort Worth, Texas. For the last ten years she has provided lactation consultations and education to mothers. Glenda has a passion to see young mothers have positive birthing and breastfeeding experiences that will lead to godly parenting. Her husband Keith serves at Southwestern as professor of missions, director of the World Missions Center, and dean of the Roy Fish School of Evangelism and Missions.

ADDITIONAL RESOURCES

Sears, Martha, and William Sears. *The Breastfeeding Book: Everything You Need to Know about Nursing Your Child from Birth through Weaning*. Boston: Little, Brown and Company, 2000.

————. *The Complete Book of Christian Parenting and Child Care: A Medical and Moral Guide to Raising Happy, Healthy Children*. Nashville: Broadman, 1997.

Spangler, Amy. *Amy Spangler's Breastfeeding: A Parent's Guide*. 7th rev. ed. Atlanta: Amy Spangler, 2000.

Wiessinger, Diane, Diana West, and Teresa Pitman. *The Womanly Art of Breastfeeding*. 8th ed. New York: Ballantine, 2010. (This is the most recent edition of this source, which is distinct from the one indicated in the footnote.)

Chapter Fifteen

Effective Preschool Education: Early Learning

Ann Iorg

Imagine you were suddenly transported to another land. When you arrived, everyone was more than ten times your weight, nothing looked familiar, you could not speak the language, and you had limited control of your body. Welcome to the life of a newborn in our world! How helpless and insecure these tiny ones must feel. God has given you and me the incredible opportunity to nurture, teach, and encourage young children—particularly during the crucial years from birth through age five. Consider some core questions and foundational answers to vital issues related to educating preschoolers.

WHAT DO PRESCHOOLERS NEED BEFORE THEY CAN BE SUCCESSFULLY EDUCATED?

The first and most basic need for preschoolers is security. Newborns are helpless and need to know someone cares for them and will provide for their needs. They need to feel secure before they can think about learning. As they get older, they need a tour guide, someone who can identify things for them and show them how things work in their world.

Besides security, small children have other basic needs foundational to their education. Eventually, as they begin to move and explore on their own, they need help in learning appropriate behavior. Children are not born with self-control. They lack the inner strength to make themselves do what is best. They are driven by their impulses. Only when they experience the consequences from living outside safe boundaries do they learn to control themselves. These consequences can come from a painful experience, like touching a hot stove, or they can be learned from loving adults who impose boundaries and consequences so a child does not have to learn everything the hard way. Preschoolers also need help learning how to care for themselves. Finally, they must learn how to get along with other people.

All these needs are evident and should be met in the first five years of life because lifelong habits are formed during those years. A newborn infant has few habits, but in a few years he repeatedly performs certain tasks and behaviors. A child begins to act in consistent ways without even thinking about what he is doing. He just does what he is accustomed to doing. Think how you, as a preschooler, began doing many things that you do today—simple routines like brushing your teeth and more significant skills like handling your anger and disappointments. Obviously, these habits can be changed, but adjustments become much harder when the actions have been ingrained for a lengthy period.

Whatever the life situation, the foundational needs of preschoolers are so crucial that parents must make sure that their child's initial needs are met. The importance of this time in life cannot be overemphasized. Parenting a young child is labor intensive. Sacrificing other activities must be done in order to devote quality and quantity time to parenting, especially during the first years of a child's life. Parents do not have to tackle these challenges alone. Many others, such as church preschool teachers, caregivers, grandparents, and friends can be great sources of support and help. However, parents must work hard to ensure that their child's developmental needs are met and that everyone is working together toward the same end. Security, discovery of surroundings, self-control, and appropriate social interaction are four big needs that must be met before a preschooler can effectively learn in more formal educational settings.

WHAT IS THE GOAL OF PRESCHOOL EDUCATION?

Once foundational needs are met during the early years of life, a second question must be considered: What is the goal of preschool education? A simplified definition of education is *acquiring the knowledge and skills necessary to do what you need to do in life.* Some think preschoolers cannot be educated. They define education as reading, writing, and arithmetic, which most preschoolers are not developmentally ready to learn. However, preschoolers are learning many things to prepare them for elementary school learning. Learning during the preschool years lays the foundation for all other learning later in life, so the primary goal for educating preschoolers is *helping them gain the knowledge and skills necessary for basic living and learning.*

This definition sounds simple but can be easily misconstrued. There are many ideas floating around about how to educate preschoolers. The problem is that these ideas keep changing, and many are contradictory. Some advocate letting children discover life on their own with very little guidance. Others claim a child's environment should be tightly controlled so he is only allowed to experience what is best. As Christians, you and I do not have to be tossed about with every wind of changing methodology. We have the Bible to guide us in every area of life—including educating young children. While not specifically outlining every detail, the overriding principles in Scripture are clear and consistent, providing direction as well as the freedom to make applications appropriate to your cultural setting, family background, and the specific needs of your children. While variety in methods and approaches is inevitable, by working toward the same goals based on a solid biblical foundation, parents can produce the desired outcomes.

WHAT KEY BIBLICAL PRINCIPLES APPLY TO PRESCHOOL EDUCATION?

The Bible makes a direct statement about educating young children: "Train up a child in the way he should go; even when he is old he will not depart from it" (Prov. 22:6). This verse is often misunderstood. Proverbs does not guarantee children will never sin or rebel. In fact, the Bible affirms that "all have sinned and fall short of the glory of God" (Rom. 3:23). Parents are assured, however, that teaching their children biblical principles is a safeguard that will follow their offspring throughout life.

Love God, Love Others

Much of what the Bible says about educating children is implied in broad principles that can be applied in many settings. Jesus taught one such principle when he was asked about the greatest commandment:

> And he said to him, "You shall love the Lord your God with all your heart and with all your soul and with all your mind. This is the great and first commandment. And a second is like it: You shall love your neighbor as yourself. On these two commandments depend all the Law and the Prophets." (Matt. 22:37–40)

Your purpose in life is to love God and love people. So, the parents' main goal is teaching their children to love God and others. All of the Ten Commandments relate to these two principles. The phrase *as yourself* is equally important for children to learn. You should treat everyone, including yourself, with equal value. You need to teach children to love God and to care for others as they care for themselves. Children must learn these principles: God cares for them; they can care for themselves; and they can learn to care for others.

Grow as Jesus Grew

A second principle for educating preschoolers comes from considering Jesus's childhood. The Bible says very little about Jesus as a child, but what is said is helpful for understanding childhood development. The Bible summarizes stories about Jesus's dedication in the temple, his flight to Egypt, and his return to Nazareth, as well as his extended stay in Jerusalem when he was twelve. Parents learn that family and church (the community of believers) are important to a child from infancy. God gives parents the primary responsibility for the safety and education of their children. God does not expect them to accomplish this task alone. Along life's journey, he intervenes directly (as in the sending of Jesus's family to Egypt), and he brings others to help along the way (as the temple teachers in the life of Jesus).

The Bible summarizes Jesus's childhood in one short, powerful verse: "And Jesus increased in wisdom and in stature and in favor with God and man" (Luke 2:52). Translations vary, but the point is clear. The essence of Jesus's childhood was growth in four areas: intellectual (wisdom), physical (stature), spiritual (favor with God), and social (favor with man). All children, no matter how challenged or gifted, can grow in those four areas. Their growth may not be incrementally equal to that of others, especially if a child has many challenges, but each child can grow. Even secular textbooks agree that a healthy child must be healthy mentally, physically, and socially.[1] Some secular textbooks even add a moral dimension.[2] Effective preschool education must include those four components. In order to live effectively, a child must gain knowledge and skills that will enable him to function mentally, physically, spiritually, and socially. All these skills work together to help a child love God, as well as love and care for himself and others.

Short Encounters, Verbal and Visual

A prominent passage related to the family in the Old Testament commands:

> Hear, O Israel: The LORD our God, the LORD is one. You shall love the LORD your God with all your heart and with all your soul and with all your might. And these words that I command you today shall be on your heart. You shall teach them diligently to your children, and shall talk of them when you sit in your house, and when you walk by the way, and when you lie down, and when you rise. You shall bind them as a sign on your hand, and they shall be

---

[1] Lynn R. Marotz, Marie Z. Cross, and Jeanettia M. Rush, *Health, Safety, and Nutrition for the Young Child* (Clifton Park, NY: Thomson Delmar Learning, 2005), 17.

[2] Jeanne Ellis Ormrod, ed., *Educational Psychology: Developing Learners* (Upper Saddle River, NJ: Pearson Education, 2008), 94–99.

as frontlets between your eyes. You shall write them on the doorposts of your house and on your gates. (Deut. 6:4–9)

This passage commands parents to teach their child to love God with all his heart, soul, and strength. The Bible explains how this teaching should take place: in short talks as the family is going about everyday life (*when you sit in your house and when you walk by the way, when you lie down and when you rise*). Not only is verbal instruction important, but written reminders are also encouraged (*write them on the doorposts of your house and on your gates*). Developmentally, all preschoolers have a very short attention span; *one minute for each year of life*[3] is a good rule of thumb. They respond best to short, repetitive, verbal and visual instructions—just as advocated in the Bible long before research in the modern era reemphasized the wisdom of these varied and comprehensive approaches.

The Bible outlines a clear purpose: you should educate preschoolers to love God and love people. God clarifies areas of growth: intellectual, physical, spiritual, and social. Finally, Scripture suggests some practical applications: teaching should permeate every day in small encounters, verbally and visually.

HOW DO PRESCHOOLERS LEARN?

God created each boy and girl with a unique personality. Traits and talents are evident early on, even in babies. One baby is content to sit and watch the world go by while another is constantly wiggling, straining to get his muscles to move him where he wants to go. God purposefully designed every person. He has a plan for every person: "In your book were written, every one of them, the days that were formed for me, when as yet there was none of them" (Ps. 139:16). When God is creating a future ballerina and a future construction foreman, he does not use the same mold.

Learning Styles

When a child is born, a parent's job is to celebrate God's creation and help the child learn to follow God's plan for his life. A child's unique personality traits affect how that child learns. Different authors have different ways of classifying learning styles, but they agree that an activity or method working well with one child may not work at all with another child. Consequently, wise teachers and parents use a variety of activities and methods with different children. One size does not fit all. Basic learning styles for children can be labeled:

---

[3] Thomas Sanders and Mary Ann Bradberry, *Teaching Preschoolers: First Steps Toward Faith* (Nashville: LifeWay, 2009), 16.

visual, kinesthetic, auditory, and *tactile.* A *visual* learner needs to see it; a *kines-thetic* learner needs to do it; an *auditory* learner needs to hear it; and a *tactile* learner needs to touch it.

Another author categorizes learners in this way: *imaginative*—needs to be with people and feel good; *common sense*—needs to know the whys and find logical sense; *dynamic*—needs to be acting on what was learned; *analytical*—needs to know all the facts.[4] Children can learn in many different ways, but all have a primary way by which they learn best. Do not be stressed by this information or get bogged down in too much analysis. As a parent (or teacher), plan to use a variety of teaching methods until you can identify the method to which your child responds most effectively.

Attention Span

No matter the learning style, all preschoolers have a short attention span. One minute per year of age does not mean you have to change activities every minute, but it does mean something new needs to happen within the activity every few minutes. If you are reading a book, the pages need to turn every minute or so to keep the toddler's interest. If working a puzzle, a new piece needs to be placed fairly often. This principle is especially important for activities like family devotions; keep them short! Some preschoolers with a calm, methodical personality may have a longer, but still relatively short, attention span.

Language

Managing the lack of language skills is another challenging aspect of early childhood education. Preschoolers are still building their vocabularies, and this takes time. Parents and teachers need to use simple words and explain new words. Showing a preschooler what you are talking about, while explaining it, works. Even words like *under, over,* and *beside* can be confusing to a young child. Show the child where you want him to look or move. Preschoolers are also very literal thinkers. Be careful to avoid symbolism. The literal mindset of preschoolers prompts them to say the funniest things. My son woke up crying on the morning of his fourth birthday. I asked, "Caleb, what's the matter? It's your birthday. You should be happy." He replied, "I am not any *bigger!*" I had told Caleb, "Wow, you are going to be so *big* when you turn four," meaning (in my symbolic mind set) older and able to do more things. But he took my words literally, and being small for his age, Caleb was disappointed when

---

[4] Marlene D. LeFever, *Learning Styles* (Colorado Springs: Cook, 2004), 20–21.

he woke up the same size as he was the night before. Consider carefully your words to avoid unnecessary confusion for young children. Even an experienced preschool-teacher mom can confuse a trusting four-year-old.

Lack of Experience

A fourth point to consider when teaching young children is their lack of life experiences. When teaching preschoolers, use a show-and-tell approach. Children lack a backlog of experiences necessary to process and understand what they are hearing. When they look disinterested, they may simply have no idea what you are talking about. When you teach about a boat, for example, a preschooler needs to see a real boat, a toy boat, or at least a picture of a boat. Better yet, put a toy boat in a little bit of water and talk about how it moves and floats. He will definitely be interested at that point, especially if he gets to play with the boat and water. As often as you can, use real objects as teaching aids. Field trips and outings are valuable to young children because they can see and experience what you are telling them. Reading picture books daily also gives them verbal and visual avenues for learning. In summary, when teaching preschoolers, implement a variety of methods, keep it short, use simple vocabulary, and utilize a show-and-tell approach.

What Should Preschoolers Be Learning?

In addition to the four basic need areas mentioned previously (security, discovery, self-control, and social interaction), what are some specific things a preschooler can learn and should be learning? Table 15.1 is a sampling of the more common skills most preschoolers can learn.[5] I have grouped the skills according to the pattern of Luke 2:52 (intellectual, physical, spiritual, and social spheres of life).

Table 15.1
⤳ COMMONPLACE SKILLS ⤳
Most Preschoolers Can Learn

Category	Skill
Physical	Sit up, stand
Physical	Feed oneself
Physical	Walk, run, hop

---

[5] Laura Berk, *Exploring Lifespan Development* (Boston: Pearson Education, 2008), 162–63.

Physical/Social	Pick up toys, put things away
Physical	Wash hands, clean oneself (bathe, brush teeth) with help
Physical	Dress oneself
Physical/Intellectual	Color, draw, paint, cut with scissors
Intellectual	Recognize some letters and numbers
Intellectual	Learn the names of colors
Intellectual/Social	Listen to others/listen to storybooks
Social	Talk
Social	Take turns or share
Social	Express love and care for others
Social	Learn to express regret and ask forgiveness (say, "I am sorry.")
Spiritual	Pray simple prayers
Spiritual	Learn basic Bible stories, simple truths, short Bible phrases
Spiritual	Learn to give money to the Lord (understand that money is for spending, saving, and sharing)

Some preschoolers, particularly older ones, because of their personalities and giftedness may go beyond the basics, such as learning to read. A parent, however, should not feel bad if her child is not reading before he turns six years old. Children who are very active often have a more difficult time learning to read early because of the tedious nature of beginning reading. Once they learn to read fast, they typically zoom ahead in their reading capabilities. Two of our children were like this. They struggled with reading early because it was too slow for them. Once they reached third grade, however, they jumped ahead several grade levels in reading because they could finally read fast. Today both of them are avid readers. Our youngest son, on the other hand, learned to read before starting kindergarten. He has a very methodical personality, so it was not a problem for him to sit still and tediously sound out letters.

If a child seems to be slower in his pace for learning, do not panic. Avoid the trap of comparing one child to another and expecting every child to advance through developmental stages at the same pace. Have a doctor check basic things like hearing, eyesight, and motor skill development. Many parents worry excessively if their child is not learning at a preconceived pace. Remember: God loves everyone, and everyone has a purpose to fulfill no matter his capabilities. God is far more concerned about your learning to love every child, regardless of the developmental pace or perceived challenges, than he is about how fast a child develops. Remember also that struggles are not necessarily a bad thing. Children, like adults, must learn that God's grace is sufficient and that he shows himself strong in our weaknesses (2 Cor. 12:9–10). Every child, regardless of his giftedness or challenges, can grow like Jesus—"*in wisdom and in stature and in favor with God and man*" (Luke 2:52). Some will develop faster or slower, but all are growing to the glory of God, not necessarily to the glory of man (by satisfying the pride of parents).

HOW DO YOU CREATE A GOOD LEARNING ENVIRONMENT FOR PRESCHOOLERS?

Preschoolers are incessantly curious and active, so learning comes naturally to them. Parents and teachers can either help or hinder the process. Creating a good learning environment begins with creating a safe and secure environment. Young children are then free to learn without worrying about what might happen to them.

Allow for Some Mess

Preschoolers need a variety of toys, books, puzzles, art materials, music, and natural items from which to learn. Preschoolers learn through play. They are not capable of focusing and sitting through long lectures. As mentioned previously, they respond best to a short, simple, show-and-tell method. Being a neat and tidy person, I have trouble understanding why all the really good learning activities are messy. My passion for helping preschoolers develop allows me to overlook the mess and focus on the learning taking place. At one weekday preschool, parents were told that Fridays were messy days, and children were to dress accordingly. One little girl exclaimed every Friday, "I just love messy days!" Adults have a harder time with this concept than the kids. Things like paint, play dough, glue, glitter, sand, puzzles, and LEGO pieces require a lot of cleanup.

Plan for Cleanup

Plan ahead to create and manage an environment, allowing for some mess. Plastic tablecloths and drop cloths are cheap, so just about anything can be covered and protected. When the activity is finished, everyone can pitch in and help clean up. Cleanup time is part of social/physical learning. As a young parent, I made the mistake of waiting until the end of the day to initiate a cleanup time. This did not work because the mess was too overwhelming for me, much less for my kids, to handle. The secret to managing a messy learning environment is cleaning as you go. Whenever one activity is finished, everyone helps clean up before moving to the next activity. Learning this responsibility for helping with cleanup is a valuable life skill. Even though children will need help to get the job done, they can still grow stronger by practicing the social skills of cooperating with others and learning how to care for their possessions.

Allow Appropriate Noise

Activity learning is also noisy. Having an environment where children can talk, sing, and laugh is absolutely necessary. However, teaching children to control their voice levels by using terms like *whisper voice* (really quiet voice), *inside voice* (quiet voice), and *outside voice* (noisy voice) is equally important. Children must learn to listen and be allowed to express themselves often, taking turns as they talk.

Avoid Excessive Clutter

While messy activities and noisy settings are to be expected, too much clutter discourages learning. Clutter in a learning environment is caused by items that are not part of the learning process. Eliminate clutter while retaining equipment and supplies directly tied to learning activities. Too much clutter in a room distracts a child. The chaos undermines learning readiness and meaningful participation in activities. If children look confused and disoriented upon entering the room, you may have too much clutter in your teaching space. Having adequate storage for equipment and supplies is an important step. You must also put things away or discard them if they are not necessary for learning. When items are left in the open, try to keep similar things together—dollhouses and accessories put together, blocks in another place, and art supplies in a different place. This helps children learn to categorize and organize.

Focus on the Learning Process, Not the Product

With preschoolers, you must focus on the learning process, not on the finished product. The value of an art project, for example, is not to produce a quality picture to impress Grandmother but to learn about colors, the consistency of art materials, and how those materials can be mixed and matched. Art is also valuable as a means of self-expression. Whether lines are straight and colors pure is not relevant to this type of learning.

Too many modern toys are a complete, finished, polished product. There is nothing left for the child to learn or do with the toy. A dollhouse built out of shoe boxes, felt, and wallpaper scraps is not nearly as attractive as a store-bought one, but the learning aspect is greater. By allowing children to choose their own colors and figure out the design, they are learning about physics, architecture, and decorating. They learn the bigger shoe boxes must be put on the bottom, or the dollhouse will fall over. They learn that some colors look good together and others do not. This dollhouse may not last very long, but it will have served a teaching purpose and then can be discarded. Taking a picture of the project will preserve the memory without having to keep the object. Remember that teaching preschoolers is about the process, not the product.

Encourage Small Groups

Finally, preschoolers learn best in small groups. In the learning process, the younger the child, the more individual attention from adults he needs. Children are easily distracted, so learning is inhibited in classrooms with a large number of children. The specialists at LifeWay Christian Resources encourage the following ratios in church preschool ministries: two babies for every adult, gradually moving to five kindergarteners for every adult, with no more than twenty in a kindergarten class.[6] Weekday preschools usually have larger numbers because of the training and experience of their teachers.

To summarize, a good learning environment is safe and secure. Parents and teachers use a variety of toys, puzzles, books, art, blocks, music, and natural items. The setting allows for some mess and noise. The class size should be small. Finally, the focus is on learning through doing, not on a having a polished product.

WHERE SHOULD LEARNING TAKE PLACE AND WHO SHOULD TEACH?

For preschoolers, home is the primary learning place. Mothers and fathers have the primary responsibility to ensure that their children are learning what they need to know. As children mature, they need more and more opportuni-

---

[6] *Kids Ministry 101: Practical Answers to Questions about Kids Ministry* (Nashville: LifeWay, 2009), 35.

ties to interact with others for their social development. Some moms are more naturally gifted in teaching and really enjoy teaching their children at home. Others may not necessarily have these skills and may want some outside help. There are many places for preschoolers to learn and socialize with other children and adults—at home, weekday preschool, Sunday school and other church activities, playgroups, and child-care programs. Parents can strengthen their teaching at home. Reading a book on child development (see footnotes) may give you more realistic expectations for your child. Books on learning styles and activity learning may also be helpful.

If you choose a weekday preschool or child-care center to augment your teaching at home, be sure it has similar values to those you are teaching at home. As the children get older, they can learn to be around other groups who do not share their beliefs, but they need first to be established in their own values and beliefs. Preschoolers need consistency in the teachers from whom they are learning in their early years.

Church venues are an important part of a child's spiritual education. Find a church that values children and has a good teaching plan.[7] If your church does not have a curriculum plan, work with other people who are committed to children and propose a plan to the church leaders. Be willing to be a teacher for the sake of your children and also for other children who, though without solid Christian teaching at home, attend your church. Children need to know that they have a whole community of believers who love them and care for them. Also, many unchurched parents will come to church if a quality children's program is offered.

Family devotions are also an important part of a young child's spiritual development. They model a personal devotion time, which children hopefully adopt for themselves as they mature. Children who are too little to read the Bible and pray on their own need Mom and Dad to show them the way. This time should be short and simple: one Bible story, one truth, one prayer. Bible stories—not cartoon videos—and realistic pictures rather than those depicting fantasy are preferred. When our children were small, we had family devotions for five to ten minutes right before bedtime. This time was a short (but important) reminder that God is important to our daily lives. We were building biblical truths into the lives of our children one truth at a time. Mealtimes also work well for a family devotional time.

---

[7] The LifeWay Christian Resources church curriculum has a thorough teaching plan based on "Levels of Biblical Learning" and "Levels of Biblical Skills." Bible stories, verses, and truths are interwoven to give children a good spiritual and biblical foundation, progressing as the child matures through the curriculum.

FINAL THOUGHTS

The preschool years are a significant time in a child's life. During these years, parents and teachers are building a foundation of beliefs and habits that will help to ground children for the rest of their lives. Security, discovery of surroundings, self-control, and social interaction are foundational for a preschooler to learn effectively in more formal educational settings. The goal of preschool education is teaching children knowledge and skills that will help them to love God as well as to love and care for themselves and others. When teaching, use a variety of methods—keep it short, simple, and use a show-and-tell approach. Following the biblical pattern, children need to learn in four areas: intellectually, physically, spiritually, and socially (see Luke 2:52). They need a safe and secure environment with a variety of toys, books, puzzles, art supplies, blocks, music, and nature items. They need opportunities to build and create, learning through the process not just the finished product. Children can learn at home, church, preschool, playgroups, or a child-care center. Parents are the primary teachers, but others can augment their efforts. Church programs and family devotions are important parts of a child's spiritual development. You can never underestimate the importance of the first five years of life.

PUTTING THE PRINCIPLES INTO PRACTICE

1. Think about the foundational needs of your preschooler. How are you helping your child feel secure, discover surroundings, learn self-control, and learn how to relate to others?

2. Read Deuteronomy 6:4–9. How are you teaching your child as a part of your daily routine?

3. Read Luke 2:52. How can you provide opportunities for your child to grow in the four areas listed: wisdom (intellectual/mental), stature (physical), favor with God (spiritual), and favor with man (social)?

4. Think about the different learning styles. To which style does your child seem to relate the best? Does he relate well to more than one style? How can you teach him according to his bent or with his way of learning in mind?

5. Think about your child's spiritual development. Is he learning Bible stories, short Bible phrases, and how to pray at home and at church? Is he learning music with good biblical truths, such as "God Is So Good"?

ABOUT THE AUTHOR

Ann Iorg is the wife of President Jeff Iorg of Golden Gate Baptist Theological Seminary. They have been married for more than thirty years and have three grown children. In addition to being a supportive wife and mother, she also has served as a preschool director and teacher at various churches for more than three decades. At the seminary, Mrs. Iorg enjoys being a hostess and teaching the student wives about the practical aspects of ministry. She also has a bachelor of behavioral science from Hardin Simmons University in Abilene, Texas, and a master of arts in educational leadership from Golden Gate Baptist Theological Seminary.

Chapter Sixteen

Teaching and Training Children

Elizabeth Owens

The childhood years, between the ages of five and twelve, are pivotal in the growth and development of children. What are your goals for your children during these years and, consequently, your goals for parenting? According to God's Word, during these years Jesus "increased in wisdom and in stature and in favor with God and man" (Luke 2:52). Let this serve as an example. Jesus completed his childhood years ready to begin the season of emerging young adulthood. A Christian adult is one who makes his own decisions under the lordship of Jesus Christ and who is willing to accept responsibility for his decisions, actions, and emotions. Your job as a parent is to teach and train your children in the things of the Lord and in life skills so they will be ready to begin assuming the responsibilities of adulthood when they enter the teenage/emerging young adult years.

CHILDREN AND THE BIBLE

The Bible gives several examples of young teens or older children who demonstrate the fruit of exceptional parenting, such as in the familiar story of Naaman, whom God cured of leprosy (see 2 Kings 5). The heroine of the story is a young maiden, who had been taken captive from her home in Israel and who was a servant to Naaman's wife. Though her name is unknown, her actions show that she had learned to love and fear God and honor his prophet Elisha, to forgive those who had caused great harm in her life, and to return good for evil. Her decisions, attitudes, and actions, remarkable in one so young, surely resulted from a heart tender to God as well as from the teaching and training of her parents in her preschool and childhood years.

Esther, another young maiden living in captivity, is taken from the home and training of her godly cousin Mordecai, who raised her, and placed into an ungodly palace full of scheming and intrigue. Her actions show that she had learned to obey God even if it meant personal destruction, to cultivate despite trials a winsome spirit that won the approval of others, to seek out and follow wise counsel, to wait patiently, to speak the truth courageously for the right time, and to accept the responsibility for the protection of those whom God had placed under her care by virtue of the position with which he had entrusted her. Surely Mordecai must have been a diligent teacher and mentor for Esther during her childhood years while she was under his care.

The exact age of Moses when he moved to the palace to assume his place as the son of Pharaoh's daughter is not known, but from that time he was raised as a prince and educated in Pharaoh's court, where he would have been taught about all the Egyptian ways and exposed to their pagan deities. Where did Moses learn to love the true God and his people the Israelites? Surely Moses received his spiritual foundation at the feet of his parents, who, in his early years, demonstrated courage and wise planning to protect the life of the child whom God would one day use to set their people free.

TOWARD MANHOOD AND WOMANHOOD

So how do we get from here to there, from a me-centered, dependent preschooler to a teen or an emerging young adult who, while still under your care and receiving your guidance and counsel, is increasingly able to make decisions and choices that will honor and serve God? Several Scriptures can point parents in the right direction.

Through Moses, God gave his people the *Shema*, directions about the teaching and training of their children (see Deut. 6:4–9). Parents are challenged to teach their children as they sit, when they stand, when they walk, and when they lie down. These positions account for virtually all your waking moments of every day. You should set aside specific times to teach your children spiritual truths and life skills, but the truth is that parents (or those to whom they have delegated the task of educating and caring for their children) are teaching and training their children all the time, whether or not they want or plan to do so. Children are observing and learning from the actions and attitudes—good and bad—of their parents throughout the day, every day.

Do you want your child to develop a self-disciplined use of time? How do you present this model? Do you want your child to be a wise steward with his money and possessions? How do you model this stewardship? Do you want your child to find joy in serving and obeying God? Do you want your child to treat others kindly and with respect? Do you want your child to have integrity in his dealings with God and others? Do you want your child to submit in a godly way to those with God-given authority in his life? All these things parents should be teaching their children by their words, but they need to be challenged continually to remember that their actions and attitudes—all of them—are also being observed by their children every day.

While John 3:16 may not seem at first like a verse about parenting, it does teach the meaning of loving according to God's definition of love. The modern world has redefined love to be a warm fuzzy feeling, the end of which can mean moving on to the next person who makes you feel good. This definition of love brings disaster in marriage and in the rearing of children. God loves you and me and showed that love by the giving of himself, all of himself, even unto his own death. This does not mean that you must sacrifice yourself to give and give to your children in order to satisfy all their desires. God's loving had a purpose—to bring his creation into a right relationship with Him. He loves you with the goal of growing you in righteousness and godliness. In the same way, this is how you are to love your spouse and your children: love is giving of yourself, even unto death, for the goodness and godliness of another.

Loving your children with God's love is difficult. It demands time, energy, and focus. It may never require the giving of your physical life unto death, but each day you must die many deaths to your own wants, desires, and schedules. It means stopping what you are doing immediately to deal with obedience issues with your children instead of continuing in what you want to do and letting disobedience escalate. It means making yourself do necessary things that you do not enjoy doing so you can model the self-discipline that you are trying to develop in your children. It may mean altering schedules and even accepting a decrease in salary in order to maintain a daily environment that will teach and train your children moment by moment in God's ways and values.

THE GREAT COMMISSION FOR THE HOME

The Great Commission found in Matthew 28:18–20 is a wonderful Scripture used to promote missions and evangelism. But it is also a marvelous guide for parenting. Your responsibility to evangelize begins at home with the eternal souls God has entrusted to your care. Certainly your foremost wish for your children is that they would recognize their own need for God's forgiveness in their lives, accept his gift of salvation, and submit to his lordship. This most important decision that your children will ever make has not been placed into your hands; it is between your child and God, and you cannot make it for him. But the spiritual condition of your child needs to be the focus of your prayers and efforts beginning before he is born, and your child needs to be able to see the fruit of God's salvation in your life and words as you pray for and teach him.

The Great Commission does not end with evangelism; neither should your spiritual focus for your children end with their salvation. Indeed, according to these verses, your work has just begun. You are to teach all that God has commanded; you are to make disciples. *Disciple* is an interesting word and related to the word *discipline*, which is associated with the rearing of children. Discipline often has a negative connotation alluding to punishment, but its meaning is actually much bigger and is something that parents should be positively pursuing all the time. Disciplining your children in a very real sense is making disciples of them, first of all disciples of the parents and of the ways of your home, but ultimately disciples of the Lord. To disciple someone is to teach and train him in the values and ways of the person he is to follow. Disciplining your children is teaching and training them in the ways (yours and God's) you want them to follow.

Now that this task of teaching and training has been established, how do you flesh it out? What exactly are parents supposed to teach, and how are they to train?

GOODNESS AND GODLINESS

Only God can change your children's hearts, but parents have the responsibility to teach their children about God and to develop habits that will make it easier for them to obey God when they are older. Parents need to demonstrate to their children their love for God and his Word. Begin telling your children Bible stories when they are babies; you should also be reading to them directly from God's Word by the time they are old enough to begin school, always ready to explain words or concepts they may not understand. Provide a plan for them to memorize Scripture. Incorporate God's Word into your daily lives; make reference to his Word as you observe nature, make decisions, shop, spend time with friends, and serve others. Show them that Scripture is useful and necessary for making the choices with which they are faced daily.

Teach your children a love for the bride of Christ, his church. Lead them by the example of your faithfulness to the local church to which God has called your family by your attendance, your giving, your service, and your supportive attitudes toward church leaders and other members. Let them see your ministries in the church as part of your joyful service to God and his people. Train them to begin ministering to the body of Christ as soon as they are able. This can be as simple as picking up bulletins and other papers from the pews after the services, helping you prepare and deliver a meal to a family in crisis with an illness, a death, a new baby, or some other need, visiting an older church member who may be lonely, making and sending a card of encouragement, and praying together for those who lead your church.

Teach and train your children to be joyful givers. Lead by your example and train them to give from whatever monies they receive. Do not stop the promptings they may receive from God to give to him more than you think they need to give. On different occasions two of our children felt led to give all of the spending money they had saved to special kingdom needs, and I was thankful that God stopped my initial impulses to tell them that they did not have to give all they had. They learned the joy of obedient giving, they learned to go without some things they wanted but did not really need, and they saw God provide for their needs.

CHILDREN AND RELATIONSHIPS

Children will learn about marriage first in the home, and parents have a responsibility to model a godly marriage before their children. Wise parents will limit their children's exposure to sources of ungodly teachings on marriage, which include television, movies, books, and music. As children get older, they will see more blatantly the effects of sin on marriages around them and in the media, and parents need to help their children use Scripture to develop discernment and wisdom to prepare them for their own marriages.

Sons need to have godly manhood modeled for them. They need to be taught what it means to be a godly husband and father, to be the protector of and provider for their future families. They need to see loving headship modeled and explained.

As your sons reach the age of ten or twelve and learn about God's plan for sexual intimacy and building families, they need to be reminded of God's definition of love. A godly man will never tell a woman he loves her and then ask her to do something that will not contribute to her growth in goodness and godliness. That is not God's kind of love. Whether your family allows dating or promotes some type of courtship model, your sons need to develop godly boundaries in how they relate to young women. Likewise, your daughters of that age need to be taught that a young man who says he loves her and then asks her to do something contrary to what will help her behave in a Christlike manner is not selflessly loving her in God's way but is rather looking out for his own interests.

Daughters need to be taught what it means to be godly women, to develop their God-given talents and gifts, to serve God joyfully wherever he has placed them. They will be blessed if they can grow up with the biblical teaching on submission described in Ephesians 5 modeled in their home. My husband

and I have observed over the years "good Christian families" rearing children who were rebellious and irresponsible from childhood into adulthood years. In many of those families we sensed an ongoing and subtle rebellion in both parents; the wives were quietly unsubmissive to their husbands, and the husbands were disobedient to God in the relinquishing of their God-given responsibility of headship. The seeds of rebellion sown by the parents seemed to be reaped and magnified by the children.

Your children need teaching and training in other relationships as well. Peers can influence your children for good or for evil, and in this regard you need to be watchful and alert. Electronic communications make this increasingly difficult for parents. Your children are your responsibility; do not be hesitant to limit and monitor all that goes into and out of your home. At the same time, begin teaching your children how to have discernment in friendships and in what they allow to be put before them. The book of Proverbs is a good place to start. Philippians 4:8 is another helpful guide. It is not wise to restrict your children terribly in the areas of friendships and electronics, and then have them leave your home at age eighteen for unrestricted freedom before you have taught them what it means to have friends, to be a friend, and to guard their hearts and minds for Christ.

CHRISTIAN WORLDVIEW

More and more the spirit of the world is against the spirit of Christ. You see it in the news, in books and movies, and in shattered relationships. How do you help your children view attitudes and philosophies through God's eyes instead of through the lenses of those whose core values are not of God? They need to know the truth first. When you know and understand what is real and true, it is easier to identify what is not. Ground your children in God's Word. Let them see you living out your daily life based on his Word, so they know that it is true and helpful.

And then you need to talk. Talk with them about what they are studying in school. Look with them at the flow of history and ideas, show them where people and civilizations deviated from God's ideas and plans, and discuss the consequences that followed. Talk with them about what they see on television or read in books. This means that you will watch much of what they watch with them and read what they read. You can show them how to discern what is good and true as you read and watch with them, and then you can point out to them the influence of sin and disobedience on people's viewpoints and choices. Your goal is to raise a discerning adult who looks at the world from God's point of view.

LOVING AND CARING FOR CHILDREN

Just as your children know that they themselves are of inestimable value to God and to you, they need to be taught to love and care for other children as gifts from God. Do your children see you greeting the news of a coming baby with joy? Do your children have opportunities to hold and care for babies and toddlers (under your supervision), and do you show them how to teach and train even little ones for Jesus? Do your children see you caring for the orphans of the world through adoption, helping and welcoming those who adopt, as well as giving to and mentoring the fatherless among us?

Do you celebrate big families? My husband and I have observed that big families rarely are invited to others' homes. Over the years we have been enriched by friends who have been blessed with many children, and with joy we have welcomed them into our home for meals. Our children have benefited from seeing big families working together to ensure that everyone receives care, the guest children have benefited from the opportunity to accept hospitality, and the moms always seemed grateful for an evening of eating someone else's cooking.

Our family keeps a high chair, toys, and puzzles ready for young guests. Our girls have learned that they can have an important ministry to young parents by playing with and entertaining the children when a family visits in our home, thus allowing the parents time for adult conversation.

CARING FOR THE HOME

In the early days of our country, many families were larger, often living on farms and in rural areas. Even young children were given jobs to do. They understood that the well-being of their family (such as having food on the table) was dependent upon their fulfilling their respective jobs. With modern conveniences, smaller families, handy grocery stores, and even household help, there seems to be increasingly less for children to do to feel important and necessary to their families.

In the garden of Eden, Adam was given work to do. Children need to know from an early age that work is a blessing from God and that they are necessary and important to their families. They need to have jobs to do, starting in the preschool years and continuing until they establish their own homes. Teaching and training them to care for their homes now will prepare them for caring for their own homes and families someday.

There are many ways to organize chores and children. Some families assign daily chores to each child, some have a weekly chore list, some do a combination of both. Some chores are assigned by age and passed on to the next child as the children grow. Others are rotated by a routine, by the parents' assignment, or by the children's choices. By the teen years a child should acquire these skills:

- knowing how to do all chores necessary for the daily and weekly cleaning and organizing of a home
- ability to do basic shopping, comparing prices and using coupons
- ability to fix simple meals
- knowing how to do basic lawn and yard care
- knowing how to use household machines and power equipment safely

The hardest part of all of this process is the beginning. It takes time to teach a child to do a chore correctly; at first it may seem easier for the parent to "do it herself." But if you are loving your child with God's kind of love, you will sacrifice your own time, patience, and energies to teach a child to do a thing correctly and well, cheering his efforts and praising his accomplishments. Children need to be taught not only the mechanics of a chore but also that work is a gift of God for which one should be thankful and that chores are an important and helpful aspect of family life. Our children know that our family's ability to minister is extended when they all pitch in to exercise care for our home. In fact, the children are working through their weekly chore list even while I am typing this chapter.

STEWARDSHIP

Teaching and training children in stewardship involves more than teaching them to tithe, although that is important. Underlying lessons teach that all the family resources come from God, demanding that we care for everything we have in a way that would please and honor him. Even though our furniture may be worn, we still treat it with care because God gave it to us to use for his glory. This principle also prepares children to treat someone else's things carefully, whether on a playground or in a home. When you know that all you have comes from and belongs to God, who allows you to use it, your children can learn by example and word to hold things lightly, to pass them on to others who have a need, and to trust God to provide for their needs.

EDUCATION

The method of educating children has become a major issue for parents. Gone are the days when all parents sent their children to public schools without worrying about what they were being taught, who was influencing their worldview, or what physical harm might come to them. There are many options for schooling your children: in public schools (both traditional and charter), in private schools (both Christian and secular), and at home. However, parents are ultimately responsible to God for the education and training of their children, and they are to choose and use the resources available under his direction. If you decide to send your children to a public or private school, be aware of what your children are being taught and of who is influencing them. Be prepared to counteract a secular worldview with the truths from God's Word.

Increasingly popular, homeschooling has proven to be an effective choice for meeting the academic as well as socialization needs of children. It also helps parents identify and nurture each child's unique interests and talents. The choice to homeschool often involves a great sacrifice of time and finances; but many parents feel that it best allows them to fulfill the commands of the *Shema* (see Deuteronomy 6), to teach and train their children in God's ways throughout each and every day, and to provide unity and stability for the family in a culture of constant busyness. Many resources are available in the form of local and state homeschool associations, textbooks, co-ops, and tutors. Homeschooling is legal in all fifty states, and the Homeschool Legal Defense Association (www.hslda.org) provides information, forms, and legal representation for homeschooling families nationwide.

A FEW NUTS AND BOLTS OF CHILD TRAINING

Children will find it easier to obey when they know what to expect. If you are going to someone's home, or to an event, and there is a certain way you need your children to behave, calmly let them know that ahead of time. Our children were able to greet new adult friends politely when we gave them that expectation ahead of time and told them how to do it. If they will need to sit quietly for a short time or to provide comfort to someone who is sorrowing, prepare them ahead of time and let them know how important their ministry will be.

Preparing them ahead of time will also help in the area of obedience to your instructions. My son was more cheerfully and easily able to obey by putting his toys away and preparing for bed when I set a timer and gave him a ten-minute warning.

Children do need to learn to obey the first time they are told to do something. This should begin in the preschool years, but it can be started in the childhood years with some explanations and training. Much of the training involves re-training yourself to expect obedience the first time. This involves the self-discipline of getting up and dealing with disobedience when it first happens, instead of nagging and finally getting angry. You are training your children in disobedience when you teach them that you are not serious about obedience until you get angry or until you get to that fraction of two that triggers your anger on your way to counting to three. Training children to obey the first time eliminates a lot of anger and fussing and prepares a child to obey God promptly when he is older.

Train your children to develop their own self-discipline. Do not completely childproof your home; rather, house-proof your child. Children need to be trained not to touch what does not belong to them (including their siblings' toys) without getting permission from the owner. Just as they have learned to take care of what God has given to them, they need to learn to respect what he has entrusted to the care of others. This may take the form of special training in your home as well as in stores. If you constantly hold their hands or isolate them in a shopping cart in a store, they will never learn to discipline themselves. This was particularly difficult for one of our daughters. I would tell her to put her hands in her pockets or to hold her own hands if she did not have pockets when we were in a store particularly enticing to her. Then I would follow her at a distance to make sure she did this. (This training of my child meant that I could not shop, but it was part of sacrificing myself for the goodness and godliness of my child.) She learned that with obedience and self-discipline came the reward of increasing freedom. When your children have learned this area of self-discipline, they will reap great rewards when a guest in someone else's home.

Do not reward undesirable behavior. For example, my children know that whining will automatically not get them what they want. They have learned to ask for things politely and to accept the first *no* as the last. (I have also learned to think carefully before I tell my children *no*.) When you give in to whining, you are training your children to nag and manipulate, and you are also teaching them not to trust your word. Just as they need to know that God's Word is trustworthy and that he means what he says, they need to know that your word is just as certain.[1]

FINAL THOUGHTS

Raising children to walk in God's ways is a God-sized task that necessitates your own dependence on him for wisdom and strength. As you teach and train your children, you find that God uses them in your life to stretch and sanctify you. May you be faithful to the task and the privilege he has given you to nurture and train your children. Remember that you are not only rearing the next generation to serve and obey the Lord, but you are also teaching and training

---

[1] Elisabeth Elliot, *The Shaping of a Christian Family* (Nashville: Thomas Nelson, 1992), 114.

the parents of your grandchildren! At the end of your life what will matter most is your children, your grandchildren, and those yet to be born, and your faithfulness to God's calling to fulfill this most important task in your life.

PUTTING THE PRINCIPLES INTO PRACTICE

1. Review the stories of Esther, Moses, and the servant of Naaman's wife. Choose one story to tell to a school-age child; discuss the godly traits that were exhibited. Help the child identify at least one trait that he would like God to help him develop. Pray for and encourage him in this area.
2. Read the *Shema* in Deuteronomy 6:4–9, and think about loving your children with God's love as described in John 3:16. Identify some aspect of your home or routine, which, with God's help, should be modified or changed to provide a godly example to your children.
3. Make a plan to lead your school-age child in reading the Bible every day and in memorizing Scripture.
4. Watch a movie or read a book that your child enjoys. Assess the worldview portrayed and discuss with your child.
5. Identify several chores that you can begin teaching your child to do. Make a plan for him to do them regularly.

ABOUT THE AUTHOR

Elizabeth (Betsy) Owens has been married to Waylan Owens, dean of the School of Church and Family Ministries at Southwestern Baptist Theological Seminary, for twenty-five years. They have four children. Their oldest, Blayne, now age twenty-one, was born to them. Joshua, seventeen years; Grace, fourteen years; and Mary, thirteen years, were all born in China and adopted as babies or preschoolers. Betsy has homeschooled the children since Blayne's first day of school. She is a graduate of West Suburban Hospital School of Nursing, the University of Illinois, and Rush University, and holds bachelor's and master's degrees in nursing. She has worked in intensive care units with adults and newborns and has taught nursing but is thankful to be at home full-time with her family. Betsy served with her pastor husband in churches in Mississippi, Alaska, and North Carolina. She currently volunteers in children's ministries at her church and with student wives at Southwestern. She and Waylan recently joyfully welcomed a new daughter into their family with the marriage of their oldest son.

Chapter Seventeen

Raising Teenagers on God's Terms

Joy Souther Cullen

My husband and I spent twenty years—from 1975 to 1995—raising teenagers. That is how long it took to move through the teen years in our household. The oldest was fourteen when our fourth and last child was born—hence, the extended time of physical changes, emotional turmoil, endless extracurricular activities, dating, broken hearts, high school, and finally the decisions leading to college. Having a baby at the beginning of those years, burying a parent, sending two children to an MK (missionary kid) boarding school, transferring from a Thai-Buddhist country to serve in a Singhalese-Hindu culture, and finally saying good-bye to all of them as they flew thousands of miles from Southeast Asia to college, probably colored those years with unusual stress. The unexpected marriage of our seventeen-year-old to her twenty-four-year-old sweetheart made us realize life and weddings do not always go as planned. So let's go back to the beginning: How does one make the journey of raising teenagers? Where's the road map? Is there a manual? Whose advice do I take?

GOD HAD A PLAN FOR EACH ONE

When my father told me God had a plan for my life, I was only seven. I had just taken the first step to discovering this place on October 8, 1948—the day I asked Jesus to come into my heart to stay. Only later did I discover the wonderful truths in Psalm 139, especially verses 13–16, not only for my life but also for our children.

> For you formed my inward parts;
>> you knitted me together in my mother's womb.
> I praise you, for I am fearfully and wonderfully made.
> Wonderful are your works;
>> my soul knows it very well.
> My frame was not hidden from you,

when I was being made in secret,
    intricately woven in the depths of the earth.
Your eyes saw my unformed substance;
in your book were written, every one of them,
    the days that were formed for me,
    when as yet there was none of them.

God had a plan for my life! God had a plan for the lives of each of our children. We had the awesome responsibility of communicating that truth to them as one of the basic biblical foundations; in fact, it was the foundational truth for their spiritual growth. When I faced a decision in my life, my dad would say, "Joy, how does this impact God's plan for your life?" By the age of nine, I had experienced God's unmistakable call to missions. So it was with great joy that this great truth was passed down to my own children: "God has had a plan for your life since before you were born. We want nothing more than for you to be in the center of God's plan every day of your life." You see, God does not reveal this plan on a big screen where you can scroll down to see all of the events of the future. In fact, he reveals his will only one day at a time—often, hour by hour. The incredible realization is that our children did not have to worry about what was going to happen the next week or the next year or even ten years later. All they needed to do was to make sure "that day" they sought his will in every decision and activity. And then the days roll into weeks and into years, and his will is revealed. And they and we are discovering that this process continues.

GOD WORKS ALL THINGS TOGETHER FOR GOOD

Romans 8:28 is another component of the spiritual legacy given to me by my parents and passed on to our children. I wonder if they got as tired of hearing those words coming out of my mouth as I did my father's. The day I realized that I had fallen in love with a prelaw student who had no call to missions caused me to fly home from Hardin-Simmons University to New Orleans Seminary to pose the question to my dad: "Do you think God is uncalling me to missions?" Dad asked in reply, "What does Romans 8:28 say?" *Oh no, I thought, not that verse again.* But I submissively quoted it: "And we know that for those who love God all things work together for good, for those who are called according to his purpose."

"Joy, do you love God?" Dad asked. "Yes, Dad. You know I do," I replied. I knew what was coming next. "Has he called you to missions—is that his purpose for your life?" I nodded with tears in my eyes. "Then," Dad exclaimed, "All things will work together for good!" Of course, I thought that God's "good" was that the relationship would end, and I would end up alone in Africa in my little grass hut—my visual image of life as a single missionary in Africa! In the end, God's plan was to "call again" that young man who had rejected missions at the age of ten due to childhood illnesses and asthma. How could we not pass on this wonderful biblical promise to our children? We had seen God work things together over and over in our lives; surely the children could see that. They certainly heard Romans 8:28 quoted enough.

Now in her mid-thirties, our youngest daughter, Catherine, has held on to that verse through the childhood injuries that resulted in a life of pain and then as a young wife enduring eight years of financial struggles while planting a church with her husband in the Northwest. How do you tell a teenager who suffers pain every day that "all things work together for good"? She loved God so much and believed that he had a plan for her life. She had to believe he had her good in his hands. Now it was funny also to hear Catherine state very clearly what this "plan" was *not* going to be—she was not ever going to marry and she would never be a preacher's wife. A word to the wise: Do not crush a teenager's dreams or tell her or him, "Don't say 'never.'" Our oldest daughter, Jane, and her best friend used to talk about backpacking through Europe as soon as they graduated from International School Bangkok! They never did, and we were glad we let them dream. By the way, Catherine met that preacher boy at Southwestern Baptist Theological Seminary and finally realized that God had worked all of the events of her life to bring her to that day when God drew them to each other in his perfect plan.

FOLLOW GOD'S WORD FAITHFULLY

By the time a child has reached the teen years, Mom and Dad's words and warnings become garbled by the world's verbiage of what is right, real, and relevant. It was important that our children had a foundation based on God's Word for instruction and direction. When I became a Christian, my pastor W. A. Criswell wrote 2 Timothy 2:15 in my Bible, beneath where he instructed me to write the date of my spiritual birthday and testimony: "Do your best to present yourself to God as one approved, a worker who has no need to be ashamed, rightly handling the word of truth."

At the age of seven, these were big words. My parents explained that to please God I would need to read my Bible every day. I was already having my own daily devotions as well as devotions at the breakfast table with my mom, dad, and brother, so reading the Bible was not going to be a problem. As I grew older, however, understanding the meaning and rightly dividing the Word of truth became the one constant that always gave me answers and comforted me in my disappointments.

Leading our children to become Bible readers began in the preschool years. We read to them until they could read for themselves. Having a quiet time in the morning was as routine as making their beds, eating their breakfasts, and brushing their teeth. If anything had to be left out because of time constraints, it was the bed making. I could make up their beds, but they could not piggy-back on our quiet times with God. Had this habit not begun in childhood, I am fairly certain a daily quiet time could not have been instilled as easily in the teen years. By then, it was akin to brushing your teeth—you just did it because you had always done it. Did they always have *daily* quiet time through those difficult, stressful years during which each of our teens was having his own bumps and bruises? No—nor have I always been so faithful. Yet as we look at these young adults in their late thirties and forties still spending time with God every morning and teaching their own children to do the same—the habit was ingrained. Why was this discipline so important for the teen years and beyond? According to Hebrews 4:12, "The word of God is living and active, sharper than any two-edged sword, piercing to the division of soul and of spirit, of joints and of marrow, and discerning the thoughts and intentions of the heart."

Laying out a scriptural plan for raising teenagers is one thing, but now that they are adults, I asked each of our children this question: What, as far as our parenting was concerned, was most important to you during the teen years?

JANE SPEAKS

Our oldest child was born while we were students at Hardin-Simmons University in Abilene, Texas. She grew up on the mission field and began to live independently at age fifteen when she moved into the Baptist Dorm in Bangkok for the rest of her teen years. She then met and married Stephen Milam, another MK from Indonesia. Following his graduation from Southwestern Seminary, they served four years on the staff of Calvary Baptist Church in Bangkok and then were appointed by the International Mission Board to serve in Southeast Asia. They have three daughters—now teens and young adults themselves. Jane says that the four most important aspects are communication, prayer, prioritizing family time, and modeling commitment to Christ. As Jane says,

Communication

Back in those days, we did not have Internet for e-mail or Skype, and even phone calls were expensive and infrequent; but you [her parents] were faithful to write me almost every day making me feel connected to you and the rest of the family. In turn, I developed the habit of writing you the details of my life from the mundane of what I ate for breakfast to the more significant hurts and pains every teenager faces. I always felt like I could be and should be completely honest with you about my life even when I knew you would be disappointed. Knowing that your love for me was unconditional allowed me to be open and honest with you.

Prayer

Throughout my growing-up years, I observed your walk with the Lord and the time you spent in his Word and communing with him. Your way of keeping detailed notes of prayer requests and his answers let me know that you were interceding for me . . . for every detail of my life. To this day, that knowledge sustains me and encourages me knowing that my mom is lifting me up to my heavenly Father. As a teenager, knowing that you prayed for me gave me the confidence to live my life trusting that God was answering your prayers. I knew you were praying for me through every test, paper, relationship, and activity . . . whatever was going on in my life.

Prioritizing Family Time

When I did live at home (eighth, ninth and part of tenth grade), you always made being there for me, when I came home from school or when I needed to talk, a priority. You have always been a busy person, but you never let your other work keep you from taking time for us. Dinner times around the table were a priority as were family vacations.

Modeling Commitment to Christ

This commitment was not just something I saw as a teenager, but throughout my growing-up years, you talked about your walk with the Lord. You shared the things he was saying to you, and then you followed through on them. Early on the importance and the fulfillment of knowing and doing God's will was instilled into me. Even though I was not a perfect teenager and I made some wrong choices, there was always that voice in my head (was that you or the Holy Spirit, Mom?) reminding me that God had a plan for my life, and if I would surrender my desires to him, he would keep me on the right path. There was nothing I wanted more than to be on God's path. You nurtured that desire in my life and encouraged me in it. What I saw in your life as you followed God, I wanted in mine.

Lest you think our experience raising teenagers is a recipe for success, let Jane tell you where I failed. She called it . . .

Boxes

Mom, it would be so much easier to say you were perfect ☺, but none of us are. So I will try to be open and honest and pray you do not linger over it. I think one of the most difficult challenges a parent faces is not to put their children in "boxes." Here is what I mean: early on we begin to describe and categorize our children according to their personalities and abilities. I do not think we as parents do this intentionally, and in some ways, people would say that we are just recognizing our children for who they are. However, I think that these boxes become labels and can even end up limiting us. I think that in some ways, each of us kids had a box. My box was the talented and smart box. I know—that sounds like a good box, but so many times I wanted to be in Julie's box—the pretty and popular box. I'm not sure how NOT to do this because even though I tried not to do it with my girls, I did. Just labeling us with our "temperaments" can make us feel like we do not have choices about who we are and who we want to become. I think finding the balance between helping our children recognize their uniqueness and yet allowing room for growth and change is the key.

JOHN SPEAKS

Our son, John, born during our seminary years in New Orleans, spent his teen years in two countries—Thailand and Sri Lanka. Following his graduation from Hardin-Simmons University and Southwestern Seminary, he spent a year with the International Mission Board teaching in northern Thailand. He and his wife, Debbie, have a son. John is Associate Pastor of Pastoral Ministries at First Baptist Church in Dallas.

John's teen years were "interrupted," to say the least. After an unfruitful and unhappy year in boarding school in Thailand, he was allowed to move home to Sri Lanka where he was homeschooled. He moved a third time and graduated from International School Bangkok when we returned to Thailand. What is John's assessment of those years?

Father Teaching the Son

John says about the years in Sri Lanka:

Those were my happiest years on the mission field. There was no television, movies, clean sugar, Cokes, or flour without bugs! Instead there were books, games, and LOTS of family experiences. When Dad travelled to parts of the island to preach or teach, the "home school" went along.

In those years, John's dad taught him how to change a tire, wire a lamp, repair a toilet, remodel a house (the 150-year-old British Baptist Headquarters where we were to live), and extinguish a huge rat population.

Family time was and is important to John, seen even now as he parents his son. Raising a teenage son on God's terms means a father and son need to have a strong relationship with God and each other.

The "Purple Book" Tradition

John and I have shared a devotional book, *Springs in the Valley* by Mrs. Charles Cowman, through the years. When he went off to college, it was falling apart, so we had it rebound in purple and gold—the colors of Hardin-Simmons University where we both graduated. Someday he will share it with his son. The "Purple Book" is an incredible link to my son. In the margins are the dates and comments related to his teen and young adult experiences. He writes,

> This book is one of my greatest personal treasures. Thank you for the shared gift of it and your words of wisdom.

The "Rebekah Letter"

When John was sixteen and living in the MK dorm in Bangkok, I wrote him a letter listing the qualities of a godly wife found in Genesis 24. I did not know that he carried that letter with him for the next seventeen years until God led him to the woman described in that letter. I keep the letter in "The Purple Book" because I want to remember that God gives wise words to parents if they will ask him for guidance for their teenagers.

JULIE SPEAKS

Julie, our third child, was ten days old when we moved from her birth city to the training center for our mission work. She was six months old when we sailed from San Francisco to Hong Kong, twenty-one days at sea and then a flight to our new assignment in Bangkok, Thailand. In her preschool years and early childhood, Julie embraced the Thai language and culture only to have to give it up and adjust to new ones in Sri Lanka at age ten. While attending North Texas University, she married a missionary kid from Indonesia. They have spent nineteen years in Southeast Asia. Julie writes from a framework of having reared four daughters.

Spiritual Heritage

> What a hard question to answer! I've thought about it a lot, though, even before being asked for this purpose. I think about it as I raise my two daugh-

ters, examining what parts of my rich spiritual heritage I do not want them to miss out on and also what hindrances I struggled through that I want to keep them from if possible. The wonderful parts that I do not want them to miss are too numerous to cover, but here are a few that are so essential they must be shared.

You taught me how to pray, how to read and meditate on God's Word, and how to get to know my Lord through worship, fellowship, and time with him. One of my favorite childhood memories was waking up in the morning—finding you in your special place with a cup of coffee and HIS WORD. You never made me feel that I was interrupting you—you always made time for me. In high school, I wanted you to be home when I came home from school. You did that for me. Even though I did not always come straight to you, I knew you were there. I took note of that even though I did not show you at the time. Unfortunately I did not give you much time in my teenage years. I was gone from home to college by age sixteen. We did have my entire childhood together though.

Importance of Loving God Totally

As a result of the way I was raised, I have focused on impressing on our daughters' hearts the importance of loving God with all their hearts, souls, and minds—knowing God's will for their lives—impressing on them to make God number one in their lives, above all else. We have taught them how to pray, encouraged Scripture memory in the classroom (they are homeschoolers), and asked them for accountability for what God is teaching them through our family altar time led by their father. Being available is the theme of my role as a mom—demonstrating to them how important they are—and that is the key.

CATHERINE SPEAKS

Our fourth child, Catherine, was born in Bangkok, spent most of her preschool years in Sri Lanka, and then spent her school years in Thailand. She and her husband, Michael, a bivocational pastor, planted a church in the Northwest and have two daughters.

Discipled by Parents

My parents taught me that God knew me intimately, was always at work in my life, and was speaking to me even as a young child. I never doubted having purpose. As a young Christian, I was expecting to hear from God and be used by him every day.

I grew up in a missionary family. My parents made me feel that I was as called to the mission field as they were. That has impacted how my husband and I include our older daughter, as we will our baby as she grows older, in our ministry. I was empowered by my parents in this, and I pray our children will be as well. So many believers are never actually discipled, but my parents truly discipled me, which is a much rarer gift than I would have expected. As an adult, I wrote a study on the spiritual disciplines (which I thought was a completely new concept to me since I had not heard that term before), only to realize that my parents had taught me so many of the disciplines without me even knowing that's what they were doing! I am especially grateful that these disciplines included studying and memorizing God's Word, praying, and journaling. My parents gave me a new Bible, devotional book, or journal at least once a year. Those gifts encouraged my personal walk with the Lord and taught me to treasure my intimate relationship with him. Even as a child, my mom set a special time and place aside for me to spend time alone with the Lord each morning. My dad encouraged my desire to wrestle with theology and ask hard questions, allowing me to feel a sense of equality in discussions and never belittling my attempts to make sense of difficult issues. My parents also made it very natural to share about our walks with the Lord and how he was working in and through us. Spirituality was not a compartmentalized part of life; rather, it encompassed all of life. This put in place a mind-set that has impacted and will continue to impact every season of my life.

Understanding God's Will

I would rather write a book on the incredible impact my parents had on me than bring up one or two of the hindrances I struggled with in my teen years. However, we all know there is no perfect upbringing. And I am personally grateful that the Lord has compassion on us as parents and that he is Redeemer. Whether my struggles came from what I saw and heard at home, what was in my own flesh to begin with, or what the church sometimes portrays, these are what I strive not to pass on.

I struggled with a perception that following God's will was like walking on a very narrow balance beam, with very little room for mistakes. This idea caused me to try to walk very carefully for fear of falling off (which for a long time led to very strict following of the rules). Then when I did come to a place in life where I felt that I had fallen off, I felt hopeless and that all was lost. Instead of experiencing true conviction that leads to repentance and restoration, I listened to the lies of the enemy and lived with a great deal of shame and failure, even with a sense that I had lost my identity, which was very much tied into my outward "performance." These experiences make me want to help my daughters live with a sense of freedom as they follow Christ, striving to love him with all that they are and at the same time basking in his grace and his power to redeem. Looking back, I believe my parents could have helped me find that same grace and redemption, but I needed to have heard that message loud and clear as I was growing up. I took the "narrow balance beam" message to be "the end" instead of knowing that there would be grace given even after failure.

Hindrance of Perfectionism

I struggled for a long time with a sense that I needed to be perfect or pretend to be perfect. I was afraid to be authentic and felt secret shame over my struggles with sin. Letting my oldest daughter see me drop to my knees in confession to the Lord and then to ask for her forgiveness is not easy when I have fallen short of his desires for me as a parent. I pray it teaches her authenticity before the Lord and others so that she will walk in forgiveness and freedom. I also pray that my children will be able to look back on their upbringing with as much thankfulness as I have for my parents for loving me, teaching me, and pouring their lives into me! I am truly blessed!

CONCLUSION

"I will sing of the steadfast love of the LORD, forever; with my mouth I will make known your faithfulness to all generations" (Psalm 89:1) was God's challenge to us as we parented our teens. We sang a lot! My children "burst into song" without any provocation. They know all my childhood choruses that are never sung anymore: "Something Happened When He Saved Me," "Oh Say, 'But I'm Glad,'" "It Is Summertime in My Heart," and "Every Day with Jesus." If you cannot sing of his steadfast love, play Christian music in your home and on the car radio. As you raise your teenagers on God's terms, remember that you are making God's faithfulness known to the generations that follow. As we have watched two of our daughters raise their teenagers, we rejoice that a third generation is discovering our spiritual legacy.

PUTTING THE PRINCIPLES INTO PRACTICE

1. Review the four passages recommended to help teenagers discover God's will for their lives: Psalm 139:13–16; Romans 8:28; 2 Timothy 2:15; and Hebrews 4:12. Set aside four different times for the family to consider what God desires for each family member. Encourage your teenagers to figure out the meaning as you listen and encourage. Suggest that they paraphrase each verse to make it personal by using personal pronouns or their names.

2. Jane described three positive ways a Christian parent should parent their teens: communicating with them (even if it means you need to learn to text); praying for them—for every test, game, and problem; and making family time a priority. Are you coming up short on any of these? On which of these do you need to focus?

3. Jane and Catherine talked about boxes and perceived parental expectations. If you have been labeling or comparing your teens, take them out of the box you may have made. Be sure they understand that you do not expect them to be perfect.
4. John values the practical skills his father taught him. The "Purple Book" and "Rebekah Letter" gave absentee guidance. Do you have a son? Who is his main male role model? Dad, are you passing on your skills to your son? Mom, what emotional links do you have with your son?
5. Every family is different. What will be your spiritual legacy to your children? Houses, land, and money pale in comparison to the value of what you instill in them spiritually—truths and traditions that they will pass on to your grandchildren and great-grandchildren.

ABOUT THE AUTHOR

With her husband, Joy reared four children overseas in the countries of Thailand, Sri Lanka, and Malaysia. Normal teen developmental issues were compounded by living as third-culture kids. They survived to appreciate their overseas experiences, discover God's will in full-time Christian ministries, marry godly spouses, and dedicate their own children to the Lord. She now delights in being a part of the lives of ten grandchildren between the ages of six months and twenty-two years, making sure to remember their spiritual birthdays, send them a Scripture for each year, and communicating with them by whatever means—phone, text, e-mail, Facebook, cards, and "room and board"—whenever.

Chapter Eighteen

Relating to Young Adults

Susie Hawkins

The challenges of parenting can be daunting, no matter the age of the child, but the *young adult* stage can be one of the most challenging of all. During the teen years, the apron strings are greatly loosened. In the young adult years, not only are the apron strings cut, but in many cases, the apron is completely ignored or outright rejected. This rejection can be perplexing and distressing to a parent, especially when she has been fully involved in all areas of her child's life. Rather than *parenting* (and all that it implies) at this stage, parents may find themselves less needed and less consulted by their children. Young adults may frequently make important decisions, regardless of their parents' approval or opinion. In this sense, parenting no longer consists of *controlling* the children. This is a new day, the time for parental influence rather than parental domination.

In this chapter, the young adult stage of life will be considered as spanning from the college years to the post-college decade (late teens through early thirties). Moving away from home to college, job, or military is usually the first step in this process, and the final step would likely be the young adult's financial independence. These changes bring about a reinvention of the parent/child relationship to an adult/adult relationship.

Parents understand that this is a crucial stage. The most important decisions of life, with lifelong ramifications, are usually made during this period—whether to attend college and where; choice of mate, friends, vocation, hobbies, and life habits. The frustration of the parent at this stage is that there is so little a parent can *do* to alter his child's behavior or choices. However, faithfully praying for the child and working to establish a healthy relationship are the two areas that are always safe.

For the young adult, these years are exhilarating, if not slightly overwhelming. During this time his life becomes his own. No longer under the watchful eyes of parents, school, or home church, the young adult has the freedom to make his own life choices. This chapter will discuss characteristics of young adults and how parents can best relate to them, yes, even enjoy them.

UNDERSTANDING YOUR YOUNG ADULT

Gary Chapman has written an insightful book on this topic, *Parenting Your Adult Child*. These distinctives are helpful in understanding the cultural changes regarding this particular group:

- Adult children typically live more than one hundred miles away, often out of state.

- Parents hope to see their children for one big holiday a year, not every Sunday for dinner.

- Many adult children do not marry until their late twenties to thirties.

- Some adult children have live-in partners of the opposite sex, sharing their lives and sometimes their checking accounts, but not marrying. They are convinced marriage is too risky, at least for a while.

- Adult children value leisure time more than their parents and feel less loyalty to their jobs.[1]

These choices are felt keenly in the family circle, especially by parents who may be disappointed or displeased with those choices. Nevertheless, parents need to support and encourage their adult children in any way they can, while not violating their own principles.

THE GOAL: FROM PARENT TO FRIEND

Moving toward a relationship of friendship does not mean that one abdicates the parental role. This interaction is unique. Usually the maturing adult child acknowledges a need for a relationship with parents, although on a new level. Being a parent at this stage means advising when asked, working on a mutually satisfying adult friendship, and, above all else, praying for your child. Naturally there will be tensions in these areas, but avoiding judgmentalism and unnecessary negative comments will go a long way toward a positive relationship that is enjoyable to both parties. While this is uncharted territory, respecting your child and his choices will enable the parent to be present in an appropriate role.

THE EMOTIONAL HEALTH OF THE PARENT

Before exploring how an adult friendship can be nurtured with adult children, the parent needs to take an honest look at herself. One common pit-

---

[1] Gary Chapman, *Parenting Your Adult Child* (Chicago: Northfield, 1999), 14.

fall of moms especially is *needing to be needed*. This is the challenge of the *empty nest*—no more little birdies to nurture and care for on a daily basis, which is the role and identity of the mother. However, while child rearing requires extraordinary time and energy, your life is not meant to be child-centric. That stage of life is only for a season. Parents who lead productive and meaningful lives apart from their adult children are doing what is best for everyone.

Consider the story of Ron, whose parents were in their forties when he was born, having thought they would never be able to have children. Due to their age and this unexpected blessing, they showered their son with love and attention to the point of spoiling him in some ways. As he matured and began the natural process of pulling away, they clung to him for their emotional well-being. When Ron married, the situation intensified. While they loved their daughter-in-law, their son was no longer *theirs*, and they felt rejected when the newlyweds did not call for several days or include them in their weekend social plans. Ron lived with the burden of feeling that his parents' happiness depended on him. This resulted in the conflicting emotions of genuine love and respect for his parents but also guilt and resentment for their inability to release him from being the center of their lives. Fortunately, his wife was able to help him come to a place of understanding and respect for his parents while maintaining his independence.

A parent also needs to guard and cultivate her own relationships with her husband, other family members, and friends. If a child is making unwise choices, parents can find it difficult to think of anything else. But investing time and energy in others is important to maintaining a balance in one's own life. Personal growth experienced through travel, developing hobbies, or discovering new interests is always beneficial to the emotional and spiritual health of the parent.

RED FLAGS: STOP!

Barbara Rainey and Susan Yates, in their excellent book, *Barbara and Susan's Guide to the Empty Nest*, identify a classic mistake parents make at this stage. Knowing that they must let go of their children, many go to extremes, becoming either a *helicopter parent* or a *hands-off parent*.[2] Helicopter parents *hover*—constantly calling, e-mailing, or texting—trying to help solve every problem, as if the child were in middle school again. These parents are much too free in

---

[2] Barbara Rainey and Susan Yates, *Barbara and Susan's Guide to the Empty Nest* (Little Rock, AR: Family Life, 2008), 97.

giving their own time, money, and energy to their child, only to be frequently used or rebuffed. By hovering, the parents communicate to their child that they do not believe he can manage his own life. During this transition period, the adult child needs to develop his decision-making skills (usually by making mistakes) and learn to cope with the pressures of adulthood. Not giving a child space to do so only slows down this developmental process and weakens his self-confidence.

Helicopter parents need to ask themselves a hard question: "Am I actually trying to manipulate my child into good behavior?" By attaching strings, especially to financial help, parents actually hurt their child more than helping him. Adult children who are continually rescued by their parents will form a very unhealthy family dysfunction that inevitably spirals downward.

The opposite of the helicopter parent is the hands-off parent,[3] who heeds the advice that parents should not interfere in their children's lives once they are married or financially independent. Believing they are doing what is best for their children, they are actually missing great opportunities for input in their children's lives. There will invariably be times when the adult child simply wants the parent's company or wants to talk over life in general. The "hands-off" approach is hurtful to young adults—they need to know that they are important to their parents, despite the changes in relationship.

One young woman has said, "I wish my parents would show more love and interest in my husband's life. They seemed really to want to get to know him when we were dating but after the marriage, things changed."

Another young single noted of parents,

> We still want you around. We don't want you to disappear out of our lives, and we don't hate you. We want you to be our friends, but we want our space. We need balance between you being our parent and being our friend. We need you to be honest with us when our friends won't be. We want you to be the person that we want to talk to about our lives, not because you pry, but because we want to involve you in our lives. If we don't call you, we will soon.

Barbara Rainey and Susan Yates describe this stage very well: "At this season we are moving from being a coach to becoming a cheerleader."[4]

Another mistake parents frequently make is taking offense at their children's preferences, especially in regard to church (or lack of), entertainment, how they use their free time, how they spend their money, how they rear their

---

[3] Ibid., 99.
[4] Ibid., 101.

children, and where they choose to live. Unless these choices involve immorality, illegality, or something equally serious, keep quiet and do not take it personally. A relationship does not need to be harmed just because an adult child makes a choice that differs from the parent's. This is easier said than done, especially when the choices touch on issues upon which the parent places high value. It should also be noted that even though a parent may remain silent and try not to criticize or be judgmental, disapproval oozing from body language is hard to miss!

One of the most common complaints of adult children is the use of manipulative guilt even if the parent does so unconsciously. As someone once said, "Guilt is the gift that keeps on giving." Making children feel guilty about their shortcomings and lack of concern or communication never brings about the desired result. Rather the adult child becomes resentful and angry. If parents are not mindful of this, they can fall into the guilt trap, which is especially destructive in relating to young adults.

In today's culture, a chapter such as this must address stepparenting. Probably no family relationship is as precarious as a stepmom's with her stepchildren, and it can be very challenging. As one stepmom quipped, "Unless the Lord builds the house, the stepmom labors in vain."[5]

The stepparent dare not try to step into the role of mother (or father, in the opposite case). The friendship connection is by far the most effective in establishing a respectful and healthy relationship. If at all possible, try to stay out of generational conflicts that do not directly involve the stepparent. Frequently these family dynamics pit the stepparent against the stepchildren in competition for the attention or love of the parent/spouse. Taking small opportunities to get to know the stepchildren, showing concern and interest, and finding common ground will hopefully bring the family to a place of mutual respect and appreciation.

Of course, these same principles apply to the in-law relationship. It is a monumental mistake to try to parent a son-in-law or daughter-in-law without first establishing a good relationship. The parental relationship in this case is a privilege you earn, not one you can assume.

In considering the many pitfalls of "parenting" adult children, note that a myriad of helpful resources on this topic are available, including Christian counseling, which has helped thousands of struggling families address their problems within a biblical framework. A prudent person takes advantage of these resources and seeks godly counsel when family difficulties arise.

---

[5] Kali and Elizabeth Schnieders, *You're Not My Mom!* (Colorado Springs: NavPress, 2005), 21.

GREEN LIGHTS: GO!

One of the qualities young adults most appreciate is a parent who is transparent about her own struggles. As parents and their children learn to relate on a friendship level, being honest with one another is vital. You will not find a young adult anywhere who does not say he wants authenticity in his relationships, especially with his family. Something about a parent's admitting, "I don't know" or "I made a mistake" is very disarming and opens wide the door of communication. The child is made to feel respected and trusted on a whole new level. This is especially true as parents share their own spiritual joys and disappointments, helping young adults navigate these important years. As one mom said, "My walk with God is personal, but not private." In other words, she is willing to share what she has learned along the journey and is not afraid to admit she does not have answers for all problems. Telling your story to your adult child (when solicited) can lead to a better understanding of your family and the way God has led you. Throughout childhood and adolescence, parents shield a child from anything that might cause anxiety or threaten his sense of security. But this is the time to let them in. They can handle it, and you will not lose status in their eyes; you will likely gain it. This simple gesture can be an important part of the transition from being "parent," who takes care of the child, to "peer" who develops a symbiotic, mutually encouraging relationship with the adult child.

The flip side of this is also true. Listening to your young adult's opinions and thoughts communicates respect and value. Age does not necessarily determine maturity, and the parent may be surprised at the wisdom of the young adult. Any healthy relationship, including this one, depends on *give-and-take.*

Another essential in creating a healthy dynamic between generations is actively encouraging young married children to honor their spouses as well as in-laws and extended family. Support your adult children in those relationships by pointing out the positives (you may have to look hard) and helping them work through misunderstandings or difficulties. Save any criticism or complaints about the in-laws until you are with your spouse or trusted friends.

All parents must observe boundaries regarding their child's privacy. Always calling before dropping by their home, asking permission to see or talk to grandchildren, and avoiding nosy questions regarding money or personal matters are basic rules that communicate respect and common courtesy. It also needs to be understood that the more enlightened party (parent or child) holds the greater responsibility in doing everything possible to make these interactions successful.

One mother has said her philosophy is "Mouth shut, but door open!" This approach is good; if followed, it can lead to a good rapport between parents and their adult children.

PRAYER-ENTING THE PRODIGAL

The heartbreaking topic of parenting a prodigal child must be addressed in this context. As so often happens, a child can be raised in a strong Christian environment by loving parents who actively serve the Lord, only to rebel and deliberately make bad choices that end in serious trouble or a rejection of the Christian faith. The irony of this situation is that a sibling raised in exactly the same way may enthusiastically embrace everything the parent has taught. Since parents tend to see adult children as their *report card* on parenting skills, the consequences of this rebellion are terribly painful. If a child *fails* by making choices the parents would never endorse, they conclude that they failed their child, even though the sibling may succeed in a career. Parents need to remember that their *report card* from the Lord is in the next life, not this one. Human nature is mysterious and difficult to understand at times. Why one child obediently follows Christ and a sibling deliberately chooses a rebellious path has perplexed parents of every generation. Even the very first married couple, living in the perfect garden of Eden, had two children who chose drastically different paths. Parents of prodigals, you are not alone.

While a parent should not *preach* to a wayward child, which rarely accomplishes the desired result, it is always appropriate to pray. *Prayer-enting* is a term coined by the mom of a young man who had "de-converted"[6] from Christ. Knowing that there was little she could say or do to convince him of his dreadful mistake, she committed herself to intense prayer for this child. This is the experience of most parents of prodigals—striving to show unconditional love while not continually rescuing the child or excusing his behavior. One mother describes her approach this way,

> My husband and I continue to use the same vocabulary we've always used, not avoiding spiritual words. We tell our son how we are praying for him, about answered prayer in our own lives, about people we know and have been praying for. The natural thing to do when one's child indicates he doubts everything he once professed to believe and hold dear is to avoid sharing spiritual things. Maybe it is to avoid conflict or out of fear that he will cease to communicate, but we feel strongly that we must continue to be true to what we

---

[6] *De-conversion* is a term used by those who at one time professed to be Christian but have chosen to become atheist or agnostic.

know. We also forward words of encouragement to our children from others and tell them when someone asks about them and indicates they are praying for them. We don't insist that they believe as we do, or condemn or whine about their spiritual condition. We leave that to God and work hard to keep the communication moving.

This mom's key sentence is that she and her husband do not complain to their child about his lack of commitment to Christ or preach to him. By not doing so, they demonstrate that they still love and respect their adult child, although they remain heartbroken over his rejection of Christ. These wise parents have refused to burn the bridge of their relationship with their son, choosing to do everything they can to model the unconditional love of God to him.

Parents of prodigals desperately need emotional and spiritual support from friends and family. Unfortunately, because of the perceived shame associated with prodigals, many parents live with enormous pain. As the family of God, we are responsible to encourage and pray for them.

CONCLUSION

The relationship between a parent and adult child can be one of the most enjoyable of life or one of the most difficult. By understanding the change in the parental role during this transitional stage of life, the parent can greatly maximize the bond between the generations. Recognizing that parental *control* has morphed into parental *influence* is vital at this stage, and parents frequently need to remind themselves of this truth.

There are no perfect parents and no perfect children. Freely giving forgiveness, grace, and unconditional love (and a big dose of humor doesn't hurt) will go a long way in creating harmonious family relationships. Scripture is clear. Children are a gift from God: "behold, children are a heritage from the LORD, the fruit of the womb a reward" (Ps. 127:3). There is no age limit on this observation of the psalmist, and so with prayer and wise actions, both parents and adult children can enjoy a rich relationship for many years.

PUTTING THE PRINCIPLES INTO PRACTICE

1. Read the story of the prodigal son found in Luke 15. Look at this story from the perspective of the adult child and his father. What do you see as elements that relate to the content of this chapter? Note verses 12, 13, 16, 17, 20, and 32.

2. What points would you add to the "Red Flags"? And "Green Lights"?
3. How can a parent best influence her adult child toward a Christian commitment?

ABOUT THE AUTHOR

Susie Hawkins is the mother of two adult daughters and the grandmother of five. She frequently speaks and teaches on topics that relate to the biblical framework of family and life in general. As everyone else, she is trying to figure out life as it happens. She holds two master's degrees from The Criswell College in Dallas, Texas, and is the author of *From One Ministry Wife to Another.* She is married to Dr. O. S. Hawkins, president of GuideStone Financial Resources of the Southern Baptist Convention.

Chapter Nineteen

Spiritual Formation through Family Worship

Malcolm and Karen Yarnell

A Fort Worth mechanic once told me that he had owned, rebuilt, and sold sixty-five cars by the time he was eighteen years old. As a child, he must have been taking apart and rebuilding everything imaginable. This man then studied at different mechanic shops; after further developing his skills, he opened his own shop for repairing foreign cars. What started as a natural gift, thinking mechanically, was fine-tuned and became his livelihood.

As a Christian parent, you will naturally influence your children for Christ through the actions and choices you make for the family. You desire for them to grow in faith in Christ. This chapter is designed to help you fine-tune your skills as you spiritually nurture your family.

Family worship can occur in a variety of settings: all family members gathering to read the Bible and pray, memorizing Scripture with Mom, having a family worship service while on vacation, offering biblically informed prayers of thankfulness at the end of the day, reading Scripture around the dinner table. Whatever the setting, the outcome of incorporating worship in the life of the family is that God's Word has been opened, God is glorified, the family is drawn closer together, the children are discipled, prayers are offered, and relationships are strengthened.

FAMILY WORSHIP

We gather together around God's Word to honor the Lord as being worthy of whatever he would ask of us.

First, you must establish a biblical basis for intentionally gathering as a family to worship. Then practical ideas are suggested for this special family time, followed by words of encouragement for parents as they share the truths of the loving Father and his Son through the guidance and strength of the Holy Spirit.

THE "WHY" OF FAMILY WORSHIP

A primary reason for family worship is to obey the Lord's instruction to families:

> Hear, O Israel: The LORD our God, the LORD is one. You shall love the LORD your God with all your heart and with all your soul and with all your might. And these words that I command you today shall be on your heart. You shall teach them diligently to your children, and shall talk of them when you sit in your house, and when you walk by the way, and when you lie down, and when you rise. (Deut. 6:4–7)

These instructions were given to the children of Israel as they were about to enter the Promised Land. On the journey, and in the promised dwelling, they would be tempted and tested. God's provision for the ensuing battles was his instruction to love him and know his commandments. Loving the Lord and knowing his Word would be the strength and shield they would need for the battles ahead. In the same way, your desire for your children is that they be victorious in the spiritual battles they will experience and that they dwell in the presence of the Lord. They will be tried and tested, as were the children of Israel.

In the New Testament, the instruction to parents to teach their children is coupled with what Jesus described as the Great Commandment: "Love the Lord your God . . ." (Matt. 22:37). Loving the Lord is interwoven with knowing his commandments (1 John 5:3). If the desire for your children is that they grow to be mighty in the Lord, then they must be taught his commands. The all-encompassing nature of the Great Commandment—*all* your heart, *all* your soul, *all* your might—is met with an all-encompassing commandment: *Teach when you sit, walk, lie down, and rise.*

THE "WHO" OF FAMILY WORSHIP

Have you ever tried to explain the Trinity to a three-year-old? I have. Usually, after I, the mother, put in my two cents, I send them to their theologian father. The exchange is often amusing. He will on occasion use "big" words, and they will respond by pretending to understand. For all of us, young and old, understanding the unity of our one God, who is also three persons, is an act of faith. Yet, in family worship, we as a family have a tangible way to live in the unity and love of our God.

Jesus prayed to the Father, "I in them and you in me, that they may become perfectly one, so that the world may know that you sent me and loved them even as you loved me" (John 17:23). Through times of family worship, we are developing that very love and unity. Being together, we direct our worship toward the God of love and share his love with one another.

While the "who" of family worship begins with a focus on God, it continues with the gathering of the family members. The goal is for all of the family to attend, but that is not always possible, considering each person's schedule of school, work, and other activities. For our family, evening gatherings have worked best. Sometimes, when evening activities are scheduled, we have our "Bible Time" at the dinner table, after eating and before other activities. Other times, we gather just before bedtime. Other families may find that starting the day with a morning Bible reading is best for their schedules.

When one parent is an unbeliever, the believing parent still has the opportunity to bless the children through worship. Recently, a woman shared with me that in her childhood home her mother was a Christian, but her father was not. Her mother was faithful to take the children to church as much as the father allowed. As a child, she saw her mother open her Bible and pray regularly. Her mother acted in a godly, kind way toward her husband. She shared Christ with her children. Today, her daughter is serving the Lord. If you are a single parent or are married to a nonbeliever, please be encouraged that the Lord will honor your efforts as you share Christ with your children.

THE "WHAT, HOW, WHEN, AND WHERE" OF FAMILY WORSHIP

God assigned the home to be the primary place for learning his Word and receiving instruction in how to live life his way (Deut. 6:1–9; Prov. 22:6). Though our family worship occurs throughout the day in a variety of forms, the focal point is a time when the whole family gathers to have Bible reading, prayer, and music. We call this "Bible Time." In a sense, the husband/father is the pastor of his family. Jonathan Edwards said, "Every Christian family ought to be as it were a little church, consecrated to Christ, and wholly influenced and governed by his rules."[1] The basic structure of the gathering for our family is for my husband to read a Scripture passage followed by sharing prayer requests, praying, and singing a hymn or chorus by all the family. This time together, which takes place three or four times a week, usually lasts ten to fifteen minutes. (Occasionally, the family plays a game of *Uno* before or after "Bible Time.") This very simple time is formative in the lives of our family members.

---

[1] Jonathan Edwards, "Farewell Sermon," in *The Works of Jonathan Edwards*, ed. Edward Hickman, vol. 1 (Edinburgh: The Banner of Truth Trust, 1990), 206.

Family worship might also include a creative activity or game that helps interpret the truth of the Scripture. Children may want to lead one part of the worship time—for example, teaching the family a new worship song or playing an instrument, reciting a memory verse, or reading the Scripture passage. Always, the focus must be worship of the Lord and hearing from his Word. Fun times together are very important to the family, but it is the truth of God's Word that will change a life for eternity.

For the family that is not musically inclined, worship and hymn compact disks are available to help. With many styles of Christian music from which to choose, every family can find something to suit particular preferences. Hymns are a treasure because they teach rich doctrine. We have chosen to purchase each child a hymnal, which is often used in "Bible Time."

Although "Bible Time" is the corporate worship for our family, spiritual nurture takes place throughout the day.

⌒ IDEAS FOR SHARING CHRIST ⌒
in the Family Context

- Do Bible studies designed for children's discipleship.
- Review what was taught in Sunday school.
- Read children's books about God, the life of Christ, or prayer.
- Read Christian allegory, such as *The Pilgrim's Progress* or The Chronicles of Narnia.
- Lead the children in prayer throughout the day, especially in prayers of thanksgiving.
- Teach Scripture one-on-one to each child.
- Post specific verses in the children's areas of the home, such as by the child's bed or at the bathroom mirror (you may use pens of all colors to write a verse on the mirror and easily erase for a new verse).
- Memorize Scripture.
- Ask the children to pray for the family needs and for others.

Helping your children memorize Scripture is a gift that will bless them for the rest of their lives. I was challenged in this area when I heard that Ruth Bell Graham spent Sunday afternoons helping her children learn Bible verses. Our church offers programs that require children to repeat memory verses. Having them recite them aloud helps them learn the verses as well as expressive public speaking skills. One friend said that every time her childhood family went on a trip, they quoted Psalm 121. Even today, she remembers and can quote this psalm.

A WORD ABOUT PRAYER

A key component to family worship is prayer time. Through prayer, the children learn to bear the burdens of others. They also see firsthand that God is real and is at work. Deuteronomy 6 concludes with the child asking the father why he is to know God's commands, and the father relays the story of God's deliverance. As adults, many times we have seen the Lord work in our personal lives as well as in the lives of others. The children will grow in faith as they see the Lord answer prayer and work in the lives of people for whom they have prayed.

Recently, my sister called from Kansas City to request prayer for her father-in-law, who was quickly deteriorating from illness. They were going to visit him, hoping to be able to share Christ with him one last time. We went through the house and asked all the children to pray for this man. Minutes later, we received a text saying that he had prayed to receive Christ as Savior. When we told the children, they were filled with joy. Their faith was strengthened because they exercised their spiritual muscles and helped carry the burden through prayer. They saw God at work. "Let them thank the Lord for his steadfast love, for his wondrous works to the children of man!" (Ps. 107:8).

Philippians 4:6–7 instructs us to pray about everything. May I encourage you to pray for your children specifically? Pray about everything! Our words to them, though important, are not as lasting or as influential as our prayers for them. The Lord knows what they need before we do, and he is the loving Father who desires to care for them (Matt. 6:32). One of my favorite prayers is "A Parent's Prayer" by St. Augustine:

> O Heavenly Father, I commend the soul(s) of my children to thee. Be thou their God and Father; and mercifully supply whatever is wanting in me through frailty or negligence. Strengthen them to overcome the corruptions of the world, to resist all solicitations to evil, whether from within or without; and deliver them from the secret snares of the enemy. Pour thy grace into their heart(s), and confirm and multiply in them the gifts of thy Holy Spirit, that they may daily grow in grace and in knowledge of our Lord Jesus Christ; and so faithfully serving thee here, may come to rejoice in thy presence hereafter. Through the same Christ our Lord. Amen.

A WORD ABOUT THE LORD'S DAY

The Puritans considered the Sabbath, or the day of worship, as being a family day—an important time for all the family to be together, whether attending worship, eating family meals, talking about the things of the Lord, or even resting and relaxing away from the week's work. This day of worship and rest set a rhythm for worship of and service to Christ and for a balance in working and resting.

One component in family worship should certainly be the participation of all the family in corporate worship. Parents must not settle for simply delivering their children to church. Rather the family together must honor the Lord's Day (Heb. 10:25).

THE "LARKSPUR" PRINCIPLE

Helen and Jerry built a house on an acre lot in a small semirural area. The first year they planted a lovely purple larkspur flower in the front flower bed. Noting that the soil was unhealthy, that winter they dug up the flower bed and spread the soil on the back slope of the property, near the creek. The next spring, to their surprise and to the delight of the entire neighborhood, the larkspur bloomed with its deep, bright purple color spreading across the slope. It was lovely. Every year the seeds multiplied into more and more bright purple flowers filling the area. They had no idea that the seeds would germinate into such a glorious scene. With children, you are sowing seeds. Sometimes, the children seem as if they are not listening, they defy what you have said, or the worship time seems routine. Believe the Lord's promise to the sower:

> So shall my word be that goes out from my mouth;
>   it shall not return to me empty,
> but it shall accomplish that which I purpose,
>   and shall succeed in the thing for which I sent it. (Isa. 55:11)

A SPECIAL WORD FOR FATHERS

This section is written specifically for fathers from another father. Mothers may consider copying and giving these pages to their husbands. A man will treasure his wife forever for this small gesture as in so doing she is affirming the important role of the father in the family.

Every father naturally wants to bless his children with the best he has to give. When we as fathers give to our children like this, we are reflecting the fatherhood of God. We love our children because God the Father loves his children. The fatherhood of God is the source and example for our own fatherhood to our children. We love our children when we mirror the love God has for us. Let me explain this through four great biblical truths. Afterward, we will determine the best gift for our children.

FOUR GREAT TRUTHS ABOUT FATHERHOOD

First, note that God's eternal nature is love. In essence, "God is love" (1 John 4:8, 16). The one God, existing in and from eternity as three persons—the Father, the Son, and the Holy Spirit—shared and shares in this mutual and glorious love before and above all creation (John 17:5, 22–23; Rom. 5:5). At the beginning of creation, God selflessly shared this divine love with creation through bringing all things into existence (Gen. 1:1–3). God made himself the Father of all people through the one man, Adam (Acts 17:26–29). He loved us so much that he created us in his own image (Gen. 1:26–28).

Second, sadly, beginning with the same Adam, humanity rebelled against God and rejected him as their Father (Gen. 2:15–3:24). One cannot emphasize enough how horrible our rejection of God's love is. The Father loved us and we rebelled against him, believing the lies of the tempter (Gen. 3:1–13). Having sinned against God and marred his image, we were removed from his presence (Gen. 3:23–24). Spiritual death is exclusion from God's holy presence; physical death follows. The punishment of eternal death awaits the souls of all those, including fathers and their children, who sin against God (Ezek. 18:4).

Third, like the father of the Prodigal Son, God the Father has never stopped loving us, even as we sold ourselves into the slavery of sin (Luke 15:11–32). Despite our rejection of him, the Father never stopped loving us. To restore his rebellious children to a proper relationship with him, God the Father sent his only and eternally begotten Son, Jesus Christ, into the world (John 3:16; Hebrews 1). Through the apostles, God the Father reveals to us the truth that this Jesus is the Messiah whom we need and that he is our only hope. Jesus Christ is literally the Son of the living God (Matt. 16:16–17). God loved us with the greatest love by giving us his Son (1 John 4:9).

Fourth, when this Word from God is proclaimed, the Holy Spirit convicts us of the truth about our sin, judgment, and the righteousness available in Christ (John 16:8–11). Those who will believe in the Son of God have their relationship with the Father restored (John 3:9–16). Those who receive the Son of God truly become children of God through faith in him (John 1:12–13). Those who believe in the Son of God are born again through the Holy Spirit (John 3:3–8). Today, God is the Father of all those who believe in his Son. The rebellion of humanity against the Father has been overcome through the death and resurrection of his Son. This reconciliation becomes ours individually through faith and regeneration by the Holy Spirit.

If perchance you do not believe in Jesus Christ as your personal Savior, please ask God to forgive you of your sins through the death and resurrection of his only begotten Son. "We implore you on behalf of Christ, be reconciled to God" (2 Cor. 5:20). Now, at this very moment, you may become a child of God. If you want to be the best father possible to your children, you must know God the Father as his child. Turn away from sin and death, and turn to God in Christ! Believe in Jesus Christ and confess that he is the Lord (Rom. 10:9–10). What a loving Father we have! He gave us life and offers us new life!

THE BEST A FATHER CAN GIVE

Through Scripture, we know that God the Father gave us life and offers new life. He loved us through creating us, but we rejected him; afterwards, he loved us through redeeming us by his Son and through his Spirit. The Son of God is also known as the Word of God (John 1:1, 14). In giving us his Word, the Father showed us the best way we can give to our children. Why is the Word the best gift that the Father could give? Because the Word, also identified with Scripture, allows us to come again into the Father's presence (Heb. 4:12–16).

Like the Father who gave us his Word, the best gift a Christian father can give to his children is the Word of God! In Deuteronomy 6, Israelite fathers were commanded to teach the truth about God to their children. The Word of God is to be given to the family in everything said and done. In other words, a father's responsibility does not end with purchasing a Bible and giving it to his child. Giving an appropriate version of the Bible is a good place to start, but we must go beyond that. We are to teach the Word of God to our children "diligently" (Deut. 6:7)—with all our effort, sharply and constantly.

A father is not to give God's Word to his family once or even once in a while, but regularly, daily, even hourly: "You shall teach them diligently to your children, and shall talk of them when you sit in your house, and when you walk by the way, and when you lie down, and when you rise" (Deut. 6:7). The Israelites were even supposed to adorn their houses and their bodies with God's Word (Deut. 6:8–9).

In my own family, we seek to open the Word of God daily in a formal time of family worship, except on Sundays and Wednesdays when we are at church. We simply open the Word of God together in a relaxed setting: (1) I read a passage; (2) we discuss that passage's implications; (3) we gather prayer requests and one of us leads in prayer; (4) my wife often leads us in a short song. The positive changes in us, which are caused by this simple but profound and life-changing routine of the daily reading of, and hourly reflection upon, the Word of God, are wonderful.

As men consider the legacies they want to leave their children, they often think of education, good experiences, and wealth. These are all good things, and we should give them to our children. However, the best thing that we can give our family is the Word of God. The Word of God is eternal. Everything else in this life will fade away, "but the word of our God will stand forever!" (Isa. 40:8). Give your family the Word of God. That is the father's responsibility as the head of the household. That memory is the best and most long lasting for your wife and children.

PUTTING THE PRINCIPLES INTO PRACTICE

1. Reflect on your childhood and young adult years:

   - How were you spiritually nurtured?
   - What did you know about God and his character from these relationships?

2. Take a spiritual assessment based on Deuteronomy 6:

   - Do you love the Lord with all your heart?
   - Do you spend time learning his commands and delighting yourself in his Word?
   - Do you share the stories of how the Lord has worked in your life with your children?

3. Meditate on Psalms 1, 19, and 119.
4. Name one thing that the Lord would have you do to nurture your family spiritually. Act on that one thing.
5. Choose to pray in a purposeful and focused way (Phil. 4:6–7).

ABOUT THE AUTHORS

Dr. Malcolm B. Yarnell III serves at Southwestern Baptist Theological Seminary in Fort Worth, Texas. Among many roles, he is associate professor of systematic theology and director of the Center for Theological Research. Malcolm and Karen parent five children from young adult to preschool age. Karen has completed a master of divinity degree from Southeastern Baptist Theological Seminary. She is a wife, mom, and Bible teacher. As she has written this chapter, she has had her hair brushed by a four-year-old, the dog jump on the bed, and the children ask a myriad of questions about language, math, and geography, since she also homeschools them.

Part Four

THE PRACTICAL
ASPECTS OF
ESTABLISHING A HOME

Chapter Twenty

Life Management Skills

Rhonda Harrington Kelley

GOD GIVES LIFE

God is the giver of life! He created the earth and sea, then said "It is good." He created the birds and fish, then said, "It is good." He created man and woman, then said, "It is *very* good." To humans, God gave life as well as purpose and responsibility. Throughout their life span, Christian men and woman seek to know God's will and fulfill their callings. Life management skills are necessary for people who use time wisely and accomplish personal goals.

From childhood, I have always wanted to stay busy and be involved in many activities. To reach that goal I have to discipline my time and manage my life. I admit that I have not always been successful, but I have learned some helpful strategies along the way. As a Christian, I have always prayed for God's guidance and searched his Word for divine direction. Philippians 3:13–14 has become my biblical basis for proper priorities. God's perfect plan for life management is to *focus on one thing*. As you focus on knowing God, he will help you forget past failures and move forward to accomplish the goal and win the prize. Focus requires discipline, a key element of a well-managed life.

In this chapter, life management skills will be suggested. Different stages of life will be described, together with a plan for balanced living. The importance of ministry, the impact of stress and pressure, and the influence of time management strategies will be emphasized. Ultimately, meaningful life will be the prize to those who "seek first the kingdom of God and his righteousness" (Matt. 6:33).

LIFE REQUIRES MANAGEMENT

Someone has said that if you do not plan your life, someone else will. How true! Every woman should try to manage her own life and determine her priorities with the help of the Lord. If you do not, more organized people will eagerly help fill your day and try to control your destiny. You must put some life management skills into practice if you desire to use your time to accomplish God's purposes.

In *Ordering Your Private World*, Gordon MacDonald presents four laws of unseized (unplanned) time. He suggests negative results when time is not managed. These practical principles have been adapted to describe unmanaged lives:

- Unmanaged lives reveal personal weaknesses.
- Unmanaged lives are influenced by dominant people.
- Unmanaged lives surrender to the demands of all emergencies.
- Unmanaged lives get involved in activities that gain public acclaim and are not necessarily important.[1]

If you want your life to matter and you want to determine your own course, begin now to manage your life. Emphasize your strengths, not your weaknesses. Seek leadership from the Lord and receive wise counsel from others, but manage your own life. Respond to urgent emergencies, but accomplish your daily goals. Invest your energy in work that has eternal benefits. Without some structure and discipline, your life will become disorganized and unproductive.

Disorganization is costly. Everyone gets disorganized at times. But, when signs of disorganization emerge, it is time to manage your life intentionally. Signs of disorganization might include the following:

- cluttered personal space (home, office, car, etc.)
- forgotten appointments or missed deadlines
- energy in unproductive tasks
- poor attitude and lower self-esteem
- less intimacy with God and strained personal relationships

Disorganization should be a wake-up call. The time has come to get organized and manage your life more efficiently.

Since I am naturally organized, I can usually keep up with the demands of my life. However, when my life is extra busy and piles begin to grow, I get anxious. I do not like to be disorganized in my life or cluttered in my workplace or home. I am a real believer in spring cleaning. When springtime arrives, I begin changing my closets and cleaning my desk. I follow the *1-2-3 Rule* and sort my belongings to determine whether I should *keep, give, or throw away*. When I manage my life and unclutter my home, it is amazing how much better I feel. Life requires management!

LIFE PROGRESSES THROUGH STAGES

While life has a definite beginning and ending, it also moves through seasons or stages. In general, women experience four life seasons, which can be associ-

---

[1] Cf. Gordon MacDonald, "MacDonald's Laws of Unmanaged Time," in *Ordering Your Private World* (Nashville: Thomas Nelson, 2003), 88–93.

ated with the seasons of the year. Springtime is the season of youth and growth; summer, of nurturing and productivity; fall or autumn, of maturing and harvest; winter, of calm completion and eventual death.[2] Effective life management adapts to each season of life. In the same way God promised an orderly progression of the seasons (Gen. 8:22), Christians should seek to have an orderly life in every stage. This requires some adoption of life management skills.

In *The Life Ready Woman*, Shaunti Feldhahn and Robert Lewis suggest ten stages of a woman's life—each impacting time and emotions. Consider them as you seek to manage your life:

1. Single adult
2. Single and engaged
3. Newly married, no children
4. Married with preschoolers
5. Married with grade-schoolers
6. Married, with young-adult children
7. Married, empty nester
8. Married in-law, grandparent
9. Late-in-life, widow
10. Glorified saint[3]

These generalizations may not perfectly fit every woman's life. Those who never marry, those who divorce, and those who do not have children will not experience every stage. However, almost every woman progresses through each stage at some time during her life. Understanding life stages helps you manage your own life and encourage others as they manage theirs.

Feldhahn and Lewis also recommend four principles that can affect decisions you make in any season or stage of life.[4]

☞ LIFELONG DECISION-MAKING PRINCIPLES

1. There is a time for everything.
2. Your core callings never go away.
3. A choice for one thing is a choice against another.
4. Make choices appropriate to your season.

---

[2] Helen Young and Billie Silvey, *Time Management for Christian Women* (Grand Rapids, MI: Zondervan, 1990), 206.
[3] Shaunti Feldhahn and Robert Lewis, *The Life Ready Woman: Thriving in a Do-It-All World* (Nashville: B&H Publishing Group, 2011), 107–37.
[4] Ibid.

I have already lived through several seasons of life. You could say that I am in the autumn years. Because I am a baby boomer, I am in denial about my age and always consider myself a young adult. In fact, our Sunday school department is Young Married 7 rather than Median Adults. I have moved into adulthood and marriage and now find myself in those subsequent years of life. Because my husband and I were not able to have children, I skipped several typical stages. Our childlessness greatly impacted my life, quickly bringing me to the stage where I have time for work and ministry. Life management skills must adapt across the years. Life progresses through stages.

LIFE NEEDS BALANCE

One important life management skill is maintaining balance. Many people can manage one or two areas of their lives, but few can balance all areas of life. Lifelong discipline is needed to maintain balance or equilibrium.

Because a Christian's life should always flow out of her relationship with the Lord, work on spiritual growth is essential. However, every Christian should also develop in other areas—physical, spiritual, mental, and social. Each area is important and is related to the others.

Balance involves even distribution or steady positioning. In our academic courses for women at New Orleans Baptist Theological Seminary, we teach the importance of balance in women's ministry. A healthy, biblically solid women's program will balance inreach and outreach, discipleship and evangelism, as well as personal growth and ministry within the church. We often share this quotation with the ladies in our classes: "Consumption without contribution makes for a stuffed Christian; contribution without consumption makes for a shallow Christian."[5] How true! Spiritual growth and Christian service are both components of a balanced life.

Life balance refers to the proper prioritizing of life and work. Many fields of study include principles of balance. In physics, a balance is an equalized weight. In art, balance refers to the distribution of lines. In finance, balance equals the amount of money in an account. In fitness, balance is the positioning of the body based on equilibrium, senses, and muscular movement. All areas of life are dependent on balance.

All these strategies must be practiced in order to maintain a balanced life. Even scheduling time away from work—time to enjoy yourself and your family—is vital to your personal productivity. Working without any breaks does

---

[5] Chris Adams (Women's Enrichment and Ministers' Wives Specialist in Training and Events for LifeWay Christian Resources of the Southern Baptist Convention) has popularized her "all-time favorite quote" but denies being its author.

not fuel creativity. When you are worn out, you are less productive. When you have proper rest, you are rejuvenated and ready to work more effectively.[6]

⌒ TIPS ⌒
for Work-Life Balance

- Build downtime into your schedule.
- Drop activities that sap your time or energy.
- Rethink your errands.
- Get moving physically.
- Remember that a little relaxation goes a long way.

My husband and I work diligently to maintain balance in our lives. We *work* hard and we *play* hard. Our days are filled with meaningful ministry. Yet, we try to build a rhythm of rest and relaxation into our schedule. We both love to read, travel, and see good movies. Early in our marriage we began an annual commitment to establish and evaluate our priorities. To achieve balance, we identify six life areas and set specific goals for each:

⌒ SIX LIFE AREAS ⌒
for Goal Setting

Spiritual
church, outreach, Bible study

Mental
school, study, reading

Physical
exercise, diet, dress

Family
husband, children, parents,
in-laws, brothers/sisters

Financial
tithe, save, share, reduce debt

Social
entertainment, vacations, projects,
community involvement

---

[6] Jen Uscher, "5 Tips for Better Work-Life Balance," *Web*MD feature, http://www.webmd.com/balance/guide /5-strategies-for-life-balance.

Specific goals in each area encourage balance in life. To maintain this balance is not easy. Natural inclinations and emergency situations constantly disrupt plans, causing imbalance. Employ some life management skills and establish some boundaries to regain balance in your life. It has been said that "balance is not better time management, but better boundary management." Life needs balance.

LIFE INVOLVES MINISTRY

A well-balanced life includes personal enrichment and ministry involvement. Every Christian needs to grow spiritually while also serving others. Busy Christians must manage their lives so that there is adequate time for ministry. Whether a lay leader or a professional in ministry, every Christian must care for the needs of others.

In *Life Management for Busy Women*, Elizabeth George suggests ten life disciplines. Several of them seem applicable to this discussion of managing your ministry in life. To ensure time for ministry now and throughout your life, you should try to practice these disciplines below.[7]

ᥫ DISCIPLINES ᥫ
for Managing Ministry Time

- Determine and develop your spiritual gifts.
- Pray for ministry opportunities.
- Accept the challenge to grow and be stretched.
- Support others in ministry.
- Pray for your pastors and spiritual leaders.
- Don't neglect your family for ministry.
- Decide that ministry is for life.

Ministry is not only commanded by God, it gives meaning and purpose to life. God desires for his children to be a part of his work on earth, and he blesses those who serve obediently. Ministry is an eternal investment in the lives of others. Though time and energy are required, God honors those who do his work. Paul expressed it this way: "Be steadfast, immovable, always abounding in the work of the Lord, knowing that in the Lord your labor is not in vain" (1 Cor. 15:58).

What a motivation for ministry! No labor is wasted, no work is insignifi-

---

[7] Elizabeth George, *Life Management for Busy Women: Living Out God's Plan with Passion and Purpose* (Eugene, OR: Harvest House, 2002), 139–47.

cant, and no effort is temporary when done for the Lord. My husband and I work hard to include personal ministry in our lives of professional ministry. Even though our livelihood is earned in ministry, we make every attempt to serve the Lord from our hearts. I am very involved in our local church, serving as a volunteer in the welcome ministry and as director of the women's ministry. At the seminary, we participate in special mission projects such as disaster relief training and mission fairs. In our city, we get involved in community ministries such as work days at local mission centers. And we enthusiastically support friends on mission trips through prayer and giving. This summer a faculty child is serving in Ghana as an intern for a children's autism center. It has been a blessing to give to her financially, pray for her faithfully, and read her blogs frequently.

Though ministry is a vocational calling, it must also become a lifestyle. Seek always to be involved in service to others. Invest your time in the lives of others, meeting their needs and sharing Christ with them. Keep your eyes on Christ and your heart open to others. Never get too busy with activities to take advantage of opportunities for ministry. Let the Lord fill your days with his work and his ways. Life involves ministry.

LIFE CAUSES PRESSURE

Life does cause pressure because its activities can make you very busy. Even the most organized person feels the inherent pressure of life. And even the most efficient managers experience the pressure of time constraints. Everyone is pressured by life—it is not a matter of *if* but *when*. It has been said that you have just come out of a storm, you are in a storm, or you are going to face a storm. So, pressure is a fact of life.

The Bible teaches how to respond to the inevitable trials in life. "Count it all joy, my brothers, when you meet trials of various kinds, for you know that the testing of your faith produces steadfastness. And let steadfastness have its full effect, that you may be perfect and complete, lacking in nothing" (James 1:2–4). Pressure is a certainty of life. When it comes, Christians are to respond to pressure with great joy. Though difficult from the human perspective, faith in God produces joy as it strengthens and matures the Christian facing adversity. And a crown of life is promised to those who endure (James 1:12).

Though life may bring major disasters and personal heartbreak, most often stress and pressure come from the ordinary demands of life. Let me suggest several "time savers" for these "time wasters."

1. *Trying to do everything at once.* Time is wasted and pressure is added when you busy yourself doing too many things at the same time. Instead, set priorities. Determine what is most important and do that first before going to the next task.

2. *Trying to do everything yourself.* Whether you want control or you like the way you do things, there is no way you alone can do everything, so learn to delegate. Seek help at home, at church, or in the community. Ask others to do their parts; then oversee the work.

3. *Reluctance to say no.* It is so easy and much nicer to say yes. But then you find yourself overcommitted and frustrated. Learn to say no—and say it with your teeth showing (smile). Seek God's direction for your response, sometimes yes and other times no.

4. *Letting the telephone interrupt.* Today our phones are with us everywhere we go. They can interfere with our work and relationships. Phone conversations and texting can waste a lot of time. Make the phone work for you. Do not answer calls or texts when at the table or talking with someone. Callers can leave a message allowing you to respond when it is more convenient. Set aside times for phone calls, texting, and e-mailing each day, but do not let them control you.

5. *Putting things off.* Small things become huge when put off. The work stacks up and multiplies, so do it now. Tackle each task as it arises. Do not put it off and let it pile up. Do it and check it off the list. Time is saved and pressure is reduced.

Although you cannot always control the pressures of your life, you can control many things. Stay focused on God and his Word. Seek to do his will and not just your own. Try not to overschedule your life, and do not forget to take some time off. Demonstrate flexibility when emergencies arise. Pressures in life will come, but respond to them in joy and confidence, knowing that your faith will be strengthened. Life causes pressure.

LIFE TAKES TIME

Meaningful relationships and work require time and energy. One of life's greatest challenges is time management. Every age and stage of life demands the discipline of time.

Did you know there are three basic facts about time that cannot be changed?

1. *We all have the same amount of time.* Everyone has twenty-four hours in a day, seven days in a week, fifty-two weeks in a year. Though some people seem more productive, we all have 24/7.

2. *We have all the time we need.* God who created the days and the nights gave us exactly the amount of time we need—no more, no less. Our challenge is to use our time wisely because time is valuable to us and to God.

3. *When you are pressured by time, it means you are doing the wrong things or you are doing the right things the wrong way.* You may be filling your time with unnecessary tasks. Sometimes even good things are the wrong things for you at the time, and often you waste time with inefficiency. Master the shortcuts and make the most of your time.

I like to stay busy, and I enjoy a variety of activities. However, I do not like to feel stressed when I am overcommitted nor do I enjoy the failure when I am overwhelmed. When I feel pressured, I step back and evaluate my life. For years, I have followed "Twelve Timely Tips" to help manage my time. I commend these to you:

⤝ TWELVE TIMELY TIPS ⤞
for Time Management

1. You have all the time you need.
2. Plan your time or others will.
3. Leave a margin for the unexpected.
4. Do one thing at a time and finish it.
5. Learn to say no.
6. Separate the important from the urgent.
7. Use shortcuts to promote efficiency.
8. Be decisive.
9. Write it down.
10. Be time conscious.
11. Work smarter, not harder.
12. Set your course and stick to it.

Do you have other timely tips? What strategies help you manage your time and your life? Time is fleeting, and life must be managed. Identify those things or people who waste your time. Determine your goals and stick to them. Find time-saving tips that work for you. Do your best, with the help of the Lord, to make the most of your time and your life. Life takes time.

LIFE GIVES MEANING

Your birth was not an accident. You are not here for your own pleasure. You are a creation of God with a plan and purpose for your life. Once you realize this fact and accept God by faith, you can begin living a meaningful life. Christians do not have to wait until heaven to receive God's rewards. We enjoy his blessings in life. In fact, Jesus himself said that he came that we might have life and have it in abundance (John 10:10). How wonderful to know that the Lord wants us to have a meaningful life.

God gives meaning to life. As you seek him and follow him, you *become* who he created you to be. As you seek him and follow him, you *do* what he has called you to do. As you seek him and follow him, you *experience* the life he has carved out for you. Life can have true meaning when you know who God is and who you are in him.

As a young bride, I read *Disciplines of the Beautiful Woman* by Anne Ortlund. When I married, I was a strong-willed, independent woman. Though I was saved and grew up in a Christian home, I brought my own agenda into my life and marriage. Upon the recommendation of a godly mentor, I read the book and it changed my life. I learned that beauty is not from outward appearance but from inward discipline. Beauty flows from a heart devoted to God. I learned to seek God for meaning in life and to set my priorities around him.

Anne Ortlund distinguishes between lifelong and daily priorities. While *lifelong priorities* are major goals to be accomplished over the years of your life, *daily priorities* are specific goals to be accomplished more immediately, and they should be guided by your lifelong priorities.[8] Ultimately, Christians can experience the greatest meaning in life as they seek God's priorities. Though the words sound simple, there is no more complex challenge than understanding and following God's will.

Through the years, I have listed my priorities and worked to follow them. Several years ago, I considered my lifelong and daily priorities as suggested by Anne Ortlund. General, then specific, they guide my life and give it more meaning.

Table 20.1

Lifelong	Daily
1. Live for the Lord. 2. Love my husband. 3. Love my family. 4. Love others. 5. Develop myself.	1. Read the Bible and pray at least fifteen minutes each day. 2. Enjoy a date night each week with my husband Chuck. 3. Talk to Mother and Dad daily and my sister Mitzi weekly. 4. Speak to and smile at everyone. 5. Exercise at least three days each week and eat a healthy diet.

---

[8] Anne Ortlund, *Disciplines of the Beautiful Woman* (Waco, TX: Word, 1977), 23–35.

God wants to give my life more meaning. He wants me to experience life abundantly. That is God's heart desire for you, too. As you focus on him and follow his plan, God will bless you beyond expectations. He will give your life meaning and purpose, and you can share this hope and his truth with others. Life gives meaning!

CONCLUSION

Life is a gift of God to be received with great gratitude. Because the years pass by quickly, you must learn to manage yourself and your time in each stage of life. Balance in life is essential. Find time and focus intentionally on each area of life—spiritual, mental, physical, familial, financial, and social.

Involve yourself in ministry to others. Leave a lasting legacy of faith as you share Christ and meet needs in his name. Face daily pressures with joy and endurance, knowing that your faith can grow stronger. Use your time wisely and pursue God's priorities for your life. Remember that God gives meaning to life and he wants you to live it abundantly. As you master these life management skills, your life will have greater meaning for you, for others, and for the kingdom of God.

PUTTING THE PRINCIPLES INTO PRACTICE

1. At this moment, is your life organized or disorganized? What is the cost of disorganization in your life?
2. List one specific goal in each area of your life (spiritual, mental, physical, family, financial, social). Now seek to maintain balance.
3. Is ministry an important part of your life now? List several ways you are involved in ministry. If not, set some ministry goals.
4. List several time wasters in your life. Identify them and then suggest a time saver for each.
5. Do you have meaning and purpose in your life? Describe who God has created you to be and what he has called you to do.

ADDITIONAL RESOURCES

Feldhahn, Shaunti, and Robert Lewis. *The Life Ready Woman: Thriving in a Do-It-All World*. Nashville: Broadman, 2011.

George, Elizabeth. *Life Management for Busy Women: Living Out God's Plan with Passion and Purpose*. Eugene, OR: Harvest House, 2002.

Kelley, Rhonda H. *Divine Discipline: How to Develop and Maintain Self-Control.* Gretna, LA: Pelican, 1992.

———. *Personal Discipline: A Biblical Study of Self-Control and Perseverance.* Birmingham, AL: New Hope, 2011.

MacDonald, Gordon. *Ordering Your Private World.* Nashville: Thomas Nelson, 2003.

Ortlund, Anne. *Disciplines of the Beautiful Woman.* Waco, TX: Word, 1977.

Chapter Twenty-One

Nest Building 101: Setting Up a Household

Pat Ennis

Ornithology is the technical term for the scientific study of birds. Birds, far more than any other animal, are notable for building homes in which to raise their young. In some cases, the nests are used for many years. Nests vary in complexity from simple ones constructed with sticks and stones to hanging and woven nests, which are the most complicated of bird architecture. Birds also establish homes in holes in the ground, wood, mud mounds, and the water. According to Psalm 84:3, "Even the sparrow finds a home, and the swallow a nest for herself, where she may lay her young, at your altars, O LORD of hosts." If our feathered friends carefully craft their homes, how much more should believers build their nests to shelter all those who abide in them?

Karina, one of my former students, and her husband are involved in full-time ministry. Married ten years, they have two sons. Her description of her peers provides the rationale for why it is important to know how to establish and maintain a home:

> So many of my peers who truly love Christ and love their families are struggling desperately with practical daily skills in the management of their homes. This can lead to great conflict and frustration in family and community life. . . . We lack both the biblical framework and the practical knowledge that can and should be instilled before we form households of our own.
>
> Establishing a home is such a great topic to address as it is much easier to begin well, allowing for some fine-tuning in each season of life, rather than having to overhaul everything mid-course. Having biblical principles in mind from the beginning allows for a structure that makes sense.
>
> I have been giving a lot of thought lately to the necessity of home management skills for the purpose of class mobility. I'm part of a community of young families that are either rising in their income and socioeconomic class or else declining considerably in their income due to personal crises or the

economy. Without a biblical framework for the purpose of the home, many with an increasing income are simply raising their standard of living with little thought for the effect of consumerism on their family relationships and the structure of their home life. On the other hand, those who have experienced significant income loss often lack the skills to do for themselves what they have been in the habit of outsourcing. This leaves them with few options, and all too often the credit card is seen as the way out. Home management skills coupled with a biblical understanding of the purpose of the home are essential to all socioeconomic classes.[1]

One of the crucial reasons for passing on a biblical framework for the home and practical home management skills is that we live in an uncertain world. Assuming that we will always have access to certain technologies or a certain income level is unwise. Additionally, having these skills frees us as Christian women to respond to the call of God to move out of our current situation. A middle-aged woman whose businessman husband feels called to the ministry will experience significant changes in disposable income. Is she prepared with the skills to adjust? A newlywed couple from an upper-middle-class background may be called to serve as "urban missionaries" in a low-income apartment complex. Will they be able to transition effectively, or will their lack of homemaking skills cause unlivable tension in their new household?

Karina's concluding question provides the rationale for the need to create a safe nest, develop a spiritual security system, learn how to furnish a nest as well as assemble your assets, and establish a scripturally based home.

CREATING A SAFE NEST

According to the 2011 edition of Injury Facts, 70 percent of all unintentional injury deaths (an estimated 90,300 deaths) in 2009 occurred in the home and community. Another 30,500,000 people suffered medically consulted injuries. About 1 out of 10 people experienced an unintentional injury in the home and community, and about 1 out of 3,500 people died from such an injury. The five leading causes of unintentional injury deaths in home and community were poisoning, falls, drowning, choking, and fires/flames.[2] What do these sobering statistics mean for homemakers creating a nest that is physically safe and sound?

---

[1] Personal communication.

[2] National Safety Council, *Injury Facts*® [online], 2011 ed. (Itasca, IL: National Safety Council, 2011), 130–31, http://www.nsc.org/safety_work/FirstAidResource/InstructorResource/Documents/Injury_Facts_2011.pdf.

Room Safety

Check out each room in your home for possible safety hazards. Be intentional in correcting them. Remember that a safety hazard is simply an accident waiting to happen. Consider creating a safety checklist for each room in your home. While each home varies in needs, the list can get you started on your personal Safety Checklist.

The Kitchen

____ Appliances and wiring in safe condition
____ Carbon monoxide detector tested monthly
____ Exhaust fan free of dust and grease buildup
____ Fire extinguisher easily accessible
____ Poisonous products and knives safely stored
____ Pot handles turned away from the range (stove) front
____ Smoke detector tested monthly
____ Spills wiped up immediately
____ Sturdy step stool readily available

Laundry Area

____ Appliances cleaned after each use
____ Dryer lint filter emptied when load of laundry is completed
____ Fire extinguisher easily accessible
____ Iron cooled before storing
____ Iron cord in safe condition
____ Laundry products safely stored
____ Smoke detector tested monthly
____ Water drained from iron when pressing/ironing cycle is completed

Bathroom

____ Doors that can be unlocked from the outside
____ Hand-grab bars in tub and/or shower
____ Medicines and cosmetics in safe and childproof storage
____ Night-light
____ Plastic or paper cups used rather than glass

Bedroom

____ Chain or rope ladder available for fire escape from second story
____ Clothes, toys, and personal items put away at night
____ Crib that meets legal safety standards
____ Fire extinguisher easily accessible
____ Light switch or lamp located near bedside and door
____ Night-light

_____ No cords under rugs
_____ Plastic bags covering clothes out of children's reach
_____ Smoke detector tested monthly

Living and Family Rooms

_____ Adequate space between the fireplace and rug
_____ Electrical circuits not overloaded
_____ Fire extinguisher easily accessible
_____ Furniture arrangement that allows for unobstructed movement
_____ Mesh screens or glass doors across the front of the fireplace
_____ No cords under rugs
_____ Sliding glass doors clearly marked at eye level
_____ Smoke detector tested monthly
_____ Television and stereo sets placed to allow adequate air circulation around them
_____ Unused outlets covered with childproof covers

Emergency Plans

Develop an emergency evacuation plan to activate when disaster is pending.

- Identify natural disasters common to your area (e.g., hurricanes, earthquakes, tornadoes). Customize the evacuation to align with your geographic region. Post it in common areas of your home. Be sure each family member understands procedures, including a meeting place to use if separated.
- Gather emergency supplies to sustain your family in case of a disaster:

  - First aid kit (noted later in chapter) plus thirty-day supply of medicines and prescriptions, along with their instructions
  - Glasses and assistive devices
  - Seven-day water supply (one gallon per person per day)
  - Seven-day supply of non-perishable foods
  - At least two flashlights and three sets of batteries
  - Small bag of clothing and personal items
  - Important personal records
  - Cash, checks, credit cards, driver's license, Social Security number
  - Full tank of gas in cars
  - Supply of pet essentials

- Establish a strategy for dealing with home fires.
- Practice the strategy so that it is a natural reflex in the event of impending danger.
- Identify an easily remembered meeting place for the family.

First Aid

Assemble a first aid kit with basic supplies:

____ Adhesive tape
____ Antibiotic ointment such as Neosporin
____ Aspirin and nonaspirin pain relief
____ Bandages
____ Benadryl antihistamine for allergic reactions
____ Cotton balls
____ Cotton-tipped swabs
____ Cough syrup
____ Digital thermometer
____ First aid instructional manual
____ Gauze pads
____ Hydrogen peroxide
____ Instant cold pack
____ Latex gloves
____ Petroleum jelly or other lubricant
____ Plastic bags for the disposal of contaminated materials
____ Rubbing alcohol
____ Safety pins in assorted sizes
____ Scissors
____ Small flashlight (keep the batteries fresh)
____ Soap or instant hand sanitizer
____ Sting and bite treatment
____ Tweezers

Keep your home first aid kit in an easily accessible central location. Place a first aid kit in your car as well. A small tackle box or even a resealable freezer bag will function well as a container for the kit, or use a hanging shoe bag and label compartments for storage of various items. The key principle is that it should be accessible and portable. Check the first aid kit at least every three months (mark this checkup on your household calendar) to replace supplies that have expired. Replenish used supplies as soon as possible. Acquire training in first aid, CPR (cardiopulmonary resuscitation), and AED (automated external defibrillator). According to the National Safety Council, 25 percent of emergency room visits could be avoided if people knew basic first aid and CPR. They urge everyone to be able to perform basic first aid. Their website states:

> Everyone should be able to perform first aid because most people eventually will find themselves in a home or work situation requiring it, either for another person or for themselves.

- First aid is the immediate help given to a victim of injury or sudden illness by a bystander until appropriate medical help arrives or the victim is seen by a health care provider.

- First aid is generally not all the treatment the person needs, but it helps the victim for the usually short time until advanced care begins.

- First aid can mean the difference between life and death, between temporary and permanent disability, between rapid recovery and long hospitalization.[3]

Medical Information

List important medical facts about each resident of the home. Some families use a journal so that medical history can be included. Post or store it in a central location and include:

- blood type;
- any allergies including reactions to medicines;
- vaccinations and inoculations;
- any physical conditions (diabetes, heart condition, chronic sinus, etc.) that could affect the emergency medical measures administered;
- names and phone numbers of physicians and dentists.

Store prescription medications out of the reach of children. Consider placing a small bell on bottles of medications that could be dangerous if taken by someone other than the individual for whom it is prescribed.

Prevent Falls

Fall-proof your home.

- Check all doormats and small area rugs. Do they all have nonskid backing?
- Keep traffic paths clear of clutter. This includes furniture that has angular or protruding parts.
- Use nonskid strips, designs, or mats in bathtubs and stall showers.
- Keep kitchen and bathroom floors clean and dry.
- Examine handrails to confirm their ability to stabilize the stair climber.
- Provide adequate lighting throughout the home.

Emergency Evacuation Preparation

Establish a strategy that allows you quickly to collect important documents (driver's license, credit cards, passports, insurance policies, wills, etc.) and

---

[3] "NSC First Aid," National Safety Council website, accessed December 7, 2012, http://www.nsc.org/safety_ home/FirstAidCPR/Pages/Firstaid_CPR.aspx.

valuables in the event that rapid evacuation is necessary. Select a secondary location to store a duplicate set of the documents.

Spiritual Security System

Develop and alarm a spiritual security system for your home. As a Christian nest builder, you have a great privilege and high calling consistently to pray for the spiritual condition of your home. The question now becomes, What do I pray? There is no better way to pray for your home than to pray God's mind and will for it. "My Nest's Spiritual Security System" gives a systematic monthly prayer plan to promote regular intercession to your heavenly Father for the protection of your home.

Table 21.1

☙ MY NEST'S SPIRITUAL ☙ SECURITY SYSTEM

Heavenly Father, in accordance with your Word,
I pray that my home will be . . .

DAY	PRAYER
1	. . . permeated with God's love (Jer. 31:3; John 14:21).
2	. . . an environment where affirming, edifying words are spoken (Ps. 19:14).
3	. . . Spirit filled (Gal. 5:16).
4	. . . a place where personal burdens are shared by all who reside within its walls (Gal. 6:2).
5	. . . filled with occupants who daily put on each piece of the armor of God (Eph. 6:10–20).
6	. . . a refuge of sincere love (Rom. 12:9).
7	. . . overflowing with genuine affection for everyone abiding in it (Rom. 12:10).
8	. . . characterized by appreciation for one another (Rom. 12:10).
9	. . . focused on putting others first (Phil. 2:3).
10	. . . distinguished by humility (Phil. 2:3).
11	. . . a model of biblical servanthood (Mark 10:45).

12	. . . a light in a dark, decaying world (Matt. 5:14–16).
13	. . . known as a refuge (Heb. 6:18).
14	. . . an environment where truth is proclaimed in love (Eph. 4:15).
15	. . . consistent in practicing instructive, uplifting, encouraging speech (Eph. 4:29).
16	. . . propelled by prayer (1 Thess. 5:17).
17	. . . distinguished by gratitude (1 Thess. 5:18).
18	. . . able to withstand the destructive tactics of the Devil (1 Pet. 5:8–9).
19	. . . a place where my family members willingly submit to one another (Eph. 5:21).
20	. . . an oasis where each member has the freedom to confess his sins to another and pray for one another (James 5:16).
21	. . . an atmosphere that stimulates you to flee quickly the works of the flesh (Gal. 5:19–21).
22	. . . prompt to embrace the fruit of the Spirit (Gal. 5:22–24).
23	. . . concentrating on setting your affections on things of eternal value (Col. 3:2–6).
24	. . . careful to embrace the character qualities that please God (Col. 3:12–15).
25	. . . a fortification for the truth that the believers who dwell within its walls are always secure in God's tender embrace (Rom. 8:38–39).
26	. . . a prepared place for my family just as heaven will be a prepared place for the members of God's family (John 14:1–4).
27	. . . a refuge where forgiveness is readily granted (Luke 17:3–4).
28	. . . content with God's provisions (Heb. 13:5).
29	. . . established on God's Word (Ps. 119:11).
30	. . . identified as an oasis where a lifestyle of holiness abounds (Lev. 20:7).
31	. . . a place that consistently seeks God's wisdom (James 1:5).

FURNISHING YOUR NEST

Are you establishing your first home or trying to help someone set up an apartment? The process can be overwhelming, both personally and financially, especially since a limited number of resources are available to provide assistance. Prior to beginning work on this portion of "Nest Building 101," I conducted a database search to see what is available to the average consumer. My search yielded seventy-seven pages and 221 million results. I thought that perhaps this section could be eliminated from the chapter since so many resources were available. Closer analysis, however, revealed that while much information is available for setting up a home wireless network, home theater, home office, and home studio, little information is available on establishing the foundations for a home. The dearth of specific resources challenged me to compile a list of "Nest-Building Nuggets."

NEST-BUILDING NUGGETS

- Loan officers, apartment managers, and utility companies will undoubtedly conduct a credit check to determine the risk factor in selling, renting, or supplying utilities to you. Be sure that your credit history is accurate before proceeding with any applications (see chapter 26).

- Focus on staying debt free. You may need to delay some purchases for a while, but the financial freedom is well worth the momentary inconvenience. Spiritually, the delay assists in building self-control (Gal. 5:24) and contentment (Phil. 4:11). It also aids in determining the difference between legitimate needs and wants.

- Exhaust the inventory of discount and closeout stores for bargain prices on many of the items listed on the "Nesting Needs Inventory" before purchasing them from an upscale store.

- Develop a priority list. Determine what you *really* need to establish your home and what can wait.

- Prior to buying major appliances and furnishings, conduct research. *Consumer Reports* and research databases provide professional brand-by-brand reports based on laboratory tests and surveys. Epinions.com contains reviews from people who have purchased and used the items reported.

- Determine what level of quality is best for your season of life. In the long run, it is usually more economical to purchase quality merchandise that will endure through a number of seasons. Pay attention to when the items are on sale. This tactic frequently allows you to purchase a higher quality item for the same price or less than a regularly priced item of lesser quality.

- Consider purchasing previously used items. The modern mobile lifestyle often means that attractive, quality merchandise is available. Remember that *previously owned* does not imply someone else's worn-out castoffs.

- Consider registering at several reasonably priced stores so that those who want to help you nest can purchase items that you will enjoy using. Be sure to purchase notes and stamps so that you can send a *handwritten* thank-you note to the benefactor of your new nest's inventory immediately (an e-mail is not appropriate even in our electronic age).

- Customize the "Nesting Needs Inventory" to complement your specific lifestyle.

NESTING NEEDS INVENTORY

Kitchen/Dining Room

Cookware

_____ Baking pans (9" x 13" x 2"; 8" x 8" x 2" or 9" x 9" x 2")
_____ Casserole dishes (preferably oven-to-table)
_____ Cookie sheets (without sides)
_____ Covered saucepans (1-qt., 2-qt., 3-qt., Dutch oven)
_____ Covered skillets (8" to 12")
_____ Custard cups
_____ Griddle
_____ Loaf pan
_____ Muffin tin
_____ Pie plates (8" and 9")

Cooking Utensils

_____ Apple corer
_____ Baster
_____ Biscuit cutter
_____ Bottle and jar opener
_____ Can opener (manual)
_____ Candy thermometer
_____ Cheese slicer
_____ Colander
_____ Cookie cutters
_____ Cutting boards (plastic and wooden)
_____ Deep-fat thermometer
_____ Funnel
_____ Grater/shredder
_____ Juicer
_____ Kitchen scissors
_____ Knives (paring, utility, chef's, carving, slicing)
_____ Ladle

_____ Long-handled fork
_____ Measuring cups (dry and liquid)
_____ Measuring spoons
_____ Meat thermometer
_____ Mixing bowls
_____ Pancake turner
_____ Pizza cutter
_____ Potato/carrot peeler
_____ Rolling pin and cover
_____ Rotary beater
_____ Rubber scrapers
_____ Salt and pepper shakers for the range
_____ Spatulas (flexible, metal)
_____ Spoons (metal, slotted, wooden)
_____ Strainer or sieve
_____ Teakettle (range top or electric)
_____ Timer
_____ Tongs
_____ Vegetable brush
_____ Whisk

Linens

_____ Cloth napkins
_____ Dishcloths
_____ Dish towels
_____ Place mats
_____ Potholders
_____ Tablecloths

Small Appliances

_____ Blender and/or food processor
_____ Can opener (electric)
_____ Coffee maker
_____ Crock-Pot (slow cooker)
_____ Electric mixer
_____ Toaster
_____ Vacuum cleaner

Tableware and Flatware[4]

_____ Cups and saucers or mugs
_____ Dinner forks
_____ Dinner knives

---

[4] Purchase these items in quantities of four or more whenever the budget permits.

_____ Dinner plates
_____ Fruit/cereal bowls
_____ Glasses (4 oz. to 6 oz., 12 oz.)
_____ Salt and pepper shakers
_____ Salad/dessert forks
_____ Salad plates
_____ Serving pieces for flatware
_____ Serving pieces for dishes (platter, etc.)
_____ Sugar bowl and creamer
_____ Teapot
_____ Teaspoons

Other Essentials

_____ Cleaning supplies (paper towels, rags, ammonia, cleanser
such as Ajax or Comet, spray bottle, etc.). See "Cleaning
Products from Your Pantry" in chapter 23.
_____ Cookbook
_____ Pantry staples (plastic wrap, plastic bags of varying
sizes, foil, waxed paper, parchment paper)
_____ Plastic storage containers with lids
_____ Tool kit
_____ Trash bags
_____ Trash can

Bathroom

_____ Bath and hand towels
_____ Bath rug
_____ Clothes hamper
_____ Facecloths
_____ Medicine cabinet basics (see first aid kit contents, page 285)
_____ Squeegee
_____ Toilet brush
_____ Toilet plunger
_____ Trash can

Laundry

_____ Bleach (chlorine and nonchlorine)
_____ Detergent
_____ Fabric softener
_____ Iron
_____ Ironing board
_____ Laundry basket
_____ Sewing kit
_____ Spray starch

_____ Stain remover
_____ Steamer

Bedroom

_____ Alarm clock
_____ Bedside lamps
_____ Blanket and/or bedspread
_____ Hangers
_____ Mattress pad
_____ Pillows
_____ Pillow cases
_____ Sheets

Office Supplies

_____ Basket or notebook to hold bills
_____ Envelopes of different sizes
_____ Notecards
_____ Paper
_____ Paper clips
_____ Pens and pencils
_____ Postage stamps
_____ Post-it notes in different sizes
_____ Rubber bands
_____ Stapler
_____ Transparent tape and dispenser

Watch yard sales and newspaper advertisements for lamps, desks, chairs, bookcases, CD racks, TVs, furniture, and other miscellaneous items. Also, mark your calendar with the information displayed on "Table 21.2: Bargain Bulletin Board."

Table 21.2
◞❦ BARGAIN BULLETIN BOARD ❧◜

Month	Bargain
January	Annual "white sales" provide a good opportunity to replenish your linens and towels.
February	Winter clothes, coats, and snow boots are usually on sale.
March	Small electronics such as digital cameras from the previous year are bargain-priced because the current year's new models are usually arriving in the stores.

April	Cookware and other household items are often on sale.
May	Yard sales abound when the warmer spring days arrive and people are contemplating a move.
June	Gym memberships are available when people begin flocking outside to exercise.
July	Retailers use the Fourth of July (and other major holidays) as an excuse to offer special bargains on everything from cars to carpets.
August	Most summer items go on sale to make way for fall items. Purchase grills, lawn furniture, gardening supplies, air conditioners, and summer clothing.
September	Back-to-school bargains abound.
October	New home appliances are often introduced in the fall, so you can buy last year's models at a discount (a good bargain since appliances rarely change drastically from year to year).
November	Holiday bargains begin early. Watch the advertisements, especially the day after Thanksgiving.
December	The week after Christmas is the best time to purchase seasonal items at super-deep bargain prices. Buy next year's holiday wrappings, ornaments, and decorations.

ASSEMBLING YOUR ASSETS

Depending on the source, 25–35 percent of your budget is normally allocated to your housing costs. Once selected, a variety of items will fill that home. You will want to assemble your assets in an orderly manner. The suggestions that follow provide you with guidelines for ensuring that you are executing faithful stewardship of all the assets God has entrusted to you (1 Cor. 4:2).

- Create and label computer folders for all your household records. Be sure to back up your files on a portable electronic device so they are easily transported in case of an emergency. You may wish to store the device—wrapped in plastic wrap, foil, and a resealable baggie—in the freezer since it is one of the last items to burn should a fire occur.

- Make a file folder for warranties and instruction books for each appliance. Place a photocopy of the sales receipt in the folder since original receipts often fade.

- Compile an inventory of your household items. Include a brief description and the serial numbers of the items. The inventory will provide you with important data for your insurance company in the event of a burglary or fire. This inventory, together with warranties and manuals, could be kept in a notebook or binder.

- Take pictures of each room of your home. Label the printed pictures and place in a photo album. Keep the digital copy with other electronic devices such as your portable data drives.

- Consider backing up your files with an off-site service such as Mozy.com.

- Many people step into eternity taking all of the knowledge regarding their assets with them. Now is the time to begin organizing your assets. Create forms using these simple templates provided here.

    - Save each in a separate file on your computer.
    - Print a copy and place with your financial records.
    - Give a copy to a relative or trusted friend.

VITAL STATISTICS FORM

First name _____ Middle name _____

Last name _____ Maiden name _____

Home phone _____ Cell phone _____

Address (including country) _____

E-mail _____

Gender _____ Race _____

Birthplace _____ Birth date _____

Social Security number _____

Marital status _____

Spouse's complete name _____

Occupation _____

Employer _____

Education _____ Degree(s) _____

Father's complete name _____

Mother's complete name _____

PEOPLE TO NOTIFY IN THE EVENT OF AN EMERGENCY

Name _____ Relationship/Association _____

Address _____

Home Phone _____ Cell Phone _____

E-mail _____

BANKING INFORMATION

Information for (insert name) _____

Date list was prepared _____

Location in my home of my banking records _____

Bank/Branch _____ Type of account _____

Signature on account _____

Username _____

Password _____

SAFE DEPOSIT BOX

Information for (insert name) _____

Date list was prepared _____

Location in my home of my safe deposit box key _____

Bank/Branch _____ Key holder(s) _____

Contents Description _____
_____

INSURANCE POLICIES[5]

Information for (insert name) _____

Date list was prepared _____

Type of policy _____ Policy # _____

Date policy issued _____

Insurance agent _____ Phone _____

Amount of policy $_____ Premiums due _____

Beneficiary(s) (if applicable) _____

Location of the policies in my home _____

REAL ESTATE

Information for (insert name) _____

Date list was prepared _____

Address _____

Tax assessor's ID# _____

Tax assessor's address _____ Phone _____

Property tax due date(s) _____

Mortgage holder _____

Loan # _____ Mortgage payment $_____

Location of loan documents in my home _____

---

[5] All policies should be documented in this way.

OTHER ASSETS

Information for (insert name) _____

Date list was prepared _____

Location in my home of the list of my other assets _____

Vehicles (include how each is titled) _____

Jewelry _____

Investments—mutual funds, stocks, bonds, CDs, retirement plans (include how each is titled) _____

_____

ONGOING HOUSEHOLD OBLIGATIONS

Telephone company _____ Account number _____

Mailing address _____

Cell phone company _____ Account number _____

Mailing address _____

Water company _____ Account number _____

Mailing address _____

Power company _____ Account number _____

Mailing address _____

Natural gas company _____ Account number _____

Mailing address _____

Cable company _____ Account number _____

Mailing address _____

Waste management company _____ Account number _____

Mailing address _____

- Assemble a list of all credit cards. Make a copy of the front and back of all credit cards.

Type of card _____

Account Number _____ Password _____

- Collect copies of other important documents for each family member such as:

  - Birth certificate
  - Marriage certificate
  - Passport
  - Academic transcripts and certifications

Location in my home of my important documents _____

- Develop a master "Log-in List" (see Table 21.3). Much of our household business is now conducted at the computer, and each organization requires specific information. Develop a master list that is readily accessible at your work space. Carry it with you when you travel, but use caution in protecting this vital information.

Table 21.3
☞ MASTER LOG-IN LIST ☜

Organization	Account #	Log-in	Password

STOCKING THE REFRIGERATOR AND PANTRY FOR YOUR NEST

Depending on geographic region, the average family spends between 12 and 14 percent of their monthly income on food and other necessities for their nest. A family's goals, values, and life cycle greatly affect the way its food budget is allocated. Consider these suggestions for stocking your nest with nutrients:

- Create a master grocery list—items you regularly want to have in your personal pantry.

  - Save it in your household folder.
  - Print multiple copies and store in a designated location in the kitchen.
  - Categorize the list according to types.
  - Alphabetize the items within the categories.
  - Date the list and circle items needed for your next grocery shopping excursion.
  - Provide extra space for items unique for each trip to the grocery store.
  - When the copies of the supply list are depleted, edit it before printing replacement copies.

- Align the list with the layout of your grocery store, discount store, or other shopping venues. You may need several versions of the list since each store is organized differently.

- Organize your list so that you begin at the side of the store with the heaviest items you will purchase so they will be at the bottom of your cart.
- Place the list in order of the aisles to avoid retracing your steps.
- Any easily damaged items (e.g., bakery, chips, fruits, and vegetables) should be the last items placed in your grocery cart.
- Never shop when you are hungry! ☺

- Use the "Master Grocery Shopping List" as a start for compiling your own.

MASTER GROCERY SHOPPING LIST

Beverages
    Carbonated beverages
    Cocoa
    Coffee
    Juices
    Tea

Cereals and Grains
    Crackers
    Bread
    Breakfast cereals—cold and hot
    Noodles
    Pasta
    Rice

Cleaning Supplies
    Bleach
    Cleanser (Ajax, Comet, etc.)
    Dishwasher detergent
    Dishwashing liquid
    Laundry detergent
    Non-chlorine bleach
    (Refer to chapter 23)

Convenience Foods
    Marinara sauce
    Soups

Dairy
    Butter or butter substitute
    Cheese

    Eggs
    Ice cream
    Milk
    Yogurt

Fish and Shellfish
    Fish fillets
    Shrimp
    Tuna

Fruit
    Apples
    Bananas
    Blueberries, strawberries, blackberries
    Grapefruit, oranges, other citrus fruit
    Grapes, cherries
    Lemons
    Melons

Meat
    Bacon or breakfast meat
    Brisket
    Ground beef
    Lamb
    Pork loin or chops
    Steaks

Poultry
    Chicken
    Turkey

Staples

Artificial sweetener
Baking powder
Baking soda
Brown sugar
Cornstarch
Dried beans
Dried herbs (e.g., tarragon, basil)
Condiments (e.g., ketchup, mustard,
      jam/jellies)
Cooking oil
Flavorings (e.g., vanilla, almond)
Flour
Mayonnaise
Peanut butter
Pepper
Popcorn
Powdered sugar
Salad dressing
Salt

Shortening
Spices (e.g., cinnamon, nutmeg)
Sugar
Syrup/honey
Vinegar

Vegetables

Beans/peas (fresh or dried)
Broccoli
Carrots
Cauliflower
Corn
Green beans
Lettuce
Onions
Potatoes
Spinach
Squash
Tomatoes
Yams

DEVELOPING YOUR NESTITUDE

Matthew 5:1–12 and Luke 6:20–22 are commonly known as the Beatitudes. When describing the Beatitudes, John MacArthur writes that *blessed* literally means happy, fortunate, and blissful:

> It speaks of more than a surface emotion. Jesus was describing the divinely-bestowed well-being that belongs only to the faithful. The Beatitudes demonstrate that the way to heavenly blessedness is antithetical to the worldly path normally followed in pursuit of happiness. The worldly idea is that happiness is found in riches, merriment, abundance, leisure, and such things. The real truth is the very opposite. The Beatitudes give Jesus' description of the character of true faith.[6]

As "Nest Building 101" draws to a close, I share with you a word I coined to summarize its contents—*Nestitude*; it is drawn from the word *nest* meaning a person's snug or secluded retreat or shelter[7] and the word *beatitude* signifying the character of true faith. My prayer is that the chapter's contents will stimulate you to establish a scripturally based home so that the Nestitudes will be evident within its walls.

[6] John MacArthur, *The MacArthur Study Bible* (Nashville: Word, 2000), notes for Matthew 5:3.
[7] *Oxford American College Dictionary*, 2nd ed., s.v. "nest."

NESTITUDES

Happy are those who intentionally acquire both the biblical framework and the practical knowledge to establish scripturally based homes.

Happy are those who create safe nests.

Happy are those who develop "Spiritual Security Systems" to protect their nests from Satan's tactics.

Happy are those who apply the "Nest-Building Nuggets" as they establish their nests.

Happy are those who compile a "Nesting Needs Inventory" to furnish their nests.

Happy are those who assemble their household assets so that biblical stewardship is practiced.

Happy are those who know how to purchase nutrients and other necessities expediently for their nests.

Happy are those who petition their heavenly Father to pass Nest Building 101 with flying colors!

PUTTING THE PRINCIPLES INTO PRACTICE

1. Starting with the sample in the chapter, create a safety checklist for each room in your home.
2. "My Nest's Spiritual Security System" is a systematic prayer plan to promote regular intercession to your heavenly Father for the protection of your home. Once you have used it for several months, customize it to meet your needs.
3. Use the forms provided under the "Assembling Your Assets" section to organize your assets.
4. Use the "Master Grocery Shopping List" to compile your own personalized list.
5. Write each *Nestitude* on a card; meditate on them as you work in your kitchen. Create your own list of Nestitudes.

Chapter Twenty-Two

Nest Building 102: Relocating a Household

Pat Ennis

True believers are much like eagles. A scriptural analysis of this noble bird of prey provides numerous illustrations that parallel the Christian life. Consider the imagery of Deuteronomy 32:11–13:

> Like an eagle that stirs up its nest,
>   that flutters over its young,
> spreading out its wings, catching them,
>   bearing them on its pinions,
> the LORD alone guided him,
>   no foreign god was with him.
> He made him ride on the high places of the land,
>   and he ate the produce of the field,
> and he suckled him with honey out of the rock,
>   and oil out of the flinty rock.

The passage describes how the young eagles first leave the comfort of the nest of their parents and learn to fly. To convince the eaglets that the time has come to leave the nest, the parent eagles "stir up the nest." That is, they rough it up with their talons and make it uncomfortable so the sticks, sharp ends, and pointy spurs stick out of the nest. Transformed from a place of comfort and refuge, the nest is no longer soft and secure. It becomes most inhospitable as the eagles tear up the "bedding" and break up the twigs until jagged ends of wood stick out all over like a pincushion. Life for the eaglets becomes miserable and unhappy.

Compounding the miserable nest life, the mother eagle starts "fluttering her wings" at the eaglets. Propelling them to the edge of the nest, she "spreads her wings." To escape her winged fury, the eaglets climb onto her back and cling tightly. The mother eagle launches out into space, carrying the eaglets on her back. All seems safe and serene as the eaglets relish the thrilling ride. However, it comes to an abrupt halt when, without warning, the mother eagle dives downward. Suddenly the eaglets find themselves tumbling down, down, down in the air, their wings flapping wildly in an attempt to grasp the air. Just as the eaglets flounder, the mother eagle swoops down below and "catches them on her pinions" and soars back into the atmosphere. Much relieved, the eaglets tenaciously grasp the wings of the mother—but not for long. After a brief respite, the mother again tosses them into the air. The eaglets struggle. This time their wings react reflexively; rather than plummeting wildly, they manage to slow their descent and stay aloft a little longer. The flight training continues until the eaglets learn how to catch the air currents, ride the winds, and soar "like an eagle."

The initial "stirring up of the nest" solicited discomfort and required the eaglets to use talents they were unaware they possessed. But because their loving mother pushed them to the edge of the nest and persevered with them until they learned to fly, they were no longer confined to its parameters. They were now free to soar in the sky as mature eagles. Eaglets are safe in the nest—but that is not the purpose for which they were created (Isa. 40:31).

Your loving heavenly Father, as the mother eagle, may "stir up your nest" and ask you to leave its comfort so that the gifts he has bestowed on you can be used to their fullest potential. That may mean relocating to another state or even overseas. Are you willing to allow your heavenly Father to mature you into a spiritual eagle that can ascend to great heights, or are you more like a barnyard chicken that is bound to the earth, scratches to exist, and is fearful to leave its comfortable coop?

NEST RELOCATION: GUIDELINES

If your gracious heavenly Father is stirring up your nest and challenging you to relocate, you have a variety of factors to consider. The "Nest Relocation Guidelines" are a foundation for you to plan your relocation so that it is a blessing rather than a burden. Customize it to accommodate your unique needs.

- Prepare your heart spiritually. Locate a Scripture passage that will provide comfort and encouragement during the challenging days. Psalm 84:11; Jeremiah 29:11–14; Matthew 28:19–20; Ephesians 3:20–21; Philippians 1:6; 4:6–7, 13, 19; and 1 Peter 5:7–8 provide a foundation for you to develop personalized moving meditations.

- If you are moving at the request of an employer or ministry, investigate any guidelines or policies for moving. You will likely save yourself time and money by asking before making arrangements yourself. For example, when I moved to Southwestern Baptist Theological Seminary, the institution had well-defined policies that included specifics regarding what costs they would and would not pay. They also had a procedure that allowed me to appeal the policies if I had special circumstances. If you appeal a policy, maintain copies of all correspondence.

- Moving internationally can be exciting. The challenge of adopting a new culture, meeting new people, and exploring new countries can make for an enjoyable experience. Research and planning will help ensure that you understand the requirements involved, including laws and regulations governing the importation of your personal and household goods. Securing the services of a professional moving company is recommended for an international relocation. Their depth of experience equips them to provide accurate, timely information. Generally, if they do not know the answer to your questions, they can refer you to a source with answers to your questions.

- A cardinal moving rule is to accomplish as much as possible early in the process. The importance of applying this rule is magnified when considering an international move. Establishing a timetable to execute the move will eliminate crisis management as the date approaches.

- When securing the services of a professional moving company, get several estimates, which should be available without cost. Prepare an inventory for the estimator so that he understands exactly what will be moved and the services you want the company to provide.

- Secure your visas and passports. Entry into most countries on a long-term or permanent basis requires appropriate visas and passports. Contact the consulate of the country to which you are relocating to ensure that your documentation is in order and that entry for both you and your goods is allowed. Some countries apply strict regulations to importing household effects, and heavy financial penalties may be applied if the appropriate paperwork is not in place. The consular representative should be equipped to advise you concerning all documentary requirements and how to apply for appropriate visas and work permits.

- Acquire vaccinations and inoculations. You and your family may need immunizations, inoculations, or booster shots before relocating internationally. You can find out what inoculations are necessary as well as those recommended by contacting the consular representative of your destination country. More than likely your family doctor will also be a valuable resource.

- Organize your personal records and valuable documents.

- You and your family should acquire complete medical and dental checkups prior to your departure. Request copies of your records to take to your new country.

- Review the content from "Nest Building 101" to determine the personal records and valuable documents you should have in your possession.

Valuables from safe boxes, jewelry, and the like should also be carried on your person in the transition.

- Consider your financial matters. When moving internationally you will need to determine your tax obligations in both your country of departure and your new country.

- Consider the transfer of funds, the closure of your current bank accounts, and the opening of appropriate accounts in your new location. The overseas department of your current bank should be able to provide assistance with the transfer of funds, a letter of credit, currency exchange rates, etc. You may want to maintain a stateside account, in which case you may wish to shop around for an interest-bearing account, which is usually available when only a few checks might be written each month.

- Acquire a current credit report (see chapter 26).

- Contact all utility companies and other services to which you subscribe and discern their procedure for terminating your relationship with them.

REESTABLISHING YOUR NEST

As a college professor I have the privilege of interfacing with many students. They teach me in subtle ways just as I impart knowledge to them in the formal classroom. I recall a lovely young woman overflowing with potential to impact the kingdom significantly. However, much like Lot's wife (Gen. 19:26), her previous residence was the place where happiness and contentment flourished. Rather than embracing Paul's perspective (Phil. 3:12–14) and finding joy in her new environment, she was transformed into a spiritual pillar of salt because she chose to look behind rather than ahead. Her choice reflected a lack of contentment, and its deficiency in her life created misery for her and everyone whose life she touched.

The word *content* (Gk. *autarkēs*, "sufficient," Phil. 4:11) primarily suggests satisfaction. The contented woman is one who actively believes that her heavenly Father is all of these things:

- a sun and shield—God provides total protection
- the giver of grace and glory
- one who will withhold no good thing from her *if* she is walking uprightly (Ps. 84:11)

As a woman embraces contentment, she matures into a thankful woman. Jerry Bridges defines thankfulness as "a recognition that God in his goodness and faithfulness has provided for us and cared for us, both physically and spiritually.

It is a recognition that we are totally dependent on Him; that all we are and have comes from God."[1] With this definition in mind she acknowledges these facts:

- Gratitude is a command, not a suggestion (1 Chron. 16:7–36; Psalm 100; 1 Thess. 5:18).

- The psalmist directs you to give thanks every morning and evening (Ps. 30:12; 92:1–3). Remember that thankfulness springs from the will, not the emotions.

- A contented woman acknowledges that discontentment, the opposite of contentment, is a sin.

- Discontentment is a characteristic of the unregenerate person (Rom. 1:18–21; 2 Tim. 3:1–2).

- Discontentment is "a questioning of the goodness of God."[2]

- Contentment is not a natural response to the challenges of life. It must be learned (Phil. 4:11). If you are truly content, you accept the "unchangeable" in your life (2 Cor. 12:9). When you are overwhelmed with feelings of dissatisfaction in areas of your life that can be changed, you go the Lord and pursue your goals according to the guidelines he provides in Scripture, while being content to endure even the greatest difficulties in the process (Phil. 4:13).

In *Calm My Anxious Heart*, Linda Dillow introduces Ella, a missionary wife and the mother of one of Linda's friends:

Ella worked as a missionary with the pygmies in Africa for fifty-two years. She had left her country, her family, and all that was familiar. Primitive does not even begin to describe her living conditions in the scorching heat and the humidity of the African bush. But Ella found no relief because electricity, air conditioning, and other modern conveniences were only a dream. Some days it was so unbearably hot that she had to bring the thermometer inside because it couldn't register past 120 degrees without breaking. Ella's daughter wondered how her mother had done it—how she had lived a life of contentment when her circumstances would have caused the hardiest to complain. Recently she unearthed a treasure, a much more significant find than gold or silver. In an old diary of her mother's she discovered Ella's prescription for contentment:

- Never allow yourself to complain about anything—not even the weather.
- Never picture yourself in any other circumstances or someplace else.
- Never compare your lot with another's.

---

[1] Jerry Bridges, *The Practice of Godliness* (Colorado Springs: NavPress, 1996), 100.
[2] Ibid., 86.

- Never allow yourself to wish this or that had been otherwise.
- Never dwell on tomorrow—remember that tomorrow is God's, not yours.

> Ella's eyes were fixed on eternity. Her tomorrows belonged to God. She had given them to Him. And because all her tomorrows were nestled in God's strong arms, she was free to live today.[3]

The key to your contentment is a joyful submission to your heavenly Father regardless of your country of residence. He superintends your circumstances (Rom. 8:28–29), he ordered your days before any of them came to be (Ps. 37:16–20), and he is sovereign (Ps. 139:3, 5, 7–10; Jeremiah 1). You question his sovereignty and goodness when you feel discontent with your circumstances (2 Chron. 20:5–12; Isa. 64:8; Jer. 18:1–11; Rom. 9:19–21). As you consider an international reestablishment of your nest, do you possess an attitude of contentment that corresponds with the New Testament formula found in 1 Timothy 6:6–8? Consider the lesson Paul teaches in a few brief words:

> Godliness + Contentment = Great Gain

> The expanded formula for this teaching might read: A consistent, authentic walk with God + an attitude of satisfaction with one's heart (regardless of circumstances) = great wealth.

Purposeful application of this formula when relocating your nest can cast the experience into a blessing rather than a blight (Phil. 4:11–12).

MANAGEMENT CHALLENGES IN A FOREIGN CULTURE

As a young believer, I read a book titled *The 100% Christian*.[4] The author's intent was to remind the book's readers that regardless of where you live, you are a Christian first and a resident of the country second. He focused as well on the reality that relocation to an international environment involves the same tasks as establishing a home in the states—acquire a place to live, arrange for utilities, unpack, stock the pantry, and so forth. However, though the tasks are similar, the challenges associated with their completion vary from country to country.

I am privileged to have friends—many are former students—residing in other countries. As I prepared this chapter, I contacted some of them, requesting that they complete a brief survey. The women listed in Table 22.1 granted me permission to use their responses.

---

[3] Linda Dillow, *Calm My Anxious Heart: A Woman's Guide to Finding Contentment* (Colorado Springs: NavPress, 1998), 11–12.
[4] C. S. Lovett, *The 100% Christian* (Baldwin Park, CA: Personal Christianity, 1970).

Table 22.1

⮫ SURVEY RESPONSES: ⮩
International Residencies

Individual	Country	Length of Residency
1. Danika	Okinawa, Japan	3 years
2. Jodi	Phnom Penh, Cambodia	6 ½ years
3. Robin	Mexico	7 years
4. Julie	Albania	12 years
5. Patti	Seoul, South Korea	2 years
6. Holly	Bolivia	17 years
7. Rosalinda	Philippines (birth); United States (current); short term in Burma, India, Hungary, Moldova, Romania	30 years (Philippines); 29 years (United States); 1 year (Hungary); short term (Burma and India); in and out over 12 years (Moldova and Romania)
8. Rose Anne	Spain	36 years
9. Sandra	Turkey	22 years

Figure 22.1

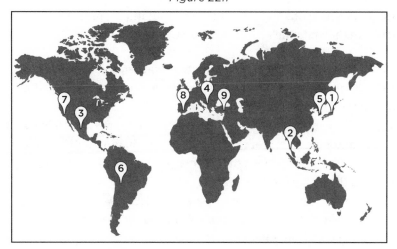

The numbers on the world map reflect the diversity of the countries represented in the survey. Consider the challenges laid out by each woman as you contemplate the necessary preparation spiritually and physically to relocate internationally. Evaluate also the homemaking skills you may need to cultivate regardless of where you are residing.

1. Danika (Japan)

Challenges Encountered: Learning to drive on the left side of the road.

We lived on a military base, but off base the houses were very different from Western standards—fewer bedrooms because they share and oddly shaped because they don't use furniture, little to no closet space, kitchens with apartment-sized fridges (they shop daily) and only a small broiler oven used for fish.

How Homemaking Skills Can Cushion the Adjustment: Organizational and management principles I learned are always helpful in a move, especially in Okinawa where we had no garage and very little closet space.

2. Jodi (Cambodia)

Callenges Encountered: I couldn't speak Khmer in a country that *only* speaks Khmer.

I didn't recognize much of the food in the markets ("wet" markets) so it was hard to know how to prepare anything.

I was expected to have someone clean my home and prepare my food. So, how was I to train someone? Again, I didn't know the language.

There are many values I adhere to as a Christian regarding diligence, joyfulness, and excellence in work, as well as a home manager regarding cleanliness, proper methods for cleaning, and sanitation. These are all new and basically unknown to the general Khmer population

How Homemaking Skills Can Cushion the Adjustment: The discipline (character development) I learned in the home economics courses helped me to be diligent in my study of Khmer.

I spent time in the kitchen learning the names of the available fruits and vegetables and how to prepare them. I experimented with different cooking methods to see which one my family preferred. Once a dish was satisfactory, I wrote down the recipe for future use.

Since I was expected to have helpers, I focused my attention on training them in the basics of home management, including food preparation, proper cleaning and sanitation, safety in the home, the basics of first aid, time management, and the basics of child care. I also sought to use this time to encourage them in their walks with the Lord, so we did some Bible study and discipleship as well. Just about everything I learned through my home economics classes prepared me to train others.

3. Robin (Mexico)

Challenges Encountered: The necessity of adjusting to the high levels of crime in Mexico City.

Corruption at all levels of Mexican society affects every aspect of household management: from time to resources to financial management, and especially the aspects of caring for our children. What each member of our household accomplishes every day as well as when, why, where, and how we live both inside and outside of our residence is continually restricted due to the high level of crime in Mexico City.

Significant financial challenges due to the high cost of obtaining basic services such as water, electricity, propane (we do not have natural gas), transportation, telephone/Internet, and bank use.

Time management. The Mexican culture values people and relationships over time, so that has been a challenging adjustment. The inefficiency of living in a huge city aggravates those challenges. Getting from place to place safely and efficiently is not always possible.

How Homemaking Skills Can Cushion the Adjustment: All the information I learned in time, resource, financial, and home management classes has proven invaluable in helping me to manage my household in Mexico.

Having a firm biblical foundation of God's design for women helps me in every moment of my day-to-day living in Mexico. God's Word is my basis for every management challenge I have faced. God's character does not change, and his Word is totally applicable in every culture—*that* has sustained me through every change I have faced.

4. Julie (Albania)

Challenges Encountered: Language barriers made everything difficult, from shopping to meeting neighbors.

Cultural barriers made it difficult to understand why people did or did not do certain things and also difficult to know with certainty what I should do or not do.

I did not have many of the amenities (reliable electricity and water, good roads, effective heating and cooling) and products that I was accustomed to using in our household in the States. I had to learn to be flexible and creative.

How Homemaking Skills Can Cushion the Adjustment: What I had learned at home and in my early years of marriage helped me to "fend for myself" in many ways, including sewing curtains, planning meals from what was available, cooking from scratch, and decorating our home using available resources.

Having some proficiency in basic homemaking skills gave me the confidence to use our home for hospitality, which is perhaps the best way for moms of young children to be involved in ministry. (You can't do much going *out* to them, so you bring them *in* to you.)

5. Patti (South Korea)

Challenges Encountered: My husband and I were stationed on Yongsan Army Garrison in the heart of Seoul. Our army garrison is surrounded by gray walls and barbed wire, and every exit leads directly into the hustle and bustle of Seoul (similar to Central Park in New York). Our army apartment was an eight hundred square foot unit constructed during the Japanese occupation and was very uninviting with its white plaster walls and concrete floors covered in dingy linoleum. My desire was to transform our home into a restful oasis. My resources were few since I could not transport my own furniture and could bring only a few accessories.

Entertaining Korean military officers and their families was very frightening to me because of the immense cultural differences of food, status, and custom.

Being so far from family and friends, unable to understand the Korean language, and adjusting to living in a huge, populated, noisy, and polluted city was a big adjustment. I'm more of a country girl. Unable to drive off post, I needed to become familiar with the subway system.

How Homemaking Skills Can Cushion the Adjustment: I tried to remember everything I was taught in my interior design and home décor classes; how to create a beautiful home on a limited budget was one of my primary goals, as was space management.

My husband and I entertained frequently. It was fun to share traditional American foods with our Korean friends, but I also had to consider their cultural likes and dislikes. Everything in the Korean culture is spicy and is eaten with chopsticks. I enjoyed "adapting" my recipes to accommodate their tastes. I tried desperately to learn to use chopsticks, and they had fun using forks.

I used my sewing machine a lot in Korea to construct runners, dresser scarves, and other accessories for our tiny apartment. We also had a large ministry on post of making quilts from velour for wounded soldiers and baby quilts to stock our Stork's Nest for young military wives giving birth so far from home and family.

However, the primary way my home economics training helped me overcome the challenges of living in Korea was through the spiritual principles that first began to be ingrained in my heart and mind as a student so many years ago. Living in Korea for two years was the time of greatest spiritual growth in my life. Not being close enough to be there for family or to talk often because of the time difference, and having all familiar support networks taken away revealed areas of my heart that needed to be transformed by God's grace. The characteristics of a Proverbs 31 woman never become outdated. The knowledge of them has been there since college, but the application of them is a constant process!

6. Holly (Bolivia)

Challenges Encountered: Balancing the old with the new, balancing the culture from which we come with the culture in which we live, are important. Examples include how my home is decorated, what holidays to choose to celebrate, living in one season of the year while remembering the other season. In South America during the month of December the store aisles have furry Christmas stockings imported from North America on one side and bathing suits on the other because it is summer.

Making long-term versus short-term plans, setting up for a three-year term with the idea of being there for twenty years.

How Homemaking Skills Can Cushion the Adjustment: The skills I learned in the classes of food preparation, sewing, finances, developing Bible studies, hospitality, decorating, beauty, being a godly woman as a wife and mother, basically submitting myself to the Lord in being the Proverbs 31 woman wherever I am, have gone way beyond the classroom. I must admit that it has not been easy. I have been stretched in not only having to set up my home but a couple of different offices. I have also grown spiritually during the years of living in Bolivia because there have been trials, temptations, challenges, and joys along the way.

Homework assignments helped in disciplining me to do the research necessary now for our current ministry.

7. Rosalinda (Various Countries)

Challenges Encountered: *Challenge:* People just drop in to discuss matters (no appointments like in the West).

Overcome Challenge: I finish my personal devotion and planning very early in the morning before people start coming. I also cook a lot of soup and fried rice so I am ready to serve any number of people who come. I usually have a tall can of cookies and crackers ready to serve anytime.

Challenge: People are not punctual—most of the time they are late for an appointment. Most people do not have cars; they use public transportation, no cell phones for a lot of people.

Overcome Challenge: Work on projects while waiting for appointment.

Challenge: Public transportation does not arrive on time; vehicles break down.

Overcome Challenge: Use time to converse with nationals; capture the opportunity for evangelism. Bring prepared sandwiches or crackers and share with others.

Challenge: Children watching unsupervised TV programs; more time playing video games than doing homework.

Overcome Challenge: Make friends with children introducing Christian action stories with songs. Help supervise homework and reward children with treats after finishing homework (with parental approval). Introduce after school Bible clubs.

How Homemaking Skills Can Cushion the Adjustment: Rosalinda's daughter, Corrine Thomas, (author of chapter 24) was a home economics major at The Master's College. Rosalinda is a strong advocate of the kind of home economics training Corinne received.[5]

8. Rose Anne (Spain)

Challenges Encountered: Every few blocks there is a marketplace where each stand sells something different: fruits and vegetables, chicken, meat, cheese and cold cuts, bread. It was a terrifying daily experience to go to the market and keep track of who was in line for each stand because the ladies would get their place in line but then leave and expect to come back to the same place. They often had heated arguments over this, and for a newcomer it was frightening.

---

[5] A biblically based homemaking program provides women with a biblically based foundation of life skills that will prepare them for their most important role of helping their husbands, nurturing their children, and managing their households.

Just furnishing our apartment was a challenge. A Spaniard cares a lot about outward appearances. Being a practical American I thought we should furnish our bedrooms first, then the living room, etc. A Spaniard decorates the entrance to her home first because that is often the only area someone sees when she comes to the door. That was the lowest on my priority list.

How Homemaking Skills Can Cushion the Adjustment: My family background was rich in hospitality, and it is as natural as breathing for me to have people in our home and make them feel part of our family.

Becoming a Woman Who Pleases God and *Designing a Lifestyle That Pleases God* by Pat Ennis and Lisa Tatlock are a tremendous encouragement to me. I use the materials often as I teach God's Word to the women and young women of our church.

9. Sandra (Turkey)

Challenges Encountered: When setting up a household, I found that apartments are rented bare. You are renting the space within four walls. You need to purchase everything from light fixtures to curtains and curtain rods, closets or wardrobes, and heaters as well as your normal furniture. The apartment comes "as is," so you are responsible to paint it and get it into working order. Turkish people frown on buying used furniture, so it is very difficult to find and awkward to explain to your neighbors.

Homemaking in Turkey comes with high expectations. The Turkish wife is an impeccable housekeeper and believes that cleanliness is next to godliness. Keeping a clean home, caring for your family, as well as being a good hostess are very important to maintaining respectability.

I've needed to learn how to make substitutions. When baking something that calls for brown sugar, I need to use normal white sugar and the local grape syrup in place of molasses. Another example would be using a local packet of dry soup mix in place of a can of cream of mushroom soup.

How Homemaking Skills Can Cushion the Adjustment: Some things don't change. The fact that you have to clean your home, do your laundry, provide meals and hospitality, and care for the many needs of your family are universal.

Being able to adapt and change your way of thinking to blend into a culture demonstrates adaptability.

Turkey is a country that is now importing more foods. I love it when something "new" is on the market and I know what to do with it. I remember when broccoli, lasagna noodles, soy sauce, peanut butter, and chocolate syrup were first available on the market here.

Prior to writing this chapter, I again conducted a database search to discern what resources are available to the individual relocating internationally. The search yielded seventy-seven pages. Hopeful that this search would prove more fruitful than the one for "Nest Building 101," I eagerly scanned the results. While information was available for international computing setup, establishing an international home-based business online, astronauts setting up home in international space, and a plethora of other topics, no resources addressed the topic of an international relocation. The scarcity of specific resources challenged me to expand the "Nest-Building Nuggets" found in "Nest Building 101."

NEST-BUILDING NUGGETS FOR RELOCATIONS

- Review the "Nest Building Nuggets" from "Nest Building 101." Conduct research and then modify the nuggets to complement your anticipated geographic change.

- Create your moving meditations as discussed earlier in this chapter.

- Research the country—its customs, its climate, its currency, its local etiquette, and even some of its conversational phrases.

- Make a decision that you will not move one thing that you do not use on a regular basis or that is not absolutely necessary for establishing your international residence.

- Get rid of everything else by holding a garage sale, posting to craigslist.org and freecycle.org (while you visit these sites, see if you can find moving boxes that someone is trying to discard), giving to a charity, or filling a trash bin.

- Apply the Titus 2:3–5 principles by cultivating homemaking skills so that you can adjust to living in any environment. A choice to do so will guard against discrediting God's Word.

EXPANDING YOUR NESTITUDES

As "Nest Building 102" draws to a close, I want to expand the list of Nestitudes begun in "Nest Building 101." It is my prayer that the chapter's contents will encourage you to establish a home, which, regardless of its geographic location, will always be a prepared place (John 14:2–3) for your family and a "city set on a hill" (Matt. 5:14) to those who touch your life.

NESTITUDES

Happy are those who allow their heavenly Father to mature them into a spiritual eagle that can ascend to great heights.

Happy are those who intentionally study and apply organizational and management principles to their lifestyles.

Happy are those who have a firm biblical foundation of God's design for women, a desire to imbed it in their hearts, and the tenacity to implement it into their lives wherever they reside.

Happy are those who apply the "Nest-Building Nuggets" as they establish their international nests.

Happy are those who petition their heavenly Father to pass "Nest Building 102" with distinction.

PUTTING THE PRINCIPLES INTO PRACTICE

1. Study the scriptural passages related to the eagle to complete the chart.

Scripture	Personal Application to My Life
Ex. 19:4	
Deut. 32:11–12	
2 Sam. 1:23	
Job 9:26	
Job 39:27–29	
Ps. 103:5	
Prov. 30:18–19	
Isa. 40:31	
Ezek. 1:10	

Ezek. 17:3	
Obad. 1:4	
Matt. 24:28	
Luke 17:37	
Rev. 4:7	

2. Sarah models for the Christian woman a strategy to relocate her nest successfully. Examine Genesis 11:29–13:1; 16:1–18:15; 20:2–12; 23:1–2, 19; 24:36; 25:10, 12; 49:31; Isaiah 51:2; Romans 4:19; 9:9; Hebrews 11:11; and 1 Peter 3:6. Develop a relocation strategy based on Scripture's report of Sarah's actions. As you observe times when Sarah was unsuccessful in completely trusting her heavenly Father, use Scripture verses to assist you in being a victor rather than a victim. Are you more like Sarah or Lot's wife? Research and meditate upon Scripture verses that will direct your attitude in a forward direction.

3. Thankfulness springs from the will, not the emotions. Spend time in the book of Psalms underlining all of the times the psalmist states, "I will." What did you learn from this study?

4. Consider the vignettes of the women who shared their experiences in "Management Challenges in a Foreign Culture." Create a list of skills you would like to develop so that the Lord is glorified in your management decisions regardless of your country of residence.

5. Expand your list of Nestitudes.

Chapter Twenty-Three

Smart Routines for Cleaning a Home

Pat Ennis

Many women looking for a theme verse for managing their homes instinctively gravitate to Proverbs 31:27 and its description of the godly woman as looking "well to the ways of her household." Others might select Titus 2:3–5, focusing on the character and responsibilities a woman should practice so that God's Word is not discredited. First Corinthians 14:40 is another logical choice: "All things should be done decently and in order."

Though each of these verses motivates a woman to create a well-managed home, the passage that drives my own household management is John 14:1–4. This tender scene described occurs in the upper room as Jesus is preparing his disciples for the devastating events that would soon occur. Fast-forwarding beyond the imminent trials, he comforts the disciples by sharing that he will soon leave to prepare a place for them in heaven:

> Let not your hearts be troubled. Believe in God; believe also in me. In my Father's house are many rooms. If it were not so, would I have told you that I go to prepare a place for you? And if I go and prepare a place for you, I will come again and will take you to myself, that where I am you may be also. And you know the way to where I am going.

Jesus promised to prepare a place for you and me. When he takes you to heaven, you will not find "under construction" signs and caution tape. Jesus will have everything ready, and you will enter a home that is fully furnished and welcoming beyond what you can imagine.

The happiest home on earth cannot compare with the life that awaits you and me in heaven—an environment void of sadness, sickness, and tears but constantly peaceful, perfect, and lacking nothing. Heaven is home for all those who turn from their sin and receive the Lord Jesus as their Savior (see Rom. 10:9–13). Heaven is the ultimate "House Beautiful": angels (Rev. 5:11); a street of gold (Rev. 21:21) twelve beautiful gates of pearl (Rev. 21:21); a pure and clear-as-crystal river of life (Rev. 22:1); a city of gold built upon the foundation of precious stones (Rev. 21:19); and from the tree of life a different fruit each month (Rev. 22:2)—no more searching for the best piece of produce (see Rev. 21:9–22:5).

However, since my heavenly Father still has work for me to accomplish on earth, I am motivated to make my home a bit of heaven on earth. The model Jesus used to prepare a heavenly home for his family is the one I have adopted as my prototype and blueprint. Just as I will not find an "under construction" sign and caution tape when I arrive in heaven, I should enter my earthly home seeing a reflection of that heavenly order and peacefulness rather than worldly chaos and disorder. Its arrangement should literally draw others to its warming hearth.

CREATING A WELCOMING HOME

If you want your home to be a welcoming environment, you will attempt daily to make those who enter its doors feel welcome. What visual images suggest welcome? First and foremost, someone's arrival should be joyfully anticipated. Whatever your season of life, the biblical mandate calls for you to prepare your heart and home to welcome family and guests. You prepare your heart by meditating on God's Word and thinking his thoughts (Phil. 4:8–9). You prepare your home to be clean and comfortable so those who abide within will joyfully anticipate returning to this prepared place. Orderliness will give to those who live there a sense of peace and emotional well-being.

A child responded to the question, "Would you like to go to heaven?"

She said, "What is it like there?"

The response came: "Why, heaven is like home."

"Like *my* home? Then I don't want to go there!"

Choosing to learn practical skills for home care will go a long way in making sure that none of our family members ever has the response of this dear child.

PRACTICAL HOME CARE

A smooth-running home needs daily care. The words *clean* and *neat* have different definitions for each family. The most important point is for everyone in the family to feel that home is a protected place, a healthy environment, and a setting that enables the extension of biblical hospitality to others.

Consider the home fashioned as a glass house with few window coverings and built on the top of a hill (Matt. 5:14–16). Everyone is able to view what is happening in the home. Not only should others see a well-managed home, but they should also see the biblical virtues of love, honor, kindness, and respect joyfully modeled. Just think of the incredible Christian testimony you would have to the community if each family in your church lived together according to God's design. The impact would be immeasurable.

Being the last person to leave my home in the morning, I attempt to establish order. If I remember my home as clean and peaceful, I will look forward to returning to its comfort. If my mental image is one of disorder, then I will want to stay away as long as possible. To make and keep my home environment pleasant, I need to have a smart home care plan.

CREATING A SMART PLAN FOR HOME CARE

As a professional home economist, I am not only trained in the theory and skills of home management, but I also possess many years of experience in applying these principles. However, despite all my education and experience, I am unable to get the vacuum to run itself, the polish and dust rag to make a connection to furniture without my hands, or the mop to glide along the floor without my assistance. I must use my training and skill to create a **Smart Plan for Home Care** that meets the needs of my home, schedule, and season of life.

Smart home care involves planning how best to use my energy, time, money, and skill. It demands choosing cleaning techniques that get the tasks done as efficiently and completely as possible. This plan also calls for everyone in the family to help so that no one person has too much to do and everyone has a vested interest in maintaining this cleanliness and order in the home. The motto "many hands make light work" truly applies to the upkeep of a home.

The boundaries of home care depend on the following:

- the size of the family
- the ages of family members
- the indoor hobbies and activities enjoyed by the family
- hospitality styles
- the size and age of the home
- the types of furnishings within the home
- the presence of pets
- the geographical location of the home
- the weather and climate of the respective seasons

These steps lead to a Smart Plan for Home Care:

1. Analyze your needs and set cleaning *goals*. Take the time to look over each room and identify clutter as well as cobwebs, dirt, or dust. In hard-to-see areas, do the touch test by running a clean finger over furnishings and surfaces to find undetected dirt. Ask yourself, "What jobs need to be done?" and then list them.

2. Set priorities. Rank the home care tasks from most to least important.

3. Assign numerical order to the cleaning tasks. Which ones need to be done first?

4. Develop a **Home Care Plan** for each room and then itemize the steps for each task. A part of preparing the plan is to answer some important questions:

   - How often does the specific task need to be done?
   - When will it be done (daily, weekly, monthly, seasonally)?
   - Who will do it?
   - How much time will it take?
   - What supplies, tools, or other materials are needed to do the task?

5. Make a weekly **Home Care Schedule**. Assign the cleaning tasks to certain days of the week. With a plan, the family can determine the workload in consideration of everyone's abilities and personal schedules. A schedule lets family members know when tasks need to be completed and divides the cleaning tasks according to age, ability level, and time schedules.

6. Allow for flexibility, such as trading tasks or changing the days on which certain tasks are done. Customize the schedule to meet your family's needs. Though another family's schedule might serve as a model, two schedules are not likely to be exactly the same.

7. Consider rotating the tasks periodically, allowing everyone to experience all the cleaning tasks so all have an appreciation of what it takes to do each task.

8. Whenever possible use the room-by-room method of cleaning, which is usually more effective than completing random tasks.

9. Include larger seasonal cleaning tasks in the schedule. Washing the windows, cleaning the garage, stripping and waxing the floors, and cleaning under the refrigerator are not done weekly, but these tasks need to be included in the schedule to ensure the entire home stays well maintained.

10. Evaluate your Home Care Schedule to make sure you are working *smart*. The *plan* should simplify your *cleaning tasks*. Evaluation is helpful. The following questions might help this process:

    - Does the schedule include daily tasks such as picking up clutter, making the beds, and hanging up or putting clothes in the hamper?

- Does the schedule encourage a room-by-room cleaning so that each room gets the special care needed?
- Do you save energy by having cleaning tools and supplies collected—perhaps in a basket or bucket or multipocket apron—before you begin cleaning?
- Do you alternate difficult and easy tasks? Have you considered tackling the most challenging task first—while your energies are fresh?
- Do you take a brief rest after a difficult cleaning task or in the middle of a long work period?
- During the brief rest, do you increase your energy with a healthy snack? A cold glass of juice can help the mind and muscles feel refreshed.
- Do you refresh your mind with soothing music?
- Does the schedule rotate cleaning tasks so that they do not become boring?
- Does the schedule include larger seasonal cleaning tasks?
- Are you constantly looking for ways to work *smarter* rather than longer and harder?

Consider using the template for a Home Care Schedule (Table 23.1) to manage your home management routines effectively. Your home schedule really depends on your standards and lifestyle. The most important steps are to develop, use, and then evaluate a schedule. For each task listed, be sure to answer the questions stated in step four in the preceding section. The schedule is helpful only if it meets the needs of your family. Remember: *If you are not managing your home, it is managing you.*

Table 23.1
HOME CARE SCHEDULE

Room _____			
Daily Tasks	Weekly Tasks	Monthly Tasks	Seasonal Tasks

ACTIVATING YOUR HOME CARE SCHEDULE

A critical element to the activation of your schedule is acknowledging that it must align with your body cycle—not your mother's or your neighbor's. You cannot force yourself to be something you are not. For example, I am *not* a morning person. Therefore, I must plan to do the challenging tasks on my schedule at a time when I function best. Since it takes me a while to wake up completely, I will not be successful if I plan to do my most difficult tasks in the early morning. However, when the late morning sun pours into the windows, I come alive. So, whenever possible, I plan to do my most difficult tasks at that time—when my attitude is fresh and my energies full. Consider these procedures as you plan your Home Care Schedule.

✑ CLEANING YOUR HOME ✑
from Top to Bottom

- *Dust descent.* Regularly dust ceiling fans; tall mantels and bookshelves; and the tops of cabinets, shelves, and doorframes, where dust can build up. Clean up dust and dirt that fall as you work your way down, finally sweeping what makes its way to the floor.
- *Shiny showers.* Prevent streaks by using microfiber cloths and a squeegee. Lemon oil applied to shower doors and walls twice a month will help repel soap scum.
- *Dust mite combat duties.* To reduce dust mite allergens:
  - encase mattresses and pillows, place strips of duct tape on the mattress case, and wash bedding in hot water every week;
  - place stuffed animals in a large plastic bag and freeze four to five hours, then remove and vacuum with a HEPA filter.
- *Fresh air.* Use a high-performance air filter and change every 3 months.
- *Finally, floors.* Vacuum and clean floors weekly, including areas under large pieces of furniture, corners of rooms, and backs of closets. A few drops of mild liquid dish detergent added to a gallon of water makes an inexpensive cleaning solution. Use water that is barely warm rather than hot water, which can break down the floor finish over time.

Some tasks are best done before you retire for the night. For example, mopping the kitchen floor in the evening works well for me. The floor also can dry completely overnight before someone walks on it the next day. How can you adjust your schedule so you receive maximum return for your energy investment?

SMART USE OF YOUR HOUSEHOLD HELPERS

Do you know that you have a whole staff of household helpers to take the trauma out of housework? They are your cleaning tools, appliances, and supplies. Take the time to get to know them well to appreciate fully what they can do. You can best make their acquaintance by becoming a reader of labels, tags, and instruction manuals. Manufacturers spend thousands of dollars to explain what their products and appliances will and will not do, yet often the manuals and labels are ignored. Before using a product or appliance, read about it, absorb the manual's content, and then use the appliance efficiently and effectively. Keep all of your labels, tags, and manuals in a notebook or expandable file for easy access. For products that come with a warranty, photocopy the purchase receipt, being certain the date of purchase is legible, and tape it to the inside cover so it is available if you need to activate the warranty.

A wide variety of cleaning tools and products are available, and you do not want to overspend in this budget area. Analyze which ones will help you to implement your Home Care Schedule. As you make your selections, consider choosing the style, color, and quality of tools that you like and that will build in you a positive attitude about the tasks these tools help you perform. Spending a few extra pennies when they are purchased will add a bit of enthusiasm to the completion of the task.

PURCHASE AND CARE OF ESSENTIAL TOOLS

Stores, both local and online, offer an array of gadgets and gizmos, all designed to make your chores easier. Since many are nice to have but not necessary, consider focusing on purchasing the basics before expanding into the extras. The basic cleaning tools include:

- basket or caddy for carrying cleaning supplies
- broom
- brushes
- bucket
- cleaning products
- dust cloths
- dustpan
- mop
- paper towels
- rubber gloves
- sponges
- step stool
- toilet brush
- vacuum cleaner

Taking the time to care for your cleaning tools will increase their life span. Consider investing a few extra minutes to pamper your cleaning tools:

- Wash and rinse brushes frequently with warm water and detergent.

- Wash and rinse mops often enough to keep them clean and odor free. Mops should be hung by the handles and without touching the floor when put into storage.

- Regularly wash sponges, dust cloths, and rags. Be sure to allow the sponges to dry thoroughly to prevent odors. Use a miniclothesline (with clothespins) attached to the back of a closet door to hold dust cloths and other cleaning rags.

- Discard oily or cleaner-soaked cloths. Because they can be combustible, storing them in a closed closet can cause a fire. If they must be stored, choose a well-ventilated area.

- Rinse buckets after each use to prevent the building up of dried cleaning product and residue at the bottom.

- Check the vacuum bag frequently. Follow the manufacturer's instructions for care and cleaning. Be sure to keep some extra vacuum bags in your storage area.

- Use cup hooks on the side wall of your storage area to hold the dustpan and any other items that can be hung.

- Look for a place other than under the kitchen sink to store laundry and cleaning supplies. These products may be poisonous, so you are wise to store them where young children will not get to them.

CLEANING PRODUCTS FROM YOUR PANTRY

What is your annual budget for cleaning supplies? Even with the help of coupons or purchasing the products at a warehouse club, the total cost by the end of the year can be hefty. One way to save money is to use resources already found in your pantry or medicine cabinet as cleaning agents (see Table 23.2). The natural products are also safer and healthier to use.

Table 23.2

✂ CLEANING PRODUCT CHART ✂

Product	Characteristics and Use
White vinegar	• White vinegar is a mild acid. • It is a good all-purpose cleaner and deodorizer. • Mixed with water, it cuts grease and dissolves film on glassware and windows
Baking soda	• Cut the lid off the box and leave on the back of a shelf in both the freezer and refrigerator to absorb odors. Replace several times a year. • Its mild abrasiveness provides a good scouring powder. • Light soil and stains on sinks, counters, and stovetops can be removed. • Mixed with water it makes an all-around, light-duty cleaner.

Ammonia	• This heavy-duty cleaning liquid agent is effective for general household cleaning. • It is available in both plain and sudsy formulas. • Ammonia is poisonous and the odor and fumes can be irritating, so use with caution in a well-ventilated area.
Salt	• Salt, a mild abrasive, can be used to absorb grease or wine stains. • Salt softens water.
Hydrogen peroxide	• Hydrogen peroxide can be used as a disinfectant. • It can also function as a bleaching substitute.

The procedures for preparing the cleaning solutions are simple and quick (see Table 23.3). You do not need to be a chemist to mix them successfully, and in most cases, they are much safer than many of the commercial products that contain toxins.

Table 23.3

⌒ CLEANING PRODUCT SOLUTIONS ⌒

Product	Recipe
All-purpose liquid cleaner	Mix together ½ cup white vinegar, 1 cup plain household ammonia, ¼ cup baking soda, and 1 gallon warm water. Dispense in a spray bottle and use it as you would a commercial brand such as Formula 409.
Window, glass, and mirror cleaner	Mix together ½ cup plain ammonia, ½ cup white vinegar, 2 tablespoons cornstarch, and 1 gallon warm water. Dispense in spray bottle.
Cleaner for ceramic and vinyl floors	Mix together 1 cup white vinegar and 1 gallon warm water. Use the solution to mop ceramic tile and all types of vinyl floors. Rinsing is unnecessary.
Heavy-duty cleaner for non-wood floors	Mix together ¾ cup plain household ammonia and 1 gallon warm water. Use on heavily soiled floors. Rinsing is unnecessary.

Wood floors	Steep two regular tea bags in 2 quarts boiling water. Allow the tea water to cool to room temperature. Remove bags. Use a well-wrung cloth mop or sponge mop (make sure it is just barely damp) to wipe the floor. The tannic acid in tea is great for the wood and leaves a beautiful shine.
Toilet bowl cleaner	Mix together ¼ cup baking soda, ¼ cup liquid detergent, and ¼ cup warm water. Use a toilet brush to distribute the cleaner inside the bowl. Allow to soak a few hours or overnight, and then brush the bowl before flushing.
Tub cleaner	Mix together 1 cup baking soda, 1 gallon hot water, 1 cup vinegar, 1 cup plain household ammonia, and 1 table-spoon liquid detergent. Dissolve the baking soda into very warm water in a bucket. Add the vinegar, ammonia, and liquid detergent. Shake or stir to mix the ingredients. **Use in a well-ventilated area.**
Ceramic tile cleaner	In a gallon-sized container, mix together ½ cup baking soda, ⅓ cup household ammonia, ¼ cup white vinegar, and 7 cups warm water. Cover tightly and shake, stir, or swish to mix ingredients. Dispense the solution via a spray bottle. Spray directly onto tile surface (cleans grout, too); then wipe with a damp sponge or cloth. The solution usually eliminates soap film.
Heavy-duty grout cleaner	Mix 3 cups baking soda with 1 cup warm water in a large bowl to make a smooth paste. Scrub the paste into the grout with an old toothbrush or sponge. Allow to sit for a while, depending on the severity of the situation. Rinse well with clear water.

Mildew removal	Use white vinegar (full strength) or isopropyl alcohol (full strength) and apply with an old toothbrush or nail brush.
	Allow to sit for a while, depending on the severity of the situation.
	Rinse well with clear water.
Furniture polish	Combine 2 parts olive or vegetable oil and 1 part lemon juice or white vinegar in a glass jar.
	Seal tightly.
	Shake well before using sparingly.
	Apply a thin coat with a soft cloth, then buff well.
Jewelry cleaner	Make a 50/50 mixture of ammonia and water.
	Soak jewelry, then brush and rinse completely.
	Do not use with pearls or opals.
Oven cleaner	Place one cup ammonia in a **glass or ceramic** bowl.
	Put the bowl on the bottom of a cold oven and leave it in the closed oven overnight. Perhaps you should make a warning sign to alert family members that cleaning is in process.
	The next morning, pour the ammonia into a pail of warm water and use this solution and a sponge to wipe away the loosened grime.
	Be careful of the fumes. They will be strong when you first open the oven door. You may want to wear a mask.
Clogged drain treatment	Pour ½ cup of salt and ½ cup of baking soda, followed by 4 cups boiling water, into the drain.
	Allow to sit overnight, if possible.
	Greasy drains usually respond to this treatment.
Sluggish drain treatment	Pour ½ cup of baking soda, followed by ½ cup of white vinegar, into the drain.
	The two ingredients will interact, creating foam and fumes, so put the drain cover or strainer back in place after pouring in the soda and vinegar.
	Allow to sit at least 3 hours or overnight.
	Follow with a kettle of **boiling** water.
	This is a highly recommended monthly maintenance technique to keep drains running well.

Carpet freshener and deodorizer	Sprinkle the carpet liberally with baking soda.
	Allow to sit overnight.
	Vacuum thoroughly in the morning.
	Start with an empty vacuum bag or receptacle because it is going to fill up fast.
Coffeemaker and carafe cleaner	Pour 1 quart of white vinegar into the top of the coffeemaker.
	With brewing basket in place, set the coffeemaker on a hot plate.
	Turn on coffeemaker.
	After approximately ½ of the vinegar has pumped through the coffeemaker into the carafe, turn it off and pour the vinegar back into the top of the coffeemaker.
	Allow vinegar to remain in the unit for approximately ½ hour.
	Turn coffeemaker back on and allow all the vinegar to pour into the carafe.
	Discard vinegar solution and flush the system by cycling through 10 cups of clear water.
	Repeat the flushing procedure.
	Do this once a month.
Garbage disposal cleaner	Empty the contents of your ice maker into the garbage disposal side of your sink.
	Remove the stopper from the opposite side.
	Turn on the hot water and the disposal. The ice will clean the inside of your disposal unit.
	This is a highly recommended monthly maintenance technique that will keep the disposal unit running well.

✑ A WORD OF CAUTION ✐

Liquid chlorine bleach is an inexpensive, effective disinfectant. **However, never mix chlorine bleach with any other product.** You could create deadly chlorine gas. **Always label** the products you create and keep them tightly covered and out of the reach of children and pets. Storage closets or cupboards containing cleaning solutions should have childproof latches installed on the doors.

THE BONUS

Surprisingly, much of the movement associated with the care of the home tones the human body in ways that are comparable to hours spent at the gym. Knowing that your loving heavenly Father allows you to multitask personal fitness with household tasks as you fulfill your biblical responsibilities for looking well to the ways of your household is exciting. Making your home a prepared place for others also helps you tone your body.

First Timothy 4:8 is a reminder that while "bodily training is of some value, godliness is of value in every way." The woman who balances the care of her home with the care of her body receives a bonus because she avoids becoming a worried, frazzled, and defensive woman who sacrifices herself on the altar of domesticity or physical fitness.

PUTTING THE PRINCIPLES INTO PRACTICE

1. Review the Scriptures that are introduced in this chapter (Prov. 31:27; Matt. 5:13–16; John 14:1–4; Titus 2:3–5). What personal goals will you set to integrate them into your home management routines?
2. Apply the guidelines for a Home Care Schedule to several rooms in your home. Implement the plan for two weeks and then evaluate. Make any modifications to ensure that you are working *smarter* rather than harder.
3. Once you have mastered the Home Care Schedule for these rooms, develop a Home Care Schedule for your entire home. Make sure your schedule includes the participation of all family members.
4. Modify the Home Care Schedule evaluation questions so they meet your personal needs.
5. Visit the websites of Heinz Vinegar (http://www.heinzvinegar.com/tips /around-the-house) and Arm and Hammer (http://www.armhammer.com). Expand and modify the "Cleaning Product Solutions" chart to meet your household needs.

Chapter Twenty-Four

Technology in the Home

Corinne Thomas

As a young girl visiting my aunt at her workplace in a large bank in the Philippines, I was introduced to technology. Large, white boxes rested on the employee desks. If I behaved during the visit, my aunt allowed me to play a software game with a skier and an abominable snowman, who would try to eat me as I slalomed down the virtual hills. To me, *that* was technology. Technology was a toy; and if obedient, I was allowed to play with this toy.

Fast-forward several years to a small mission office in San Dimas, California. My mother and I had just returned to California from our first trip to the former Soviet Republic of Moldova. She had agreed to volunteer at the mission office a portion of each week. There I was introduced to something called a "Mac." When turned on, a smiling version of the cute bitten apple would pop up on the screen, simultaneously chiming. This "thing" had something magical called "AOL" that connected me to hundreds of other users through *the Internet*. It was a bigger toy than the one in the Philippines! The mission director taught me an important principle about computers—they are like a toolbox, and your job is to find the best ways to use the tools to help achieve goals.

So, what is technology? A toy? A tool? Something as specific as a computer? What about the book you are holding in your hand right now? Is technology good or bad? Mention the word *technology* and different ideas surface from a variety of sources—it is blamed for society's ills, such as obesity and addictions, and praised for society's advancements, including space shuttles and the ability to save a life in utero.

When it comes to dealing with technology as a Christian with or without a family, keep these Scriptures in mind:

Know the truth, and the truth will set you free. (John 8:32)

For everything there is a season. (Eccles. 3:1)

There is nothing new under the sun. (Eccles. 1:9)

Test everything; hold fast to what is good. (1 Thess. 5:21)

KNOW THE TRUTH, AND THE TRUTH WILL SET YOU FREE

Within the context of John 8:32, Jesus is speaking to a group of Jews (Pharisees and scribes included) at the temple. He had just pardoned the woman caught in adultery (vv. 1–11) and declared that he was the light of the world, sent to do his Father's will (vv. 12–29). "As he was saying these things, many believed in him" (v. 30), and to these new believers he says, "If you abide in my word, you are truly my disciples, and you will know the truth, and the truth will set you free" (vv. 31–32). What was this truth about which he spoke? The truth was the message of salvation, the truth about redemption. Knowing that truth would set one free from the power of sin.

There are those who attempt to paint technology as a savior. Others would argue that technology is a sin from which we must be freed. There are many sources of information and opinions when it comes to various forms of technology. *Find the truth and be free.*

MYTHS AND TRUTHS ABOUT TECHNOLOGY

Two myths are commonly associated with technology:

- Technology is an add-on to life.
- Technology is any tool invented after I was born.

Examine each myth. Would you affirm either?

Technology, by definition, is "the application of scientific knowledge for practical purposes."[1] From the beginning of time, civilization has experienced technological advances—discovering fire, the wheel, the printing press, computers, and the list goes on. Consider the options of washing your clothes in machines instead of by hand. Consider travel in cars, buses, airplanes, or by horseback. Technology cannot be considered an add-on to life because technology has become a major part of twenty-first-century life. Whether you write with a quill, a ballpoint pen, or a stylus on a Wacom tablet, you are still writing. The point is, you find new ways to do old things. Technology is not a "tool" invented after you were born. God has continually blessed his creation with technological advances.

Regardless of the time period in which you live, two things remain constant:

---

[1] *Oxford Dictionaries*, Oxford University Press, s.v. "technology" [online], accessed August 5, 2010, http://www.oxforddictionaries.com/view/entry/ m_en_us1297439#m_en_us1297439.

- new things; and
- opinions about those things.

Usually, new things will be heralded with either excitement or disgust. Opinions will come from experts or the "man on the street." To whom should you listen? Whom can you trust? Consider these guidelines:

- *Consult more than one source.* Like any good researcher, find out if there is consensus about a product. This takes time and effort but is well worth it.

- *Determine who the credible experts are.* Any field has its well-known experts, and the same goes for technology reviews. Discern who among individuals or groups of individuals is considered a reliable source for the latest on new technologies.

- *Ask your friends.* Is there someone you know who is a tech enthusiast or who may already own the product you might purchase? Ask for her input. Of course, as with any review, execute caution. Some people are very enthusiastic while others are negative. Use discernment!

FOR EVERYTHING, THERE IS A SEASON

One of my best childhood memories was spending a summer on a farm in Graysville, Pennsylvania. The farm was owned by the parents of a woman my mother met in Thailand, where my mom was working among refugees and the woman was serving with the Peace Corps. Both women ended up in Pennsylvania, where I was enjoying the farm animals, exploring wherever I pleased, and savoring the food. Then we had to leave.

In my young naïveté, I could not imagine anything better than being on that farm. Having that "ripped" away from me felt devastating. I cried on the way to the car. I cried in the backseat of that car. I cried as we drove across the states to Ohio. I cried when we *got* to Ohio. I learned a big lesson that summer, and I continue to be reminded of it—change happens. Places change, people change, and eventually everything on this finite earth will change. Even the relics of times past are still changing because of outside forces of nature or human beings. Change happens and will continue to happen until the Lord returns.

CHANGE HAPPENS . . . AND CAN HAPPEN QUICKLY

Of all the realms of change, changes in technology seem to progress the fastest. For example, here are some major technological advances in the last two hundred years alone:

1752 – Benjamin Franklin presents the lightning rod.

1797 – Eli Whitney, inventor of the cotton gin, gives the US interchangeable parts.

1806 – The coffee pot with a metal sieve is created.

1807 – Robert Fulton's steamboat changes transportation.

1814 – The cast iron tipped plow changes farming.

1830 – The electromagnetic motor is built but has no practical use.

1833 – The sewing machine is invented.

1837 – Power tools come on the scene thanks to Thomas Davenport.

1857 – The passenger elevator is introduced.

1876 – Alexander Graham Bell patents the telephone.

1879 – Incandescent lightbulbs hit the scene.

1880 – R. G. Rhodes improves the ear trumpet with his primitive hearing aid.

1885 – The first skyscraper is erected.

1888 – The Kodak portable camera is available.

1889 – The dishwasher makes its appearance.

1891 – Initially shown as a novelty ride, the escalator is born.

1902 – Air-conditioning enters.[2]

The list includes only inventions in the United States and reaches only to the early 1900s. Since then, cars—both gas-powered and electric—commercial airplanes, a man walking on the moon, space stations, record players, CDs, DVDs, personal computers, cellular telephones, and the Internet have all come on the scene. Only the Lord knows what the future will bring. That phrase may scare some and excite others, which brings to the surface an important point about change: *Change will happen; through the Lord's strength our reactions to change can be controlled* (Phil. 4:13).

COMMON REACTIONS TO CHANGE

Growing up on the mission field with my widowed mother, we developed a strong mother-daughter bond. Just by looking at her, I could tell what my mother was thinking in certain situations. She was able to do the same with me.

Then I grew up. Of course, I had been growing all along, but the older I got, the more complex life became. There were a few years in high school when my mother likely thought she had a completely different person living with her than the one who had traveled by her side for a number of years. I was changing; she was changing. Maybe I was changing more, and she did not want to lose her little girl. As all parents know, children mature and change.

---

[2] See "Technology Timeline: 1752–1900," *American Experience*, Public Broadcasting Service (PBS), http://www.pbs.org/wgbh/amex/telephone/timeline/timeline_text.html.

My mother and I had a few options. We could get angry—angry at each other, angry at the situations in which we found ourselves, angry at God. We could ignore the changes taking place and try to live like nothing new was happening. Finally, we could choose to trust the Lord with whatever was going on and love each other as Christ loved us as we navigated the new challenges and blessings God had brought into our lives. I was blessed that my mother generally chose the second or third option. I, unfortunately, tended to choose the first and still do sometimes. Praise the Lord for continuous growth.

Change can be scary. You become accustomed to things, places, or people, and when something changes, a bit of you will have to change, too. Just when you have learned some new technology, another *newer* technology comes along to replace or enhance it, or the technology may disappear entirely. This may lead you to feel incompetent or insecure in your skills. Do not fall prey to a defeatist mentality. Do not choose anger. Do not choose apathy. Choose to move forward with discernment, knowing that the Lord already knows what was, is, and what will be. Consider the following guidelines for dealing with change:

- *Do not be ruled by fear.* You are well within your rights to hole up in a bunker out of fear and ignore the changes occurring around you. However, you are then depriving the world of your Christian witness. While you may not be the next game changer in technology or you may not see a need for a particular technology in your life, someone else may. That person may need a human being who can show her the love of Christ. Do not lose a potential friendship because of your fear of change in any arena.

- *Do not get caught up in the crowd.* On the flip side, do not blindly follow the crowd. Just because 90 percent of your friends are buying a new piece of technology does not necessarily mean you need one, too. Neither does it mean that your friends are necessarily sinning by making such a purchase. Keep your wits about you and use discernment in all things.

- *Trust in the one who never changes.* The Word promises that "Jesus Christ is the same yesterday and today and forever" (Heb. 13:8). In a world full of constant change, rely on your heavenly Father to sustain and be faithful as he has promised (Isa. 41:10, 13).

THERE IS NOTHING NEW UNDER THE SUN

"When I was a child, my family did not own a CD player. We played records!" Even though demographically I am still in the "young generation," I sometimes find myself explaining to younger people how *I* used to do something "back in the day." But as I reflect on those times when I feel old, I realize that there really is nothing new under the sun. If you stop and think for a moment about technology as a tool, what does technology allow you to do (or prevent you from doing) that you could not do as a child? My grandmother may have listened to records; my mother may have listened to records and cassette tapes; I have listened to cassette tapes and CDs; my students download their favorite MP3s to play on their digital music players. But we are all looking for the same thing. The styles may be different, the mediums may be different, the content may be different, but we were all seeking the same enjoyment that music brings.

HUMAN NATURE NEVER CHANGES

Human beings are sinful. Because of the fall, sin will continue until the day the Lord returns and takes believers to live with him forever in glory. That said, some things will never change, even if technologies change. Consider four sinful attributes that have spanned the ages and their application to technology:

- *Anger*—In a sinful world, there are sinful human beings who can make mistakes or purposely orchestrate hurtful events. Sinful human beings *think* they know everything about a story, a situation, or a person. However, eventually they must accept that they are finite; only God above can truly judge a person's motivations and actions. That does not stop some people from lashing out in unholy anger. In an age of new technologies, they are given new media to show anger, whether it be through an e-mail sent thoughtlessly, hurtful comments posted in a public forum, or use of slander by some other technological means. The tone of expression may keep you and another person from face-to-face encounter, but your words or actions are no less meaningful or hurtful. "Be angry, and do not sin; ponder in your own hearts on your beds, and be silent" (Ps. 4:4).

- *Greed*—As long as people live, greed and selfishness will exist. The Lord knew what he was doing when he included, "You shall not covet" (Ex. 20:17) in the Ten Commandments. In fact, he ended the list with this command, and to this day all people struggle with it. You want, not necessarily what you cannot have, but what you *do not* have. You do not have to learn this sinful trait; children and adults alike suffer from it. In modern society, the acquisition of technology can be seen as a status symbol. Believers must fight the urge to hoard technology merely to keep up appearances. Your neighbor may no longer have an ox or a donkey, but she may have a better GPS, home theater system, or faster Internet connection. "You shall not covet" indeed.

- *Idolatry*—In *Worship: The Missing Jewel*, A. W. Tozer writes, "Now we were made to worship, but the Scriptures tell us something else again. They tell us that man fell and kept not his first estate; that he forfeited the original glory of God and failed to fulfill the creative purpose, so that he is not worshiping now in the way that God meant him to worship."[3] Not only do you and I not worship God the way he meant us to worship, but we also replace him altogether with idols. Our sinful desires allow us to turn anything into an idol. Once technology has crossed the line in your life from being a tool to being your savior or your reason for living (although most would not phrase it that way), you know you have an idol in your life.

- *Lust*—"The righteousness of the upright delivers them, but the treacherous are taken captive by their lust" (Prov. 11:6). One intense topic related to technology is pornography. The proliferation of sexually stimulating images in marketing and entertainment makes it virtually impossible to avoid some form of exposure to temptation and lust (for example, magazine covers in grocery stores, billboards, posters in malls). However, the Internet (available both on computers and cell phones) and numerous other media have made pornography readily accessible, magnifying the dangers to children and adolescents of usage of this technology that is not protected and monitored by adults who care about the harmful effects and addictive power of even incidental exposure to erotic material.[4] Pornography is not a new problem, having been around since ancient times, but the level of vigilance required, especially in the home, to guard your heart and to help your spouse, children, and friends guard their hearts, has escalated.

PRACTICAL STRATEGIES

Consider these practical strategies for dealing with your humanity:

- *Know that you are a new creation in Christ.* "Therefore, if anyone is in Christ, he is a new creation. The old has passed away; behold, the new has come" (2 Cor. 5:17). You may still have your sinful nature on this earth, but if you are in Christ, you are no longer who you used to be. You have Christ in you; you are a new creation, and "he who began a good work in you will bring it to completion at the day of Jesus Christ" (Phil. 1:6). You are not alone. Draw on his strength as you fight your sinful nature.

- *Search your heart.* It is much easier to blame others (or things) for your challenges than to acknowledge the fact that the root of a problem is most likely . . . *you*. Pray with the psalmist, "Search me, O God, and know my heart! Try me and know my thoughts! And see if there be any grievous way in me, and lead me in the way everlasting!" (Ps. 139:23–24).

- *If you are justifying it, avoid it.* There is nothing wrong with listening to music. There is nothing wrong with surfing the Internet. There *is* something wrong

---

[3] A. W. Tozer, *Worship: The Missing Jewel* (Camp Hill, PA: Christian, 1992), 6–7.
[4] See William M. Struthers, *Wired for Intimacy: How Pornography Hijacks the Male Brain* (Downers Grove, IL: InterVarsity, 2009).

with doing those things if your motivation and your end goal does not glorify God (1 Cor. 10:31). Just as you should be wary of justifying eating a sugary doughnut while on a diet, so should you be wary of trying to justify using technology in ways that grate on your conscience.

- *Run.* Some things cannot be avoided or foreseen, but you *can* choose to remove yourself from a compromising situation. When that pop-up with a questionable link appears on your screen, do not hesitate and ponder the consequences of clicking on it. Close it. Run. If you know you are prone to some sinful behavior, no matter how insignificant it may seem, and you find yourself in a situation that encourages that behavior, follow Joseph's example and run (Genesis 39).

TEST EVERYTHING; HOLD FAST TO WHAT IS GOOD

What should you do with technology? Is technology a tool or a toy? Is it good or bad? The response may irritate you, but the truth is: it depends heavily on you, your needs, your personality, your culture, your contexts, and your convictions. If you have a family, consider your family's needs, personalities . . . the list could go on and on. However, as 1 Thessalonians 5:21–23 teaches, there are some things to keep in mind:

- *Test everything.* You do not become knowledgeable about technology by reading one review, trying one product, or by sequestering yourself from it. Trial, error, and research will help you determine how technology can assist you and your family in your daily tasks.

- *Hold fast to what is good.* If something is indeed good, hold on to it. If something proves to be more detrimental to you, abstain from it. What works for one family may not be good for yours. That is why you must "test everything," then "hold fast to what is good" (v. 21).

- *Abstain from every form of evil.* Some things are clearly wrong (for example, pornography, illegal downloading), but others may fall into gray areas. Are you buying that new television because you want to impress your neighbors? If so, you just crossed the line from buying a piece of technology for its function (a beautiful viewing experience) to purchasing it to boost your ego (pride). Are you going into debt unnecessarily to acquire what has been marketed as the latest and greatest? Such a choice reflects your heart's issues, and with God's help, you can deal with them.

As you navigate the waters of technology and how you can use it, my prayer for you echoes that of the apostle Paul, "Now may the God of peace himself sanctify you completely, and may your whole spirit and soul and body be kept blameless at the coming of our Lord Jesus Christ" (1 Thess. 5:23). May the God of peace guide you, give you wisdom, and keep you blameless until the coming of the Lord, not just in matters relating to technology, but in all aspects of your life.

Lord, thank you for blessing us with the wonders of technology and the benefits they can give us. Give us discernment and perseverance. Grant us peace in change. Search our hearts and know our motivations. Shower us with mercy and grace, as we test everything, and the wisdom to hold fast to what is good. Allow us to bring glory to you in all we do. Lord, come quickly! Amen.

PUTTING THE PRINCIPLES INTO PRACTICE

1. *What technologies are you currently using in your life?* Have you stopped to consider that you may be using technologies without realizing it? Take a moment to think through the different technologies you are using and the benefits (or pitfalls!) they bring you. If you cannot think of any benefits, maybe you should reevaluate that technology's role in your life.

2. *How are you using technology?* What you use is important, but *how* you use it is even more crucial. Is a particular technology helping you with certain tasks, or are you using it to shirk responsibilities? Out of fear, have you avoided technologies that might actually be a great way to connect with others and share the love of Christ?

3. *Who is holding you accountable for the technologies you use?* God created you to live in community; no one is an island. While you may feel like you have a solid grasp on your technology use, is there someone you can trust to hold you accountable in that area? Do you have a friend who can gently remind you that it might be wiser to turn the computer off and get together face-to-face for coffee? Who can give you good advice on different technologies?

ABOUT THE AUTHOR

Corinne Thomas graduated from The Master's College with a bachelor of science degree in home economics—family and consumer sciences. During her time as an undergraduate, her research focuses included HE-FCS and immigration as well as integrating technology effectively in educational programs. This led her to pursue a master of arts in education and human development with an emphasis in educational technology leadership from The George Washington University in Washington, DC. Corinne believes that technology is a great tool for education if understood and used correctly. Currently, she serves as assistant director of Instructional Design and Technology at Loyola Law School in Los Angeles, CA.

Chapter Twenty-Five

Is Working at Home for You?

Glynnis Whitwer

When I first started working at home, a former coworker joked that my days would be filled with eating bonbons and watching soap operas. I was not sure what a bonbon was, but I did know the lure of soap operas. He was wrong. My busy days at home were far from the pampered life he had imagined.

When I worked in the corporate world, I was guaranteed breaks and an hour for lunch. Since my office was in an upscale retirement community with a full dining room, an employee benefit was low-cost lunches. Not only was the food fantastic, but I enjoyed the lunchroom conversations with friends, as well as the impromptu after-work gatherings. There was excitement as we worked toward the completion of a project or celebrated the accomplishment of meeting a goal. I worked for wonderful people, and their praise and encouragement fed my self-esteem.

Sounds great? It was. I really loved my job. My life looks very different now. My work breaks involve starting a load of laundry or cleaning the kitchen. Lunch consists of reheated leftovers or a sandwich. Although my husband works at home, most days we grab our lunches and each head back to work. My after-work impromptu gatherings with friends are nonexistent, and for the most part, I pat myself on the back when I have completed a task.

Would I ever go back to work outside the home? Not unless God sent me a personalized memo and told me so. I absolutely love being home, but working at home is not for everyone. It is, however, for those whom God has called to walk this path.

How do you know if home-based work is right for you? Only you can know, but from my experience, God usually calls you *to* something rather than away *from* something. For example, perhaps you dislike your job. At one time I did. In fact, I wanted to be anywhere but at work. I liked what I was doing, but the working conditions were difficult, and I was losing creativity and self-confidence. During that time, I was ready to do anything else. If I had made a move to work at home during that time, I would have been doing it for the wrong reasons.

If I had started working at home for the wrong reasons, I would have quit years ago. Why? Because it is really hard. It is difficult to know when to stop working, how to balance work and home; and then there is the fear of not always knowing when you will be paid next.

Knowing I am called by God to work at home enables me to put one foot in front of the other, trusting God in greater measure and growing in my faith. When the difficult times come, I am learning to press into God more and lean less on my own power.

Once a woman acknowledges that God is calling her to work at home, she has some work to do. Many women are currently working outside the home and will need to put together a transition plan. Doing this work in advance of making an employment change will help you be successful in the long run.

WHERE DO YOU START?

Whether you are married or single, the first place to start in making the transition to home-based work is to uncover the real cost of your labor in the marketplace. When you take a detailed look at your work-related expenses, you will discover what is necessary for you to live on one income if you are married, or you will learn what part of your current net income comes from your work.

Before you start, gather pertinent information, such as pay stubs and receipts of expenses if you have them. Sometimes your check register can work just as well if you record debits/ATM transactions as well as checks. There are some great calculators online that will walk you through this process (see Crown.org), but an old-fashioned pencil and paper work great too.

Determine Your Net Spendable Income

The first step involves identifying your net spendable income. I think it is easier to work on a monthly basis, so start by determining your gross monthly income. Your gross income is how much you make before taxes or any other withdrawals, such as insurance or retirement investments.

Then you will need to subtract some nonnegotiables. There are four main expenses in this category: federal income tax, state tax, Social Security tax, and your tithe back to God. The first three should be found on your paycheck stub:

- *Income taxes* are a big expense for all Americans. Unfortunately, the federal tax system is set up so that in a two-income family, both incomes are added together to determine the tax bracket, which can put you into a higher tax bracket. When considering possible savings in a two-earner family, consider if the first income would drop into a lower tax bracket without the second income tacked on. Sometimes the extra earnings provided by a second income, when offset by expenses, do not, in fact, provide enough additional income to justify a woman's time away from family needs and responsibilities.

- *State income tax* varies by state. You will need to do some research to determine your state's policy.

- *Social Security tax* is based on a simple idea. While you work, you pay taxes into the Social Security system, and when you retire or become disabled, you, your spouse, and your dependent children receive monthly benefits based on your reported earnings. Also, your survivors can collect benefits when you die. Normally, the employer pays part and you pay part.

- *The tithe* on the second income is another substantial expense. For families who give 10 percent of their income, this can be an area where you will "save" money. Of course, every Christian needs to ask the Lord what he would have them do in this area. We should give with a cheerful heart rather than looking for opportunities to "save" in the area of giving. However, if you feel called to give 10 percent of your income and your income drops, this would be a financial expense that will change.

When you have subtracted taxes and tithe, you will come up with your net spendable monthly income. This is what you have left to spend on the expenses of life.

Identify Work-Related Expenses

As you work your way toward determining your net income, the next step is to identify your work-related expenses. These are expenses you would not have if you were at home, such as child care and commuting. Here is a list of common work-related expenses:

- child care (either full-time or part-time)
- transportation
- meals and snacks during work
- clothing (such as uniforms or business attire)
- dry cleaning for clothing required for work
- personal grooming/services (professional manicures, acrylic nails, pedicures, makeup, hair care, and perfume or cologne)
- business gifts

Estimate Expenses That Could Be Avoided by Being Home

Some expenses are hard to nail down as directly related to work. You might not be able to list these when you create your cost assessment. But if you can, then by all means, include them in your list.

- home maintenance
- meals in restaurants
- guilt gifts to children
- increased health care costs (for you and your children)
- miscellaneous (professional dues, books, or special equipment)

If some of these expenses occur only once a year, add them together and divide by twelve to get your monthly expense.

The Final Step

When you have listed all your monthly work-related expenses, add them up and subtract that number from your net spendable income (after taxes and tithe). This is what you really bring home from your job.

When you look at that number, you have to decide how you are going to make it up once you are home. You might discover that you can save that amount by shopping smarter or reducing expenses by moving to a smaller house or apartment. You may be able to eliminate some debt before you quit your job and realize that you do not need to make it up at all. Another option is to earn money from home.

DESIGNING A TRANSITION PLAN

Many variables come into play when setting a start-date goal for working at home: your current debt, how much money you need to make, and how you want to make it (telecommuting, direct sales, or some home-based business started from scratch). For instance, if you will start telecommuting for your current employer and in your current position, you might be able to start in a few weeks. If you need to research options for earning money, give yourself some time.

Once you have set a realistic goal for the date of your transition, write it down and post it in clear view. Then, make a list of everything you need to do before that date and start chipping away at the tasks.

Pay Off Debt and Reduce Expenses

To be a wise steward of what God has given you, the best way to make a transition to working at home is to pay off debts while reducing expenses. You will want to start working at home with the best possible financial condition. Look at every item on your budget and be ruthless. First make easy changes, such as eating at home instead of at restaurants, ironing your own work clothing, and shopping at secondhand stores. Then consider more difficult changes such as selling a new truck that guzzles gas and buying a less expensive, smaller car. You might even need to move into a more affordable home or apartment.

Start Working from Home before You Quit

If possible, research different opportunities and begin working from home before you quit your job. This extra money can pay off your debt, or you can begin to save. If you do start your own business before resigning from your current position, be very careful not to do any personal business on company time. Also, while still employed, do not in any way undermine your employer by soliciting his customers as your future customers. These are unethical business practices and could lead to a lawsuit.

WORK-AT-HOME OPTIONS

The options for making money are varied and numerous. An old-school thinking process might lead you to believe you will need to sell a product to your neighbors and friends (makeup or plastic storage containers). While good options are available in this arena, the vista for working at home has expanded exponentially in the past few years. Home workers can choose from among three major categories of employment:

- Telecommuting (for your existing company or a company that hires work-at-home employees)
- Starting a home-based business (from scratch, purchasing an existing business, or buying a franchise)
- Investing in a direct sales business (makeup, for example)

Each employment opportunity requires a unique set of personal skills to be successful. For instance, if you love talking with people and developing relationships face to face, then a direct-sale business might be for you. If you would rather interact with your computer than a person, certain home-based businesses might be more suitable. If talking on the phone makes your head ache, do not go near some telemarketing jobs.

WHAT IS RIGHT FOR YOU?

Likely you already have an idea of the type of work you will do from home, but for those who are unsure, I encourage you to do a personal assessment.

Consider God as a master painter. He has colored your life with these special characteristics:

- Your personality
- Your likes and dislikes
- Your talents
- Your physical ability
- Your learning style
- A bent toward being an introvert or extrovert
- Your spiritual gifts—teaching, prayer, or administration

As you consider which type of home-based work is right for you, take a look at your uniqueness. Be honest in your evaluation of your weaknesses and strengths. The way God designed you is exactly how he wants to use you. If you are unsure about what type of work you want to do from home, take time to complete a thorough personal evaluation. Here are some areas to consider:

- Your professional skills and experience
- Your personal strengths, such as being a hardworking or self-disciplined worker (including your spiritual gifts in this category)
- Your personal weaknesses, such as lacking in organization or not being internally motivated

Once you have completed this assessment, you are prepared to consider the options. God wants you to be successful, and, based on your personality, some work will suit you better.

WHAT IS TELECOMMUTING?

Because I am on staff with Proverbs 31, a national women's ministry, I am officially considered a teleworker or telecommuter. Each month I receive a paycheck, I have a boss, and I am accountable to the ministry for the quality and timeliness of my work.

As the editor for the ministry magazine, I interact with the ministry's home office in Charlotte, North Carolina; work with a graphic designer in Greensboro, North Carolina; use a printer in Birmingham, Alabama; and coordinate proofreaders, editors, and authors literally around the world. I am able to do this with a minimal investment in equipment and by using the Internet.

A teleworker, by the most common and broad definition, is employed by a company. She may be paid as an employee or as an independent contractor—but she is *not* self-employed.

Where to Find Telecommuting Jobs

Telecommuting jobs can be found everywhere. They might seem a little like Easter eggs hidden in your backyard. You know they must be out there, but they are not in plain view. There is not a telecommuting column in the newspaper want ads yet. The warnings against scams ring loudly in your ears. A friend's failed attempt at telecommuting is fresh in your mind. Are there legitimate telecommuting jobs to be had? Absolutely!

The trend toward companies hiring teleworkers is growing rapidly:

> The number of Americans who worked from home or remotely at least one day per month for their employer ("employee telecommuters") increased from approximately 12.4 million in 2006 to 17.2 million in 2008 . . . . The rise in the number of telecommuters represents a two-year increase of 39 percent, and an increase of 74 percent since 2005.[1]

Telecommuting is somewhat like homeschooling, which was once on the fringe of society but now has a strong voice in the marketplace. Working at home, once done by a select group of workers, is becoming a viable alternative for all levels of employment.

With the dominance of knowledge work in the business world, those people with the knowledge can usually work anywhere if given a computer, phone, fax, and any other needed equipment for the job. Companies are adapting to this wave of workers and creating fair policies to do so.

Finding a quality telecommuting job will likely take more screening work on your part than a traditional job because many telecommuting jobs are not advertised as such. In fact, the employer might not even realize a job has the potential to be done at home.

The first place to start identifying a teleworking position if you are employed is within your own company. In fact, it could be your current job. Ask yourself, how much of your job could be done from home? Before you yell "All of it!" and rush in to your boss's office with the good news, you should be prepared with a written proposal. Your boss might not share your enthusiasm. If that is the case, better to be armed with supporting information for why and how it could work.

A telecommuting proposal does not have to be a formal document—just an objective look at how you could do some, or all, of your job from home. Consultant Gil Gordon says the predominant attitude you are likely to encounter is skepticism, not rejection. So be prepared.

---

[1] The Dieringer Research Group Inc., "Telework Trendlines 2009: A Survey Brief by WorldatWork," accessed April 27, 2010, http://www.worldatwork.org/waw/adimLink?id=31115.

Your employer will want to see how this move will benefit the *company*, so be careful not to list how it benefits *you*, which would be obvious. Here are some common employer benefits you might include in your proposal:

- *Increased productivity.* You might outline the different distractions you face at your job, such as time lost due to common interruptions (phones, salespeople), commuting issues, or challenging work environments (high noise level, uncomfortable temperatures). This could either work in your favor if you are a strong employee or work against you if you have a history of whining. Blaming other people or challenging situations for your lack of productivity will not get you very far.

- *Less need for office space.* Depending on your employer's needs, your office and parking space may be a high premium. Include this in your proposal if it is.

- *Reduced employee costs.* Every employer spends money for miscellaneous expenses to house an employee on site. Normally, home workers assume the cost for office products, which could add up over time. This is a detail you would work out with your employer. In addition to the small expenses, which add up, doubtless your sick days would decrease. That is a big benefit to an employer. The State of California hired Fleming LTD to assess the savings of telecommuting employees. They arrived at an annual savings of eight thousand dollars per employee! This did not even include the savings on sick days.

- *Retention of a knowledgeable employee.* If you are a valued and knowledgeable employee, your company will benefit by retaining you. If you know training costs for new employees, here would be a great place to include them.

In addition to the benefits, offer practical information on how you will approach different aspects of your job. Your thoroughness will show your employer that this is not an off-the-cuff idea.

If your current position does not lend itself to telecommuting, and if you have a good history with your company, consider changing positions. Approach this new position with the same type of proposal. If you are not familiar with the position, be diligent in your research. Also, be open to the idea that you might have to work in the office for a while before transitioning home.

How to Discern Scams from Legitimate Jobs

Because almost all telecommuting jobs involve the Internet, you will find most jobs through this avenue. However, some warnings are in order. First, a legitimate company will not ask you for any money up front. A telecommuting job is like any other job. There may be some requirements after you are hired, but if someone wants you to send a fifty dollar application fee—*run*! Additionally, if they give you a 900 number to call, claim you will make thousands in a week, say you do not need experience, or claim the work is easy, watch out. Those are common red flags that you are about to get scammed. A true job will be presented as such—real work!

There are two common approaches to finding a telecommuting job outside your existing company. The first is a website that lists such jobs. One of the most popular is craigslist.org. This is a massive site that requires some digging on your part. Enter the type of work you want including keywords that indicate "telecommuting" or "work at home." Common keywords include:

- Telecommuting
- Telecommute
- Telework
- Teleworking
- Home-based
- Home-based employee
- Home-based employment
- Home-based jobs

Other established websites listing current openings include:

- Christian Work-at-Home Ministries (CWAHM.com/wordpress/)
- Work-at-Home Moms (WAHM.com)
- Telecommuting Mommies (TelecommutingMommies.com)
- Workaholics4Hire (Workaholics4Hire.com)

There are also legitimate organizations where you pay a fee to receive job listings. Solid companies are Telework Recruiting (TeleworkRecruiting.com) and FlexJobs (FlexJobs.com).

HOME-BASED BUSINESS CHOICES

The other options for working at home center on building your own business. The two most common categories of home-based businesses are these:

- starting a home-based business from scratch; or
- investing in a direct sales or network marketing business.

Starting from Scratch

You have had this dream for years. It could be assembling gift baskets, planning children's parties, or making and selling specialty cookies. This type of business almost always starts with your unique talents or experience.

If you have never owned a dog, never worked in a pet shop, and never had experience or instruction in obedience training, then you probably should not start an animal behavior business. Just because you *want* to learn a skill does not mean you will be successful at it. In other words, start with something you know.

You may have the perfect vision of the business you want to start. If not, the possibilities are almost endless. But how do you make a decision on what is right for you?

Janet Drez, author of *Putting the Pieces Together: A Christian Woman's Guide to a Successful Home-Based Business* advises women on what type of home-based business to choose. She recommends asking yourself questions such as:

- What did you enjoy most about the last two positions you held?
- What did you like least?
- What did you enjoy studying in high school or college?
- What hobbies do you enjoy?
- What do your friends and family tell you that you do well?
- What is your family background? Traditions?
- What are your spiritual gifts (1 Cor. 12:7–11; Rom. 12:6–8; Eph. 4:11)?
- What types of people do you enjoy being around?
- Do you need a business that is done mainly in your home (bookkeeping), or are you able to make appointments?
- If there were no limits or feasibility issues, what type of business do you think you would like to start?
- Where would you like to be in two years in all areas of your life?

Armed with this information, you can proceed to brainstorm the variety of business opportunities available.

Important Considerations

As you pray about your options, there are other things to consider. Here is a quick overview:

- Is there a market for your product or service? You may love the idea of canning zucchini pickles, but that does not mean other people will rush to buy them. Do research into where you would offer your product, who else is doing what you want to do, and how well they are doing.

- Can you do the work from home legally? Do diligent research to make sure you are meeting all municipal and homeowners' association guidelines before investing any money.

- Do you need any special permits? Check with your city and state governments.

- Do you need to increase your homeowner's insurance?

- There is usually a steep learning curve when starting a home-based business. Business is complicated—but not impossible to understand. I encourage you to become a learner by tackling one subject at a time. The better educated you are, the better your chances of success in whatever work or business you choose. Some components of business you can learn on your own, and you must look to experts for others.

Here is *very* good news. Likely your community has free support services for you as a business owner. Every government agency wants you to succeed. Small businesses are critical to the health of a community, and free information abounds. Here are some places to check for the technical pieces of the business puzzle:

- Small Business Administration
- State Department of Commerce
- Local Chamber of Commerce
- Internal Revenue Service
- City government
- State government
- Local library
- Your bank

If all else fails, use an Internet search engine and type in "Starting a business in (*your city and state*)."

Invest in an Established "Direct Sales" or "Network Marketing" Business

Chances are you know someone who loves her direct sales business. You have probably been to a party, looked at a catalog, or had a friend go on about how her product has changed her life. When I was growing up, Tupperware parties were the rage. I bought my first bud vase as a high schooler at a Princess House Party (see PrincessHouse.com). And I have lost count of my friends who have sold Avon or Mary Kay at one time or another. Direct sales companies can offer wonderful ways to make income at home, whether it is pocket money or a full-time income, depending on how much time you want to invest.

By definition, a direct sales business is one in which a product or service is sold from one individual to another, and the seller is paid a commission based on her personal sales. Think of the old-time Fuller brush salesman who went door to door.

Today most direct sales companies are also network-marketing companies, meaning a salesperson recruits a network of other salespeople (called a *downline*) from whom she receives a percentage of their sales in addition to her own. This sponsor tree can continue with an unlimited potential for residual income.

You must differentiate between legal and illegal network-marketing companies. In a legitimate company, commissions are earned only on sales to the end user. When participants make money solely by recruiting new participants into the program and receiving a sign-up fee, that is an illegal *pyramid scheme*. If you are investigating a company unknown to you, analyze the compensation plan to make sure you are being paid from actual sales.

Another way to be sure of legitimacy is to check with the Direct Selling Association (DSA.org). This is a major industry organization that monitors activities worldwide. To be a member, a company needs to fulfill a one-year application process and abide by a code of ethics.

STANDING STRONG IN OBEDIENCE

The joys of working at home far outweigh the difficulties, but difficulties have a way of sidelining even the stoutest heart. Staying committed to God's call on your life will require care and attention, and a commitment not to quit when it gets difficult.

When you decide in advance that you will stay true to your calling to work at home, you can face the difficult days and the times when God seems distant. When you choose in advance to trust God even when you cannot explain your circumstances, your faith grows. It is awesome when you come through a challenge and look back and see how God worked through it all. Set your eyes on heaven and trust God's goodness. When you face an uphill battle, you will see it as a stairway to greater intimacy with God instead of a reason to quit.

Hebrews 12:1 gives encouragement for those challenging days: "Therefore, since we are surrounded by such a huge crowd of witnesses to the life of faith, let us strip off every weight that slows us down, especially the sin that so easily trips us up. And let us run with endurance the race God has set before us" (NLT).

At some point in your work-at-home journey, you may wonder where God is. You might wonder why he has not solved a problem, or why he has allowed something bad to happen. When your work at home is not going according to your plans, you may be tempted to think you misheard God. When that happens, do not give up. Hang on and anticipate with joy how God is going to answer your prayers.

PUTTING THE PRINCIPLES INTO PRACTICE

1. Evaluate carefully whether or not your financial situation actually requires additional income, since time invested in the home workplace is also time away from meeting the needs of your family. Why do you need additional income? Do the accompanying expenses allow an appropriate profit margin?
2. What skills, experiences (professional/personal), volunteer work, and passions do you have that could be incorporated into making money at home?
3. What resources do you currently have within your home that could be used to make extra money?
4. Consider your current home situation. What challenges do you foresee having when you start working from home? Think in terms of relationships, work space, scheduling, and financial outlay.
5. Consider each challenge you have identified, and suggest a creative solution.
6. What are the benefits of working at home for you personally? List those benefits and review them when you feel overwhelmed or discouraged.

ABOUT THE AUTHOR

Glynnis Whitwer is on staff with Proverbs 31 Ministries as the senior editor of the *P31 Woman* magazine. She is also on the Proverbs 31 speakers team and speaks at women's conferences, retreats, and special events around the country. She is one of the writers of *Encouragement for Today Devotions*, published online and e-mailed to subscribers by Proverbs 31, with over three hundred thousand daily readers.

Whitwer is the author of *When Your Child Is Hurting: Helping Your Kids Survive the Ups and Downs of Life* (Eugene, OR: Harvest House, 2009) and *work@ home: A Practical Guide for Women Who Want to Work from Home* (Birmingham, AL: New Hope Publishers, 2007). She and her husband, Todd, and their five children live in Glendale, Arizona, where they are active in the Vineyard Church North Phoenix. Together they run two home-based businesses—Rose Lane Cottage, an Internet retailer (RoseLaneCottage.com), and an environmental consulting firm.

Chapter Twenty-Six

Too Much Month at the End of the Money?

Pat Ennis

The events on Wall Street in the fall of 2008 are a reminder that no invest-ment in this world is ever secure. Regardless of the safeguards and the sup-posed guarantees, the economic climate can change in an instant. Like the falling autumn leaves that characterized the season, retirement portfolios dropped significantly in 2008, as they have done in cycles throughout history, leaving individuals of all ages asking the question, "Does an impoverished lifestyle lie ahead?" Economic uncertainty can evoke a myriad of negative responses—especially for people whose trust is in money rather than God. Believers, however, should have an entirely different response if their dollar theology is sound.

DOLLAR THEOLOGY

The cornerstone of *dollar theology* is that believers are accountable to God for the resources that he entrusts to them. The principle of stewardship is woven throughout the New Testament. As you read the following passages consider how they influence your dollar theology.

- Matthew 24:45–51 and Luke 12:42–48 describe the parable of the faithful steward and remind us that every person possesses natural abilities, wealth, and possessions in trust from God. Eventually, God will require an account of how each was used.

- The parable of the unjust servant in Luke 16:1–13, especially verse 9, illus-trates that even the wicked sons of this world are shrewd enough to provide for themselves against coming evil. Believers ought to be more shrewd because they are concerned with eternal matters, not just earthly ones.

- Matthew 6:20 admonishes believers to "lay up . . . treasures in heaven."

Regardless of your season of life, if someone analyzed your checkbook register, what conclusions would he draw about your spiritual values? How do your spending habits reflect your spiritual values?

FINANCIAL PRINCIPLES

A number of financial principles, if followed, can eliminate the potential of a dreary retirement:[1]

- You cannot be financially bound and spiritually free (Matt. 6:19–24).
- Give to the Lord's work (1 Cor. 16:2; 2 Cor. 9:6–8).
- Learn to save money in every season of life (Prov. 13:11).
- Learn to spend less than you earn (Prov. 21:20). Be creative in finding the best price and using coupons.
- Don't borrow money for pleasure items, such as vacations (Eccles. 5:10).
- Control your credit cards and pay before interest accrues (Prov. 22:7).
- Plan adequate life insurance to protect your loved ones (1 Tim. 5:8).
- Be self-insured for life insurance by the time you retire (Prov. 13:22).
- Have a retirement plan in progress by age forty; but if you are late, start now (Prov. 13:22).
- Own your own home debt-free by the time you retire (Prov. 13:22).
- Have a workable budget, which demands discipline and planning (Prov. 24:3–4).
- Understand that tax laws apply to you—pay your taxes (Matt. 22:15–22).
- Have an estate plan that includes a will and/or living trust.
- Remember that there is a difference between debt and obligations.
- Have cash in an emergency fund.

Critical to the successful implementation of these principles is the application of Malachi 3:10, a reminder to "bring the full tithe into the storehouse."

Practically speaking, you cannot afford *not* to tithe. This I know from personal experience! Regrettably, tithing was not a part of my family's financial goals. My conviction is that the numerous financial calamities that befell my family were related, in part, to the absence of giving to the Lord a portion of our monthly resources.

Conversely, my spiritual growth aligned with the procurement of my first professional position. I noticed that as I consistently wrote my tithing check *first* each pay period, my financial resources were multiplied. Practically speaking

---

[1] Jim Rickard, director of the Stewardship Services Foundation, recommends many of these financial principles. The Stewardship Services Foundation (see http://www.ssfoundation.net) is a privately funded, non-profit corporation established for the singular purpose of serving the evangelical Christian community. The Foundation offers individuals and churches several important stewardship services:

- estate planning seminars, which include counseling on wills and living trusts
- income tax seminars, including the preparation of federal and state returns for ministers
- family finance seminars
- church leadership seminars

the order in which you write checks should not make any difference. Yet, to this day I intentionally practice the order, and as long as I am also a careful steward of the remaining resources, I never have too much month at the end of the money.

When I transitioned from full-time secular education to Christian education in the late seventies, I knew my financial structure would be affected. However, I was surprised at the magnitude of the effect. My first check from Christian Heritage College was $400 less than my final check from San Diego City Schools. I knew that it was inappropriate to place a price tag on the giftedness God had bestowed upon me, so rather than fretting over how I was going to bridge the financial gap, I again committed my needs to him and focused on Philippians 4:19. God has promised to meet all of your needs—not all of your wants. He promised to "give increase to the Philippians in proportion to his infinite resources, not just a small amount out of his riches."[2]

While God does indeed promise to meet all of your needs, God also calls you to exercise faithful financial stewardship with your resources. Learning to manage your money, cultivating financially responsible credit habits, understanding that credit can be either a friend or foe, making wise consumer decisions, and knowing how to craft a consumer concern letter are all components of faithful financial stewardship.

MANAGING YOUR MONEY

You may be inclined to laugh at the mention of managing your financial resources, which you may think are few. However, as you continue reading the chapter, you will realize that you do have resources to be managed, regardless of your season of life.

Failing to have a budget or spending plan is like trying to navigate through an unfamiliar city without a road map. You most likely will get lost. Recall the teaching of Proverbs 29:18 "Where there is no prophetic vision the people cast off restraint [or the people are discouraged]."

A *budget* is simply a road map for using the money you have to its maximum potential. Designing a personal budget, or *spending plan*, is not difficult. However, to build a successful budget you must know your personal goals and determine your expenses.

Setting Personal Goals

Every successful spending plan is based on clearly defined personal goals—the things you really want. They can be short term, like saving for a new pair of

---

[2] John MacArthur, *The MacArthur Study Bible* (Nashville: Thomas Nelson, 1997), note for Philippians 4:19.

shoes, or long term, such as having enough money to make the down payment on a home. Most goals require more money than what you have right now. That is why goals must be written down. Once they are in place, you are ready to build your budget.

Building Your Budget

Consider using the following steps to build your budget.

- Pray (John 14:13; 15:16; 1 Pet. 5:7–8; James 1:5).
- List your income and expenses to develop your budget or spending plan.
- You must know the following information to be successful:

  - *Your income*—salary, retirement benefits, gifts, and loans.
  - *Fixed expenses*—tithing, house payment or rent, car insurance, gas, utilities.
  - *Variable expenses*—clothing, entertainment, gifts.
  - *Savings*—an established percentage of each paycheck. Since you should learn to get along with what you have, this amount should be determined before any money is spent from the first paycheck.

- Create a weekly spending plan.

  - Once your income and expenses are determined, you need to chart them weekly.
  - This step allows you to develop a spending plan or budget.
  - Once you have charted your expenses for a month, evaluate whether or not your plan is helping you to reach your personal goals.
  - Revision is necessary if there is too much week at the end of the money. No one can survive unless she spends less than she earns.

- Project your retirement income. You may wish to complete the helpful form, "Projecting Your Retirement Income," located at the conclusion of this chapter, as a personal evaluation tool for lessening the potential of a dreary retirement.[3]

CREDIT—FRIEND OR FOE?

Credit is basically a promise to pay in the future for what can be bought or purchased today. It can be a friend or foe depending on how it is used. Regrettably, the twenty-first-century consumer often makes credit a foe rather than a friend by failing to pay the credit card balance at the conclusion of each billing cycle. In my local newspaper, I noted an editorial that clearly calculates what

---

[3] Provided by Jim Rickard (see footnote 1).

transpires when credit balances are allowed to linger. Sue Prout imagines the scenario of walking into a store and seeing a sign:

"This item is marked UP 18 percent or 20 percent or 28 percent or more."

She continues:

If you use your credit card to pay for your purchase and you do not pay off your credit card in full each month that is what you are doing. Do the math and you might realize what you are doing to yourself for instant gratification.[4]

When my parents stepped into eternity, they left me an inheritance. Although the amount of money in the bank was not significant, after all of the medical and funeral expenses were paid, our home and rental property were mortgage-free. The inheritance my parents left allowed me to begin my life without them on a firm foundation. In today's culture, many children inherit nothing of substance and may, in fact, have to deal with a loss of security because of debt. Perhaps even more tragic is the example of irresponsible spending they have observed in their parents.

Christians and Credit

A Christian should diligently search the Scriptures to determine whether credit is a friend or foe. Exodus 22:25; Psalm 37:21; Matthew 5:42; and Luke 6:34 are a few of many verses that permit and give regulations regarding the borrowing of money. Despite the freedom to use credit allowed by Scripture, many Christians cite Romans 13:8 as a prohibition against borrowing money or using credit. However, Paul notes that all financial obligations must be paid when they are due. Rather than ruling out the possibility of using credit Christians are to:

- Practice self-control (Gal. 5:23).
- Examine motives for using credit to ensure its use is not based on what someone else has (Ex. 20:17).
- Purchases should not reflect a lack of contentment (Phil. 4:11; Heb. 13:5).

These principles enable credit to function as a friend. Then you are ready to consider how to establish and maintain good credit.

---

[4] Sue Prout, "Do the Math," *The Signal Newspaper* (Santa Clarita, CA), November 28, 2008, http://www.signal scv.com/archives/6406.

Establishing Credit

- You may inquire at your local bank for options. Also, if you do not have credit (or adequate credit history), the key is to start small. One credit card or a small loan can get the ball rolling.

- An Internet search will yield a number of options. Most will suggest that you compare the offers and apply for the credit card of your choice by filling out a secure online application.

- Make sure your lender reports your on-time payments to one of the three credit bureaus, Equifax (Equifax.com), ExperianSM (Experian.com) or Trans-Union (TransUnion.com)—and preferably to all three. If your on-time payments do not get reported, you are accumulating debt without building credit. Only credit accounts that report your borrowing and repayment activity will count toward your credit history.

Establishing a Good Credit History

- Always pay off the balance in full when the statement arrives. This prompt and complete payment shows the card company that you are fiscally responsible. You are using credit as it was intended—as a short-term loan.

- Pay on time. By paying your bills on time each month, you are showing the lender or creditor that you have enough cash flow to cover your expenses. If you pay late and the creditor reports your late payment to the credit bureaus, you may have damaged your credit history.

- Keep your total credit card charges well within your credit limit. Your credit score will be penalized if your balance is above that limit since creditors assume that you may be having financial difficulties and, thus, are a riskier borrower.

- Regularly read your credit report. Credit bureaus will provide you with one free copy per year if you contact them. Errors and negative information can damage your credit history and your credit score, so you will want to regularly check your credit report to see what was recorded. By establishing and maintaining a good credit history, you will be able to borrow money when you need it at the most favorable terms and conditions being offered.

Building a High Credit Score

A credit score is a three-digit number that represents your entire credit history. Credit scores are designed to predict how risky you will be as a borrower and what your chances are of making good on loans and other financial obligations. The scoring system analyzes how you manage each piece of credit (such as credit card accounts, mortgage or home equity loans, car loans, school loans, and other debt) and then calculates your credit score based on how you have handled your debts over time.

Various companies use different formulas to come up with a credit score. While all the formulas look at roughly the same information (such as your outstanding debts, whether you pay on time, whether you carry a balance), one formula may give more weight to certain factors than others, so these companies could assign you different credit scores. These are the components that go into the calculation of your FICO credit score (the most widely used model):

- Payment history: 35 percent
- Amounts owed: 30 percent
- Length of credit history: 15 percent
- New credit: 10 percent
- Types of credit used: 10 percent

When trying to build a high credit score, the most important thing you can do is pay all your bills on time and in full. If you want a high credit score when you become a "senior saint," you must cultivate financially responsible credit habits in your youth.

Cultivating Financially Responsible Credit Habits

Mary Hunt is a graduate of The Master's College. As creator and editor of *Debt-Proof Living* (formerly *Cheapskate Monthly*), a monthly newsletter that premiered in January 1992, Mary combines her expertise in business with a message that overspenders and those burdened with debt seem ready to hear. Her credo is *"Bringing dignity to the art of living below your means."*[5] In 2009, Hunt shared "Seven Habits for a Financially Fit New Year." If embraced, these habits can assist in the cultivation of financially responsible credit habits. You can visit her website to read them.[6]

CONSUMER DECISIONS

Making sound consumer decisions is another way to avoid having too much month at the end of the money. Knowing some key consumer terms can help you find your way through the decision-making maze.

---

[5] Found at http://www.debtproofliving.com/DPLNewsletter/CurrentIssue/tabid/164/Default.aspx.
[6] The newsletter website is EverydayCheapskate.com; Hunt's main website is DebtproofLiving.com. The "Seven Habits" are available from http://www.creators.com/lifestylefeatures/advice/everyday-cheapskate/7-habits-for-a-financially-fit-new-year.html.

- When you work you are a *producer,* helping to fulfill the wants and needs of consumers.
- When you save your money in a bank or invest in stocks and bonds you are an *investor.*
- When you spend money you are a *consumer* or anyone who buys goods and services.
- According to the law, *consumers* have many rights. Typing the words *consumer rights* into an Internet search engine yields numerous sources that will educate you about the laws.

Sound consumer choices depend on *comparison shopping,* which involves evaluating a number of competing products. Consider the following criteria when making a major purchase:

- Quality of workmanship
- Ease of use
- Conditions of the *warranty* (the manufacturer's terms of repairing or replacing the item if it does not perform according to its advertised expectations)
- The features most important to the consumer
- Cost of the item (the lowest cost is not always the best buy)
- The importance of purchasing a name brand (often quality merchandise with market history will outlast cheap knockoffs)
- The best place to purchase the item (many choices are available, such as retail and discount stores, catalogs, the Internet, thrift stores, and garage sales
- The reputation of the merchant or seller
- The season of the year (can affect product availablity and the price to be paid)

The choice is not a good one if the consumer does not really need the item.

CRAFTING A CONSUMER CONCERN LETTER

As a Christian consumer, what do you do when you have a problem with something you bought? Your first response as a believer is to glorify God in the handling of the situation (1 Cor. 10:31). Then consider the following practical tips:

1. Review the labels or instruction book to see if you are using the product properly. If so, return it to the store and ask for the person who handles complaints. Take with you the sales receipt, tags, and labels. If possible, the product should be returned in its original bag or box. Keep focused on the importance of being polite even though you are unhappy with the product.

2. If the store is unable to resolve the problem, write to the manufacturer. Consider these tips on how to write a letter or e-mail (most companies have a contact feature on their websites):

- Address the correspondence to the person in charge of complaints at the company headquarters. You can probably get the name of the correct person to write by phoning the company (contact information is usually on the label) or by checking the company website.

- Proofread the correspondence. It should be free of spelling and grammatical errors.

- If corresponding via the website, write the message offline and proofread it, then copy and paste it into the contact portion of the website.

- Keep the correspondence brief, but make sure it contains:

  - what you bought,
  - where you bought it,
  - when you bought it,
  - how much you paid for it,
  - what is wrong,
  - the name(s) of anyone already contacted,
  - a copy of the original sales receipt (do not send the original), and
  - your name, address (include zip code), and phone number.

- The tone of the correspondence should be businesslike and polite.

- Keep a copy of the correspondence.

- If you do not receive a response in a reasonable amount of time, follow up with a second inquiry.

- If the situation is not resolved to your satisfaction, contact one of the federal agencies responsible for enforcing consumer laws. An Internet search will give you contact information for the Office of Consumer Affairs (part of the US Department of Commerce), the Federal Trade Commission, and your local Better Business Bureau.

As you think of your finances, would you be considered a faithful steward? Do you focus on managing carefully what you have instead of coveting what you do not have? Regardless of your response, completing the activities in "Putting the Principles into Practice" can sharpen your skills. Remembering that all you have belongs to the Lord should assist you in cultivating spending habits that ensure extra money for you at the end of each month.

PUTTING THE PRINCIPLES INTO PRACTICE

1. Conduct a Scripture search of the word *money*. Use a concordance (either book or electronic). Create a chart like the one below to record your research.

Scripture	What the Verse Says to Me
1 Corinthians 4:1–2	I am to be a good manager of all the resources God has given to me.

2. Review the principles listed in the section "Dollar Theology." What do they teach you about money and how you should use it? Develop a personal dollar theology. To launch your study consider the following verses: Proverbs 11:24; 13:11; Ecclesiastes 5:10; Malachi 3:10; Matthew 6:24; Mark 12:41–44; Luke 6:38; 1 Corinthians 9:6–8; 1 Timothy 6:10. Study the life of the widow (Mark 12:41–44). How does her example impact your dollar theology?
3. Customize the "Building My Budget" form located at the conclusion of these questions to record your weekly income and expenses.
4. Develop a list of *comparison shopping* strategies to consider when making a major purchase.
5. Write a practice consumer concern letter following the suggested guidelines. If needed, make an Internet search for the guidelines for writing and formatting a standard business letter.

ADDITIONAL RESOURCES

Ennis, Pat, and Lisa Tatlock. *Becoming a Woman Who Pleases God: A Guide to Developing Your Biblical Potential*. Chicago: Moody, 2003.

———. *Designing a Lifestyle That Pleases God: A Practical Guide*. Chicago: Moody, 2004.

Hunt, Mary. *Debt-Proof Living*. Los Angeles: DPL, 2005.

———. *Live Your Life for Half the Price*. Los Angeles: DPL, 2005.

MacArthur, John. *Whose Money Is It Anyway?* Nashville: Word, 2000.

The website for Quicken: Quicken.com.

❦ BUILDING MY BUDGET ❧

Use the form below or develop your own to record your weekly income and expenses. Once you have used the chart for several weeks, revise it, if necessary, to best meet your personal goals.

CATEGORY	AMOUNT
Income	$
Salary	
Gifts	
Loans	
Total Income =	$
Fixed Expenses	$
Tithing	
Rent/House Payment	
Car insurance	
Gas	
Total Fixed Expenses =	$
Variable Expenses	$
Clothing	
Entertainment	
Gifts	
Total Variable Expenses =	$
Savings	$
An established percentage of each paycheck.	
Total Savings =	$
Grand Total =	$

PROJECTING YOUR RETIREMENT INCOME[7]

1. Consider annual income needed in retirement at 80 percent of take-home pay (if you own no home, then figure 100 percent of your current take-home pay).	$
2. Evaluate your expected Social Security benefit (for a projection of your benefit call the Social Security Administration at 800-772-1213 and ask for Form SSA-7004).	$
3. Do you expect pension benefit from other work sources—for example, from your spouse's work?	$
4. What is your expected income from retirement benefits (line 2 plus line 3)?	$
5. What annual retirement income is needed from savings and investments (line 1 minus line 4)?	$
6. To determine amount you must save by retirement in today's dollars, divide line 5 by .05 = needed savings.	$
7. What amount have you saved already?	

a. IRAs	b. Employer savings plans	c. Other investments (include all CDs, mutual funds, bonds, stocks, investment real estate, and any other assets available for retirement)	d. (Optional) If you wish to count a portion of your home's value as savings, enter its present value minus the anticipated cost of a home in retirement.	e. Total retirement savings (add **a** through **d**)
a. $	b. $	c. $	d. $	e. $

8. Finalize the amount of retirement capital still needed (line 6 minus line 7e)	$

Amount of contributions per year into a retirement account. Example: Assume you invest $2,000 per year into a tax-sheltered plan until age 65:
8% Annual Return
Start at age 40—at age 65 you will have $169,000
Start at age 50—at age 65 you will have $60, 986

---

[7] Provided by Jim Rickard (see note 1).

Chapter Twenty-Seven

Decorating Your Home with *Silent Witness*

Georg Andersen, ASID

Silent Witness: The Language of Your Home (Wheaton, IL: Tyndale House, 1999) by Georg Andersen, American Society of Interior Design, with James McAlister, should be in every woman's library. Inspired by Andersen, Dorothy Patterson has adapted, with Andersen's permission, his very effective presentation on weaving Christian testimony into the warp and woof of your home with a silent but powerful testimony.

Many Christians fail to employ effectively one of their greatest resources for influencing others for Christ—that is, their homes. Any home can become aesthetically pleasing and hospitable. Its words of *silent witness* will influence others, sending a message about your beliefs, priorities, and purpose in life. The essence of a home is inexorably bound to the way life is as expressed through its furnishings and accessories as well as through the lives of its occupants.

Physical components of a home and the thoughts behind them *say* a lot about its occupants and their activities. Your homes do not speak with words per se, but they subtly reveal interests and priorities, including the place God has in your life, your concerns for others, the value that you put on your family, and how you spend your time. Your home becomes a silent witness to the multifaceted work of God in your life. Many miss the joy of seeing gifts and ministries developed. Instead of serving as launching pads, their homes become more like anchors.

Do you experience CONTENTMENT—accepting God's present provision of shelter and clothing as sufficient—with your home, or do you expend energy pursuing physically or emotionally something beyond the means that God has provided? When FAITH—visualizing God's plan and responding accordingly—and CONTENTMENT are taken together, they are a powerful resource for blessing your home. Coupling a vision of what can be with a satisfaction that what you as a believer have in God's divine scheme is sufficient to keep you on track.

People do not come into your home to look at *things*; they come for a "banquet of the heart." They long to sense the spirit of the home and to enjoy the fellowship that they inwardly desire. In a word, they are seeking expressions of SINCERITY—the genuine, earnest desire to help others without any thought of personal gain. Hearts are touched, not by opulence, but by intent and concern. In fact, design is more of a continuum than a onetime action. It is the process of putting together unrelated things—juxtaposing even the valuable and the trivial if you desire—to develop the "words" of testimony that you want your home to share. You can bring the Master's touch and life to otherwise inanimate surroundings. Your home will reflect who you really are in Christ.

The "first words" your home speaks are significant. With a bit of forethought the first word can be preprogrammed. And it should undoubtedly be ANTICIPATION—the eager expectation that God's promises are true and that he will work through your circumstances to fulfill them. There should be a subtle (but still compelling) element of mystery in your home. ANTICIPATION hints of what lies beyond. Not even best friends tell everything about themselves in a single sitting. Nor does the God of creation ever fully reveal everything about himself. Part of the beauty of building relationships is the discreet process of mutual revelation and discovery behind ANTICIPATION.

On the outside jamb of the front door of some houses a *mezuzah* is found. Andersen received one from a Jewish client and used it in his home with honor. A *mezuzah*, the tiny box Jews put on their doorposts, contains some excerpts from the Law on a parchment scroll (Deut. 6:4–9). The family is thereby reminded of the place of God in their lives and the importance of their service to him. What ANTICIPATION a *mezuzah* can build in Jewish visitors to your home!

THE WELCOME ROOM

Just beyond the front door is what most people unimaginatively call an entrance or foyer, which has been jettisoned by Andersen in favor of a *Welcome Room*. Your homes must express welcome clearly throughout its rooms with many words of *silent witness*. Jesus said, "Come to Me, all who are weary and heavy-laden" (Matt. 11:28 NASB). A warm, enthusiastic greeting at the door from the hosts immediately puts a guest, who feels at home even among strangers, at ease. With ENTHUSIASM—the outward expression of the joy that is in your heart—what you feel on the inside finds in your surroundings an outward display that is contagious.

Before going into your Welcome Room, try to determine what color is the visual unifying "ribbon." If you are not sure, look at the walls, flooring, ceiling, and fabrics to get a clearer picture. The first goal in analyzing any room should be to determine its color theme. Designwise, color is probably the greatest unifier in a room. The effective application of a *particular* color can do more to cause a room to be cohesively successful than any number of carefully selected (or even costly) objects. Once you have determined the thread of color that runs throughout the furnishings of a room, you may want to use it on the walls or ceilings to pull things together. Ceilings, by the way, are usually the most neglected surface in a room, but you can use color and patterns there as well. Andersen coined the term "ribbons of color" both to describe and validate the assemblage of numerous but seemingly unrelated patterns and colorations in one space or room. A fabric or a rug with varied colors is the "lead" fabric. Start with a lively patterned fabric, and let one of its colors translate to a single color in the next piece. These colors—whether they are blue, violet, red, gold, or green—essentially "move" into the adjoining piece of furniture. But you are not just limited to a single color in this transition; you may use any combinations of these same colors.

Design is much like the frame on a painting: It should enhance and embellish but not overshadow. If proper design technique can be engaged in your home in order to bring the words of silent witness unobtrusively to the forefront, so much the better.

THE DAILY ROOM

In bygone days, Norwegian family life centered in the *dagligstue* or "daily room." It was much more the hub of activity than its rather limp, westernized "family room" counterpart. In the *dagligstue*, families interacted, friends were entertained, relationships were built, and memories were forged.

The *Daily Room*, the center from which most activity radiates, reflects an attempt to facilitate informal but meaningful interactions in the spirit of the *dagligstue*. Order and flexibility, which are not mutually exclusive, cooperatively form the foundation for a successful Daily Room.

The best room is not confusing in its layout and does not appear so precious in its appearance that people do not want to use it. Consequently, order is possibly the most important element of any well-designed room. Your rooms, in a user-friendly way, should speak of ORDERLINESS, which is the arranging of your surroundings to maximize their usefulness in a very practical way. For example, when putting together a floor plan, keep it logical by remembering the sizes of your furniture, noting especially pieces that can fit only into one particular place.

Your Daily Room can silently speak of FLEXIBILITY, which means not being rigid in your approach to achieve your goals by arranging seating in the round to avoid the confinements of the "conversational groupings" that appear decorative but thwart conversation and interaction. Try not to force seating patterns artificially. Most people seem to love this arrangement, which will go a long way toward restructuring the circumstances that create the small clumps of people that naturally exclude those who are more reticent. Seating in the round helps break down the constraints of contrived "conversational groupings" that seem to be in vogue, echoing the theme that everyone should be able to participate, whether they are there for a structured meeting or for casual conversation. A house is to be lived in, literally touched and felt until you are a part of it.

Homemakers must understand the importance of not hiding everything if their homes are to be used and useful. Be creative about the way you organize your home. Nothing gives a home instant age and a finished appearance like beautiful wallpapers, whether patterned or strongly textured. Toys and photos proclaim the presence of life. Your home should not just look but should also feel and touch and hug. SENSITIVITY, perceiving the real needs of those with whom you have contact, can affect both ORDERLINESS and FLEXIBILITY. If people can sense that you perceive needs they have not overtly revealed, then you are in a position to minister with sensitivity and usefulness. Work with the space you have to keep your room friendly, inviting, and uncomplicated. There still must be a method to the madness, however, lest disarray take over and reign.

Every room in the house should have a "cozy corner," a term coined by Edith Dean, who with Andersen coauthored *Interior Decorating: A Reflection of the Creator's Design*. This spot consists of a comfortable chair in which to read the newspaper, watch the news, or listen to music. An adequate reading light should be next to that chair.

A successful room will have warmth and comfort coupled with logic and substance, and with careful attention to proportion. If you can feel the hurts of others and tear down natural barriers to their hearts by the way you arrange your home, they will sense your concern without your having to say a word.

THE LIVING ROOM

On the surface an object is no more than what it appears to be. A shoe is a shoe is a shoe, so to speak. But if the shoe is an old baby shoe, its leather and stitching are but shadows—victories and defeats, tragedies and triumphs, struggles for maturity and independence—of a departed childhood. Parents understand,

and stories that bind relationships can be shared. Such items can become catalysts for discussion times that draw people together with memories of home. A sentimental object can have great power for nurturing a warm, companionable atmosphere in a home. Could there be a better vehicle than a *Living Room*, where seemingly ordinary objects might envelop stories that will forge lifelong bonds?

Numerous illustrations of RESOURCEFULNESS, or making the most of resources available to you, are possible in the *Living Room*. A bit of CREATIVITY may work well both aesthetically and economically. Three words of witness, like good friends, usually run together: RESOURCEFULNESS, CREATIVITY (seeing new ways to get around roadblocks to achievement), and THRIFTINESS (avoiding unnecessary expenditures). They cooperate with one another. While a picture-perfect room certainly may be assembled totally from new items, many prefer furnishings and accessories with a history. In this case, both CREATIVITY and RESOURCEFULNESS can be blended harmoniously to make use of these historical treasures. In proper mixture, THRIFTINESS is a natural result.

Seemingly unrelated patterns and things, if put together with an attitude of authority, can result in a unique cohesiveness unattainable with preplanned matches. Such mixtures take the edge off the widespread misconception that everything has to be a perfect match and fit. Design has little or no value unless the heart gains control, regardless of how things seem to fit in a technical sense. Careful shopping with attention to construction and materials can produce some excellent buys, even from discount furniture stores.

From a design standpoint, wall coverings offer almost limitless combinations of colors, textures, and patterns. Very practical, they have a typical life span of ten to twenty years, two to four times that of paint. Though they cost more to install, they provide the better long-term investment. Books, too, may act as a strong ribbon binding rooms together.

THE SETTLING ROOM

The home should be the oil that settles the troubled seas of life. While bedrooms naturally evoke an image of settling down for the night, the picture need not—indeed should not—end so simply. The master bedroom may be the place where many difficult issues of life are brought to resolution, settled, as it were, in a peaceful, joyous, and harmonious way. That is why the master bedroom is the *Settling Room*.

The Settling Room speaks of PATIENCE, which is agreeably giving up your expectation of a speedy resolution to a difficult circumstance. Such peaceful interludes are vital in order to afford time to listen, to pray, to think. As you find yourself trying to consider family needs, a place to get away is not a luxury.

Though each room in a house has its own purpose, there is something particularly unique about the Settling Room (and bedrooms in general). This room is the last you see at night and the first you see in the morning. In a figurative sense, its usage can help you mark out your days—even emphasize the extreme importance of each one—as you greet both evening and morning in this room.

The design of the Settling Room—from color scheme to furnishings to family accessibility—contemplates restfulness and quietness because DISCERNMENT, or the ability to separate cause and effect, is necessary to nourish family relationships. There you can pursue relationships with each other, the family, and with God himself. Not much will happen without some quietness and unhurried solitude. The Settling Room offers the need for several types of specialized lighting. Overhead lighting can be dimmed to a candle-like radiance that flatters the room and illuminates a special piece of artwork. Light from tall table lamps will spill onto the bed for reading; if needed, they are supplemented by a spotlight projector above the bed. Some people prefer a separate spotlight—each with an independent switch—for each half of the bed.

If your bedroom is large enough (or if you can plan for new construction), try to eliminate the need for dressers and tall chests of drawers. Small bedside chests make a practical place to keep hosiery, underwear, and sleepwear. Relegating storage to well-organized closets or dressing areas will release more space to the bedroom itself.

THE HOSPITALITY ROOM

The Bible is filled with accounts of strangers who were compelled by hospitable people to share their food and lodging, as well as the shelter and provender necessary for animals. Though the basic idea is straightforward enough, there is an aura of mysterious importance embodied in HOSPITALITY, which is eagerly sharing the resources of your home to benefit others (Heb. 13:2). HOSPITALITY naturally emanates from the kitchen or *Hospitality Room*.

GENEROSITY (not being stingy with resources that could be used to benefit others) does not mean that you have to give away a lot of money, but it does include the attitude you have toward the possessions and resources under your control. What distinguishes a house from a home? All houses have walls and floors, but GENTLENESS, the display of tender care and concern in reaching out to others, sparks a nurturing and warm atmosphere. The hospitality of your own home will build up a good self-image in your husband, encourage your children, and express love to those whom you call brothers and sisters within the family of God.

THE MINISTRY ROOM

In Bible times, having overnight guests was more the rule than the exception. When travelers were on the road, they could *depend* on having someone take them home for the night. A well-used guest room has such potential for meeting needs and healing hurts; for this reason it becomes the *Ministry Room.* Consider the Shunammite woman who often observed the prophet Elisha traveling by her house. Noting his situation, she first began to reach out by inviting him to share food with her family. But she did not stop there (2 Kings 4:9–11).

Elisha's schedule was unpredictable, and his arrival time was not known in advance. He just showed up . . . dirty . . . tired . . . lonely . . . discouraged. He may even have had other people with him. But the eye of the Shunammite woman looked beyond the obstacles to a man with needs. She and her husband acted with COMPASSION—not withholding time and resources to meet the needs of others.

One option for allowing your guests as much freedom as possible is to provide a very informal array of breakfast foods—cereal, fruit, bagels, and the like—that may be accessed whenever they are ready. That removes the tension that can arise by forcing them to adhere to family schedules and tastes. Good lighting and a handy table surface for books or a laptop computer allow guests to steal away and work in comfort if they desire. Keep artwork the same quality as in the rest of the house. Do not use your guest room as a graveyard for items that you do not really want.

The Ministry Room is greatly enhanced if it has its own bath. Two twin-sized beds provide more flexibility than a double bed, and a portable alarm clock and a television are thoughtful provisions. You can also provide some reading material, but do not be didactic in your selections. If the room does not have its own bath, a freestanding towel rack with bath towels and facecloths identifies for your guests which linens to use. Providing fruit and possibly a hot-cold thermos is a great idea for late arrivals. An inexpensive luggage rack for the suitcase of your guest is a handy item.

Providing a guest book encourages your guests to sign and leave a memory of their visit. Do not cover every surface with fragile knickknacks, which could be in constant peril of being knocked over. Depending on the season, a small fan or portable heater might be in order if the room is not individually zoned. Finally, try staying overnight in the room yourself to see where it might fall short. Perspective and attitude are all-important in how you envision meeting others' needs.

THE BANQUET ROOM

If serving is really your desire, you will need ATTENTIVENESS (shifting your focus to the needs of those who cross your path) to elevate your awareness of others' needs. Legend records that King Arthur seated his knights at a round table to reduce quarrels over who might have the seats of greatest honor. Political protocol often relies on the same tactic to establish mutually agreeable ground. A large round table is preferable for similar reasons; guests are put more on the equal footing that believers will enjoy at the wedding feast of the Lamb.

Aim for a mixture of lighting types. Some should be overhead, via spotlights, a lantern, or other hanging fixture. Both carpet and rugs (on wood or other hard surfaces) work well, and bare floors are especially pleasant in summertime. If you use a rug, try to fit the table and all chairs on the rug, allowing space to slide the chairs up to and away from the table without struggling with the rug. When you hold the resources at your disposal with an open hand and are AVAILABLE (giving up your right to determine how your time and resources are spent), you will get them back—and in abundance.

ALERTNESS suggests an acute awareness of the significance of the times and circumstances in which you find yourself. Even if you have an honest, deep-rooted desire that your home extend its arms to embrace others, you cannot compel your guests to come again. There must be something more binding—mutual investments in the lives of one another. And while that will take time, there is a far more brilliant facet to the treasured gemstone of lasting relationships. Will your guests be haunted by a lingering conviction that your home's last word and first word are both ANTICIPATION? If so, they will want to return without compulsion, and the words "Come again" will not even be necessary. But say them anyway.

PUTTING THE PRINCIPLES INTO PRACTICE

1. Take a tour of your home with notepad and pen in hand. What does it reveal?

   - Interests and priorities?
   - The place God has in your life?
   - Your concerns for others?

- The value that you put on your family?
- How you spend your time?

2. Is your home a "silent witness" to the multifaceted work of God in your life?

> Develop a strategy to allow it to become an environment where gifts and ministries are developed. Evaluate your progress monthly by identifying your home's strengths and offering practical suggestions for improvement.

3. Write a description of your home. What would be your family's reaction to the statement, "Some individuals can't wait to get home . . . others can't wait to leave"?

4. Using the chart below, establish goals that will cultivate a welcoming environment in your home.

⸂ CULTIVATING A WELCOMING ⸃
ENVIRONMENT IN MY HOME

Room	The Equivalent Room in My Home	Goals to Cultivate a Welcoming Environment
Welcome		
Daily		
Living		
Settling		
Hospitality		
Ministry		
Banquet		

A number of character qualities are necessary to create a home with a "silent witness." Begin internalizing each by:

- preparing a meditation card for each character quality defined in this chapter. Write both the character quality and its definition on the card;
- locating Scripture verses and passages that align with the character quality;
- placing the cards in a prominent location;

- recording on the back of the cards specific incidents where you intentionally manifested the qualities; and
- meditating daily upon at least one character quality, definition, verse, and incident of application.

ABOUT THE AUTHOR

Georg Andersen is well known in the international design world. His expertise is attested by the extensive list of hotels, hospitals and medical facilities, banks, retirement facilities, restaurants, corporate clients, educational institutions, churches and synagogues, country clubs, theaters, art galleries, and residential clients whose names appear on his résumé. He has lectured widely. His work has been featured in numerous magazines. He and his wife, Annabelle, a full-time homemaker, are the parents of Katrina, Kristian, and Kirsten. The Andersens also are blessed by two grandsons.

Chapter Twenty-Eight

Decorating Your Home with Love

Lisa O'Harra

GET STARTED

There is a difference between a *designer* and a *decorator*. The designer has a degree from an accredited college or university through the design and architecture department. Designers are licensed by the state in which they practice. They are often affiliated with a design organization such as American Society of Interior Design (ASID). To maintain her license, a designer is required to keep up with annual continuing education. A designer thinks beyond mere finishing touches for a room; she begins with function, floor plan, and form, which are blended into design concepts.

The decorator does not have a formal education in design. She has a flair for putting things together, including fabric and paint, but she has not been trained to make educated structural decisions. When you begin a project, you must know your needs, whom you are hiring, and what you will receive in return. The journey from an ordinary house to a customized home begins with the relationship between a consultant and the client, whose trust, friendship, and respect the designer will gain over time.

If you are considering an extensive remodeling project, addition to your home, or the construction of a new home, consider hiring a designer to guide you through the project. She will be worth every penny you spend. This decision will provide experience and expertise that will save you headaches, mistakes, and money as you pursue your project.

In addition to wanting a warm and inviting home, Christians should desire for Christ to be the center of their homes: "But as for me and my house, we will serve the LORD" (Josh. 24:15). In this chapter you will be provided helpful and interesting information on how to incorporate educated principles and creative practices for your home. Ideas about how to reflect your faith in your design choices will be presented.

Function, style, and budget are just a few of the key elements to keep in mind when redesigning a space. Some people have a gift for being able to visualize space, color, and lighting in advance, and others need help to bring these elements together. If you do not know how to arrange furniture, select color, mix fabrics, or hang art, call a designer to help you in the process. Do not be afraid to ask for even a little help. There are many designers who will work on a consultation basis only. They will come into your home, get you started, and save you from the consequences of expensive mistakes. They can often point out easy changes, create an overall budget, and plan the work in manageable phases.

Your home should be a reflection of you. You want your family and guests to experience the best you can offer. God provides your home as a secure place to nurture and rear your family and enjoy your guests, and he wants you to represent you and him well. The finest homes reflect the tastes, travels, collections, passions, and the faith of their owners. Cookie-cutter homes are just that—"the same ole same" that anyone can do. Determine to do your best and bring your personal style to your home. Let your light shine for the Lord and be excited about the ways God has blessed you, however great or small.

KNOW YOUR TERMS

Many terms in the design language may be confusing, especially considering the fact that terms change over time. Here are the updated terms for some old words.

Your grandmother referred to her "davenport" or "couch." The updated term for the lovely piece of furniture to which your children and husbands seem bound when you need their help is the *sofa*. There are still curtains, but those are the simple *window treatments* that hang inside the window. The more lavish window treatments that hang to the ground on beautiful rods or brackets are called *draperies*. Many times these are custom-made, but they do not have to be. The wall-to-wall carpet is just that, *carpet*. The *rug* is the single floor covering that lies independently on the floor.

The drawn or painted masterpiece of art on the wall is *an original*, while the mass-produced piece is a *print, poster,* or *giclée (zhee-klay)*. A *giclée* is a piece of art that has been touched up with paint over the paper on which it was printed. Then there are the signed and numbered prints that are not one-of-a-kind but are more valuable than a poster. They are limited in the number produced by the artist or publisher. The fabric around your bed was referred to as a "dust ruffle," but the new term is *bed skirt*, which sounds a little more generic.

Faux (pronounced *foh*) *finish* is a wall's special treatment, which goes beyond a coat of paint. A *faux finish* can be a combination of texture, glaze, or paint or two of the aforementioned. Sometimes metal or glass or gauze is added to the finish. All of the above can be priceless, pricey, or inexpensive. Know what you are purchasing before you pay.

FOCUS ON YOUR HOME

When you begin to focus on your home, consider some basic guidelines. First, with what colors do you live easily? Bring a little of that color into each room. Second, define your style. This evolution may happen over years. Some people love the style in which they were reared, and others want to be different and create a style of their own. You travel, you gain confidence in yourself, and you gain more education as you age. These things may help you create your own style:

- Prepare a budget. I advise you to wait for what you want, not buying just to fill a room with "stuff." Again you are wise to return to phases of the designing/decorating project.

- Make a priority list of all you need. Begin with rooms that everyone will see and enjoy.

- Consider your family's lifestyle. Do children or aging parents live with you? Their presence will impact your decisions as you focus on your home.

- How long will you live in this house? Is this a forever house or just a step to getting what you want? Buy smart and be flexible with any major purchase if you are in a starter home. You can make a more substantial investment if it is a forever home. Do not overspend on trends, and beware of spending money you do not have.

- Are you about to remodel? I do not recommend any major remodeling unless you can focus on the project. Too much outside interference can cause you to make poor decisions. Know your local building code requirements, and get at least two or three bids to make sure you are getting the price and quality you expect.

- Consider carefully your selections of the finishes and fabrics. If you have a very active family, choose finishes that cannot be destroyed with one drop of a toy car on the coffee table. Fabric choices are essential to your lifestyle, whether formal or casual. You will want something easy to clean and not quick to show wear and tear in the midst of an active lifestyle. "Whatever is lovely . . . think about these things" (Phil. 4:8).

ELEMENTS OF DESIGN

When you move into a home, you have a bare shell. What you do with a home makes it lovely and your own. The elements of a room are floor, walls, and ceiling. The additions to a room are paint, wall coverings, draperies, lighting, and accessories—including art. As you plan a room's use, consider function and budget.

If you are doing a remodel, order your steps carefully. First, plan the scope of your project. Get bids on the project and interview contractors and designers. If you have a contractor, he will supervise your job and its timeline. Items for the job should be ordered to make sure everything you need is available for the job process to run on time and according to plan. Only then should the demolition begin.

Next, schedule any reconfiguring of the space. After walls are moved and before they are sheetrocked, have any electrical and plumbing work done. Then arrange for any cabinets to be installed as well as any new windows, doors, and millwork trim. Next in line is your stain work, followed by the painting—ceilings first, then woodwork, and walls last.

While painting is in process, the tile work may also be done. Special finishes and wall coverings come next. The flooring will be installed last. This is followed with any touch-up paint if needed. Last comes the installation of furniture, window coverings, art, and accessories. Finally, your lovely home or room is complete.

PLAN YOUR KITCHEN

The best kitchen design is very personal and requires planning. Do your homework before you begin a kitchen remodel. Do not overcrowd your kitchen. Consider flow of use—from the time you carry groceries in the door and put them away to how you use these items and prepare food. Your refrigerator and preparation area should be close together. Before you remodel, organize your needs for cabinets and drawers. Learn about sinks, faucets, lighting, countertops, flooring, and appliances. Keep in mind that this room is the most used in a home and one of your largest investments. Plan wisely. "This is the LORD's doing; it is marvelous in our eyes" (Ps. 118:23).

UPDATE YOUR ROOMS

Updating a room or rooms can be expensive. If you are moving into a new home, you may have spent your entire budget on the move. Here are twelve simple ideas to make a quick update to a room with minimal expense:

1. Add new pillows for a splash of color or pattern. You can buy ready-made pillows, have beautiful custom pillows made, or make them yourself. If you cannot afford fabric, consider recycling an old drapery panel, vintage tablecloth, skirt, or tapestry.

2. Change or add candles. Changing a candle size, texture, or color can make an impact, especially when candles are grouped on a table or tray. Make seasonal changes by sprinkling dried fruit or flowers around the candle.

3. Rearrange your bookshelf. Add points of interest with new photo frames, small green plants, vases, plates on stands, and favorite accessories. To break up straight rows of books, lay books flat and stack small items on them. Paint the back of a bookcase to draw interest to the items on the shelves.

4. Paint provides a fast and inexpensive impact. Be careful not to close in the room when doing an accent wall. The trend right now is to paint the walls and ceiling the same color unless you are using an extremely dark color. If picking the latter choice, paint the ceiling several shades lighter than the walls.

5. Rearrange the furniture. Try not to clutter the room with too much furniture. Instead of lining the furniture up in a room, make interesting groups of furniture. Removing just one piece of furniture can often improve the function and look of the room. Keeping fewer, but interesting, pieces of furniture in a room is better than a traffic flow that is too tight. Take that old chair and repaint or stain it and cover with a new fabric for a fresh look.

6. Change out the hardware on the cabinets. Be careful to reuse the existing holes. Changing a finish can quickly add a new update without much effort. Consider including new doorknobs and hinges.

7. Change a lampshade. Think about changing its shape and texture. Putting dimmers on existing light switches can make a dramatic change to a room's ambiance. Changing out the glass on a fan will update the fan and draw your attention to the new glass and away from the old fan. Consider updating light fixtures in a bathroom. This choice can be very inexpensive or customized and more pricey.

8. Bathrooms can be an easy improvement. By changing out the towels and rugs or shower curtain you can freshen up the room. If there is money in the budget, install a new glass shower door and possibly new faucets.

9. Make a statement in the kitchen. The style these days is "less is more." Declutter the tops of those cabinets. Remove old greenery and replace with some interesting objects and a few pieces of greenery for a much cleaner, updated look. Instead of redoing all the cabinets, consider new door and drawer fronts as well as new hardware. New countertops could be the ultimate update.

10. Replace window coverings. The style now is to have more tailored window treatments. The straight drapery panels are sleek and not overdone. Valances

tend to be more tailored with box pleats and not a lot of fullness. Window coverings enhance and set a tone for the room. A good seamstress or skilled homemaker can take a dated pair of draperies and rework them to a more tailored style if budget is an issue. Styles change about every eight years, so be wise with your investment.

11. Mirrors can add dimension to a room. But be careful to note what you are reflecting in the mirror you hang. A mirror that reflects a blank wall is not very interesting. Mirrors should be used to enhance a room.

12. Add fresh flowers to set a mood and add beauty. Consider fresh flowers on a table, countertop, or mantle—in groupings or in a single vase. Using plants around your home is better for the environment and improves the quality of air you breathe.

With all changes, you should consider the amount of time you will enjoy the change and make your investment a smart decision. For home resale value, the smartest investments are improvements to the kitchen and master bath.

PLAN TO LANDSCAPE

Do not forget the home's exterior. What does the approach to your home look like? Adding nice planters near the entry and a wreath on the front door provides a welcoming look. Keep flower beds neat and tidy. Remember your back patio or terrace. Outdoor living is quite popular and is a wonderful way to expand your living space. There is a wide range of pricing for outdoor planters and plants.

Mixed with garden sculptures and water elements, the patio can make a peaceful place for meditation and Bible study. There are many outdoor fabrics available. Look for pretty cushions for outdoor furniture at discount fabric stores or custom order them. These fabrics are now made to endure the heat and weather and resist fading and mold. Think about bringing the outdoors inside by making your patio or deck attractive as you view it from your interior rooms. Here is a great place to add color and texture to your environment.

DISPLAY YOUR FAITH

There are many ways to display your faith in your home. Beautiful crosses in media ranging from metal to painted to carved to glass are available. Consider an attractive wall grouping. Scriptures can be displayed in many ways. An artist might paint a verse around the top of a room, window, or door. Framed Scripture quotations can be displayed on the walls, shelves, or tables. A Bible should be visible in each home. Favorite Scriptures can be painted on ceramic pieces. You might consider giving each person in the family a gift that features a favorite Scripture—a plate, the rim of a bowl, or a picture with a plaque. Decorative pillows are available with Christian symbols for beds, chairs, or window seats. A bulletin board for notes on the family schedule might include a favorite Scripture. Be bold and show your faith and share your faith with those who come to visit you.

A PERSONAL WORD

This chapter has discussed how to get started on a project, how to focus on your home, how to understand terms, and how to update your home. I hope this will help you put into practice principles that will make your home meet the needs of your family. God expects you to extend hospitality in your home and share with others the joys he has given you. My prayer is for your home to be blessed with the gift of good decision making for your family and home.

PUTTING THE PRINCIPLES INTO PRACTICE

1. What changes do you need or want to make to your home? Do you need to organize, remodel, or move?
2. What is your style? How will you go forward in developing your personal style and displaying your faith in your home?
3. If you feel called to extend more home-based hospitality, how will you plan for this?
4. What home projects do you need to start and finish this year? How will you accomplish these projects?

ABOUT THE AUTHOR

Lisa O'Harra is a licensed interior designer in Fort Worth, Texas, where she has lived and practiced interior design for thirty years. She earned a bachelor of fine arts degree in interior design from Texas Tech University. She has worked on many amazing projects, including two seminaries, offices, homes, and even a yacht.

Lisa lives on seven acres with her husband, two dogs, and two horses. She has one son and two stepchildren. She is active in her church and is very involved in a community, faith-based children's organization that reaches out to at-risk kids. She feels God has blessed her with the gift of creativity, and she is honored to use her talents to the glory of God.

Chapter Twenty-Nine

Biblical Hospitality

Mary K. Mohler

The word *hospitality* has many connotations. The hospitality industry is massive, including food service and accommodations. Hospitality suites are designated rooms stocked with refreshments and set apart with many conveniences to serve speakers and others. Many universities offer majors in hospitality administration and management. This word is part of the secular vocabulary. Yet hospitality (Gk. *philoxenia*, "love of strangers") is a biblical matter as well. Consider these familiar passages:

> Contribute to the needs of the saints and seek to show hospitality. (Rom. 12:13)

> Do not neglect to show hospitality to strangers, for thereby some have entertained angels unawares. (Heb. 13:2)

> Show hospitality to one another without grumbling. (1 Pet. 4:9)

Note that the first and last are simple imperatives. Both Paul and Peter clearly instruct all believers to show hospitality. No exceptions are given because of gender, gifting, or availability. Peter has good reason to add the phrase "without grumbling," as he had certainly heard of complaints among those who had grown weary in providing for the needs of others. How interesting that Paul, in his detailed description of a widow qualified for aid, includes that she should have a reputation for being hospitable (1 Tim. 5:9–10). The writer of the book of Hebrews makes an unusual reference to "entertaining angels unaware" as one faithfully practices hospitality. Hospitality, although often identified by biblical scholars as a spiritual gift of service, is also a command to all believers. Perhaps you have no idea how the Lord may choose to bless your sincere efforts to produce results beyond what you can ever imagine.

Fascinating accounts of hospitality are found in both the Old and New Testaments. Many of Jesus's miracles were performed in a context of hospitality, including the wedding at Cana in Galilee, the feeding of the five thousand, and the raising of Peter's mother-in-law. Much has been written about the importance of this mandated ministry, and yet it seems to be regarded by many as a thing of the past.

C. S. Lewis gives an inspiring example of the role of hospitality in the early church:

> For we all wish to be judged by our peers, by the men "after our own heart." Only they really know our mind and only they judge it by standards we fully acknowledge. Theirs is the praise we really covet and the blame we really dread. The little pockets of early Christians survived because they cared exclusively for the love of "the brethren" and stopped their ears to the opinion of the Pagan society all round them.[1]

Nothing has changed in terms of the need for affirmation and encouragement from "the brethren." What has changed is the willingness to recognize that fact and act upon it. We are all commanded to practice hospitality joyfully as did the early church. How grateful we should be that our homes do not resemble the sparse and cramped hovels of biblical times. How sobering it is to realize that the obedience of the early church to this simple command had amazing results.

WHAT IS THE DEAL WITH THE "LOST ART" OF HOSPITALITY?

Have you heard of the "lost art" of biblical hospitality? What used to be common among Christians has been relegated to the category of a practice from the distant past and often is missing from the twenty-first-century lifestyle. Perhaps you should be heartened by the fact that many are seeking to recover what they consider to be a lost art and even suggesting innovative ways to do so. One of the purposes in this chapter is to analyze briefly the reasons for the decline. From there the focus is on what the unchanging biblical mandates are and how you can apply them.

What Changed?

The advent of technology brought with it big promises of mass quantities of saved time, but that was a lie. The conveniences are wonderful, but they brought with them less free time, not more. To prepare a turkey and all the trimmings in just a few hours matters not if you have neither the time, interest, nor skill to do so. Too many women are simply not at home more than a

---

[1] C. S. Lewis, *The Four Loves* (1960; reprint, Orlando, FL: Harcourt Brace, 1988), 79.

few waking hours per day. They are buried by the demands of employment outside the home. Running a household under such pressures, they are not about to invite guests into this chaotic atmosphere. Others are overwhelmed by responsibilities and easily rationalize that they are contributing to the greater good in a myriad of ways. They will be only too happy to enumerate those ways, but having guests in their homes is just not for them. Still others would be very eager to return to the patterns of their grandparents who welcomed strangers and friends with open arms, but sadly they have no idea how to do so. Their mothers did not teach them how to cook. They know of no mentors who would be willing to help them now. The thought of embarking on what seems like a daunting task causes them to join the ranks of those who lament that hospitality is clearly a lost art and a faded memory.

RECOVERY 101

One of the best ways for the so-called lost art to be recovered is by modeling hospitality in varied ways whenever you have the chance. The message needs to be proclaimed loud and clear: there is no singular method used to practice this art. Misconceptions abound. Many women who multitask and brilliantly handle complicated issues seem to fall prey to intimidation when it comes to this topic. Others somehow see it as beneath their level of importance and mentally relegate it to those who like to wear aprons and bake cookies. How paradoxical that hospitality management is a worthy profession while doing hospitality at home is merely for the simpleminded or old-fashioned? Satan loves both of these mind-sets since the end result means that hospitality is not practiced and opportunities are purposefully missed.

Semantics Count—What Do You Really Mean?

As you consider the topic in general terms, you must define *biblical hospitality* since it is an often-misunderstood practice. One of my favorite definitions comes from my dear friend, Dorothy Patterson. She simply and succinctly states that it is "the unselfish desire to meet the needs of others." Many people equate food with hospitality, but notice that food is not mentioned in this helpful definition. Although providing a meal is one way to meet the needs of others, it is not the only way. Also note that this definition says nothing about impressing recipients or seeking reciprocation. Yet another key part of the definition is the word "unselfish." Hospitality is not about the provider. It is not about showing how creative, innovative, organized, proficient, and gifted you are. It is about *selflessly* sacrificing your time, efforts, and some degree of finances. It is about taking the risk to let your guard down and invite people to get to know you beyond a superficial level. It is about abandoning the sinful tendency to be self-absorbed and instead seeking to do whatever is necessary to meet the needs of others.

Another apt definition comes from an unlikely source. I heard about a hundred-year-old great-grandmother who had been welcoming guests to the town that she had called home all her life. When someone noted how welcoming the little burg was, the grandmother quipped, "Well, when you come to our town, we just want you to feel better when you leave than when you came." What a great way to describe biblical hospitality! If you provide a weary traveler with a filling meal, homemade or not, or a warm bed, he will feel better when he leaves than when he arrived. If you welcome a friend in crisis into your home and truly listen to her despite the fact that your house is not in perfect order, she will feel better when she leaves than when she came. If you pause to help your neighbors and then invite them to your patio to visit and to tell you about themselves, they will leave encouraged and often feeling better about themselves. Hospitality is not to be equated with five-course gourmet meals and formal wear. Hospitality is to be equated with selfless caring for others. Remember that the world is filled with people who feel isolated, lonely, and unloved. Simple acts of hospitality can lift anyone's spirit in unexpected ways.

The familiar portrait of a godly woman describes her as one who "looks well to the ways of her household" (Prov. 31:27). When you do the same, you will find that extending hospitality beyond your own family is much easier. Too many women are overwhelmed with homemaking. Perhaps they did not have it modeled for them as they grew up, or perhaps they are too busy to make it a priority. Thus the importance of recovering biblical homemaking takes on yet another level of validity in restoring hospitality to its rightful place.

Biblical Hospitality Serves to Promote Evangelism and Discipleship

The mission field for many of you is your neighborhood. You must go out of your way to be good neighbors long before you have an opportunity to share your faith and testimony. If neighbors see you as aloof and unfriendly, they will not likely want to pursue a friendship. If they see you as neighbors who do not take care of your yard or follow neighborhood guidelines, they will likely have a negative impression that will be difficult to overcome. You should be motivated to be friendly and trustworthy neighbors who take pride in your own home.

When my children were preschoolers, I started a coffee group. I have fond memories of our meeting every Friday morning in each other's homes for fellowship and some lively conversation. Many who assumed that a Baptist preacher's home would be a frightening place came to find out that they had nothing to fear. We had some very candid discussions about everything from parenting to politics, all while chasing our toddlers around the house. Those women came to know that I was far from perfect but also far from the judgmental Bible-thumping stereotype whom they had envisioned. They came to trust me as a friend who cared about them and was deeply concerned about where they would spend eternity. Spending time in my home, receiving a caring note, enjoying a meal, or knowing that I was there to offer to help in crisis all served to show hospitality by fleshing out Christ's love in everyday life. Hospitality and evangelism can thus be melded together to God's glory.

Discipleship can be enhanced in a similar way. As recipients of hospitality, new believers can greatly benefit as they observe marriage, parenting, and homemaking playing out in your home. They will learn valuable truths as they see that your Christianity is not just a Sunday activity but a lifestyle that permeates all you do. What valuable and practical lessons about the Christian life can be learned by simple, informal visits by a new believer as you simultaneously welcome and mentor her.

Biblical Hospitality Sometimes Does Provide Food and Lodging

Note that food and lodging should not be the primary focus of this topic, but they can play important roles. Those who have the gift of hospitality seem to enjoy this aspect. They thrive on planning menus for company. They anticipate preparing their guest room as they try to think of all the things that might make their guests feel right at home. Hospitality will look different for each household. The Lord equips each of you uniquely, which can be reflected in how you reach out to others, assuming you choose to do so. Some women look at those who practice hospitality with flair and gusto and wrongly assume that since they cannot duplicate such excellence with their own respective skill sets, they need not try at all. This is folly. Although it is certainly more enjoyable for those who have the spiritual gift, those who do not have it are nonetheless commanded to show love in Christ's name, and he will give the ability.

WHAT IS YOUR BLISS?

Neither my husband nor I own a pair of jeans. We rarely use paper plates. We host many formal dinners with multiple courses in our home. Hosting guests while sitting on the floor wearing jeans and eating from take-out containers is not likely to happen in our home. However, that does not make our style of hospitality any more or less genuine than those who opt for less formal settings. The motivation of the heart is what counts here. Am I trying to impress my guests with my crystal and silver? Are you trying to impress your guests with how laid-back you are by avoiding such things? If the answer to either of these is yes, then hospitality has not been shown. Make yours flow out of whatever your natural style is. You will still have to work at it, especially if you are reluctant to jump in, but know that the Lord will bless your efforts in ways you would never imagine.

No rules apply for guest rooms either. You do not have to live in a palace to offer lodging to a weary traveler. In biblical times hosts welcomed guests for weeks at a time even though they barely had room to house their own families. If you can offer a room with a decent mattress where a guest can get a good night's sleep and provide access to a bathroom—all with the appropriate levels of privacy—then you should do so whenever possible. You do not have to have designer linens on the bed or a Jacuzzi in the bathroom. However, if you are one who enjoys assembling a welcome basket and providing sample sizes of toiletries or other forgotten items, then go for it. Your guests will appreciate your efforts even if they fail to let you know. The motivation of your heart to provide for them does not go unnoticed by the Lord.

Many acts classified as hospitality may surprise those who equate it only with food. Remember that we defined *hospitality* as "selflessly meeting needs of others." Consider how biblical hospitality can do just that in the twenty-first century.

Biblical Hospitality in Writing Is the Gift that Keeps on Giving

You may have attempted to show your gratitude to someone only to have him stop you and say, "Oh, that was nothing. Don't mention it." Occasionally this response is prompted by awkwardness or embarrassment. When you are able to show gratitude in writing, you can choose your words wisely to express yourself with honesty and sincerity. Writers of kind notes may be surprised to know that those notes are often read and reread by the recipients. I have heard of handwritten notes found tucked away in Bibles and later discovered by family members after a loved one has died. Words of encouragement offered with genuine love are powerful. On the other hand, notes written by obligation can be detected with ease. When the Holy Spirit brings someone unexpectedly to mind, realize that this is not a random thought. Act on this prompting. Pray for the person. Send a greeting of some kind whether or not it is an obvious occasion. Your words may be the only encouragement received by the recipient all week long. Does this meet the criteria of unselfishly meeting the needs of others? It certainly will if it is done with some forethought and not out of obligation. Even those who try to shut down verbal compliments will appreciate heartfelt words of gratitude. This too is biblical hospitality. Remember to acknowledge gifts as well as meals or lodging provided for you. I like to assume that many people rank words of encouragement as one of their greatest needs. What a privilege to be a blessing to believers and unbelievers alike by following through on good intentions to practice hospitality in writing.

What Was Your Name Again?

Can you associate with the common problem of being introduced to someone and immediately forgetting that person's name? Many people do not listen well when meeting someone new. You may be preoccupied and thinking about something else and then feel reluctant to admit that you were not paying attention. The wrong assumption is commonly made that those who remember people's names are just "great with names," as if they have a genetic marker for that. The truth is that those who are adept at remembering names invest time and effort in learning them. Consider it an act of encouragement and, yes, an expression of hospitality to call someone by name. Do you know anyone who is not pleased to be called by her name? You, too, can master this skill, but it is an intentional act. Listen carefully and then try to remember the name by either saying it to yourself, if you are an auditory learner, or by picturing it in writing, if you are a visual learner. These two steps alone will make a difference in your ability to learn names. If you are attempting to learn a group of names and have access to a written roster, make notes on that list that will help jog your memory when you gather again. Refreshing your memory by reviewing even briefly will serve to reinforce both the name and perhaps something about that person and help you remember her in the future. Remembering names is another small yet meaningful way to demonstrate to others that you care.

YOU ARE SOMETIMES BLESSED TO LEARN THE BENEFIT

All it takes is one story from someone whom you have blessed to spur you on to continue. One rainy morning in our campus center, I saw a young man approaching from a distance. By the time we met, I felt confident enough that he was the husband of one of my student wives that I called him by name (a feat that is certainly not always the case). I could tell that I got it right as evidenced by his rather surprised look. I was pleased but thought nothing further of it. Months later, I ran into him and his wife at a campus-wide event. He told me with great joy about this day in the distant past when he was headed into the post office, hoping for some good news on a dreary day. He had just flunked a midterm exam and was beginning to wonder if he had made a mistake in tearing up roots and moving his family so far away from home. And then he ran into me. And I called him by name. He described how the Lord used that to brighten his mood and to encourage him in the midst of his gloomy day. The telling of that story in turn was a huge blessing to me. Not only was I pleased that the Holy Spirit prompted me to recall his name and thus encourage him, but I was also highly motivated to continue intentionally to learn names since it really does make a difference.

BIBLICAL HOSPITALITY IS A BLESSING ALL AROUND

This chapter has only begun to explore a few of the aspects of applied biblical hospitality. Valuable lessons are learned by your children when they grow up in a home where hospitality is offered freely and frequently. Children will want that same atmosphere in their homes as they grow to adulthood. If they have never seen hospitality practiced, they will have little to emulate. If they can recall only how their usually calm mother was transformed into a nervous wreck whenever company was coming, that will have an influence as well. Please take away the important truth that although it is not rocket science to perform, hospitality can be used by the Lord to bless believers and unbelievers in ways that you will not understand this side of heaven. If you are one who thrives in this area, be thankful and keep looking for opportunities. If you are one who has either minimized or deemphasized your responsibility to practice hospitality, resolve to improve as you start small, compare yourself to no one, and genuinely seek to be a blessing by your unselfish desire to meet the needs of others.

PUTTING THE PRINCIPLES INTO PRACTICE

1. Give serious thought to what the Bible teaches about hospitality, both explicitly and implicitly. Consider one of the many examples of hospitality in practice. Study it and ask the Lord to teach you something new by application.
2. Do you love all things related to hospitality? If so, you likely have the spiritual gift (in addition to the biblical mandate). Do not apologize for this. Who might benefit from your excitement and creativity? How can you encourage her in this area without making it look too easy?

3. Do you struggle to make time for hospitality? Do you know someone who models it well and could serve as your mentor? You do not want to mimic her style, but you can adapt to your own situation what you learn from her.

4. Consider the hospitality ministry of writing notes as a simple yet meaningful way to encourage others. Ask the Lord to bring people to mind whom you could bless. Act on it as you set aside even an hour per month to send notes or cards to encourage those whose good work is well acknowledged as well as those whose good works are unseen by many.

5. Are you intentional about calling people by name? Do you diminish the importance of this discipline by thinking memory is easy for others but not for you? Resolve to listen carefully the next time you are introduced to someone. Make an effort to honor her by learning her name.

ABOUT THE AUTHOR

Mary K. Mohler is the wife of Dr. R. Albert Mohler Jr., president of The Southern Baptist Theological Seminary in Louisville, Kentucky. They have been happily married for twenty-eight years and have two young adult children, Katie and Christopher. Mary loves her role as homemaker. She also enjoys hosting many seminary events in their home as she practices hospitality with groups of all sizes. She directs Seminary Wives Institute, an academic program for student wives. One of her favorite courses to teach in the program is her annual hospitality elective.

Part Five

PLANNING AND PREPARING HEALTHY MEALS

Chapter Thirty

Nutrition and Healthy Eating: Making Wise Choices

Kimberly Toqe

You will eat approximately 1,095 meals this year. Assuming an average life expectancy of seventy-five years, you will eat approximately 82,125 meals in your lifetime. Consider the opportunity you have to influence your family's health. Although a single daily choice of what to eat might seem rather insignificant, those choices made over and over again can have a significant impact on your health and ultimately on your life.

The daily choices you make regarding food and nutrition are important. But, why? No matter what you do, you are not going to add even a moment to your life. God determines the span of your life, and your days are already numbered (Ps. 139:16). If God gives you life as long as he purposes, then he will sustain you until that time is complete. However, knowing that does not give you a license to indulge your flesh and pander to every appetite of your body. To do so would be sin. "Or do you not know that your body is a temple of the Holy Spirit within you, whom you have from God? You are not your own, for you were bought with a price. So glorify God in your body" (1 Cor. 6:19–20). You are God's creation, and he expects you to protect, nourish, and care for your body because he purchased you and you belong to him. The goal in life is to glorify God, and caring for your body is just one way you can honor him (1 Cor. 10:31). You make the choice to discipline yourself in your eating habits with the aim of being healthy to serve God at your best.

God has prepared an amazing variety of foods for the nourishment and sustenance of his creation (Gen. 1:29–31; 9:3), but God has given food for more than sustenance. He has also created food for enjoyment. God has given a vast variety of flavors and tastes for the pleasure of his creation. You are able to enjoy your food while making wise food choices. This chapter will introduce you to key habits that are designed to help you make healthful food, eating, and exercising choices for you and your family.

KEY #1: VARIETY

The children of Israel wandered in the wilderness for forty years, and during that time God sustained them on nothing but manna and the Word of God (Neh. 9:21; Deut. 8:3). Manna was a special food provided by God to sustain the Hebrews during the exodus from Egypt. The nature of that manna is not known, but it resembled the coriander seed and was white, tasty, and sweet like honey (Ex. 16:31). Most important—it was nutritious. In fact, manna was the single perfect food, supernaturally supplied by God to meet all the nutritional needs of his chosen people.

The modern day has no single, perfect, complete, balanced food that can be consumed exclusively to sustain life. All foods are missing at least one essential nutrient. In the same way, there is no one food group (grain, vegetable, fruit, dairy, or protein) that supplies all the nutrients your body needs. The best way to get all of the nutrients your body needs is to combine a variety of foods from different food groups so that nutrient surpluses in some foods will compensate for nutrient deficits in others. The key to a healthful diet is to eat a wide variety of foods from each of the different food groups every day.

The food you eat is broken down during digestion into nutrients that are carried to every cell in your body. The cells then use the nutrients to perform specific and unique life-sustaining functions in the body. There are more than forty different nutrients in food that are essential for your overall health, and each of these forty nutrients falls into one of six categories: carbohydrates, fats, proteins, vitamins, minerals, and water.

Carbohydrates: Simple Yet Complex

Carbohydrates are your body's main source of energy. Most important, carbohydrates provide the only form of energy (*glucose*) that your brain is able to use. Carbohydrates are divided into two categories: simple and complex. *Simple carbohydrates* include sugars that occur naturally in foods such as fruits, vegetables, milk and milk products, as well as sugars that are added when foods are processed or refined. *Complex carbohydrates* consist of starches and dietary fiber. *Starches* are found in certain vegetables such as corn, potatoes, peas, and beans, as well as various grains and breads. *Dietary fiber* is found in vegetables, fruits, and whole (unrefined) grains. Unlike whole grains, refined grains are not a good source of fiber. Grains lose nutrients during the refining process; while some nutrients are added back to the grain, fiber is not. Both sugars and starches are broken down during digestion and absorbed into every cell in your body. There they are converted into energy. However, dietary fiber is unique in that it cannot be digested by the human body; therefore, fiber cannot be used as energy fuel for your body. Fiber instead aids in digestion and offers protection from some diseases.

Unfortunately, carbohydrates have developed a bad reputation in recent years. Blamed for causing weight gain, they have been blacklisted from many diets. This is an unfair analysis of carbohydrates. Remember that carbohydrates are an essential part of a healthful diet. They are the main power source for your brain as well as your muscles. The problem is not the consumption of carbohydrates but the amount and type of carbohydrates being consumed, a topic to be addressed later in this chapter.

Which carbohydrates should you avoid and which should you consume? Processed foods with refined carbohydrates, such as white flour and/or added sugar, are generally high in calories and low in vitamins, minerals, and fiber. They are often referred to as *empty calories* because of their minimal nutritional value. These simple carbohydrates are absorbed quickly into your body. On one hand, they can cause your blood sugar to spike, creating energy highs; on the other hand, they can cause blood-sugar levels to crash, creating energy lows. (Beware: You may find these sweet, simple carbohydrates included in the ingredient lists of processed and prepackaged foods. They are easily identifiable because many of them end in *ose* such as sucrose, fructose, maltose, and glucose.) The best plan is to consume a variety of fiber-rich complex carbohydrates found in vegetables, fruits, legumes, and whole, unrefined grains. These complex carbohydrates supply important vitamins and minerals. Because they are digested more slowly in your system, they help stabilize and balance blood-sugar levels, preventing energy highs and lows.

Fat Facts

Fat is an essential part of every diet. Like carbohydrates, dietary fats supply energy to your cells. If you consume more energy from fat than your body needs, the excess energy is stored in your body's fatty tissue. Body fat provides an efficient way to store energy for later use as well as insulation to protect your organs and bones.

There are two types of dietary fat: saturated and unsaturated. Most *saturated fats*—which are predominantly found in foods from animals, such as red meat and dairy—are solid at room temperature. Most *unsaturated fats*—which are primarily found in foods from plants, such as vegetable oils, seeds, and nuts—are liquid at room temperature. There are two types of unsaturated fats: monounsaturated and polyunsaturated. Canola oil, olive oil, almonds, pecans, pumpkin seeds, and avocados are examples of foods that are high in *monounsaturated fats*. High concentrations of *polyunsaturated fats* are found in sunflower oil, soybean oil, walnuts, flax seeds, and fish. Omega-3, one type of polyunsaturated fat, is essential to your diet. Because your body is unable to make omega-3 fats, they must come from the foods you eat. Certain fatty fish, such as salmon, halibut, and albacore tuna, as well as various plant sources such as chia seeds, flax seeds, and walnuts, are excellent sources of omega-3 fats.

Fats have also been given a bad reputation in recent years. They, too, have been blamed for causing weight gain, and these have been blacklisted from many diets. Yet, fats are an essential nutrient for good health, and not all types of fat are equal. Consider both the amount and type of fat you are eating as you would with carbohydrates.

How do you distinguish between harmful and healthful fats? Saturated fats are often considered "bad" fats because they have been shown to raise total cholesterol levels by increasing both harmful low-density lipoprotein (LDL) and helpful high-density lipoprotein (HDL) levels in your body. LDL is responsible for carrying cholesterol, a fatlike substance, to your arteries and increasing plaque deposits/formations. HDL is responsible for removing cholesterol from artery walls and carrying it to your liver for excretion or reuse.

Trans fats are another type of "bad" fat. *Trans fats* are formed when liquid vegetable oils are heated in the presence of hydrogen gas. This process, known as *hydrogenation*, transforms a liquid fat into a more semisolid fat and makes it more stable and less likely to spoil. Sources of trans fat include many commercially prepared foods, processed foods, and snack foods as well as margarines and shortenings. Trans fats are worse than saturated fats because they not only increase harmful LDL, but they also decrease helpful HDL.

By contrast, unsaturated fats are considered "good" fats because they have been shown to help decrease your total cholesterol and help lower your LDL levels. However, even healthful fats are high in calories, and if unused, those calories will be stored as extra body fat. Consequently, a variety of foods containing healthy unsaturated fats should be enjoyed, but not in excess.

Body-Building Proteins

Every cell in the human body contains protein, which is critical for many bodily functions. *Proteins* are responsible for building, maintaining, and repairing body tissue as well as forming hormones, contributing to immune function, and helping maintain the body's fluid balance. Additionally, your body can use proteins as an energy source if calories are in short supply.

Proteins are made up of *amino acids*, which bond together in various sequenced combinations to form specific proteins. The proteins in your body are constantly being broken down. Proteins continually need to be replaced through daily food consumption. Proteins found in the food you eat are digested into amino acids that your body uses to replace these broken-down proteins. Unlike fat, amino acids are not stored by your body; they must be consumed on a daily basis to ensure that your body has all the necessary amino acids for building needed proteins.

Twenty different types of amino acids are found in various foods you consume. Your body is able to make eleven of those twenty amino acids. These are known as *nonessential amino acids* because your body can synthesize them when necessary. The remaining nine amino acids cannot be synthesized by your body; they must be obtained from a food source. Foods that contain all nine essential amino acids are known as *complete proteins*. Animal products like meat, poultry, fish, eggs, milk, and cheese are considered good sources of complete protein. Foods known as *incomplete proteins* lack any one of the nine essential amino acids. Incomplete proteins are found in plant-based foods such as fruits, vegetables, grains, legumes, and nuts.

Nearly all plant protein sources are low in one or more essential amino acids. Therefore, you must consume a variety of plant proteins to obtain sufficient amounts of all essential amino acids. *Complementary proteins* are two incomplete protein sources, which, when added together, create a complete protein source, providing adequate amounts of all the essential amino acids. Some examples of complementary protein combinations are grains and vegetables (e.g., pasta and tomatoes), vegetables and nuts (e.g., green beans and almonds), nuts and legumes (e.g., tahini and chickpeas), and legumes and grains (e.g., beans and rice).[1] Whether you choose to eat complementary proteins or complete proteins, you should eat a wide variety of protein-rich foods every day in order to guarantee that your body has all the essential amino acids available to build needed proteins.

Vital Vitamins

Vitamins, essential compounds that help regulate chemical reactions in your body, in themselves do not yield any energy, but they help facilitate body reac-

---

[1] Gordon M. Wardlaw and Anne M. Smith, *Contemporary Nutrition*, 7th ed. (Boston: McGraw-Hill, 2009), 226.

tions that produce energy. They are required in small amounts for normal growth and bodily maintenance. Every vitamin plays an important and unique role in promoting overall health. Since each vitamin is responsible for a unique task, one vitamin cannot replace another vitamin. You must consume vitamins by eating foods from the various food groups every day because your body is unable to make enough of the vitamins required to prevent vitamin deficiencies.

Your body needs thirteen different vitamins. Four of these (A, D, E, and K) are *fat soluble*; they are stored in your body's fatty tissue and liver and are eliminated slowly from your body. Because these vitamins are stored, they present a risk for toxicity. Eating foods high in vitamins A, D, E, and K will not lead to toxic levels of fat-soluble vitamins in your system. However, large doses of fat-soluble vitamin supplements can lead to toxicity. The remaining nine vitamins (Bs and C) are *water soluble*; they cannot be stored in your body and need to be consumed daily.

Minerals Matter

Minerals are a group of essential nutrients that give your body structure and regulate your bodily processes. They support nervous system functioning, fluid balance, muscle contractions, and many other cellular processes. Minerals, like vitamins, do not yield any energy, but they help facilitate the bodily reactions that produce energy.

Your body needs approximately sixteen different minerals in food. These sixteen minerals are divided into two categories based on a body's daily requirement. *Major minerals* are needed in amounts greater than 100 milligrams per day. Calcium, potassium, sodium, and chloride are major minerals. *Trace minerals* are needed in amounts less than 100 milligrams per day. Iron, zinc, fluoride, and iodine are trace minerals. The amount of minerals absorbed from food varies greatly. As a general rule, minerals from animal products are absorbed better than minerals from plants. To help prevent mineral deficiencies, eat a variety of foods from the different food groups every day.

Water: Liquid Asset

Virtually every life-sustaining process in your body requires water. Humans can survive only a few days without it. Water is responsible for a body's fluid and temperature regulation. Water is also used to carry nutrients to your cells and waste products out of your body.[2] Your body is approximately 60 percent water

[2] Institute of Medicine Food and Nutrition Board of the National Academies, *Dietary Reference Intakes for Water, Potassium, Sodium, Chloride, and Sulfate* (Washington, DC: National Academies, 2005), 74, accessed December 14, 2011, http://www.nap.edu/catalog.php?record_id=10925.

weight.[3] To function optimally, your body must maintain its water weight. Your body loses an average of nine cups of water each day (in healthy sedentary adults) through sweat, urine, bowel movements, and even breathing. This means that water needs continually to be replenished in your system. Replacement water can come from a variety of sources. While drinking water and other beverages is the main way to hydrate your body, you can also *eat* your water. On average, food contributes up to 20 percent of your daily intake of water.

KEY #2: BALANCE

Calories Count

Calories are units of energy. Carbohydrates, fats, and proteins are the main sources of calories. Each of these nutrients supplies your body with much-needed energy. However, some supply more calories than others. Comparing gram for gram, fat supplies the most calories: nine calories per gram of fat. Carbohydrates and proteins both supply four calories per gram.[4]

So, how many calories does your body require each day? The number of calories needed by your body varies from person to person and is determined by your age, gender, height, weight, physical condition, and activity level. "Estimates range from 1,600 to 2,400 calories per day for adult women and 2,000 to 3,000 calories per day for adult men."[5] (There are numerous online tools that can estimate your individual calorie need.) Of the total number of calories that you need, the Institute of Medicine recommends that 45–65 percent should come from carbohydrates, 20–35 percent should come from fat, and 10–35 percent should come from protein sources.[6]

Learning to control calorie intake from food and beverages is essential to achieving calorie balance. Your goal each day should be to balance the number of calories consumed with the number of calories expended. If daily you consume fewer calories than you use, you will lose weight. Similarly, if you consume more calories each day than you use, then you will gain weight because your body stores the excess unused calories in the form of fat. Just eighty extra calories a day, the number of calories found in one medium apple, in one year will add up to an extra eight pounds per year (1 pound = 3,500 calories). How

---

[3] Ibid., 77.

[4] United States Department of Agriculture [USDA] and United States Department of Health and Human Services [USDHHS], *Dietary Guidelines for Americans 2010*, 7th ed. (Washington, DC: US Government Printing Office, 2010), 14–15, accessed December 14, 2011, http://www.health.gov/dietaryguidelines/dga2010/DietaryGuidelines2010.pdf.

[5] USDA and USDHHS, *Dietary Guidelines for Americans 2010*, 13.

[6] Institute of Medicine of the National Academies, "Report: *Dietary Reference Intakes for Energy, Carbohydrate, Fiber, Fat, Fatty Acids, Cholesterol, Protein, and Amino Acids*," released September 5, 2002, accessed August 24, 2012, http://www.iom.edu/Reports/2002/Dietary-Reference-Intakes-for-Energy-Carbohydrate-Fiber-Fat-Fatty-Acids-Cholesterol-Protein-and-Amino-Acids.aspx.

do you prevent this? You must balance your calorie intake with your energy output. Think of it as a nutrition budget. In the same way that you budget your money, you should consider setting up a *budget* for your calories. At the end of each day you want to have a balanced calorie budget.

Rethink What You Drink

Have you ever considered how many calories you are drinking? Liquid calories from beverages can add up quickly. Soda, juice, smoothies, sweet tea, sweetened coffee, energy drinks, weight-loss drinks, and even "flavored water" can contribute a significant number of calories to your diet. These beverages are often high in calories because they are high in sugar. The average 20-ounce soda, the size of many medium cups at fast-food restaurants, contains almost 70 grams of sugar and 250 empty calories and offers no nutritional benefits. Even 100 percent fruit juice, which offers some nutritional benefits, is still loaded with sugar and calories. A 20-ounce glass of orange juice contains nearly 300 calories. Pour a glass of apple juice or grape juice and the calories increase even more.

You do not have to give up your favorite drink completely, but be aware of how many calories you are drinking. When you choose to consume liquid calories, consider the overall impact to your daily calorie intake. Your goal is a balanced calorie budget, and one of the easiest ways to balance your calorie intake is to reduce the number of liquid calories you consume.

Not Just Quantity but Quality

If you are going to have a balanced diet, you must consider not only the quantity but also the quality of food you eat. A well-balanced diet involves eating the right amount of food to provide optimal, but not excessive, amounts of energy for your body. Additionally, a well-balanced diet involves eating the right type of nutrient-dense food that provides substantial amounts of vitamins, minerals, and other essential nutrients within an appropriately limited number of calories. The goal is to get the maximum nutritional value from the calories you consume.

A balanced diet includes nutrient-dense foods from each of the five food groups. Eat a rainbow of colorful fruits and vegetables. The more brilliant the color, the higher the concentration of vitamins and minerals—the brighter the better. Choose whole grains such as brown rice, oatmeal, and foods made with whole-wheat flour. Select quality protein sources including fresh fish, lean meat, eggs, beans, and nuts. Opt for dairy products, such as low-fat milk or yogurt or kefer, which provide a rich source of calcium in a form that is easily digested and absorbed by the body.

KEY #3: MODERATION

Too Much of a Good Thing

Average Americans consume many more calories than their bodies need, having transitioned from eating until they are satisfied to eating until they are "stuffed."[7] Additionally, Americans tend to be moderate in their consumption of healthful foods, such as dark-green, orange, red, and yellow vegetables, legumes, fruits, and whole grains, and excessive in the calories consumed from processed foods, "bad" fats, and foods and drinks that are high in sugar (and other sweeteners), salt, additives, and preservatives.

Making Moderation Your Mind-set

Too often people take an all-or-nothing approach toward healthy eating. However, eating healthily does not mean completely denying yourself all your favorite treats but rather disciplining yourself to eat these foods in smaller quantities and less often than you might like. Learning to practice moderation in your journey to healthful eating is an essential key that is easier said than done. Moderation should be applied not only to the amount of food consumed but also to the types of foods consumed.

Enough, but Not Too Much

Americans have a portion distortion. Super-sized "single" servings, all-you-can-eat buffets, and oversized serving plates and cups tempt you continually to overeat. As portion sizes have grown in recent years, so has America's waistline.[8] The problem: people are consuming too much food. One of the most important and crucial components of healthful eating is learning to moderate serving sizes. Eating smaller portions is one of the easiest ways to control the number of calories being consumed.

Avoid portion pitfalls by learning to recognize what *a single serving* of food actually looks like. This understanding will allow you to recognize when you are consuming excessive numbers of servings in a meal.[9]

---

[7] United States Department of Agriculture, "Profiling Food Consumption in America," in *Agriculture Fact Book 2001–2002* (Washington, DC: US Government Printing Office, 2003), 14, accessed December 14, 2011, http://www.usda.gov/factbook/2002factbook.pdf.
[8] National Center for Chronic Disease Prevention and Health Promotion, Division of Nutrition and Physical Activity, "Do Increased Portion Sizes Affect How Much We Eat?" Research to Practice Series, no. 2, May 2006 (Atlanta: Centers for Disease Control and Prevention, 2006), accessed December 14, 2011, http://www.cdc.gov/nccdphp/dnpa/nutrition/pdf/portion_size_research.pdf.
[9] Wardlaw and Smith, *Contemporary Nutrition*, 46–47.

Table 30.1
SINGLE-SERVING SIZES

Food Portion	Comparable Size
Meat or fish (3 ounces)	A deck of cards
Vegetables (1 cup)	A baseball
Fruit (1/2 to 2/3 cup)	A tennis ball
Pasta, rice, cooked cereal, or mashed potatoes (1/2 cup)	One-half of a baseball
Peanut butter or salad dressing (2 tablespoons)	A golf ball

Minimum Calories, Maximum Nutrients

In recent years, commercially prepared foods, as well as processed and pre-packaged foods, have become the staple of the American diet. Much of the average American's monthly food budget is spent on these convenience foods, which are often high in calories, sodium, fat, sugars and sweeteners, artificial flavorings, preservatives, colorings, and additives. However, the concern is about more than just what is being added to the food; it is also about what is being taken away. Processed foods have been stripped of many of their natural nutrients, calling for moderation in your consumption of prepackaged foods. Instead, eat food that is as close as possible to the way God created it. Select fresh, whole, unprocessed foods that are complete with all their rich and natural nutrients intact.

KEY #4: EXERCISE

Active Living

Caring for your body requires more than healthful eating. Regular physical activity must be combined with good eating habits, yet most Americans do not get nearly enough exercise. Just as the principles of variety, balance, and moderation should guide your daily food choices, these same principles should guide your daily physical activities.

- *Variety.* Change up your physical activity/exercise routine on a regular basis to ensure that you exercise all the different major muscle groups (arms, shoulders, chest, stomach, back, hips, and legs). Vary the duration, frequency, and intensity of each activity.

- *Balance.* Various physical activities provide different health benefits. Having a balanced approach to physical activity includes *aerobic* activity (e.g., brisk walking, jogging, biking, swimming, water aerobics), *muscle-strengthening* activity (e.g., push-ups, sit-ups, weight lifting), as well as *stretching.*[10]

- *Moderation.* You have to move it to lose it, but do not overdo it! The US Department of Health and Human Services recommends incorporating a minimum of two and a half hours of moderate physical activity into each week. *Moderate-intensity* activity increases your heart rate and breathing but still allows you to be able to talk comfortably while performing the activity. If you are too out of breath to talk, the activity is *high-intensity.* If you are able to sing, the activity is not vigorous enough.[11]

Make the Move

If you are not already active, become more active. Some physical activity is better than none. There are countless benefits to regular physical activity and exercise. Increased physical activity results in increased calorie use. Increased calorie use can help prevent weight gain, help maintain current weight, and even result in weight loss. In addition to controlling weight, exercise can help heighten your energy level, increase your stamina and endurance, build up your physical strength, boost your metabolism, lower your blood pressure, improve your bone health, lift your mood, and enhance your sleep quality.

FIT FOR SERVICE

God intends for you to care for your physical body so you can maintain your strength and be fit to serve him. Caring for your body involves disciplining yourself in your eating habits and physical activity as well as training yourself to accept variety, balance, and moderation as being necessary healthful habits rather than optional guidelines. As long as God grants you life, you are to care for and nourish the body he has given you.

PUTTING THE PRINCIPLES INTO PRACTICE

Adapt the template to become a food diary for a week, recording your intake. Write down the amount of food and beverages, including water, consumed. (Be as specific as you can; do not forget to write down the "extras" such as sauce,

[10] United States Department of Health and Human Services, *2008 Physical Activity Guidelines for Americans*, 22–24, accessed August 24, 2012, http://www.health.gov/paguidelines/guidelines/default.aspx.
[11] Ibid., 22–23.

gravy, dressing, butter, ketchup, and sugar.) Evaluate your diet to see if you are making wise food choices.

ꕥ SAMPLE FOOD AND ꕥ BEVERAGE DIARY

What Did You Eat?	How Much?

1. Do you eat the same thing day after day, or do you eat a wide variety of healthful fats, carbohydrates, and proteins to ensure that your body will have all the necessary nutrients it needs? What specific changes can you make to incorporate more variety into your diet?
2. Do you budget for how you are going to spend your daily calories? Are you including different foods from each of the food groups? What specific changes can you make to incorporate more balance into your diet?
3. Do you consume super-sized portions? Are you moderate in your intake of junk food that is high in calories and low in nutrients? What specific changes can you make to incorporate moderation into your diet?
4. The Institute of Medicine recommends that a daily adequate intake (AI) of water and other beverages is around nine cups for women and thirteen cups for men.[12] How do you measure up? If necessary, what will you do to increase your daily water intake?
5. The Bible does not give clear commands regarding what to eat or what to drink, but it does give principles that should help guide your choices. Can you think of a general biblical principle that should be applied to your eating habits? Where is this principle found in Scripture?

ABOUT THE AUTHOR

Kimberly Toqe was the assistant test kitchen chef at Lawry's Foods before starting her own culinary consulting company. She works primarily as a recipe writer and developer, and a culinary educator. She has been a nutrition professor at the Le Cordon Bleu California School of Culinary Arts and currently

---

[12] Institute of Medicine Food and Nutrition Board of the National Academies, *Dietary Reference Intakes for Water*, 145–47.

teaches nutrition in the Home Economics–Family and Consumer Sciences Department at The Master's College in Santa Clarita, California. Kimberly earned her bachelor of science degree with a double major in biology and home economics from The Master's College and earned her master of science in nutrition, dietetics, and food science from the Family and Consumer Sciences Department at California State University, Northridge.

Chapter Thirty-One

Food Safety in the Home

Janet Taylor

Although a practical and necessary topic, food safety is probably not on the priority list of most. When you think of this topic, your imagination may bring to mind unpleasant images of rotten food and illness.

Why think about food safety? Why should you bother to follow the rules? You may have never become seriously ill—even when you have not followed proper food safety practices—but some facts may be helpful.

The Centers for Disease Control and Prevention (CDC) estimates that "roughly 1 in 6 Americans (or 48 million people) get sick, 128,000 are hospitalized, and 3,000 die of foodborne diseases."[1] You want to avoid being one of these statistics and protect your family. Many who have experienced a bout of foodborne illness or food poisoning would want to avoid another bout at all costs. In addition, if eating some food brings an illness, any possible nutrition the food might have provided is also lost. These reasons are good enough to spend a little time learning how to handle food with care.

RISK VERSUS ACTUAL ILLNESS

The main goal in food safety is to minimize the risk of illness. Most illness caused by foods results from harmful microorganisms or *pathogens*. The majority of these cases are attributed to bacteria, but viruses, parasites, and molds can also be responsible. According to the CDC, in the United States "eight known pathogens account for the vast majority of [foodborne] illnesses, hospitalizations and deaths."[2] These microorganisms exist everywhere. The goal of safe food handling is to minimize the number of harmful microorganisms on foods.

Note that not all microorganisms are harmful. Some useful and beneficial microorganisms are found in cheese and yogurt and in yeast for breads. Some illnesses are caused by the sheer number of bacteria ingested, referenced as *foodborne infections*. Some illnesses are caused by the consumption of a toxin

---

[1] "CDC 2011 Estimates of Foodborne Illness in the United States: Findings," Centers for Disease Control and Prevention website, accessed August 29, 2012, http://www.cdc.gov/foodborneburden/2011-foodborne-estimates.html.
[2] Ibid.

that is produced in the food by bacteria. This type of illness is called *foodborne intoxication.*[3] In either case, the goal of food safety is to keep the microorganism population as small or as nonexistent as possible in order to decrease or prevent the risk of illness.

If there are so many microorganisms and cases of foodborne illness, why don't you get sick every time you eat food? Psalm 139 describes the wonder of the marvelous body God has given you. The human body has amazing resilience to infection and is able to fight off illness. However, sickness has occurred ever since the fall in Eden.

Whether or not an individual becomes ill depends on his overall state of health and the degree of his exposure to microbes or toxins. Often you are unable to prevent illness, but you do not want to cause foodborne illness because of unsafe food handling and preparation. Before discussing some of the important food handling and safety principles to prevent illness, consider some of the scriptural principles guiding food preparation in the home.

BIBLICAL PRINCIPLES

The book of Proverbs describes an exemplary woman who looks after herself and her family, which includes providing for their physical health and well-being. "She looks well to the ways of her household" (Prov. 31:27). This woman takes care of the physical needs of her family. She is on the lookout for their best interests. She is not lazy (Prov. 31:27). Proverbs often speaks of the dangers of laziness. "Whoever is slack in his work is a brother to him who destroys" (Prov. 18:9). You should not neglect sound food safety principles just because you are too careless or you do not want to bother incorporating these principles into your preparations or feel such meticulous care is just too much work. The work of food preparation, even if it seems routine and repetitive, requires diligence and vigilance, especially in regard to food safety.

"Whoever is slothful will not roast his game, but the diligent man will get precious wealth" (Prov. 12:27). "The soul of the sluggard craves and gets nothing, while the soul of the diligent is richly supplied" (Prov. 13:4). And Paul reminds us that all work is ultimately for the Lord, not men, not even those we love. "Whatever you do, work heartily, as for the Lord and not for men" (Col. 3:23).

The Lord has also given to homemakers a stewardship responsibility for their families and for the food that he provides. You do not want to waste foodstuffs. "It is required of stewards that they be found faithful" (1 Cor. 4:2).

---

[3] Department of Food Science and Human Nutrition of Clemson University, "Differentiate between the Major Types of Foodborne Illnesses—Infection, Intoxication, and Toxin-Mediated Infection," foodsafetysite.com, accessed August 29, 2012, http://www.foodsafetysite.com/educators/competencies/general/definitions/def5.html.

Because you want to be entrusted with more important eternal tasks, you should want to be faithful with the routine and even the mundane. "One who is faithful in a very little is also faithful in much, and one who is dishonest in a very little is also dishonest in much" (Luke 16:10). This chapter focuses on food safety issues most often neglected or misunderstood.

THE FOOD HANDLER'S PERSONAL HYGIENE

Many foodborne illnesses are caused by the food handler. Personal hygiene is frequently the issue and one over which you do have control. For that reason, attention will be given to how to improve safety in food handling.

Although everyone knows that before beginning work in the kitchen your hands must be thoroughly washed, everyone is not always as careful about rewashing after interruptions. Answering the telephone is an example of a common interruption that is often overlooked. While observing students working in the lab, I have often noticed how easy it is to brush hair away from the face or scratch the nose without realizing it. These actions are so common that you may let them pass without rewashing your hands. Think through common actions that could cause interruptions and prepare for them ahead of time. In the lab setting, I have students tie their hair back from their faces so it will not hang down into the food. In professional kitchens, nets or hats are used. There should be a plan for managing hair in the home setting as well.

EQUIPMENT SANITATION

Many pieces of equipment and utensils are used in food preparation, and any of them can harbor microorganisms. Some have flat surfaces that are easily cleaned; others have small openings and hidden recesses that can be difficult to clean. We do not often think of the dangers of neglecting the tools used for preparing food. Consider now the care of equipment used in most kitchens.

- *Can opener and cutting blades.* Whether hand or electric models, clean can opener blades thoroughly after each use. Knives and kitchen shears should be washed in warm soapy water before being used on the next food item. Repeated washing of your tools may seem like unnecessary work, but if you neglect this step, you may pass bacteria from one food item to another.

- *Electric blenders.* The blades, plastic ring attachments, and rubber washer should be separated before washing to allow for thorough cleaning of accumulated food on all parts. If the blender does not come apart, be very careful as you clean the underside of the blades. For safety, any electric appliance should be unplugged before cleaning.

- *Utensils and preparation equipment.* Place these in the dishwasher, if possible, as this will give the most thorough cleaning. The water in the dishwasher cycle is hotter than can be tolerated by the hands. Many models have a temperature boost that allows for even hotter temperatures for the safest cleaning.

- *Dishwashers.* Since the dishwasher is the most important method of sterilization in the kitchen, its regular cleaning is essential. When the dishwasher is empty (*no dishwashing detergent*), start a regular cycle and let it run until the bottom begins to fill with water. Then add 2–3 cups white vinegar to the bottom and allow the cycle to finish. Doing this even once a quarter will keep your dishwasher fresh and remove stains and mineral buildup.

- *Cutting surfaces.* Frequently clean any surface that comes in contact with food, such as cutting boards. There is some debate concerning which type of cutting board, plastic or wood, is safest. Research suggests that the real issue is the cleaning and sanitation of the cutting boards, not so much the material from which the board is made. Having two cutting boards—one for meats, the other for produce—helps to avoid transfer of bacteria from the first food that was cut on the board to the next food being prepared. Besides washing the cutting board well (preferably in a dishwasher), use a mild bleach solution as a rinse, particularly after cutting animal products.

- *Dish towels.* Hand-washed items are often dried without much thought. A fresh dish towel should be used each time food is prepared. This prevents the moist towel from the previous food preparations from contaminating the freshly washed dishes and utensils.

FOOD STORAGE TEMPERATURES

Foods should be cooked and stored at the proper temperature to keep the number of microorganisms to a minimum. Microorganisms grow best at temperatures generally comfortable to humans. The range between 40° and 140°F is frequently called the temperature *Danger Zone* because bacteria multiply rapidly at these temperatures.[4] Foods should not be left at these temperatures for extended periods of time. Generally, two hours is the maximum amount of time foods should stand at room temperature. In really warm weather or with highly perishable protein foods, this two-hour time frame should be shortened to one hour maximum.

Cold temperatures slow the growth of microorganisms, so perishable foods should be stored in the refrigerator following the meal, at temperatures below 40°F. The refrigerator should be kept at 40°F or slightly below and should be monitored regularly with a refrigerator thermometer. When placing foods

---

[4] United States Department of Agriculture Food Safety and Inspection Service (USDA FSIS), "Safe Food Handling: 'Danger Zone' (40°F–140°F)," Fact Sheet, accessed August 29, 2012, http://www.fsis.usda.gov/FactSheets /Danger_Zone/index.asp.

in cold storage, large portions of food should be divided into smaller quantities and refrigerated or frozen separately. Otherwise, the center of a large piece of food might remain warm enough for bacteria to grow to a dangerous level. This is a special challenge when you are preparing large amounts of food and trying to store it in the refrigerator.

The rule of keeping perishable foods out of the "temperature danger zone" is often violated, particularly at holidays or other gatherings where food is set out at room temperature for people to eat and snack on most of the day. The best plan is to serve only small portions of food at a time and bring out a fresh platter of food as needed. If greater quantities of food are needed for longer time periods, another option is to use warming or steam trays like those used for large buffets to keep the food above 140°. Either of these methods will ensure greater safety of the food to be enjoyed.

Storage safety rules are also often ignored when there is not enough room in the refrigerator for large amounts of food or soon-to-be-prepared food. Unfortunately, some of the foods—maybe the holiday desserts, such as the pumpkin and custard pies—are left out at room temperature. This is a food safety hazard, since these items contain milk, eggs, and other perishable ingredients that call for refrigeration.

Refrigerator Storage

The door of the refrigerator generally does not stay as cold as the inside of the refrigerator compartment. Items that need to stay 40° or below should not be stored on the door. Eggs and milk are best stored inside the refrigerator. Milk also needs to be covered when stored to prevent dust and microbes from contaminating it. Meats need to be well wrapped. Allowing the raw meat juices to drip onto other foods may cause contamination.

Refrigerators are very efficient. It is no longer necessary to cool foods to room temperature before placing them in the refrigerator, nor is it necessary to place foods on a certain shelf location for coldest storage. Drawers are helpful for preventing cross contamination and for keeping produce at the appropriate humidity.

Length of Cold Storage

How long foods are stored is another important aspect of food storage. "Use by" or "Best by" dates on food packages are a useful tool, as are "Sell by" dates. Check these dates while still in the supermarket. We have found, while doing lab shopping, that the stores do not always check these dates regularly, particularly on slower-moving items. Usually foods with "Use by" dates have rather long expiration dates. Foods with "Sell by" dates, such as milk and eggs, should be good for a week after the date on the carton or package if properly stored at refrigerator temperatures.

The longer an item is stored, the more safety and quality issues arise. This is especially true for meats, poultry, and fish. Ground beef and pieces of poultry and fish should be refrigerated for use only one to two days after purchase. Less than twenty-four hours is best.[5] If you do not plan to prepare and cook the meat in that length of time, it should be frozen. Larger cuts of meat, such as steaks and roasts, can be refrigerated safely for three to five days before cooking but should also be frozen immediately if you are not planning to use them within that time frame. Length of storage times for other foods can be obtained from government websites.

Foods in frozen storage should be stored at 0°F, and this temperature should be checked on a regular basis. Long-term storage is not recommended in refrigerator freezers, as they are usually not able to keep this low temperature consistently.

One misconception is that freezing temperatures kill all microorganisms. This is not the case. Many will survive at these low temperatures and thrive after the food is thawed, so care must still be taken with these foods. Placing the freeze date on the food package is helpful in using these foods in a timely manner for safety and quality.

Storing Food in the Car Trunk

The temperature in the car trunk is usually much warmer than the outside air. Leaving foods in the trunk for any length of time is not good for food safety. Foods left in the car will perish more quickly. Schedule buying food as your last stop before heading home. Foods should be brought home as soon as possible after purchase and stored at the proper temperatures.

One time, I missed unloading one small package from my trunk. The next day, I noticed a peculiar odor in the garage. When I finally located the source of the odor, it came from a small bag of chicken, which had been left in the trunk. The smelly chicken had actually turned black from the rapid growth of microbes caused by the high, and thus unacceptable, temperature inside the trunk.

Baby Bottles and Lunch Boxes

Storing baby bottles in a diaper bag or purse also presents a food safety challenge. Since baby formula, breast milk, and even open bottles of juice are all

---

[5] United States Department of Health and Human Services (USDHHS), "Storage Times for the Refrigerator and Freezer," FoodSafety.gov, accessed August 29, 2012, http://www.foodsafety.gov/keep/charts/storagetimes.html.

perishable and good ground for microorganisms, they should be kept cold. If they are going to be out of the refrigerator for longer than two hours, or even one hour if the weather is warm, they should be packed with a cold source, such as reusable ice packs.

Packed lunch boxes for school or work should also include a cold source to keep perishable items cold. Although most lunch totes are insulated, they do not keep foods at 40° or lower, and many lunches include highly perishable foods that are consumed hours after being prepared. The cold source will ensure their safety. Juice boxes (preferably the kind that are 100% juice) can be frozen and placed in the lunch box as a cold source and then at lunch time enjoyed as an iced juice.

PREPARATION FOR COOKING

Thawing meats for cooking is a critically important safety concern. I have some old cookbooks that talk about thawing large turkeys in a brown bag on the countertop. This is **NOT** considered safe. Many people have told me that they still use this practice of room-temperature thawing of meats, but it greatly increases your risk of illness. The outside layers of the food thaw quickly and are sitting at room temperature; the bacteria are reproducing rapidly on the outside while the inside is still frozen.

There are three acceptable methods to thaw meats, fish, and poultry.[6] The first method is to put the frozen food item in the refrigerator until completely thawed. This method is probably best because no portion of the food ever rises above refrigerator temperatures. However, it does take the longest time, perhaps several days for large roasts or birds to thaw, and meantime the item thawing takes up room in the refrigerator. If you use this method, place the meat on a tray or plate so the juices from the thawing meat do not drip on and contaminate other foods.

The second thawing method is to use the microwave. The microwave can be set on the defrost setting, or 30 percent power, and set for the weight of the meat. If a large piece of meat is being thawed, you may find the defrost setting begins to cook the outside or thinner portions of meat, so you may need to decrease the power to 10 percent toward the end of the process to avoid cooking the meat.

The third accepted method for thawing meats is to place the pieces in a pan or sink of cold water. The meat should be left in the wrapper while doing this. The water should be checked and changed every half hour to ensure that

---

[6] United States Food and Drug Administration (FDA), "Lifelong Food Safety—Chill," accessed August 29, 2011, http://www.FDA.gov/Food/Resourcesforyou/healtheducators/ucm083063.htm.

it remains cold. Warm or hot water should not be used to speed up the process, since doing so would thaw the outer layers too quickly and promote microorganism growth. Regardless of the thawing method used, meats should be cooked immediately after thawing to avoid further bacteria growth or contamination.

WASHING AND COOKING FOODS

The rinsing of poultry (or meats) before cooking is no longer recommended because the washing might cause splattering over kitchen surfaces, contaminating those surfaces.[7] Foods must be cooked to the right temperature to ensure that the microorganisms in these foods have been killed. The color of meats or juices is not a good indicator that the meat has been cooked adequately. A meat thermometer should be used to determine doneness.[8] Inexpensive thermometers can be purchased for about ten dollars. They are easy to use and last for a long time. More expensive instant-read or digital versions are available, but the inexpensive ones work just as well. It may be desirable to own more than one type of meat thermometer to be used in different cooking applications. The thermometer should be placed in the thickest portion of meat and should not touch the bone since this will give a false temperature reading.

Recommended end-point temperatures for cooking meats have changed somewhat in recent years. These temperatures should be double-checked periodically to ensure that you have the latest safe-cooking temperatures.

- Poultry should be cooked to 165°F. This includes poultry that has been ground. It is not recommended that stuffing be placed inside the bird; but if you do so, the stuffing itself should read 165°F. Test the temperature of the poultry as well as the stuffing.

- All cuts of pork should be cooked to a minimum 145°F with a three-minute standing time. This is lower than the previous recommendation of 160°F. Ground beef with all of its exposed surface area needs to be cooked to at least 160°F.

- Steaks and roasts of beef, veal, and lamb should be cooked to 145°F for rare, with higher temperatures for more well-done results.

- All types of leftovers should be reheated to 165°F.[9] Other end-point temperature recommendations can be found on the government food safety websites.

---

[7] United States Department of Health and Human Services, "Food Safety Myths Exposed" (Myth #5), Food Safety.gov, accessed August 29, 2012, http://www.foodsafety.gov/keep/basics/myths/index.html.
[8] United States Department of Agriculture Food Safety and Inspection Service, "Appliances & Thermometers: Kitchen Thermometers" Fact Sheet, accessed August 29, 2012, http://origin-www.fsis.usda.gov/Fact_Sheets/Kitchen_Thermometers/index.asp.
[9] United States Department of Health and Human Services, "Safe Minimum Cooking Temperatures," Food Safety.gov, accessed August 29, 2012, http://www.foodsafety.gov/keep/charts/mintemp.html.

- Cooked foods, which can also be a safety risk if they are not handled properly after cooking, should be eaten or stored in the refrigerator after cooking. The two-hour safety rule applies to cooked as well as to raw foods. Just because foods have been cooked does not guarantee their safety indefinitely.

Foods that are eaten raw do not have heat applied to kill potentially harmful bacteria; these foods must be handled carefully. Produce eaten raw must be carefully washed to ensure its safety. Vegetables, particularly, must be washed thoroughly as they generally carry larger amounts of dirt, being grown closer to the ground. Preventing cross contamination is also very important when handling foods to be eaten raw. Foodborne illness carried by produce has been more common in recent years. Proper growing and handling practices need to be followed by both the grower and consumer.

AT-RISK POPULATIONS

Besides abiding by the general safety recommendations for all people, certain family members may need to take extra precautions because they are at greater risk of foodborne illness. This special group includes infants, toddlers, pregnant women, the elderly, and those with chronic illness. Extra care must be taken with their food preparation.

When preparing meals for those at greater risk, certain foods should be avoided, such as unpasteurized dairy products and juices, as well as undercooked eggs, meat, poultry, and fish.[10] Specific handling requirements may be necessary as noted elsewhere.

ADDITIONAL FOOD SAFETY INFORMATION

If you would like further information on the proper handling of foods, the causes of foodborne illnesses, information on reporting food illness, and other topics related to food safety, the websites of the Food and Drug Administration (FDA), United States Department of Agriculture Food Safety and Inspection Service (USDA FSIS), and the Centers for Disease Control and Prevention (CDC) have fact sheets, podcasts, and information on food safety. The federal government also runs the Meat and Poultry Hotline (1-888-674-6854), which will answer specific questions about meat and poultry safety issues. The American Dietetic Association and county agricultural extension services provide food safety information.

---

[10] United States Department of Health and Human Services and United States Department of Agriculture, "Chapter 10: Food Safety," *Dietary Guidelines for Americans, 2005*, accessed August 29, 2012, http://www.health .gov/dietaryguidelines/dga2005/document/html/chapter10.htm.

Commercial growers and processors have their part in the food safety chain, but if the homemaker/food preparer does her part in putting into practice sound food safety principles, she will make a big difference in ensuring that the food served at her table is safe to eat and enjoy.

PUTTING THE PRINCIPLES INTO PRACTICE

1. Which, if any, food safety principles have you forgotten or neglected in your food preparation?
2. In the safe storage of foods, what temperatures are most important?
3. Identify areas of food safety about which you need to learn more.
4. Which principles of biblical stewardship are demonstrated when careful food handling practices are observed?
5. How can the biblical qualities of diligence and watchfulness be practiced when preparing food to ensure safety?
6. What consequences come because of a neglectful or lazy attitude in handling, storing, and preparing food?

ᗊ THREE Cs ᗈ
for Safe Meat Preparation

Cold: Slow bacteria growth effectively with refrigeration below 40°F.
Cook: *E. coli* bacteria generally die after exposure to 145°F for 20 seconds, but for heat to reach every surface area within ground meat is difficult. Use the 160°F official standard for cooked hamburger.
Clean: Sterilize all surfaces—use a solution of either bleach or vinegar— exposed to raw meat before using with prepared food. Wash cutting boards in the dishwasher. Never put cooked food on a surface that has been exposed to raw meat (no cooked burgers on the platter that had raw meat).

ABOUT THE AUTHOR

Janet Taylor teaches food science courses in the Home Economics–Family and Consumer Science Department at The Master's College in Santa Clarita, California. She received her degree in Food, Nutrition and Dietetics from University of California, Berkeley. She and her husband, Robert, live in the San Fernando Valley where she enjoys preparing meals for family and friends. The Taylors worship and minister with the believers at Living Hope Evangelical Fellowship in Santa Clarita.

Chapter Thirty-Two

Kitchen Equipment for the Home

Janet Taylor

One of the first lab exercises undertaken in the beginning of a food preparation course is to analyze the lab and identify the kitchen equipment inventory. Considering the wide assortment of kitchen equipment, the beginning student needs time to learn the location of needed utensils and how to use them most effectively. In the home kitchen, the food preparer, of course, would know where her equipment is located, since she would have determined its location. But she must ask herself if that equipment is stored efficiently. Does she have the most useful tools readily at her disposal? These questions are to be explored in this chapter.

THE FOUNDATION: BIBLICAL PRINCIPLES

First, consider the biblical principles that should guide your thoughts and actions. You are familiar with advertisements for food products or kitchen appliances. These ads attempt to lure you by saying how quick and easy they are to prepare or use. The culture tries hard to convince you that ease, convenience, and speed are the primary concerns in food preparation. However, are these the guideposts by which you, as a Christian, want to make your decisions?

Why do you work and in what manner should you do this work in your kitchen? Everything, including your food preparation, should be done as service to the Lord. This service should always be with wholehearted effort because of your desire to please the Lord. Scripture speaks to these issues.

Colossians 3:23–24 states, "Whatever you do, work heartily, as for the Lord and not for men, knowing that from the Lord you will receive the inheritance as your reward. You are serving the Lord Christ." In addition, 1 Corinthians 15:58 says, "Therefore, my beloved brothers, be steadfast, immovable, always abounding in the work of the Lord, knowing that in the Lord your labor is not in vain."

You should not do your work by trusting in your own abilities but by relying on the Lord to accomplish his good pleasure. Second Corinthians 9:8 states, "And God is able to make all grace abound to you, so that having all sufficiency in all things at all times, you may abound in every good work." And Colossians 1:10 offers this exhortation: "So as to walk in a manner worthy of the Lord, fully pleasing to him, bearing fruit in every good work and increasing in the knowledge of God." Serving the Lord in this way enables you to serve others with your good works—not in pride, but in humility.

Time is a gift of the Lord. Psalm 121:8 says, "The LORD will keep your going out and your coming in from this time forth and forevermore." Food preparation is hard work at times and can be time consuming. Therefore, your use of time is important. You want to be a good steward of the time the Lord has given you. However, speed in preparation is useless if the meal is of poor quality or even ruined because of carelessness. You should prepare the food with excellence so that it provides nourishment and enjoyment for those who will enjoy the fruit of your labor. Your purpose should be to produce a quality meal—not to show how fast you can prepare it.

Purchasing kitchen equipment also requires careful stewardship of the resources that God owns and provides for you to use. Psalm 112:3 says, "Wealth and riches are in his house, and his righteousness endures forever." All kitchen equipment comes at a cost, and how you choose to spend God-given resources requires careful consideration and prayer. A piece of food preparation equipment that fits into the household budget should not be just for show. If the equipment actually helps to make a quality product for the family or for others, then the purchase may be considered good stewardship of your resources. You will not become good stewards by purchasing the latest or most expensive gadget simply because it has every new feature or because it will impress others.

Being a good steward of the time the Lord has given you, as well as of your financial and kitchen resources, allows you to serve the Lord more effectively. The time and money saved are not for the purpose of spending these resources on yourselves or for your ease and pleasure, but for more effective service to him.[1]

KITCHEN HAND TOOLS

Some essential hand tools are necessary to perform the basic tasks for meal preparation. The specific pieces and the number of the tools may vary, but the basic preparation tools in any household will be similar.

---

[1] Pastor Dave Maddox inspired the development of these biblical insights.

While setting up the home kitchen, the first in a list of necessities are tools for the measuring of ingredients. Most recipes for the homemaker in the United States are written with volumetric measurements, which would require measuring cups and measuring spoons. Measuring cups for both dry and liquid ingredients are essential for accurate and reproducible results in the kitchen. Liquid measuring cups are usually glass with a spout for easy pouring and a space above the largest measuring line for transfer of the measured liquid without spilling. Liquid measuring cups generally come in 1-, 2-, and 4-cup sizes, and all three are needed for the most accurate measuring possible. Dry ingredient measuring cups normally come in a set with several different fractional cups. The common sizes are ¼, ⅓, ½, and 1 cup, and other sizes are available. Dry measuring cups should have a level top surface, making it easy to smooth the ingredient in the cup with a spatula or knife.

Measuring spoons are available in plastic or metal with slightly varying shapes. The ease of removing the measured ingredient from the measuring spoon and the ease of cleaning are features to be found in the most useful measuring spoons. The other consideration is the number of spoons in the set. In a foods lab, two measuring spoon sets per station are assigned, with at least one of the sets containing a ⅛ teaspoon, a useful size for many spices. My personal set has a 1½ measuring teaspoon. Although this amount can be measured using other spoons, you may find it to be a handy size to have in your measuring set.

Some other essential kitchen items fall under the heading of safety equipment. A reliable meat thermometer and an egg separator should be included for prevention of foodborne illness. The thermometer will ensure appropriate end-point cooking temperatures of meats. If the eggs need to be separated, the egg separator will prevent bacteria on the outside of the shell from entering the recipe being prepared. For personal safety, several heavy-duty potholders or oven mitts are essential pieces of kitchen equipment. A home fire extinguisher is also a good investment for family safety.

Cookbooks and books on food preparation often include lists of essential kitchen equipment and even foods to have on hand (see chapter 21 for a suggested list). To see what modern cooks consider the most essential, a small survey was conducted among good cooks known to this author, asking what they considered to be the ten most essential pieces of kitchen equipment. The following lists display the results of the survey. The following list reflects what the majority of those surveyed found to be most important pieces of kitchen equipment. The survey participants were asked to limit their selections to ten pieces of essential equipment, so participants were not to list every utensil and tool they use or recommend. Not everyone mentioned each item on the list.

Kitchen Equipment Musts

____ Colander
____ Cutting board
____ Kitchen timer
____ Large stainless spoon/slotted spoons
____ Measuring cups and spoons
____ Mixing bowls
____ Paring knife/set of knives
____ Pots and pans
____ Rolling pin
____ Rubber spatulas
____ Spatulas or turners
____ Strainer or sieve
____ Whisks
____ Wooden spoons

To make the cooking tasks more efficient, most kitchens have more than one of many of the items in the "Kitchen Equipment Musts" list. Various sizes of colanders, whisks, strainers/sieves, mixing bowls, and cutting boards also make the task easier. Strainers and colanders now come in collapsible form, which is helpful when storage space is at a premium.

Many choices are available when considering the types of materials used in the manufacturing of these basic kitchen tools. Some materials are better for preparing certain food, and you may want to reserve them just for those foods. Cutting boards made from wood, bamboo, and plastic play roles in the kitchen. Mixing bowls of either glass or stainless steel were mentioned in the survey. Newer types of spatula/turners and whisks are made from silicon and are useful for nonstick surfaces since they do not leave scratches. They are manufactured to withstand high temperatures, do not conduct heat to the hands, and usually are dishwasher-safe.

Quality needs to be considered when selecting kitchen equipment. This maxim is true with all the equipment mentioned above, but particularly with knives, pots, and pans. Cost, although a good indicator, cannot be the only criterion for judging quality. The highest-priced item does not always guarantee the best quality. What is the very best quality may not be necessary.

Deciding the needed number and types of knives should be based upon what is likely to be prepared. Choose a knife that feels comfortable to grip in the hand for extended cutting tasks. A good quality knife should be constructed with a full tang, meaning that the blade should extend the full length inside the handle. The rivets should be smooth with the handle of the knife. There are many different materials from which the handle can be made, but it should not crack or corrode. One should wash knives by hand to keep them in the best condition. Consumers today have several choices other than traditional metals for the knife blade, materials such as ceramic and color-coded knives. Knives can be bought individually or as a set of varying sizes, serrated or not. Several cooks mentioned a good quality paring knife as one of the absolute essentials. A utility knife, bread knife, and chef's knife are also useful to the home cook.

The marketplace offers a vast array of pans. The choices also change regularly, so pans considered good quality in the past may no longer be available. For the various meal preparation cooking tasks, pans of varying sizes are desirable. Features to consider when selecting pans include:

- their weight,
- the handles, and
- the material from which they are made—both the bottom and the cooking surface.

Although a heavyweight pan is desirable for evenness of heat transfer, a pan that is too heavy for the cook will be tiring and hard to lift. The handles of the pan should conform to the hand for ease of lifting, and they should not hold heat when the pan is used, a protection against serious burns. The substance material from which a pan is made is important for delivering heat to the contents therein. Metals commonly used in the manufacture of pans today are stainless steel, cast iron, aluminum, and copper. Each metal has positive features as well as drawbacks, and they vary widely in cost.

For the cooking surface, several cooks mentioned the desirability of having a large nonstick frying or sauté pan, particularly for low-fat cooking, which is popular today. These nonstick surfaces have improved considerably over the years. They do not flake off and are much easier to clean than earlier versions. Many pans now available also have a nonreactive anodized surface, one coated with protective film. Finally, the consumer may want to compare the warranties available on knives as well as pots and pans before making a final selection.

Additional Kitchen Tools

Additional kitchen tools and equipment mentioned by some of the survey participants help round out the kitchen utensils. The "Additional Kitchen Tools" and "Baking and Miscellaneous Supplies" lists are not exhaustive lists since there is variance, depending on the types of food preparation. However, they do provide a good foundation for building a well-equipped kitchen.

Additional Kitchen Tools	*Baking and Miscellaneous Supplies*
____ BBQ utensils	____ Baking pans
____ Candy/frying thermometer	____ Cake pans
____ Egg whisk	____ Casserole dishes
____ Funnel	____ Cookie sheets
____ Garlic press	____ Cooling racks
____ Grinder for nuts/spices/coffee	____ Cupcake or muffin pans
____ Manual can opener	____ Double boiler
____ Hand juicer	____ Jelly roll pans
____ Kitchen scale	____ Loaf pans
	____ Pie pans
	____ Teakettle
	____ Vegetable steamer

Specialty Tools

The kitchen hand tools in this category may not be essential to preparing meals for the family, but they make some specialty tasks easier to perform, thereby making food preparation more enjoyable for the cook. These pieces of equipment are more individual and specialized depending on the needs and desires of the individual preparing the food. In a household, the number of tools in this category will also depend on the available storage and budget, keeping biblical principles in mind. These pieces of equipment may be acquired over time, as the need arises. Kitchen and restaurant supply stores have many tools in this category, such as garnishing tools, specialty pans, cake decorating tools, cookie presses and cutters, and salad molds.

Electric Appliances

Students in a foods lab are required to use at least two different electric appliances for each of the hospitality meals they prepare. They then evaluate these appliances according to criteria similar to the following.

Time Savings

Does the appliance save time in food preparation? Does the time to set up, use, clean, and re-store the appliance really save time over doing the task by hand? Are you able to do other tasks while the appliance is operating, which saves you valuable time? For example, if you are making a chicken coating, is it more efficient to crush whole wheat crackers by hand with the rolling pin and then stir in the desired spices, or would the food processor perform the task more efficiently?

Ease of Use

How easy is it to use the piece of equipment? Does it take a long time to gain mastery in using the appliance? Is the assembly of the appliance easy, or must the instruction booklet be used every time the appliance is used?

Safety

How safe is it to use this piece of equipment? In using or cleaning equipment, are there safety issues that may make this purchase unwise, especially if it is to be used by young family members? Is the appliance of low or doubtful quality, making it unsafe for repeated household use?

Cost

Is it a cost-effective item? Will you use it enough to make the initial cost and upkeep costs reasonable, or will it sit on the counter unused? Do the higher priced models have additional features that are necessary and valuable to you, or will a less expensive model serve your needs just as well?

Storage

Does the storage area required for the appliance take up too much valuable counter or cupboard space? If you are limited to just a few appliances because of space or cost, which ones will they be?

End Results

Do the results achieved using an electric appliance yield a food product comparable to or better in quality than making the recipe or a portion of the recipe by hand?

The Best and Most Popular

These guidelines are especially helpful to the initial establishment of a household. Many new appliances have a short life in the marketplace because they do not meet one or more of the criteria above. One is not wise to purchase an appliance just because it is the latest piece of equipment or looks nice, especially if you are in doubt about making that food product or have not habitually made it previously. Unfortunately, the consumer generally cannot try an appliance before purchase. Choosing a more proven appliance and model and checking consumer ratings may be wise when making the large investment required for electric appliances.

Even though the survey participants have different culinary interests, many of the electric appliances that appeared on their lists are those most used in a well-run kitchen. Appliances cited most frequently were stand mixers, hand mixers, food processors, and toasters or toaster ovens. Appliances frequently mentioned were slow cookers, blenders, electric can openers, coffeemakers, grinders (for coffee and spices), and microwaves. Many people may consider the microwave as a standard part of the kitchen like a refrigerator or a range, so they may not have included it on their appliance lists. Other appliances mentioned reveal the variety of products and cooking options available: bread makers, rice cookers or steamers, electric knives, electric griddles, electric woks, ice cream or yogurt makers, and juicers. Students who, as part of food lab experiences, have evaluated the features and desirability of labor-saving kitchen appliances, have also ranked these same appliances as most desirable:

- Hand and stand mixers
- Slow cookers
- Food processors

STORAGE OF EQUIPMENT

The home kitchen may have the appropriate number of tools for meal preparation, but if they are not easily accessible and thus available for use, meal preparation will still be difficult. Assuming that your current kitchen layout cannot be changed, how should the kitchen equipment be stored in the home?

If possible, the small electric appliances and kitchen tools should have a home away from the countertop but within easy access. A clutter-free kitchen will be easier to clean and, therefore, less likely to contribute to foodborne illness. Less clutter also gives more countertop area in which to prepare the meal.

The same types of equipment are usually grouped together for greatest efficiency—for example, pots and pans, baking dishes, and wooden spoons. Kitchen equipment should be stored as close as possible to the work area in which it is going to be used. This cuts down on the number of steps and the amount of time and effort needed to collect the necessary equipment to complete the task. If several people are involved in the food preparations, this can also help avoid collisions and accidents.

For personal safety, knives should be stored in a block instead of loose in a drawer. For easy access to kitchen utensils, drawers can be divided into sections and organized as to types of equipment: rubber spatulas, measuring spoons, and potholders.

Many home cooks do not feel that they have adequate kitchen storage space. Cooks may find it periodically necessary to sort through their kitchen equipment and eliminate unneeded duplicates and tools rarely used. One question in the Los Angeles County Food Safety Quiz yielded results showing that "26% of the total participants responded that kitchen shelves and cabinets were not clean and dust free."[2] Fewer items make cabinets easier to clean, thereby giving greater food safety and allowing for easier access to equipment.

⤜ ORGANIZE YOUR KITCHEN ⤝

- Place necessary tools within easy reach, not just where they fit neatly into a space but strategically located where they will be used most efficiently.
- Use all available space creatively:
    - under cabinets
    - on walls
- Make things easy to find for family members or friends who might offer help in the kitchen. Labels and lists can help even the chief cook keep things easily accessible and efficiently stored.
- Avoid counter clutter. Everything indeed should have an assigned place, and every place should be selected with reasoned planning.
- Clean and clean some more.

CONCLUSION

Daily food preparation can be more efficient and enjoyable if the right kitchen tools are available for use and if those tools can be easily retrieved and replaced after use. Consideration of biblical principles will help with the selection of those tools.

---

[2] Centers for Disease Control and Prevention, "Use of a Self-Assessment Questionnaire for Food Safety Education in the Home Kitchen—Los Angeles County, California, 2006–2008," *Morbidity and Mortality Weekly Report* 59, no. 34 (September 3, 2010): 1098-1101, accessed March 24, 2011, http://www.cdc.gov/mmwr /preview/mmwrhtml/mm 5934a2.htm?s_cid=mm5934a2_w.

PUTTING THE PRINCIPLES INTO PRACTICE

1. Compare and contrast biblical and secular worldviews of food preparation.
2. In what ways do principles for biblical stewardship affect the purchasing of kitchen equipment?
3. Which criteria are most important to you when selecting a small electrical appliance?
4. In what ways could you rearrange your kitchen cabinets and drawers to make food preparation more efficient?

Chapter Thirty-Three

Family Mealtime

Liz Traylor

"Suppertime!"

The screen door squeaked as my mother pushed it open, stuck out her head, and hollered those welcomed words. My brother and I climbed down from the tree house and headed inside to wash our hands. We were hungry! Our after-school snack was long gone, and we had played up an appetite. We sat in our places across the table from each other, and Mother and Dad sat at either end. My father was often late because of work, but we knew he was coming. Mom kept his food warm.

Time for dinner. Words of security and promise. Until the day my brother and I graduated from high school, we were expected to be there for the evening meal. We talked, shared our day's activities, and made plans for the future—though I cannot recall a single specific conversation. Every moment of family mealtime was preparing us to be better students, citizens, friends, family members, and Christians. Thanks, Mom!

Fast-forward twenty years. I open the back door and repeat my mother's words: "Suppertime!" My children slide down from their fort and into their chairs. Usual seats, of course. It is tradition. It is comfortable. It is home.

THE EXAMPLE OF JESUS

In Mark 6, Jesus sent the twelve apostles out two by two, without luggage or lunch boxes, to cast out demons, heal the sick, and preach repentance. They returned tired, no doubt, but ecstatic. Back in Jerusalem, Herod had beheaded John the Baptist, and the local disciples buried John's body. It was a successful, stressful, and sorrowful time in Jesus's life. His words are recorded in Mark 6:31.

> And he said to them, "Come away by yourselves to a desolate place and rest a while." For many were coming and going, and they had no leisure even to eat.

Stop and have dinner. Jesus understood the power of being together to share a meal—whether in a boat, reclining at a table, or sprawling on a hillside.

How have you and I missed such an important lesson? Why have we replaced eating together with "coming and going"? While times have changed and families have changed, the positive effects from sitting down and eating a meal as a family have not.

BENEFITS OF FAMILY MEALTIME

There are many beneficial results from eating together as a family.

Fulfills Our Basic Need for Sustenance and Companionship

Everyone has to eat, and eating alone can be quite dreary.

Provides an Opportunity for Parents to Pass on Their Christian Beliefs and Values

> Hear, O Israel: The LORD our God, the LORD is one. . . . And these words that I command you today shall be on your heart. You shall teach them diligently to your children, and shall talk of them when you sit in your house. (Deut. 6:4, 6–7)

Since the family usually sits when eating, what better time to talk about the Lord God than during breakfast, lunch, and dinner?

Builds Unity

By consistently eating together, parents get to know their children—what they are thinking, how they are feeling, and what is important in their lives. Children have dependable quality time with their parents. When mealtime is nonconfrontational, enjoyable, and even fun, the family unit grows stronger and everyone benefits.

Fosters Family Heritage

The give-and-take of table conversation introduces children to their ancestry. Culture and customs are handed down, and family stories become teaching tools. For example, when children hear how Great-grandpa survived the Great Depression, they learn that they, too, can be resilient. They realize that they are part of a larger group that shares a special bond. They belong.

Makes Memories

Many of the moments you treasure revolve around food. I still laugh about trying to pull the greasy turkey wishbone with my brother or about fighting with my cousins over who got to sit on the piano bench during dinner at the family reunion. And we all reminisce about Grandma's cookie jar.

Improves Overall Health

Families who eat together regularly consume more fruits and vegetables, ingest more vitamins and dietary fiber, drink less soda, and eat less fat than those who do not.[1] Parents and children are better able to make good food choices away from home, and healthy eating habits are more likely to continue throughout life.

Helps Fight Obesity and Avert Eating Disorders[2]

When a family consistently plans and serves nutritious, well-balanced meals, children learn what an adequate portion size looks like and what actually makes up a meal. When meals are provided at regular intervals, family members are less likely to snack voraciously in between.

Prepares Children with Life Skills

Children must learn how to be civilized human beings so they can function in society. Mealtime gives them a chance to practice manners, to develop the ability to converse, and to apply Jesus's teaching to treat others as you wish to be treated (Matt. 7:12).

Enhances Education

Preschoolers who eat meals with their families are better prepared to learn to read. They hear new words, practice their growing vocabularies, and grasp sentence construction from simply participating in table talk. Soon to follow are better grades, better scores on achievement tests, and better preparation for higher education.

Eases the Stress of Adolescence

The National Center on Addiction and Substance Abuse (CASA) studied twelve hundred teenagers to find out how to intercept destructive behavior in their lives. The survey included various socioeconomic, religious, racial, and ethnic groups. The results were the same for one- or two-parent families and regardless of the mother's employment status.

The survey's discovery was surprising and astonishingly simple—family mealtime. The more often teenagers eat with their parents, the less likely they are to consume alcohol, smoke cigarettes or marijuana, experiment with

---

[1] Martha Marino and Sue Butkus, "Background: Research on Family Meals," *Eat Better; Eat Together*, Washington State University Nutrition Education website, accessed February 6, 2011, http://nutrition.wsu.edu/ebet/background.html.

[2] Laurie David, *The Family Dinner: Great Ways to Connect with Your Kids, One Meal at a Time* (New York: Grand Central, 2010), 12.

drugs, and participate in promiscuous sexual activity. They are less likely to be bored, stressed, depressed, or suicidal.[3]

The research also showed that at the very age teens need their parents and the security of family dinner the most, parents slack up on continuing the mealtime ritual. Even though kids are busy with friends, school, activities, and jobs, and may exclaim, "Oh, Mom!" in disgust, they still need and want their parents' guidance and stability.

While family mealtime does not guarantee that children will always choose wisely, the facts speak for themselves. CASA has refined and repeated the survey regularly since 1996 with the same results. When children eat regular meals with their families, they are more likely to be well-adjusted kids.

What are we waiting for? Set the table!

HOW TO BEGIN (OR MAINTAIN) FAMILY MEALTIME

Make a Commitment

If you believe in the worth of eating together regularly, act on it. If "regularly" begins with once a week, start there. But sitting down together for dinner (or breakfast or lunch or even snack time) at least five times a week should be the goal.

Is it hard work? Absolutely, but your attitude makes all the difference. Instead of lamenting, "Woe is me, I have to cook!" pray, "Thank you, God, I have food to feed my family." Be grateful and the grudge will go.

So, pull those high chairs up to the table and strap in your babies. Buy booster seats for the toddlers or let them sit on phone books like we did. Even though your initial efforts may be chaotic, you are establishing an important ritual. Do not give up or give in. Make family mealtime a priority.

Schedule the Time

To have a family mealtime, participation in nonessential activities must be limited. Our culture maintains that a productive child is one who is involved in multiple after-school endeavors. A young adult with a long list of extracurricular involvement on his college application is considered an efficient student. Advertisers want you to assume that eating in the car is normal. Our culture is wrong.

The most important opportunities you can give your children are not lessons or clubs or volunteering or sports. The opportunity they need the most

---

[3] Miriam Weinstein, *The Surprising Power of Family Meals: How Eating Together Makes Us Smarter, Stronger, Healthier, and Happier* (Hanover, NH: Steerforth, 2005), 34.

is to be part of a safe and stable family, and the easiest way to promote that kind of family is by eating together regularly. Block mealtime on the calendar. Consider it an event. Even though family members may not enjoy it at first, let them know that the pleasure of their company is required.

Clear the Table
Never allow your dining area to become a storage facility. Designate another place for keys, backpacks, and mail. Except for the occasional school or sewing project, the table should be a special place in your home. This is where your family gathers to spend time with one another.

Restrict the Technology
Turn off the television. (Not down. Off!) The same goes for the computer. Ban electronics during family mealtime. No games, no gadgets, no phones. Parents must comply and set the example before expecting the kids to do the same. If this is a new rule, get ready for resistance. The only technological exception is a device that provides pleasant background music for dinner.

Dedicate these moments to each other. Slow down and unwind. Look one another in the eyes and smile. This is your family, and you are blessed.

HOW TO USE FAMILY MEALTIME WISELY

Relieve the Tension
The whole process of eating is surrounded by too much stress. Everyone seems to be consumed with body weight and the latest diet. Food courts cater to kids' favorites and children become picky eaters. Moms try to appease their children by becoming short-order cooks. This all needs to stop, but how?

First, parents must set the right example and get their own eating habits under control. Second, according to Ellyn Satter, a nutritionist with forty years of experience, the parents' job is to put simple, healthful meals on the table at regular intervals. The kids' job is to eat—whether a little or at all.[4] This approach will cause mealtime tension to dissipate. Research shows that children by instinct will choose and eat a well-balanced diet if they are offered one.[5]

Be persistent in offering nutritious foods to your family. A child may need to try a new taste ten to twenty times before he decides he likes it. When he sees the grown-ups eating and enjoying a food, curiosity will usually prevail.

[4] Ibid., 128–29.
[5] Ibid., 143.

Mealtime tension may also be lowered by reconsidering how you use food. Do you allow food to be a bargaining tool (for example, promising dessert if kids eat all their vegetables)? Do you use food as a reward for good behavior? Do you require children to "clean their plates" under threat of punishment or guilt? When children whine or beg for what they want to eat, do you capitulate to keep them happy?

If you answered affirmatively, your children are learning that they can manipulate results by eating (or not), that they should overeat to escape consequences, or that Mom is a pushover. Neither parent nor child benefits. Food becomes a source of conflict, and associating stressful situations with mealtime can cause food issues later in life.

Family mealtime is not so much about the food as it is about being together, so relax. Every meal does not have to include a salad, a meat, and a vegetable, no matter what the food pyramid suggests. Simplify your menus and lower your culinary expectations. Occasionally serving pizza or takeout will not cause children to become fast-food junkies.

Involve the Family

Every child can participate in mealtime preparation according to his or her level of ability. Spread a shower curtain on the floor in the kitchen and let the baby sit on it with a pot of water and a wooden spoon so he can "cook" like Mommy. Invest in a sturdy step stool so toddlers can wash and tear lettuce for a salad. Teach children to measure ingredients, sift flour, and stir batter. Turn over entire recipe preparation to teens.

Divide age-appropriate responsibilities, assign the tasks, and make a chart or mark a calendar so everyone knows what he is supposed to do. One mother of five monogrammed aprons with her older children's assignments: "Table Decorator" (selects centerpiece and table linens; sets the table), "Chief Cook" (helps with food preparation and cooking), "Head Waiter" (delivers food and puts away leftovers), and "Bottle Washer" (loads dishwasher and/or washes dishes). They rotated jobs weekly.

Kids who help cook their own food usually eat their own food, so put everyone to work in the kitchen. Of course, it is slower, messier, and often frustrating to include your family, but the experience is rewarding for all.

Encourage Creativity

It does not take much to make a meal special, and a little variety keeps family mealtime interesting.

- Ring a bell, blow a whistle, or strike a gong to proclaim, "Dinner is ready!"

- Vary the centerpiece—flowers or greenery, unusual fruit that can be eaten, favorite stuffed animals, a child's collection, photographs, craft or toy creations, goldfish (in clean water), or a large bowl for nature items found on a walk. The possibilities are endless.

- Invest in washable table linens and use them.

- Learn napkin folding with your children (Internet websites abound).

- Purchase whimsical napkin rings at clearance sales, or make your own: ribbon, yarn, or rope tied around napkins, or slip napkins through child-decorated, cardboard tube sections.

- Add color with bright place mats, festive napkins, bandannas, table runners of wrapping paper, team jerseys—anything that livens up the table.

- Have a special plate, a special seat, or a special tradition to honor birthdays, accomplishments, or "good job" days.

- Schedule a fiesta night, costume night, dress-up night, crazy night where nothing matches, or party night for no reason at all.

- Vary the location. Use the good china and white tablecloth in the dining room. Spread a quilt in the backyard for a picnic or on the floor in front of the fireplace in winter. Set up a card table on a porch or balcony, or sit on cushions around a coffee table and eat stir-fry.

- Vary the service methods:
  - Blue Plate—plates are filled in the kitchen and delivered to the table.
  - Buffet—prepared food is set out and diners serve themselves.
  - Country style—serving bowls of food are passed around the table.
  - English—plates are stacked in front of the host; he serves the meat, the hostess serves the vegetables, and plates are passed to the guests.
  - Family style—one person serves the entrée on all the plates and passes them; side dishes are passed around the table.
  - Formal (or Russian)—each part of the meal is served separately (appetizer, soup, salad, main course, dessert); used dishes are removed before the next course is served (family members may take turns being the waiters).

Enlist your family to come up with new ideas and be creative. You may take a few extra minutes to make your mealtime more memorable, but it is worth it.

Set the Table Properly

Traditionally, according to respective cultural settings, there is a socially acceptable way to set the table, and your family should know what that looks like before they have to attend a business dinner or a job interview at a fancy restaurant. Many cookbooks include diagrams for formal and informal table settings, or information is available on the Internet.

To help children learn where everything goes in an informal place setting, make a "set the table" place mat for each of them. Trace a dinner plate, glass, flatware, and napkin in their proper positions on a place-mat-sized piece of poster board and laminate or cover it with clear adhesive plastic. By the time the place mat is worn out, the children will no longer need the assistance.

Instill Good Manners

Children watch their parents and act as they act, so use good manners at every meal. Remember, however, that the evening meal is when everyone is usually hungry, worn out, and tired of being nice all day or obedient at school. Be calm and patient. Whisper suggestions to an errant child, or have a cue word that reminds everyone to "mind their manners." (My mom cleared her throat—loudly!)

Pour on the praise for manners remembered instead of administering punishment for mistakes. Look around the table and tell each child one thing he or she is doing right. Include Dad, too.

Our family sometimes lapsed into pseudo-English accents and exaggerated our politeness to a ridiculous level. "'Dah-ling,' would you be ever so kind as to pass the 'mah-velous' potatoes my way?" Silly, but it worked.

✑ BASIC MANNERS ✑
Every Child (and Adult) Should Learn and Practice

- Wash your hands before coming to the table.
- Boys should pull out the chairs for girls to sit down first.
- Eat only after everyone is seated and you have thanked God for your food.
- Put your napkin on your lap; use it to wipe your hands and dab your mouth.
- Use the words *please* and *thank you* appropriately.
- Ask instead of grabbing, as in, "Would you please pass the bread?"
- Pass salt and pepper together, but always taste your food before you shake.
- Use your fork unless the food is meant to be eaten with your fingers.
- Eat one bite at a time, chewing slowly.
- Swallow before you talk.
- Keep elbows off the table.
- Thank the cook.
- When visiting ask the hostess, "May I help you clear the table?"

Teach your child how to use a knife and fork to cut meat correctly. The handle of the knife is held in the right hand with the index finger pointed and resting on the blade. The handle of the fork is held in the left hand, tines pointed down, with the index finger pointed and resting on the handle. (Left-handers may switch utensils.)

Americans usually put the knife down, switch the fork to the other hand and eat. Europeans cut a bite of meat, leave it speared on the fork, and move it straight into their mouths. Either way has gained acceptability when dining.

Learning manners takes time. Be consistent meal after meal and you will eventually see results—children who can dine anywhere with confidence.

Practice Conversation

All children need to learn the art of conversation so they will be at ease at school and in social situations. They need to be able to express their opinions and articulate their thoughts and feelings in an effective way. That takes practice, and mealtime is the perfect opportunity for verbal interaction.

Establish these five rules:

1. You will talk one at a time and keep your voices at a reasonable level.
2. You will listen when others are talking and will not interrupt.
3. You will talk about pleasant subjects—nothing gross, gory, or disgusting. (This rule is especially hard for boys.)
4. You will discuss problems and difficulties later and will not argue or fight at the table.
5. You will have Colossians 4:6 as your guide: "Let your speech always be gracious, seasoned with salt, so that you may know how you ought to answer each person."

The most important topic of conversation in a Christian home is God. When you speak warmly and wisely at your table about him, and about Jesus, the Spirit, and the church, spiritual conversation comes naturally to your children.

Mealtime is an excellent place to practice Scripture memorization. When our children were preschoolers, my husband and I taught them Deuteronomy 6:5 by saying the verse aloud and letting them fill in the blanks: "You shall love the LORD your God with all your *heart* and with all your *soul* and with all your *might*." They yelled the last word and broke the "keep your voice at a reasonable level" rule, but we did not mind.

Topics for family conversation include the following:

- *Current events.* Discuss news stories, weather, world happenings, what one would do first if he were mayor or class president.

- *Geography.* Using a globe centerpiece, find and discuss countries they are studying, where ancestors came from, what nation is largest, where they would like to travel.

- *Foreign languages.* Learn words and phrases such as *hello, good morning, please, thank you,* and *good-bye* to use when serving international foods.

- *Entertainment.* Discuss movies, television, websites, or music they have seen and heard. Decide whether each meets the criteria of Psalm 101:3—"I will not set before my eyes anything that is worthless."

- *Nature.* Use nature item centerpieces or look out the window; ask how things grow, how God teaches birds to make nests, where rain comes from. Then go look up the answers.

- *Schoolwork.* Ask which spelling words are hardest, what was the most ridiculous thing they had to learn today, what they would change about school if they could.

- *Friends and classmates.* Ask, "What was the nuttiest (coolest, most boring) thing that happened to you (your best friend, someone else) today?"

- *Family.* Name all the aunts, uncles, and cousins and where they live. List all potential family vacation spots. Have an "ask your parents anything about their childhood" forum.

- *Memories.* Have everyone fill in the blank: "I remember when _____" or "When I was younger, I _____" or "My best Christmas was _____."

Some days all attempts at harmonious communication will be abject failures, but keep at it. Plan a conversational idea, jot it on a sticky note, and put it by your plate. Ask specific questions instead of the general, "How was your day?" As children grow, the conversation will flourish.

Extend Hospitality

When I was growing up, there were often guests and other family members at our table. Our pastor and almost every visiting evangelist enjoyed my mother's good cooking. My grandparents lived nearby and came regularly, bringing fresh garden vegetables to add to the meal. Miss Alabama even dined with us once. I thought everybody had as much company as we did, but I was wrong.

Many families rarely invite others to join them for dinner. Maybe everyone is too busy, or they do not cook enough to be confident, or they simply do not eat at home much anymore. Whatever the excuse, when hospitality is neglected, parents and children miss out on the blessings and educational opportunities that result from including others in family mealtime. Yes, it is a lot of trouble, but the value outweighs the effort.

In biblical days, strangers were often part of family mealtime. Hebrews 13:2 is a reminder of one of the inherent benefits: "Do not neglect to show hospitality to strangers, for thereby some have entertained angels unawares." Go ahead and invite the preacher to dinner, entertain the new church members, feed an international student from a nearby college, and when the Lord leads, bring home a total stranger. You may have angel feet under your table.

SUPPERTIME

The modern media has tried its best to make moms and dads believe that cooking good food at home for the family they love is drudgery, demeaning, and not worth the time, but women are wising up and learning the truth. All the hours and energy you put into family mealtime really matters. Eating together makes a difference—in you, your children, your family, your home, your nation, your world.

Come on in. It's suppertime!

PUTTING THE PRINCIPLES INTO PRACTICE

1. Think about what mealtime was like in your childhood home. How has that affected your approach to family mealtime in your own home? What would you like to change about your family mealtime? What will you do about it?
2. Copy several benefits of family mealtime and post in a prominent location. When you are tempted to give in to fast-food temptation, read your list.
3. Have a family meeting to define the goals for family mealtime. Determine what adjustments can be made in the weekly schedule to have family mealtime on a regular basis. Make these adjustments.
4. With input from family members, decide the division of responsibilities for mealtime and the consequences for failure to comply. Implement those decisions.
5. Ask the family whom they would like to invite for dinner. Extend the invitation, plan the meal, and practice manners and conversation in preparation.

ABOUT THE AUTHOR

Liz Traylor, a native of Alabama, lives in Pensacola, Florida, where her husband, Dr. Ted Traylor, has been the pastor of Olive Baptist Church since November 1990. They have two adult children, both graduates of the University of Mobile. Their daughter, Rachel, is employed with Regions Bank in Pensacola and is married to Brad Hinote. Their son, Bennett, is team sports coordinator at Olive Baptist Church and is married to Amanda.

A creative writer and inspiring speaker, Liz participates in the music and drama ministries of her church and speaks at a variety of events across the country. In 2008, she served as president of the Southern Baptist Convention Ministers' Wives Conference. Her heart's mission is to teach the Bible—alive and applicable to women's lives today.

ADDITIONAL RESOURCES

Wilson, Mimi, and Mary Beth Lagerborg. *Table Talk*. Colorado Springs: Focus on the
    Family, 1994.

Chapter Thirty-Four

Ideas for Holiday Celebrations

Mary K. Mohler

What thoughts are evoked at the mention of simmering peppermint hot chocolate, freshly baked cinnamon rolls, and sugar cookies decorated with lots of white icing? Do you think of Christmas baking and wish that December was right around the corner? Perhaps instead you are relieved that it is many months until you must tackle the food challenges of the Christmas season.

Holidays in general, and Christmas in particular, are wonderful occasions to let your creative juices flow as you seek to make your own family and your guests feel welcome and loved. The focus of this chapter is to think through practical ways to use your kitchen to bring glory to the Lord as you celebrate milestones and holidays with your family and friends.

For some readers, this is a welcome topic. They thrive on jumping in and leading the way. They anticipate the arrival of the annual cooking magazines whose covers boast of marvelous new ways to celebrate with flair. Others begin to wonder if they can finagle their way (again this year) to farming out as much of the seasonal food responsibilities as possible. If you struggle with fulfilling the biblical mandate to practice hospitality in the first place, then holiday celebrations can be thorny at best. Be assured that detailed descriptions of how to prepare a six-course feast from scratch, complete with show-stopping desserts guaranteed to impress, are not what lie ahead.

Imagine the mother of four who is hosting her parents and extended family for a week at Christmastime. She has to consider daily meals, Christmas Eve snacks, Christmas brunch, and the all-important Christmas dinner. She must consider seasonal foods while being mindful of her dad's cardiac rehabilitation diet, her nephew's gluten-free requirement, and her aunt's aversion to anything remotely spicy. If she tries to throw meals together while walking down the aisles of the supermarket, or worse yet, after she gets home, she makes her task more difficult and raises her inclination to dread the rolling around of next December.

WHAT IS THE PLAN?

Whatever your particular scenario may be, you must have a plan that is crafted well in advance and will serve to make holiday hospitality a joy for both the hostess and the guest. By early December most families know who plans to be where for Christmas. Consider that to be the perfect time to start crafting a plan. Keep in mind that the plan needs to be flexible, with the aim of bringing calm and order—not of driving everyone crazy. Many of the seemingly mammoth endeavors you face are not so overwhelming when you break them down into pieces and manage them one step at a time.

SIX SIMPLE STEPS FOR PLANNING YOUR HOLIDAY MEALS

1. Start with Prayer

Do not mistake this step as an attempt to spiritualize the topic of food. The truth of the matter is that the Lord cares about all details of your life and seeks to teach you on many different levels. When you prayerfully plan even your holiday menus, you turn the task from being a headache, as is the case for some, or an extravaganza, as is the case for others, into an opportunity to bless your family and guests in ways that you would not have imagined. Pray for clarity of purpose as you are mindful of the occasion. Pray for energy as you multitask. Pray for patience as you deal with personalities that differ from yours. Pray for wisdom to implement your plan efficiently but with flexibility. If you are nervous about it all, pray for calm! If you tend to go overboard to impress and draw attention to yourself, pray for humility and restraint. Pray for opportunities to use even meals served at holidays not only to nourish your guests physically but also to nourish them spiritually as you share Christ's love. Pray the wise words of Proverbs 16:3, "Commit your work to the LORD, and your plans will be established."

2. Write It Down!

The second step is to brainstorm on paper so you can visualize the big picture. Even if you are not a visual learner, you will be amazed at how clarifying it is to see on paper what needs to be done. When you look at how many meals you are planning and how many guests are involved, you can begin to compartmentalize factors such as guest lists, recipes, shopping, make-ahead dishes, décor, and garnishes—to name a few. Craft a master plan that categorizes every holiday-meal task you think should be a part of your consideration. Hospitality planning forms are available for this purpose. The one I created to suit my needs is useful for me to revisit when the same type of occasion arises again. The more I am able to put on paper, the more I am able to press forward confidently without feeling overwhelmed.

3. Where Is That Recipe?

Next, do a recipe search! For some women, unfortunately this may mean searching through piles of paper for that perfect chocolate cake recipe ripped from the newspaper months ago. The preferred method is to search through your organized recipe collection and select some tried-and-true recipes for that family dinner and perhaps pull out some special ones that you set aside to try on an approaching holiday. Those who lack confidence in the kitchen are wise to stick with recipes that fit their skill level and are known to be crowd pleasers. Beware jumping in with an attempt to whip up that magazine-cover soufflé, which in reality is tricky to pull off. Know that you will gain confidence as your experience grows. Be sure to include those eagerly anticipated family favorites. By the way, if you always make that favorite food using a certain recipe, do not change it. Recently I heard about a mom who decided to change her famous sweet potato casserole. Instead of making the crunchy topping loved by her family, she served a marshmallow topping, which she had gotten from a website. Variation is great but not when it comes to doctoring up a traditional food.

If there are no such requests at your house, take heart. Your celebration does not need to be centered on food, but consider taking an informal poll asking what kinds of foods your family enjoys. Some people seem to be uninterested in food or have very limited tastes, but they are in the minority. Try to find at least one favorite food or dish for your family or friends. Some will have a comfort food that elicits fond childhood memories. To prepare someone's comfort food is a special gift.

As you plan, include recipes that can be prepared completely in advance. Not every recipe you choose requires being made from scratch. The goal is to achieve a nice balance between dinner that comes out of a box (and feels reconstituted) with one that is so labor intensive that the cook is exhausted. Shortcuts can be such a blessing. Our grandmothers did not have most of the options that we now have. Let's be grateful for them and use their legacy wisely.

4. So Simple, Yet So Profound—Work in Advance

Perhaps the most logical step may also be the most neglected. So many women get overwhelmed, particularly in December, because they have set themselves up with far too much to do in the short time allotted. These are usually the women who secretly look forward to January 2 when it will be over and life can get back to normal. The carefully made master plan in step two should help here. If you struggle with procrastination, break the plan into small pieces so that progress can be made incrementally as the events approach. For example, setting the table in advance seems wise. I am always surprised when I hear about hostesses going through cupboards and drawers looking for glasses and silverware as the guests are arriving. It does not have to be so. Plan ahead, especially on tasks that are not food related. This list includes housekeeping tasks, table décor, and even your family's wardrobe. Be sure that clothing is set out and ready. The completion of each task on the list will ease your mind and allow you to deal with final tasks that must be done at the last minute. If the event is not a sit-down meal, consider preparing the buffet table by setting out the serving pieces in advance and labeling them with sticky notes. Little tricks like this will make placing the hot and cold food much easier as you are not scrambling to find appropriate dishes and serving ware as the buffet line forms.

5. Let the Fun Begin

The fifth step may not seem like a step. Enjoy yourself as you enjoy the art of practicing biblical hospitality. The time to be concerned with menu planning is over. If the beef is a little tough, you can consider tweaking that recipe next time, but now you must focus on making your guests feel welcome and wanted. Things will go wrong despite great planning. Trust me; in my eighteen years of hosting many events in my home as a part of our seminary ministry, I have a long list of stories. Some of these are more humorous now than they were at the time. Be aware that your guests are watching your reaction when mishaps occur. Will it ruin your mood if the rolls are burned? Will you deal with it in such a way that your family and guests know that their presence with you is more important than food issues? Your attitude should reflect that you have diligently sought to serve them a delicious meal but that your desire is to serve them and not impress them. You want to meet their needs by feeding them well but also by listening to them and encouraging them.

6. So, How Did It Go?

Keep good records. This sixth step is often neglected but can serve to build confidence and make your task easier the next time. If you have brainstormed on paper in the first place, this step will be a breeze. My form has a section on the back to facilitate record keeping. It has space for me to record three things.

First, what recipes were especially well received? Did anyone request any recipes? If so, I try to follow up by sharing those right away. Second, is there something I would do differently or not use again? If a recipe fails, you will likely remember it, but here is a place to record that. Do not try a failed recipe again unless you know for certain that you did not follow it carefully. Too many great recipes abound, so just toss the bad ones. The third section allows space to record any special needs or prayer requests that my guests may have shared. Make sure to follow up on these. Hospitality is not all about food. Be sure to look for ways to bless your guests long after they leave your table.

Your records will be a great aid as you standardize certain events that come in cycles on your calendar. Did the luncheon that you hosted for new neighbors last year go well? Adapt it as necessary, but there is no need to start from scratch as you plan a similar event with different guests this year.

Having a plan in place will not only calm your nerves, but it can also serve to excite you about the coming days. Your personal style will dictate the elaborateness of the plan. If you have the gift of hospitality, you will especially enjoy "pulling out the stops," likely at Christmastime. Do not apologize for this. Your neighbor may not share your enthusiasm, but her gifts may lie in other areas. Use the home that the Lord has given you and the love for others that he has instilled to welcome with gusto your family and your guests during this wonderful season.

IS IT A TRADITION—OR IS IT A RUT?

Consider infusing your Christmas and other holiday celebrations with at least a few traditions. Are you a woman who grew up with treasured traditions and happily established a slew of them for your own family? Many families embrace and joyfully anticipate those time-honored occasions. Perhaps a few family members cringe at the thought of "dyed-in-the-wool" routines, which they see as little more than frivolous. Others would doubtless feel robbed if a particular tradition was jettisoned from the plan. Be sure to talk to your family about traditions. You may be surprised to learn what traditions they value and which ones they consider almost meaningless. Could it be that some traditions are carried out year after year because your family is under the impression that you value it when in fact you think you are doing it for them? Talk about it. Find out if you have some traditions that are merely ruts. A rut is something you do because you have always done it but with no known benefit.

I heard about a family that made a big deal about scheduling everyone to pile in the car, travel quite a distance, and in the cold chop down what seemed to be the best Christmas tree in God's creation. They hauled it to the car and journeyed back home to unload and decorate it. During an honest discussion, they discovered that the actual decorating of the tree—not the hunt for spruce itself—was the fun part. The entire family was relieved the next year to put up their purchased tree, without drooping limbs and falling needles. They built a new tradition around laying a fire in the fireplace and nibbling on treats while they decorated the tree. Cutting down the tree was a rut and not a tradition. Be sure that you have some true traditions. Sometimes the simplest ones are the most treasured. Traditions contribute to a family's uniqueness while giving its members a sense of cohesiveness and belonging.

A student once shared that her favorite Christmas tradition was getting new pajamas on Christmas Eve. Her mother continued this tradition even as the daughter reached her early twenties. The student observed, "I love it because no matter how old I get to be, this tradition still makes me feel like a kid again."

If you grew up in a family that did not celebrate traditions, or worse yet, in a dysfunctional family that provided few fond memories, resolve to leave that behind and establish some lasting traditions. The Lord will bless your efforts to draw your family unit closer together while making fun-filled yet meaningful memories.

TAKING IT TO THE NEXT LEVEL

Perhaps you are looking for ways to maximize your opportunities to make hospitality count. Try to dovetail, not only when you are preparing recipes from your kitchen but also when you are planning events. For example, when my daughter was in high school, I was very intentional about teaching her home economics in a practical way. She compiled a spiral card file containing recipes in various categories, which she could confidently prepare. During the last two years of high school, her "final" test each semester was to plan and prepare an entire meal on her own. For the fall semester, we devised a way to combine that project with a cookie-making party that she hosted for her friends. Each brought her favorite cookie recipe along with any unusual ingredients, and we provided the rest. Dozens of various Christmas cookies were baked in our kitchen and packaged on disposable plates with cookie tray cellophane purchased from discount stores. Katie set the dining room table using Christmas dishes and a festive tablescape. She had prepared a lovely meal prior to the guests' arrival and served it after the cookies were done. We took many pictures of the finished products before delivering them to various area families who would especially need or appreciate them. The event served to be an outreach to both Katie's friends and to the recipients of the homemade treats as well as a teaching opportunity for me to help my daughter gain confidence in practicing hospitality on several levels.

DREAM BIG!

No doubt there are some readers who look forward to letting their creative juices flow as they think about food celebrations at Christmas, Thanksgiving, Easter, Fourth of July, and family birthdays, just to name a few. Hosting an extravaganza for all of these would not be wise, but most of us who enjoy this topic tend to have a favorite holiday that we happily anticipate. Many women amass a collection of décor, tableware, special bakeware, and recipes for specific holidays. This is a good thing. Have fun as you truly celebrate by pulling out your special tools and going to work. You are making memories for your family and friends every time you do. Always keep in mind that you are not seeking to impress as you "go crazy with a theme." Your goal is to create, with lots of good food, a festive environment that draws attention to the guests and the occasion and not the hostess.

WHY NOT JUST CALL THE CATERER?

I enjoy making pies of many varieties in my homemade pie crusts. Every fall, we host two large groups for a dessert party that is all about pies. We started this tradition long ago. I start planning the next year's varieties months in advance and certainly include many varieties that are repeated every year by popular demand. I remember one year when a guest learned that I prepared the pies myself. He simply said, "Oh, just call the bakery!" He was not intending to be offensive but clearly did not see any value in investing many hours in planning, shopping, mixing, baking, and garnishing dozens of pies when there are bakeries that do that with ease. Clearly, a pie party could be enjoyed in a home by serving purchased pies. The cost would be significantly higher due to the labor involved, and some would argue that there is no pie like a homemade one. However, I do not wish to call the bakery because I genuinely enjoy making and serving my own pies. Some women would not take this on for anything, but keep in mind that they likely undertake projects I would not even consider. The Lord uniquely gifted each of us as reflected in our diversity of skills. Sometimes we need a nudge to pursue those gifts and hone in on our skills, but the Lord will bless our efforts as we do. Use your gifts and talents as the Lord leads and do not apologize for them or minimize them. Your guests, family, and friends will discern if you are serving them out of a genuine desire to please or seeking to impress and garner high praise. True hospitality is all about the former and nothing of the latter.

BE A KEEN OBSERVER

Books, magazines, and websites are great resources for holiday celebrations. They are geared to various levels of expertise and interests, yet these same resources can be overwhelming if you do not have a system to organize them. Consider using several file folders to collect ideas, so you can add to them year round and access them easily. Imagine the joy of planning a birthday party when you can pull out the file and sort through references and clippings that you may have forgotten you had saved. Be sure to record on paper and file away ideas that you have observed in other settings. Do those chocolate truffle Christmas trees that you saw in a magazine look like a great centerpiece? Give them a try! Would you like to host a Fourth of July party this year and plan a family-friendly menu to serve on your patio? Begin to look for ideas months in advance and drop them in your file. Children's birthday parties are great occasions to begin to teach your children about hospitality. Let your elementary-aged children join in the planning. They can give input not only about the choice of theme and menu but can also think about how to make their young guests feel welcome. What kind of goodie bags could be made to go along with the theme? The focus of the event moves from the birthday child to the guest. In the process, many great memories made can be more meaningful than an afternoon at the local pizza and game venue.

SPECIAL CONSIDERATIONS AT CHRISTMASTIME

Holiday and birthday celebrations aside from Christmas are often spaced out during the year to ease planning. Christmas carries with it so many extra responsibilities. Even women who welcome the added tasks realize that the usual homemaking routine does not go on hiatus just because it is December. Laundry still piles up while Christmas cards are being prepared. Dust still collects while decorating must be done. Families still need meals while gifts are purchased and wrapped. Unless the homemaker has a plan in place, she is easily overwhelmed by the combination of it all. The food element is best handled by segmenting the usual meals from the special foods of the season.

Simplify Family Meals in December

Plan your December meals to allow extra time for the myriad of tasks ahead. Whenever you make casseroles in November, double the recipe and freeze the extra entrées, to which you can add a salad and have a meal. If you have thought about trying one of those freezer meal plans, this might be a great time! Pull out your Crock Pot, pressure cooker, oven cooking bags, and other conveniences. Include some easy menus with shortcuts and quantities that will ensure leftovers.

Get Baking!

Christmas cookies make for great memories. Most families have favorite varieties that are only enjoyed once a year. New homemakers can start by choosing one variety—and it does not have to be made from scratch to be a favorite. As children get old enough to develop tastes, moms can expand perhaps to include a chocolate variety, a sugar cookie, and a specialty cookie. I usually make about ten different kinds for the family and gift giving. Here is a typical list:

> sugar cookies, coconut macaroons, cranberry white chocolate chippers, cookie bonbons (crushed chocolate sandwich cookies dipped in chocolate), peanut butter cups in peanut butter cookies, snickerdoodles, seven-layer bars, pralines, and pecan shortbread.

I make my shopping list and purchase the ingredients all at once. I prepare them all over a two-day span. Most years, I add only one new variety to the mix. Some are made from scratch. Others make use of Christmas candies or mixes. When my daughter was in junior high and high school, we worked as a team, which multiplied the fun. I cover about fifteen quality china dinner plates with the various cookies and wrap them in cellophane as gifts. I keep careful records of what family receives what particular Christmas china pattern. I shop in the summer when Christmas china is on sale. The families enjoy the cookies and have another plate to add to their collection each year. I make multiple batches of each recipe so there are always lots of cookies for my own family. Parchment paper-lined cookie sheets and a cookie scoop make the baking day so much easier. If this sounds like too much work, keep in mind that the two-day process yields fifteen gifts plus all the Christmas cookies my family will need!

Moderation in All Things

Everyone enjoys splurging a bit during special celebrations. If that means you work out a bit harder the next week or cut out desserts in January, so be it. Have fun but be wise in not going overboard or tempting family members who are prone to over do. The Lord is glorified when you serve your family and others whom he brings to your table with delicious, satisfying meals. Never forget that the motive behind your food preparation is to serve and not impress. Use your personal style to be a blessing to others even as you are mindful that the Lord graciously provides for your every need.

PUTTING THE PRINCIPLES INTO PRACTICE

1. Do you consider yourself one who looks forward to opportunities to bless others with your creative holiday menus? If so, how can you effectively mentor those who are truly clueless but desire to share your enthusiasm?

2. Are you often asked to bring napkins, whipped topping, or bakery bread to holiday gatherings? If so, is that because others know you have no desire to prepare food using recipes? How can you lean in a bit more toward developing an interest in cooking while being mindful that you can use shortcuts?

3. Considering the six steps of event planning outlined in this chapter, can you identify what is your strength? Your weakness?

4. If you asked family members to write down their favorite Christmas traditions, would they have any trouble listing several right away? Do you think you would be surprised at their lists?

⤣ EVENT PLANNING GUIDE ⤢
AND CHECKLIST

Event: _____

Date: _____ Place: _____ Time: _____

Added to Prayer Notebook ____

Invitations (send out 2–4 weeks ahead when possible)
Invitations mailed? ___ Internet invitation sent? ___ Telephone invitations? ___

Deadline for responses _____

Guest List: (see attached list for names, addresses, telephone numbers, e-mails)
Total expected: _____

Attire: (circle)

Semi-formal   Sunday dress   Business   Business casual   Casual

---

Type of Meal—Plan at least one week ahead: (circle)
Breakfast Brunch Lunch Dinner Reception Tea Dessert Buffet Other

Menu
Entrée: _____

⠀⠀⠀⠀⠀⠀⠀⠀⠀Prepared by: _____

⠀⠀⠀⠀⠀⠀⠀⠀⠀Recipe location: _____

⠀⠀⠀⠀⠀⠀⠀⠀⠀Freeze (ahead or after)? _____

Appetizers: _____
_____
_____

Salad/Soup: _____
_____

Side dishes: _____
_____

Dessert: _____

Beverages: (circle)

    Water (purchased/filtered?)   Hot tea   Iced tea   Ice

    Coffee (regular/decaf?)   Soft drinks   Milk   Punch

Grocery List: (Prepare at least 3 days before and include everything not in your regular pantry stock)

Produce:

Meat/Fish:

Canned/Dry goods:

Dairy/Eggs:

Frozen items:

Beverages:

Table Linens

Tablecloth(s): _____   Place mats: _____   Napkins: _____

China pattern: _____   Serving dishes: _____

_____

Flatware: _____   (silver, pewter, stainless, gold plate, other)

Stemware: _____

Decorations (Is there a theme? _____)

Tablescape: (sketch or describe)

Flowers: _____

Candles: (include color, size, number) _____

Have cards been prepared to identify items in the buffet menu? _____

Seating Arrangement?

If yes, are place cards completed? _____

Hostess
(should be seated closest to the kitchen)

Host

Menu cards? Table _____ Individual _____

If tea/buffet, sketch anticipated plan for placement of menu items, etc.

Music Selections: (instrumentalist, ensemble, recording?)

_____

Wardrobe of Hostess: _____

Serving Help? _____

Babysitter Secured? _____

Follow-up

Things to remember about my guests: (Are there food allergies? Have there been recent celebrations, happy events, or sorrows? Are there special interests?)

_____

_____

_____

_____

Favorite foods/beverages of guests (recipe requests from the past)

_____

_____

_____

Recipes I will not make again or will prepare differently:

_____

_____

_____

Chapter Thirty-Five

Making Your Kitchen a Springboard for Ministry

Mary K. Mohler

Do you have memories of spending time in a kitchen that was a fun, safe, and uplifting place to be? Perhaps it was your grandmother's kitchen where she always seemed to have your favorite foods ready to serve. Perhaps it was the kitchen in your own childhood home where your mother faithfully greeted you after school and you joyfully shared more family meals than you can remember. Some children do not have memories like this. They would sadly admit that they were latchkey kids. Some had mothers who loved them dearly but honestly did not know how to use the oven. Still others have memories of a divided home where strife was rampant and memories grim. Hopefully, those children had friends whose homes were filled with laughter and great aromas of delicious foods.

Common sense dictates that every woman strongly desires for her home to be a place where awesome memories are made and delicious meals are shared. Ideally she would want family and friends to know they are always welcome to stay for dinner. The kitchen, which used to be known as the center of activity in the home, is now less often frequented. People are less likely to ask friends to drop by and more likely to meet at a restaurant to avoid what they perceive to be the hassle of hosting friends in their homes.

HOMEMAKING IS AN HONOR AND A PRIVILEGE

Let me be clear: I consider it my dream job to be a full-time wife and mother. I realize that there are many moms who would like to be at home but for any number of reasons are not. I am eternally thankful to the Lord that he not only gave me a wonderful husband but that my husband has always fully supported my desire to be at home. People who do not support the importance of stay-at-home moms ask questions: "What do you do all day?" "Is it boring just to be around kids?" "Why not use your degree to contribute to society?" I am ready for an answer to all of these, but one question I was asked recently took my breath away. Someone from another culture asked, "Why do you babysit your own kids?" I recovered and then used that question as an opportunity to explain that I believe my calling as a wife and mother cannot be filled by anyone else.

YOUR KITCHEN MUST BE A WELCOMING PLACE FOR YOUR FAMILY FIRST

What do you say to your family if good smells coming from the kitchen and food served on real dishes always means that company is coming? The Lord has given you a family, whatever the number of your family circle, as a tremendous gift to be enjoyed to his glory. You know that you are commanded to practice hospitality, but that does not mean that you neglect your own precious family in the process. The daily atmosphere at home should reflect Christ's love. The commonly accepted notion that family meals are a thing of the past should be clearly contradicted at your house. Your husband and children should have no doubt that you take delight in providing delicious and nutritious meals for them. Making everything from scratch is not necessary to provide a delicious and nutritious meal.

I well remember when my then-eight-year-old daughter Katie came into the kitchen one night while I was making an ice cream roll cake. She walked slowly all the way around the island and came over to where I was, all the while silently assessing the situation. She glanced at the appetizing dessert and asked, "Is that for *people* or is that for *us*?" If I replied that it was for us, I was implying that we were not people, but I knew what she meant. Fortunately, I had made a second one for the family, and it was already in the freezer. Making fun desserts only when guests are coming tells my family that they do not warrant special attention.

Favorite Meal Night

Ever since he learned to talk, my son has been a foodie. Christopher can tell you what he had for dinner on Tuesday two weeks ago, and he would like to know what he should expect to enjoy next Tuesday. When the kids reached school age, I started what became a fun tradition related to meals. We made a special summer calendar on the last day of school. We marked out vacation dates and other summer activities. We also scheduled four dates called "favorite meal night." Each one of us got to choose the entire menu for that night. This did not require much extra work for me since they were choosing from favorite recipes that I used throughout the year. Favorite meal night was a simple way to show my family that I loved them. Christopher, not surprisingly, seemed to enjoy it the most. While enjoying a meal when the summer was still many months away, he would sometimes get a serious look on his face, saying, "I just might have this on the menu for my favorite meal night." I was amused but tried to remain serious, as I assured him that he need not rush his decision.

Keep It Simple but Special

Many simple yet memorable ideas abound for ministering to your family through the kitchen. Perhaps you have heard of one that preschoolers particularly enjoy. Try having a "backward" night for dinner. The kids wear their clothes backward when they greet their dad at the door. They delight in having dessert first and appetizers last. Another fun idea is to arrange for a babysitting trade with a friend or neighbor for an evening. Your husband will arrive home to find a beautiful candlelit dinner prepared for just the two of you. Although you may know this is being done for fun on no particular occasion, be sure you tell him that quickly lest he fear he forgot an important day!

You Do Not Have to Be Betty Crocker

Please do not stop reading because you do not enjoy cooking or you simply do not know how. We are not talking about advanced skills, nor are we implying that your family and friends will feel special only if you prepare gourmet meals and show-stopping desserts without any shortcuts. We seek to be wise women who look "well to the ways of [our] household" (Prov. 31:27). Many women love to cook, bake, meal plan and browse through stacks of cooking magazines. They have favorite online recipe sites and blogs. On cable they watch food shows. They have bookshelves full of cookbooks. Make no apologies for your interest in these things. However, many women do not have culinary interests or talents. They undoubtedly have interest in other areas of homemaking in which others may be lacking. Yet mealtime for families is not an optional activity. A wise woman will work to develop simple menus that satisfy hunger and provide nutrition. She may choose to forego the use of cookbooks and magazines unless they help her meet her goal of providing quick and easy meals. No right or wrong methods are mandated. The red flag is a scenario in which wives and mothers proudly declare that they do not cook and have no interest in developing even a simple plan.

Women in this generation are so blessed to live in an era when conveniences abound. They do not have to grind their own wheat, knead their own bread, harvest their own produce, or pull feathers out of chickens. They have microwave ovens, slow cookers, pressure cookers, and convection ovens. Grocery stores are stocked with mixes, shortcuts, delicatessens, and frozen prepared meals, which make meal planning a breeze. Certain families tend to have rather limited interest in food and are not interested in trying new things. All of these factors play a part in determining just how much cooking is actually done. The key factor is that the motivation of the heart is to show love to your family while providing meals for them without any sense of dread or obligation. Make sure your children know that even if cooking is not your favorite activity, you are happy to do it without grumbling. Realize that your children are watching your attitude across the board. Beware! Daughters who observe their mothers acting as if meals are a burden will be more likely to carry that same attitude into adulthood.

Menu Planning 101

The important subject of meal planning is not the focus of this chapter; for kitchens to be used as springboards for ministry, wives need to have in place even a simple plan. Homemakers use a wide spectrum of plans that range from very general to very complex. Choose the method that meets your family's needs based on your interest, skill, budget, and tastes. One mom I know plans an entire month at a time. She does not do bulk cooking, although that works great for some families. She simply makes a plan using rotating dinner menus that are kept in a binder with recipes and shopping lists. She wisely uses a few frozen entrées from recipes that she doubled last month. She is always careful to incorporate recipes using produce that is at the height of its season and checks the grocery advertisements before she finalizes her plan. She enjoys planning ahead, and her family always knows what is for dinner. Another friend is much more general in her planning. She simply plans by the day of the week using categories: Monday may be international night; Tuesday, casserole night; Wednesday, soup, salad, and sandwich night; and so on. She has a rough idea in her head of what she will make but does not put it on paper until she makes her shopping list. Both ways work fine, as would other options.

EXTEND YOUR GOOD WORK TO PLAN FOR GUESTS

Once you have embraced using your kitchen to bless your family, you will more readily extend that ministry to those whom the Lord will bring to your table, if you are willing to host them. How much easier to welcome guests for a meal when you already have a system in place for your own family. If you have done some type of meal planning, adding a guest or two occasionally on short notice is not a big deal. When you plan in advance to have guests for dinner, you simply select a menu that you have already used and enjoyed. Dress it up a bit with garnishes or special touches, but that is optional. Satan prefers that you keep to yourself and fail to open your home to others. He is skillful at placing traps along your path, but you do not have to fall for them.

The Time Trap

Every woman has exactly 168 hours to spend each week. A major portion of how that time is spent may be out of your hands, but the remaining discretionary portion is within your control. If every hour is so jam-packed with activities that there is seemingly no time for family, let alone reaching out to others in a demonstrative way, immediate adjustments are needed. You are not meant to be all things to all people. The epidemic of overcommitted Christian families, whose children are enrolled in seemingly every available activity, poses a definite danger to your ability to fulfill your biblical responsibilities. A fine balance must be maintained between being self-absorbed to the point of being unwelcoming and so frazzled by constant activity that family dinners are almost nonexistent, and opening the home to others is unthinkable. Sometimes long-range planning is the simple solution. A family can look at the calendar and find a date to invite the neighbors or new friends for dinner. The date may be even a month away. Once the date is confirmed, a simple plan can be executed that includes a meal plan with some make-ahead recipes as well as a strategy to prepare the home for guests by working at it a little bit at a time. The goal is not to impress the guests but to serve them in a kind and welcoming way. The family can pitch in and learn that it does not have to be a daunting task to share Christ's love with others.

The Money Trap

Learning to budget those 168 hours wisely is possible, but every family does not have the same financial resources to use each week. Many parents face challenges on a weekly basis just to feed their own families. The thought of adding extra mouths to feed is not even a consideration for them. They justify their situation and hope that it will not always be the case. Remember the words of Scripture? They say nothing about showing hospitality if you have time or if you can afford it. You must not waste opportunities. Be creative. Host a potluck event. Have a couple over for a simple dessert and coffee. Do not wait until you can afford to serve filet mignon. A hot dog served with a smile is always preferred to a filet served with an attitude of impressing.

The Inferiority Trap

What a shame for believers to wish to open their homes but simply lack the training and the confidence to do so. They think that only fine china and candlelight can be used if "company" is coming. They either do not have such finery or do not want to pull it out of storage. Maybe it is not the food aspect that is the most frightening but the fear of conversation. Sometimes the wife is eager to invite others into the home, but the husband is reluctant. He is rather introverted and works hard all week. When he comes home, he wants to crawl into his man cave and be left alone. He loves his wife and kids, but even they get on his nerves after a while. The last thing he wants is a swinging door with people—needy or otherwise—with whom he might struggle to keep up conversation hanging around his home. A wife who finds herself in this situation is heartbroken and may try to resist, becoming like the proverbial dripping faucet and nagging about the issue, but she feels strongly about being a blessing to others through her home. She has the option to host lunches for friends and neighbors. A better option might be to suggest to her husband that they host a couple for a dessert, setting a definite start and end time. She should do her best to make it a positive experience, so that her husband will see the benefits of this fellowship as well as observing her giftedness for making people feel loved and welcome. She can even prep him about conversation starters to keep things interesting, not awkward. All of this must be a matter of prayer for this diligent wife.

Opposites Often Attract

The converse scenario arises when a husband loves to invite people to the home, sometimes on short notice, but he has become reluctant to do so because it sends his wife into a tailspin. One of two different mind-sets is often in play here. First, Disorganized Darla lacks the confidence to have a meal ready and her home tidy and presentable. She is like many women who are overwhelmed by home management. Second, a wife like Perfectionist Peggy may be convinced that those guests need a gourmet meal followed by a tour of every room in the house. She is never going to have the house in a suitable condition according to her own standards.

Both of these situations will cause friction in a marriage with the end result usually being that guests are not invited and opportunities are lost. Darla's situation can be remedied by her realization that she must make time daily to manage her home. The goal of having a clean and uncluttered home should be ever on her mind as she consistently completes simple tasks. She will see improvement and immediate rewards (see chapter 23, "Smart Routines for Cleaning a Home"). Perfection is not the goal. What a joy it will be to walk into your home without shame or embarrassment! The main rooms should be straightened up daily not only for the benefit of your family; if unexpected guests come, there is no need to panic. Long-term projects like closets and garages can be worked on as time permits.

Peggy can be commended for her well-organized home, but she needs to realize that her unrealistic standards are causing her to miss opportunities to use her beautiful home as a welcome refuge for others. What joy she will bring to her husband as she adjusts her attitude, being thankful that he wants to bring guests and being ready and eager to accommodate them.

Shared Interests

In some cases, couples have shared interests that include hospitality. They love to open their homes to others and make it look easy. Their enthusiasm is a blessing to those they serve. In all likelihood, both husband and wife are excited about creatively opening their home, unlike the situation with Darla and Peggy and their spouses. A much more serious situation exists when both the husband and the wife have no desire to open their home to other couples. Unless a change of heart occurs, likely many opportunities will be missed.

The Procrastination Trap

The temptation to rationalize about how the next season of life will be less hectic is common. One can think that opening a "real" house will be easier than trying to fit guests into a small apartment. Then, one can delay due to the blessed arrival of little ones in the home, followed by the idea that once the kids are in school or perhaps out of school, inviting friends and neighbors into the home will be more manageable. Satan loves this rationale because the day when it is convenient enough to make changes never arrives. An old saying in the business world pertaining to the timing of marketing products fits well here: "Shoot when the ducks are flying." You must take advantage of each day as an opportunity to thrive—and not wish away whatever season of life you now enjoy. Young mothers in particular can feel stressed by the pressures of motherhood. They often have interrupted sleep patterns to add to their unpredictable schedules. The days when preschoolers are in the home must never be wished away but savored as one of the most precious seasons of life. Moms must "shoot when the ducks are flying" in terms of adapting their schedules to maximize this key time while at the same time not using it as an excuse to be unavailable. In that young mother's realm of influence, there are doubtless other moms of preschoolers who would greatly benefit from home-based fellowship. They are not looking for a spotless floor or fancy tapas. They desire simple fellowship and support. Do not miss the opportunity to provide it. You can state clearly that at this stage of your life, late-night or even after-noon ventures are not going to work for you as you try to keep your children's needs a priority.

USE YOUR KITCHEN AS A SPRINGBOARD BY PROVIDING MEALS TO BE DELIVERED

The fruit of your kitchen can bless families and individuals in wonderful ways as you reach out and bless those in need for any number of reasons. Neighbors who face illness, who have experienced a death in the family, or who are wel-coming a new child will all be grateful for home-cooked meals prepared out of genuine love and concern. Since you are unlikely to serve the same fam-ily twice in a normal time span, you are smart, at least to some degree, to standardize your meal to be delivered. Choose carefully what menu items to include. Some suggestions are:

- Use reliable recipes that you have proven to work well.

- Choose entrées that will retain their quality even when reheated due to any delay in mealtime or when used for leftovers.

- Realize that those recovering from illness as well as nursing moms will need to avoid spicy foods.

- Since the family receiving your meal has likely had lots of take-out dinners and fast food, try to make the meal look as little like prepackaged food as pos-sible. This does *not* mean that a meal has to be fancy or made from scratch. For example, if you are taking a salad as part of the meal, it is fine to use the short-cut of bagged salads, but take the greens out of the bag and add some additional vegetables, which you may put in separate sandwich bags so that you create a kind of "salad bar." Consider including some homemade dressing and croutons.

- Deliver the meal in disposable containers so that dishes do not need to be washed and returned.

- If you can recruit others in your church or neighborhood to help, consider using one of the free websites created just for this purpose. These centralize the schedule and ensure that the recipients can state preferences. The sites also help prevent the family from receiving lasagna four nights in a row, since those who sign up are asked to indicate what they will bring.

- Consider giving themed gift baskets filled with thoughtful yet inexpensive items, and baked goods from your kitchen are a great alternative when meals are not needed.

YOU CAN DO IT

The possibilities are endless for using your kitchen as a springboard for ministry. Do not underestimate the importance of your willingness to be used by the Lord to bless others and provide a safe haven for them. You must be intentional about looking for opportunities, as they will not come knocking if you are not prayerfully seeking them. Know that you will certainly gain confidence with experiences, so start small and learn from your mistakes. The Lord may choose to use something as simple as opening your home to do amazing things for his glory by virtue of his perfect plan.

PUTTING THE PRINCIPLES INTO PRACTICE

1. Evaluate your childhood memories of time spent in kitchens of your own home or in your relatives' or friends' homes. Do you easily recollect treasured traditions? Do you have to struggle to come up with anything you would like to duplicate?
2. Would your family be shocked to find your dining room set up just for them when company is not coming? If so, sketch out plans to make your family feel special on a regular basis.
3. Does the thought of a short-notice dinner guest coming tonight cause you great stress, or would you start thinking of what you have on hand that could easily be stretched?
4. Which, if any, of the common excuses listed keeps you from opening your home to guests on a regular basis? Are you and your husband united in your desire to welcome guests? How do you work together?
5. When you envision offering good food, sweet fellowship, and genuine care in the context of your home, do you get excited about how the Lord may choose to use your humble efforts? If not, make this a matter of prayer.

Part Six

MAKING WISE
CLOTHING DECISIONS

Chapter Thirty-Six

Crafting and Complementing Your *Life Message*

Pat Ennis

What is your *life message*—or have you never really considered the need to develop a statement that guides your decision-making process? Crafting a life message requires a working definition. The term is derived from two words:

Life—the period between the birth and death of a living thing, especially a human being.[1]

Message—a significant point or central theme.[2]

Therefore, a life message is the significant point or central theme that provides the grid through which an individual makes her decisions in the period between birth and death. A Christian woman's life message begins when she is adopted into God's eternal family (spiritual birth) and continues until she draws her final breath; it is predicated on several biblical truths:

- She is a new woman in Christ (Rom. 3:10, 23; 5:8, 12; 6:23; 10:9–11, 13; 2 Cor. 5:17).
- She consistently seeks to grow into conformity to the image of Christ (2 Pet. 3:18).
- She actively pursues the application of biblical principles into her life (Ps. 19:7).
- She purposes to model godly character (Psalms 86; 145).
- She avoids comparing herself with others and refuses discouragement during the growing process (Phil. 3:13–14).
- She has control of her body, which is presented as a living sacrifice to the Lord (Rom. 12:1–2).

---

[1] *Oxford American College Dictionary* (New York: Penguin Putnam, 2002), s.v. "life."
[2] Ibid., s.v. "message."

- She refuses to yield her body as an instrument to sin (Rom. 6:12–13).
- She acknowledges that her body belongs to Christ (1 Cor. 6:15).
- Realizing that her body is literally a temple inhabited by the Holy Spirit (1 Cor. 3:16), she chooses to glorify God in her body (1 Cor. 6:20).
- She becomes a student of her body so that she knows how to control it with honor (1 Thess. 4:4).
- She understands the need for accountability to the body of Christ to maintain her purity (Gal. 6:1–2; James 5:19–20).

One's life message should focus on passions that will have eternal value. Very early in my Christian walk my spiritual mentor, Verna Birkey, gave me a motto that has consistently motivated the living out of my life message: "I am a personal representative of the living God, on assignment to make God visible to others around me." Perhaps the questions that I use to evaluate my application of this motto will help you evaluate your effectiveness as a personal representative of the living God, on assignment to make God visible to others.

- With what issues do you want your name associated?
- When your Lord calls you home or comes for you, what evidence of your faith will others find when they sort through your belongings?
- Will they be drawn to the one who loved and redeemed you, or will they only be impressed by your accomplishments, accolades, and possessions?
- When you meet your Lord, will he say of you, "_____ (*your name*) has chosen the good portion, which will not be taken away from [you]" (Luke 10:42)?

Your response to these questions provides the foundation for the crafting of your life message. When I contemplate my responses, I want my name associated with challenging women of all ages to embrace enthusiastically God's special instructions to women. When I step into eternity and others sort through my belongings, I want my reading and viewing materials, files, correspondence, and all of the other items associated with my life to reflect my faith. I trust that throughout my life as a believer *all* to which I put my hand— not just that I had good organizational or management skills—will validate that I have loved the one who loved and redeemed me. And, when I meet my Lord, I yearn to hear him say without hesitation, "Pat Ennis, you chose the good portion, which will not be taken from you. Well done, my daughter. Welcome home!" My response to the questions provided the foundation for the crafting of my life message, which is

- to love my Lord with *all* of my heart (Matt. 22:37);
- to walk worthy of my calling (Eph. 4:1–3); and

- to train the younger women to fulfill the Titus 2 mandate so that God's Word will not be discredited (Titus 2:3–5).

My life message then provides the guidelines for my garment selection—the focus of the remainder of this chapter. Before you launch into its contents or make any new clothing purchases, please complete the questions of "Putting the Principles into Practice" at the end of the chapter.

SELECTING CLOTHING TO COMPLEMENT YOUR LIFE MESSAGE

Modesty is a recurring theme in both the Old and New Testaments. Based on the root word "modest," defined as "moderate, limited, or small; not excessively large, elaborate, or expensive,"[3] this virtue is one by which all Christian women should select their clothing. So important is the virtue that an entire chapter of this book asks and answers the question, "Is Modesty an Obsolete Virtue?" Modesty is the foundational criterion for selecting clothing to complement your life message.

Besides making certain that your clothing is modest, does not arouse sexual attention, and is not revealing or overemphasizing of the figure, consider the number of garments comprising your wardrobe. Too many garments can reflect that you focus more attention on the outer appearance than on the complementing of your character (1 Cor. 12:23; 1 Tim. 2:9). Carefully selecting garments to align with one's season of life and its accompanying responsibility allows the Christian woman to practice modesty.

Quality workmanship is another key criterion. A carefully selected garment constructed with quality workmanship will serve you through numerous seasons, thus allowing your clothing budget to be stretched, fulfilling the definition of modesty, and applying the Scriptures that address modesty. Quality workmanship helps ensure that the wardrobe will not require constant replenishing. This is especially true for the maturing woman whose size is more stable than for a teen who is changing sizes continuously. Chapter 39 provides helpful hints for selecting well-made garments.

FASHION TERMS

An understanding of how the fashion world works may help you select garments that complement your life message. Consider the fashion terms listed in Table 36.1.

---

[3] Ibid., s.v. "modest."

Table 36.1
✑ FASHION TERMS ✑

Term	Description
Fashion	A way of dressing that is currently popular and yet within classical boundaries
Trend	The direction in which a fashion is currently going, usually affected by the culture
High Fashion	The latest and, often, the most extreme styles worn by elite fashion leaders and sold in limited markets
Style	The shape of a garment and also a fashionable look in clothes
Fad	A fashion adopted by a limited group of people for a short time and usually quickly adopted with lots of enthusiasm and then abandoned

Human nature craves variety or novelty to add interest and zest to life. Strangely enough, you and I also seek the security found in the familiar. We want something just like we had before—only different. Most women want to be unique in their dress and still wear trendy clothes. Paul Poiret, a famous fashion designer of the 1920s, stated, "all fashions end in excess."[4] The statement is reminiscent of Ecclesiastes 1:2:

> Vanity of vanities, says the Preacher,
>   vanity of vanities! All is vanity.

Perhaps Christian women should understand fashion terms so they may dress attractively without allowing their interest in fashion to "end in excess."

COLOR ME BEAUTIFUL

The gracious heavenly Father is the author of beauty. While you should worship the Creator rather than what he has allowed to be created, you have the privilege of utilizing all of his gifts to you. One of his special gifts is color.

The *color wheel* is a tool for combining colors attractively. Colors are sorted into three basic groups: *primary*, *secondary*, and *tertiary*. The color wheel is a tool used to create color schemes such as *monochromatic, analogous, complementary, split complementary*, and *triad*. All colors have three dimensions: hue,

---

[4] N. Jardine, J. A. Secord, and E. C. Spary, eds., *Cultures of Natural History* (Cambridge: Cambridge University Press, 1996), 396–397.

value, and chroma or intensity. These are often known as their physical properties. Tables 36.2–36.4 can help you effectively use the color wheel.

Table 36.2
❧ THE COLOR WHEEL ❧

Term	Definition
Primary Colors	Red, yellow, and blue. All other colors are made by mixing these three colors.
Secondary Colors	Orange, green, and purple (violet). They are created by mixing primary colors. Mixing red and yellow makes orange. Mixing blue and red creates purple or violet. Mixing yellow and blue makes green.
Tertiary Colors	Six colors are created by mixing secondary colors with primary colors. For example, red, a primary color, combined with orange, a secondary color, makes red-orange.

Table 36.3
❧ COLOR SCHEMES ❧

Color Scheme	Definition
Monochromatic	Uses a variety of values or intensities of one color. The monochromatic color scheme will most easily achieve harmony. A color scheme that uses a range from light blue to dark blue is a *monochromatic color scheme*.
Analogous	Uses colors that appear next to one another on the color wheel. If green is one color, blue-green and yellow-green are the other two colors that create the *analogous color scheme*.
Complementary	Uses colors directly opposite one another on the color wheel. If yellow is one color, its *complement* is violet or purple.
Split Complementary	Uses one hue (color) and the two colors on each side of its complement. If yellow is the hue, red-violet and blue-violet are used to build the *split complementary color scheme*.
Triad	Made up of colors equidistant on the color wheel. If red is one of the hues, blue and yellow are the other two colors that make up a *triad color scheme*.

Table 36.4

ᐂ THE DIMENSIONS OF COLORS ᐂ

Dimension	Definition
Hue	The name of the color family such as blue, yellow, or red. *Hues* are often described as being *cool* or *warm*. *Cool* hues (green, blue, and violet) are found in the sky and water; *warm* hues are derived from the sun and fire (yellow, orange, and red).
Value	The lightness or darkness of a color. Adding white or black to the *value* of a color makes it lighter or darker. A *shade* is made by adding black to the color; *tint* is made by adding white to the color.
Chroma or Intensity	The brightness or dullness of a color. The *intensity* of a color can be made less bright by adding either black or the complementary color (the color directly opposite on the color wheel).

Color can help you accentuate your assets and camouflage your liabilities. Table 36.5 will be a useful tool in accomplishing this goal.

Table 36.5

ᐂ USING COLOR TO YOUR ᐂ BEST ADVANTAGE

Challenge	Hue	Value	Chroma
Increase body size	Choose warm hues such as yellows, oranges, and reds.	Select light tints, strong value contrasts, or light, high values.	Use pure, strong, brilliant, saturated, high-intensity colors.
Decrease body size	Pick cool hues (blue-purple, blue-green, and blues).	Opt for low, middle values, shades, weak or no-value contrasts.	Use weak, grayed, low-intensity colors.

CAPITALIZING UPON YOUR COUNTENANCE

Do you realize that your countenance reveals the condition of your heart? Proverbs 15:13 is a reminder that "a glad heart makes a cheerful face," while Proverbs 15:15 states that "the cheerful of heart has a continual feast." John

MacArthur suggests that "the joyous, inward condition of the wise man's heart (Prov. 14:21) is described as a perpetual feast. Real happiness is always determined by the state of the heart."[5] After becoming better acquainted with you, has anyone ever said, "I thought that you didn't like me," or "I used to think you were aloof"? If so, you may wish to consider how facial expressions can affect the communication of your life message. See if you connect with some of your acquaintances.

The neckline of your garments, including collars and lapels, can help you capitalize on your countenance. You will need to evaluate your face shape to have an accurate assessment of what type of necklines are most flattering for you. The process is simple.

You Will Need:

- A mirror large enough for you to see your face and upper body from one foot away.
- Hair clips to pull hair away from your face and expose your ears.
- A top that reveals the full length of your neck and upper chest.

View yourself in the mirror and pose these questions:

- Following my hairline and jawline as the outer border of my face, what is the overall shape?
- How wide is the widest point of my forehead when compared to my jawline?
- Is the widest point of my jawline wider than my forehead?
- How prominent and rounded are my cheekbones compared to my forehead and jawline?
- With the answers to these questions, you will be able to determine the shape of your face. A friend or relative can also assist in the analysis.
- Use Table 36.6 to determine your face shape and a suggested flattering neckline.

---

[5] John MacArthur, *The MacArthur Study Bible* (Nashville: Word, 1997), note for Proverbs 15:15, "continual feast."

Table 36.6

∽ COMPLEMENTING YOUR FACE SHAPE ∽

Face Shape	Flattering Neckline	Unflattering Neckline
OVAL Egg-shaped with jaw and forehead of equal width. The length equals one-and-a-half times the width.		
TRIANGULAR The jawline is fuller or wider than the forehead.		
HEART Forehead is wide; jaw is narrow.		

Face Shape	Flattering Neckline	Unflattering Neckline
SQUARE Forehead and jaw are equally wide and have definite square corners; length and width of face are equal.		
RECTANGULAR Face is long and equally wide at the forehead, cheeks, and jawline; jawline and forehead have squared corners.		
ROUND Face is short and broad; prominent cheeks.		

The neckline is often the most eye-arresting area of a garment. This effect can be created by color and accessories. Make certain that the ones you choose reinforce the life message you wish to communicate.

REFURBISHING YOUR SPIRITUAL WARDROBE

Garments do not define the Christian woman. Her garment choice is merely an outward manifestation of what is in her heart. The fact that she was bought by Christ at an incredibly high price should challenge her to select garments that reflect her status as an adopted daughter of a royal family. Concurrently, her character should align with her new nature. Just as you remove soiled garments and replace them with suitable ones to attend a special occasion, as a new woman in Christ, you should replace negative character qualities with positive ones. Consider the "Refurbishing of Your Spiritual Wardrobe" summary and discern if there are character qualities that need renovating in your spiritual wardrobe.

Table 36.7

⤙ REFURBISHING YOUR ⤚
SPIRITUAL WARDOBE
Colossians 3:8–14

Put Off vv. 8–10	Put On vv. 12–14
Anger/Wrath Malice Slander Obscene talk from your mouth Lying	Compassion/Kindness Humility Meekness Patience Forbearance Forgiveness Love

First Peter 3:3–4 reminds you to be more concerned about your character than about your outward appearance. The verse does not condemn all outward adornment. However, Christian women are to concentrate on developing a chaste and reverent Christlike character and then select clothing that complements it. Remember that you discredit your heavenly Father when you look dowdy or unkempt. Once the Christian woman's spiritual wardrobe is refurbished, she is then ready to focus on clothing selection that complements her life message.

THE WELL-DRESSED WOMAN

The well-dressed woman never gives the impression of artificiality. She is usually someone who wants to be pleasing and interesting to others, but she has neither the time nor the desire to spend all her waking hours attaining this goal. Several qualities define her. The "Put Off—Put On" personal profile builds upon the "Put Off—Put On" format of the spiritual wardrobe. It allows you to determine how well your wardrobe complements your life message. An interpretation, or scoring guide, is located at the conclusion of this chapter.

Upscale department stores and high-end boutiques frequently provide a personal shopper service to help their clients select clothing and accessories that align with their lifestyles and professional demands. Many personal shoppers offer advice on makeup, hairstyling, and colors, in addition to shopping assistance. Some even provide an entire "makeover" service, including posture and public speaking skills, for clients who wish to change their image. These services are helpful but are also often expensive. Christian women have the most reliable personal shopper available, the timeless Word of God. As its truth is applied to their clothing choices, they will find that what they are wearing will consistently support their life message (Prov. 31:18, 21, 25; 1 Tim. 2:9–10; 1 Pet. 3:3–4).

PUTTING THE PRINCIPLES INTO PRACTICE

1. Develop the "Spiritual Inventory" located at the conclusion of this chapter.
2. Create an "Individual Assessment Tool." The instructions follow the "Spiritual Inventory."
3. Craft your personal life message.
4. Evaluate your face shape to have an accurate assessment of what type of necklines are most flattering for you.
5. Consider responding to the "Put Off—Put On" personal profile assessment. Use the interpretation scoring guide to discern the extent to which your clothing choices complement your life message. What did you discern from completing the assessment? Craft personal goals to bridge any gap between your life message and the current status of your wardrobe.

"PUT OFF—PUT ON"
PERSONAL PROFILE

In what ways do you perceive that your clothing choices influence your life message?

Place the number that best reflects your response to the statement in the space provided.

Use the following scale:

1 = Strongly Disagree	3 = Agree
2 = Disagree	4 = Strongly Agree

1. ＿＿＿ Once dressed, there is no evidence that I am conscious of my clothes.
2. ＿＿＿ My clothing enhances my character.
3. ＿＿＿ I am able to resist fashions that are unbecoming.
4. ＿＿＿ I choose to refrain from wearing garments that may be a stumbling block to others.
5. ＿＿＿ I capitalize on my physical assets.
6. ＿＿＿ I seek to camouflage my physical liabilities.
7. ＿＿＿ I endeavor to be content with the clothing I have.
8. ＿＿＿ I use the color wheel as a tool for combining colors attractively.
9. ＿＿＿ I use the neckline of my garments, including collars and lapels, to capitalize upon my countenance.
10. ＿＿＿ I have evaluated my face shape to have an accurate assessment of what type of necklines are most flattering for me.
11. ＿＿＿ I am realistic in recognizing that every age group has charm and do not find it necessary to appear younger or older than I am.
12. ＿＿＿ I know that individuality in dressing does not just happen. It is the result of knowing oneself, planning, and constantly developing good taste.
13. ＿＿＿ I know good quality and design.
14. ＿＿＿ I am able to use self-discipline when tempted with clothing and accessories not suited to my life message.
15. ＿＿＿ I know that the smallest detail counts in clothing and the way it is worn.
16. ＿＿＿ I know the basic facts about my clothes—size, fabric, quality, performance expectation, etc.
17. ＿＿＿ I am generally satisfied with my clothing purchases.
18. ＿＿＿ With each clothing purchase, I strive toward improving the quality of my wardrobe.
19. ＿＿＿ I seek to understand the terms used by the fashion world.

20. ____ I am aware that if I select garments with quality workmanship, my wardrobe will not require constant replenishing.
21. ____ I believe that modesty is the foundational criterion for selecting clothing to complement my life message.
22. ____ I realize that I am the only one who can decide what I want my clothing to do for me.
23. ____ I am attentive to the regional differences in clothing choices and dress accordingly.
24. ____ I consistently seek to refurbish my spiritual wardrobe.
25. ____ My clothing complements my life message.

____ **"Put Off—Put On" Personal Profile Total**

"Put Off—Put On" Personal Profile Interpretation

Total all the numbers indicating your responses to the statements. Then find the corresponding range of scores listed below:

100-90

My clothing choices complement my life message.

89-80

I have a strong understanding of how my clothing choices complement my life message. I regularly apply this understanding to my clothing choices.

79-70

I have a basic understanding of how my clothing choices complement my life message. I usually apply this understanding to my clothing choices.

69-60

Further research and application are needed for my clothing choices to complement my life message.

✑ SPIRITUAL INVENTORY ✑

Method of Preparation

1. Read each primary Scripture and summarize the concepts taught.
2. Under each category find a minimum of *five* Scriptures that allow you to assess your spiritual condition.
3. Rewrite each Scripture in the form of a question.

   Example: 1 Peter 5:7—"Do I purposely cast my anxieties on the Lord?"

Topics for Evaluation

Spiritually Renewed. Develop principles from Philippians 4:6–7.

1. Do I deliberately bring thoughts of little or big needs to Christ's control?
2. Do I choose to worry about problems instead of casting them on the Lord?
3. Is a large part of my day characterized by a *conscious* peace because I have committed the details of my life to God?

Renewed Thoughts. Develop principles from Philippians 4:8.

1. Do I choose to control my thinking according to the guidelines listed in Philippians 4:8?
2. Do I choose to direct conversations on the telephone, in church circles, and within the family in these channels?
3. Has my thinking this year exhibited increased delight in God and his beauty, works, and people?

Compare Psalm 119:37 with Ephesians 4:17–18 and Romans 12:2. Develop principles from these verses.

4. Is Philippians 4:8 a criterion by which I select my music, television programs, and reading material?
5. Do I allow my mind to dwell on (*list two Scriptures per category*):
   a. mental emptiness?

   b. vanities of the world about me?

   c. insignificant occurrences of the world about me?

6. How do I evaluate my conformity to the world in (*list two Scriptures per category*):
   a. personal philosophy of life?

   b. personal goals?

✒ PERSONAL ASSESSMENT TOOL ✒

Following the "Spiritual Inventory" format, prepare a personal assessment tool that specifically addresses *your* individual needs. The personal assessment should contain:

1. An *introduction*, which

   - States the *purpose* of the assessment.
   - Provides *instructions* on how to complete the assessment.

2. Specific *categories* that are defined in your own words and that reflect what needs to be measured.

   - A *minimum* of five categories are required.
   - A *minimum* of five verses under *each* category are required.

   (5 categories x 5 verses for each category = Total of 25 verses minimum.)

Categories for Consideration

Contentment	Meekness
Controlled Tongue	Modesty
Critical Spirit	Morality
Faithfulness	Motivation
Forbearance	Obedience
Forgiveness	Patience
Gentleness	Peacemaker
Holiness	Personal Time
Humility	Positive Attitude
Impatience	Priorities
Integrity	Productivity
Intolerance	Servanthood
Irritability	Service
Joyfulness	Strength
Leadership	Striving for Excellence
Loyalty/Commitment	Unselfishness

Once your individual assessment tool is developed, periodically set aside time to evaluate your spiritual growth. As you gain maturity in the areas, prayerfully consider adding others to your list following the same procedure outlined in the original instructions.

Chapter Thirty-Seven

Is Modesty an Obsolete Virtue?

Pat Ennis

As a Christian woman, your body is the temple of God. You desire to please your heavenly Father, and you have the challenge of selecting clothing that brings glory to him (1 Cor. 6:19–20). Your appearance is the first thing people will notice about you and thus creates an impression of who you are and what your influence will be. You are often faced with a dilemma of choosing between contemporary fashion trends and the commitments to purity and holiness of your faith. What do you do when fashion and faith are in conflict? Does wholeheartedly embracing biblical standards for modesty mean you must eliminate from your wardrobe anything fashionable?

Scripture does present principles that help you make reasoned and appropriate decisions. Almost as soon as the Christmas decorations disappear from retail stores, fashion choices shift to cooler colors and lighter-weight fabrics. While lightening the color depth and fabric weight for spring and summer garments, at the same time the fashion industry tends to minimize the amount of fabric contained. Nothing is so fashionable as a simple dress with classic lines, easy and comfortable fit, lovely color, and fine fabric. That dress will get more mileage if your adornment includes jewelry and other accessories. (See chapter 38, "Beautifully Balanced" for more about classic designs.)

> Know what *you* can wear and do not let the cultural media or insecure friends push you into choosing styles and colors not right for you. Do not deceive yourself into thinking you look like someone you are not. Accept your age and physical limitations as well as your potentialities.

FASHION VERSUS FAITH—MUST THEY BE IN CONFLICT?

Modesty (Latin *modus*, "measure") is an out-of-fashion word frequently linked to the Victorian era. The word has evolved to mean a "measure" of propriety or humility as in someone characterized by a demeanor without excess. By definition *modesty* means "having or showing regard for the decencies of behavior, speech and dress."[1]

Spiritually, *modesty* is an issue of the heart. In the New Testament, modesty goes beyond the adornment of clothing to include inner beauty and attitude. Modesty calls for avoidance of anything that is impure or short of biblical standards. If your thoughts are focused on the attributes found in Philippians 4:8–9 ("Whatever is true . . . honorable . . . just . . ."), your external appearance will likely be modest. Your sense of modesty will be regulated by your commitment to Christ. Beauty and fashion are not condemned by the Bible, but they must be expressed through the lens of a biblical worldview. Perhaps the following scriptural principles will guide your clothing choices:

- *Romans 12:1–2.* Christians are *in* the world but not *of* the world. A mature believer develops the ability to separate herself from an ungodly society, including the selection of clothing if that garment is contrary to biblical principles.

- *1 Timothy 2:9–10.* Clothing is to be modest and should be selected with propriety, i.e., according to what is appropriate, and moderation (a command for Christian women who desire to please God in clothing selections). These principles can be applied to the style of clothes as well as the quantity of clothes. All should reflect the principle of modesty.[2]

- *James 1:13.* Women should not dress in such a provocative way so as to encourage immoral sexual thoughts or behavior. The heavenly Father tempts no person with evil, and his children should not draw another into evil. Modesty can protect a woman from vulnerability to sexual predators and encourages men to treat her with respect.

Throughout Scripture there are examples of aesthetically pleasing clothing for both men and women.

- The garments for the priests were constructed by skilled artisans (Ex. 31:10; 35:19).
- The children of Israel were instructed to attach blue tassels on their garments to remind them of their need to trust and obey God's commands (Num. 15:37–38).
- The wise woman of Proverbs 31 wore garments of fine linen and purple (Prov. 31:22).

---

[1] *Random House Webster's College Dictionary*, 2nd ed., s.v. "modesty."
[2] See Pat Ennis and Lisa Tatlock, *Designing a Lifestyle That Pleases God* (Chicago: Moody Press, 2004), 221–257 for further elaboration.

- The people of Zion were challenged to "awake . . . [and] put on your beautiful garments" (Isa. 52:1).
- One of our Lord's garments was woven without seams (John 19:23–24).
- The attire for the marriage supper of the Lamb is fine linen (Rev. 19:8).

These Scriptures demonstrate that for godly men and women, fashion and faith are to complement one another rather than be in conflict!

TRUTH IN LABELING

Labels provide important information. When I shop, I first look at the product's label to determine that I am purchasing what best meets my need. As a consumer purchasing groceries, I expect an item's label to provide accurate information about the nutritional value, serving size, and perhaps even instructions on how to prepare the product so I will get the best results. I also know that the federal government requires accurate labeling on products produced in America. I would be upset if I purchased a mislabeled product only to discover upon opening that the package contained a different product.

Just as I assume that the label on a product is accurate, so God's Word challenges me to dress in such a way that my outward appearance is an accurate label for my character. According to Mark 10:19, failure to do so sends a conflicting message to others. As you contemplate your fashion choices, consider responding to the "Truth in Packaging Inventory."

⌖ TRUTH IN PACKAGING ⌖
INVENTORY

- As a label for your character, what does your clothing communicate about you?
- What values determine the clothing that you wear?
- When you select your clothing, what are your first thoughts?
- When you dress for the day, whom do you want to please?

THE EYE STOPS WHERE THE LINE STOPS

The shape of a garment is created by design lines. The actual shape of the garment has a lot to do with your shape. Lines create the mood of the garment. They are either straight or curved. Straight lines tend to look formal, severe, and businesslike. Curved lines suggest delicacy and softness. They can make a person appear rounder, friendlier, and less formal.

Lines can be used for both structure and decoration in a garment. Structural lines are created by seams and darts—the construction that holds the garment together and creates the fit. A skirt, for example, can be straight, A-line, very full, or very tight. A jacket could have a diagonal line or a zipper down the front. Trim, logos, and insignias that are added to a garment provide decorative lines. Pockets, collars, and lapels create edge lines. Whether you use structural, decorative, or edge lines, the design principle is the same—the eye stops where the line stops. Consider using "The Emotional Effect of Line" chart as you select your garments.

Table 37. 1

❧ THE EMOTIONAL EFFECT OF LINE ❧

Horizontal lines carry the eye across the figure, making it appear shorter and wider.

Downward sweeping lines are sad and can cause the wearer to look tired and depressed.

Vertical lines add apparent height. They make a person look taller and slimmer.

Upswing lines are buoyant and soften an angular structure of face or figure.

Sharp angles add interest, but in excess they are displeasing.

Curved lines are graceful and flattering to the figure. They suggest softness and easiness.

 Sunbursts add height when used on hats. They are slenderizing and graceful in pleated skirts.

 Diagonal lines make a person look either slimmer or heavier, depending on whether the line is more vertical or horizontal.

 V-shaped lines are slenderizing unless they are too wide or flattened out, in which case they broaden the figure.

 Broken lines run perpendicular to one another. Broken lines shorten the length of long, straight lines.

When a woman of any age allows the line to stop at a private part of her body, she may be allowing others to focus on areas that are not meant for their eyes. If you are seeking to glorify the heavenly Father, you will choose only to reveal private body parts to the person you marry.

Wearing slacks is smart for the appropriate occasion. Someone once remarked, however, that pants should look as good "going as coming." Even some secular specialists in etiquette have suggested that since pants are never as conservative as a dress, they may not be the best choice for church where traditionally the most conservative behavior and dress are expected.

Clothing must be pressed and spotlessly clean. Learn to do spot cleaning and check hems. Be sure lingerie straps do not slip. Observe your appearance in a full-length mirror in a well-lighted room, checking back as well as front. You are wiser to be understated rather than overdressed.

MODESTY IS APPLICABLE TO ALL AGES AND BOTH GENDERS

Teaching modesty begins in the crib. Teens are unlikely to dress modestly if they were dressed in skimpy clothing when they were children. If parents dress their children modestly when they are young and set a good example themselves, they are not likely to have modesty become a major issue for their children when they are older.

Given that, according to the Scriptures, faith and fashion do not have to be in conflict, let's focus on some facts that will assist women in making modest clothing choices.

- Your face displays your character. Draw attention to your face by selecting garments that showcase it.

Figure 37.1

Tying a pretty bow at the neck of a blouse involves the same principle as tying a man's bow tie or even your shoelaces. The trick is to move the ties from the top underneath.

1. Cross the two ties, right over left. With your left hand, pull the top (right) tie under and then over the bottom (left) tie.

2. With your left hand reaching under the top tie, pull up the bottom tie to make a loop. Hold it with your thumb and forefinger of your left hand.

3. While holding the loop in your left hand, with your right hand, put the top tie around and then under the loop you're holding in your left hand.

4. Continuing this motion, pass the top tie behind the loop you're holding in your left hand (behind your thumb).

5. Change hands: with your left hand pull the tie that you've started through the back (step 4). With your right hand pull the other loop to the right. Pull both these loops gently through.

- Tight clothing outlines the body and often draws attention to parts that are private. Provide adequate wearing ease in your garments. You should be able to sit, walk, or even bend down comfortably without inappropriate revelations of flesh. Overexposure is not the key to femininity or good fashion, rather it destroys the illusion of mystery. Subtlety is a wonderful tool.

- Tops that expose the waist, hips, or midriff cause the eye to stop at that part of the body. Make sure your choices model the teaching of James 1:13.

- Low necklines cause the eyes to focus on the chest. Select garments that move the eyes to the face.

- Underwear should not become outerwear.

- Slogans, logos, or insignias placed in a private area of the anatomy cause the eye to stop there. Select garments on which slogans, logos, or insignias rest against a neutral part of your body.

- Test your garments for wearability. Do this by positioning yourself in front of a mirror to observe what others see:

    - Bend over to check how revealing your neckline is.
    - Sit down and cross your legs to check the length and circumference of shorts and skirts.
    - Bend over to see how far your skirt or shorts move up.
    - Take a large step to examine skirt slits.
    - Place your hands above your head to see how much of the midriff is exposed.
    - Check what part of your anatomy any writing, logos, or insignias emphasize.

Customs of dress frequently change with the seasons, and fashions are as fickle as the wind. Wise is the woman who directs her energy to ensuring that her fashion and faith always meet and complement one another.

PLANNING A WARDROBE

Being fashionable calls for understanding how to select the clothes most attractive on you and avoid garments that emphasize your figure faults or weaknesses. Enhance your assets and camouflage your weaknesses. A woman can be attractive to men and admired by other women.

- Select a color scheme so you can mix separates to increase your number of outfits.
- Choose items of clothing that fit your lifestyle.

- Be sure your fabric selection is wise (colorfast, nonshrinking, firm and close weave to withstand wear).
- Consider your budget for the best stewardship.
- Develop your personal life message with the help of your wardrobe, conveying the inner image you choose.

PUTTING THE PRINCIPLES INTO PRACTICE

1. Study Deuteronomy 22:5; Proverbs 11:22; 31:21–25; Romans 12:1–2; Philippians 4:8–9; 1 Timothy 2:9–10; 1 Peter 2:21–3:22; and James 1:13. Develop your personal modesty philosophy.
2. Complete the "Truth in Packaging Inventory." How will the results of the inventory influence your future clothing choices? Based on Scripture, establish personal clothing guidelines to help you groom your character so that your outward and inward beauty complement each other.
3. Respond to the following statement, "Precious in the sight of God is the woman who acknowledges that God's brand of modesty is always in style" (see 2 Tim. 1:9; 1 Pet. 3:3–4).
4. Study the life of Sarah, a woman who possessed inner and external beauty, character, and modesty (Gen. 12:11–20; Heb. 11:11; 1 Pet. 3:6). How did this study influence your life?
5. What is your response to this question: "Must fashion and faith be in conflict with one another?" Support your response with Scripture.

Chapter Thirty-Eight

Beautifully Balanced

Beth Mackey

Every morning millions of alarm clocks launch people into a day full of decisions to be made, one of the first being, "What should I wear?" Each of you is your own personal stylist. For some, the choice of what to wear does not begin at the store but with the considerations of fashion, figure type, faith, and how they interact.

Fashion may be defined as current clothing styles dictated by culture. Figure type is the way God made you as described in Job 10:11 and Psalm 139:13–14. These verses speak of God's formation of you in your mother's womb and state that you and I are fearfully and wonderfully made. Faith in Christ introduces the spiritual aspect and how everything in your life interacts with your faith. Christian women must honor God with clothing choices. When all three of these dimensions (fashion, figure, and faith) are in balance, you can make effective choices.

Emily Post, one of the foremost figures in the arena of etiquette—doing the right thing in the right way—made this observation: "The woman who is chic is always a little different. Not different in being behind fashion, but always slightly apart from it." Christian women are not to be "of the world" even though present in the world (John 17:16; cf. 15:19). This principle serves a Christian woman well as she considers the wardrobe for her outer frame. Again consider this balance in how you present yourself.

EFFECTIVE CHOICES

If you consider only one or two of these areas at a time, your clothing choice is out of balance. If fashion is emphasized (i.e., feminine details such as a pretty bow or a particular style of clothing), the inner person loses focus.

> Do not let your adorning be external—the braiding of hair and the putting on of gold jewelry, or the clothing you wear—but let your adorning be the hidden person of the heart with the imperishable beauty of a gentle and quiet spirit, which in God's sight is very precious. (1 Pet. 3:3–4)

Figure 38.1
✑ FASHION, FIGURE, AND ✑ FAITH IN BALANCE

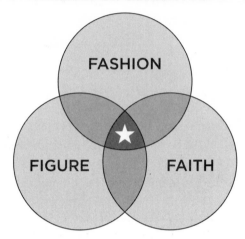

A preoccupation with the external appearance loses sight of portraying "the imperishable beauty of a gentle and quiet spirit." An emphasis on fashion alone could easily lead to choosing extreme styles that may appear more like a costume or be less attractive for the figure. If faith alone is emphasized, the clothing may seem dated, unattractive, poorly fitted, or *frumpy* in an effort not to draw attention to oneself. If the figure is emphasized, clothing could appear to be immodest or in poor taste.

In Ephesians 4:1, Paul talks about walking in a manner that is well-balanced. "I therefore, a prisoner for the Lord, urge you to walk in a manner worthy of the calling to which you have been called." The word *worthy* (Gk. *axiōs*, "bringing into equilibrium" or "equivalent" and thus "suitable" or "proper") has the sense of "balanced," the idea of living your life in harmony with your position in Christ. When fashion, figure, and faith are in balance, you are more likely to be a positive representation of who you are in Christ.

CLOTHING SELECTION

Some women seem to have the natural ability to coordinate clothing well, but for most this fashion package does not come easily. When shopping, women who are novices need to seek help from godly, experienced, and more mature women. Younger women who have a good sense of clothing style, accompanied with a desire to be pleasing to God, should not be overlooked. Understanding the basic principles of line and design will help you develop *good taste* in clothing selection and can be more useful than just relying on fashion advertise-ment or personal preference. Developing your personal style is never without a few bumps in the road. Perhaps you are seeking a measure of classic sophisti-cation instead of a girlish fad. To be tasteful without being seen as stodgy and to find figure-flattering but not revealing garments are worthy goals.

ELEMENTS OF DESIGN

The elements of clothing design include balance, proportion, color and texture of fabric, line, as well as form or shape. The arrangement of these elements comprises the design. There is harmony in a design when all of these elements work together to create an attractive garment.

Balance

Balance is the distribution of the design from a center point. Balance may be symmetrical or asymmetrical. *Symmetrical balance* occurs when a design is divided into two equal parts. One side is the mirror image of the other. A sym-metrical design is considered to have *formal* balance. *Asymmetrical balance* is uneven or *informal* balance, which occurs when a design, divided equally from the center, has parts that are not identical.

Proportion

"Proportion may be defined as the pleasing relationship of areas. Proportion is the design principle concerned with the relation of the size of the parts to the whole and to each other."[1] Fashion lines make visual divisions or parts in a gar-ment. The divisions relate to one another to create *proportion*. If the divisions in a garment are uneven, then it has *pleasing proportion*, which is more interesting than a garment with evenly divided parts. A pleasing proportion can also be seen in the design of a dress that has a definite waistline and the skirt hem at mid-calf. The bodice length of this dress is considered one part, and the skirt length is equal to three lengths of the bodice length. Thus, the ratio is one to three, which is interesting or eye pleasing to the viewer. Another example of visually uninter-esting proportion can be seen in a man's suit. The hem of the suit coat visually divides the body into two equal parts creating uninteresting proportion.

Inverted proportion occurs when the waistline of a garment is lowered. The larger part of the garment proportion is at the top. Examples of this can be seen in a *drop-waist* dress and in a jacket with a lowered hemline. An example of *poor proportion* is the miniskirt. This phenomenon also seems to remove

[1] Mary Kefgen and Phyllis Touchie-Specht, *Individuality in Clothing Selection and Personal Appearance*, 4th ed. (New York: Macmillan, 1981), 302.

something of the feminine mystique by revealing so much that nothing is left to the imagination. Because the style is divided into two equal halves, it is visually considered to be in poor proportion. The proportion is improved when colored hosiery is added to create the total outfit. Then the leg length becomes part of the proportion.

The size of the design on the fabric is also a consideration. The person wearing a garment with fabric design should be in proportion to the size of the design. For example, a tall, heavy person should not wear a very small print.

Color

Color affects proportion in two ways. When several colors are used in an outfit, a line is formed where the colors transition. The eye follows the color but stops at the color change. The principles of the use of line (see "Line" below) should then be considered. Always ask the question, "How does this line complement my figure?"

Texture

The surface texture of the fabric should be in proportion with the size of the body wearing the garment. Thus, a very petite person should not wear a garment with a bulky texture. One example of texture is *pile* (fabric with weaving, tufting, or knitting to provide looped or velvety surface) found in corduroy, velveteen, or velvet. *Pile* that is too heavy on a petite figure is out of proportion with the figure. Other texture considerations are fabric with a *nap* (process that creates fuzziness as fabric is woven with a slack twist), *flocking* (a tuft of wool or cotton fiber often used for stuffing bedding or furniture), or *fur*.

Line

Clothing portrays two kinds of lines: *straight* and *curved*. Straight lines add strength and boldness. They are stiff and without motion, so they generally do not add beauty. The stiffness of straight lines can be broken up by using soft fabrics that take on the shape of the body. A stiff fabric will tend to stand away from the body and hold the straight line. Curved lines add movement and softness. *Restrained-curve* lines are the most beautiful. This is the natural curve you see in the branches of a tree, the shape of mountains, or the curves of the human body. The restrained curve makes a transition from straight lines to *rococo curves* (the small wavy line seen in ruffles).

The goal in dressing is to create a well-proportioned figure. With the use of line, the eyes can be diverted to create the visual illusion of a well-proportioned figure. The phrase "the eye follows the line" means that the eye will travel in the direction of the line until another line tells it to stop or change direction. For example, the eye follows a vertical line until a horizontal line causes the eye to stop, which then shortens the vertical line. The eye then follows the horizontal line.

- *Vertical lines* are very slimming. If two vertical lines are close together, they remain slimming. If they are placed far apart, they divide the body into three separate panels that add width and shorten the figure, such as what is called a *princess line* in a dress. This line is better suited for a younger than a more mature figure. It tends to accentuate weight in the bustline and midriff. The princess line can also emphasize bony hips if a figure is thin.

- The *T line* shortens and widens the figure. The T line can be seen in the obvious waistband of a skirt, wide collar, *bateau neckline* (one that follows the line of the collarbone and is high in front and back), yoke in the bodice of a shirt, and empire waist. The eye moves up the garment until it stops at the waistband, neckline, yoke, or empire waist. The empire waist garment will add height because the longer the eye moves upward before it comes to a horizontal line, the taller the figure appears. However, it will accentuate the bust because the empire line stops just below the bustline.

- The *broken T line* or *arrow line* tends to make the figure appear shorter and adds width. This line can be seen in the seam placement of *raglan sleeves* (these extend to the neckline with slanted seams from the underarm to the neck). In an arrow-shaped midriff section, the broken T line accentuates the bustline as well as making the figure appear shorter and wider.

- The *magic Y line* will add height and is slenderizing. This line can be achieved with vertically placed trims or a deep V-neckline.

Different types of lines affect the look you portray. See Table 38.1 below.

Table 38.1
⌒ MENTAL OR EMOTIONAL ⌒ EFFECT OF LINE

Type of Lines	Direction	Effect
Horizontal	Parallel to the horizon, carrying the eyes across a figure	• Makes figures appear shorter or wider
Vertical	At right angles to the horizon, carrying the eye up and down	• Adds height, slenderness, strength, and stability

Diagonal	At a slant	• Tends to give a feel of motion or restlessness • Closer to vertical means more slenderizing • Tends to widen a figure rather than slenderize if lines are too thick • Too many sharp angles— displeasing to the eye
Curved	Sweeping up or down	• Appears graceful • Upsweeping—creates a dynamic, forceful feeling • Down-sweeping—gives the feeling of sadness and can make the wearer look depressed
Sunburst	Multiple lines extending outward, away from one or more center points	• Graceful and tends to slenderize (e.g., pleated skirt)

Form

The *silhouette* is the most basic line of the dress. A study of the history of costume reveals three primary forms:

- tubular or straight
- bell or curved
- bustle or back fullness

Depending on the use of the garment, all three of the silhouettes are evident in present-day clothing. Wedding dresses are a common place to find examples of bell or bustle silhouettes. A sheath dress is an example of a tubular or straight silhouette. Other lines in a garment can be seen in the construction lines of the seams and darts, decorative lines, and structural lines found in the collars, pockets, or lapels.

Just as garments have *silhouettes*, so do bodies. There are four types of body silhouettes:

- *hourglass*—small waist with a balanced hip and shoulder width
- *triangle*—shoulders narrower in comparison to the hips
- *inverted triangle*—wide shoulders in comparison to the hips
- *rectangular*—shoulders and hips that are balanced in width but with little or no waist indentation

The body silhouette can be determined by measuring the shoulders (across the back from end to end of the shoulder), the waist, and the hips (around the fullest part of the hips) and then comparing these measurements to the description of each type of silhouette. To visualize the silhouette, with a washable marker trace the body outline onto a full-length mirror. The person to be drawn should stand with feet together, arms slightly away from sides, and straight posture. Have another person trace around the outline of the body. Compare the outlined shape with the silhouette descriptions that determine the body silhouette. Once the body's silhouette has been established, the goal is to use line and design principles to disguise or enhance that silhouette to be eye pleasing. Table 38.2 offers guidelines for selecting garments for the slender, ample, tall, and short or petite silhouettes. The "Guidelines for Classic Fashion" and "Tips for Shopping for Clothing" will help you keep your clothing choices beautifully balanced.

Table 38.2

Silhouette Type	Flattering	Unflattering
Slender	Horizontal stripes Gathers and ruffles Layers in contrasting colors Patch pockets Double-breasted coats and jackets Plaids and light colors Scarves	Vertical stripes Sleeveless Large prints and dark colors Deep V-necks One-piece or one-color outfits Clingy fabrics Large accessories
Ample	Vertical lines Flowing fabrics Darker colors or monochromatic color schemes A-line skirts Dresses with defined waist Matching belts Permanent press fabrics to limit wrinkles	Horizontal lines Bulky, stiff fabrics Sharp color contrast Cuffed pants Double-breasted jackets Large ruffles and lace Large prints
Tall	Anything with horizontal stripes Two-piece outfits with contrasting colors Large accessories and patterns Cuffed pants Longer jackets and double-breasted jackets Straight, flared, or pleated skirts Moderate flats	Vertical lines Matching separates Small accessories and small prints Severely tailored clothing Short-waist or bolero jackets (loose, waist-length, open at the front) Short skirts Flat shoes

Short–Petite	Anything with vertical lines	Anything with horizontal lines
	V-necklines	Large accessories
	One-piece dresses	Drop-waist dresses or blouses
	Princess styles and high waist styles	Cuffed pants
	One-color or monochromatic color schemes	Contrasting colors
	Pencil skirts or small flared skirts	Extremes in skirt length
	Short jackets	Large prints

GUIDELINES FOR CLASSIC FASHION

- When you are trying to choose between pants or a skirt/dress, choose the skirt/dress.

  - In this unisex age, this choice sets you apart as distinctively female.
  - A good fit for pants considers the width of your hips, the size of your legs, and how the pants fit your derriere. Finding a skirt is almost always more flattering.
  - Consider the color, the fit, and the ease of the garment's movement.

- For the most finished look, plan your socks to match your pants. If you like to play with color and texture, blend together with care.

- Shoes should be closer in color to your pants or skirt unless you choose to match up with your accessories as an accent.

- Do not fixate on size—try on garments for the size that fits and looks good. If you cannot breathe in it, leave it; if you cannot sit down, try again! If you do not want anyone to know the size, cut the label out after you purchase the garment.

- Never select a garment directly from the hanger. Try it on for size and style. Study yourself in a mirror rather than quickly settling on an attractively displayed garment.

- Do not purchase at half price a garment for which you would not pay full price. Go for quality instead of quantity.

- A slip can add bulk, show folds, and certainly look tacky if it shows. It is needed if fabric is sheer. Foundational garments can help make you slimmer and more trim but should be selected as carefully as outerwear.

- Give attention to your footwear—scuffing, worn heels, and misshapen form are signs of lack of care.

- Invest in a full-length mirror and take a head-to-toe look before you go out the door.

- Keep a mystique about you—dress modestly, leaving something to the imagination.

- Make your imperfections challenges to address and not excuses to overlook.

- Consider the right makeup, appropriate hairstyle, and flattering clothing as a canvas for the outworking of your gentle and quiet spirit, and always include a God-glorifying smile.

- Prune your wardrobe seasonally. Try on the garment to determine fit, discarding if it is not a good fit or uncomfortable. If it needs repair or alteration, make the adjustment or discard it. Update with accessories already on hand or consider purchasing a piece to rejuvenate your outfit for a new and fresh look.

- Rotate your garments, especially undergarments, in a regular pattern.

- Seek to coordinate accessories (purse, shoes, jewelry, scarf, etc.) with clothing for a polished/finished look. Using fewer accessories equals more in a polished and fashionable look.

✑ TIPS FOR SHOPPING ✑ FOR CLOTHING

- Use personal discipline:
  - Shop with a list of what you need.
  - Consider your budget. The safest procedure is to take cash. When it is gone, you are done!
  - Avoid impulse buying. Something you do not need or cannot afford is not a bargain. Genuine bargains offer the best quality at the least cost.
- Look for good quality—often that means buying "brand names," and sometimes that calls for paying a bit more.
- Buy pieces that you can mix and match to give your wardrobe the greatest versatility.
- Pray about what you need and trust God to provide for you (Phil. 4:19).

The most important decision when getting dressed does not occur in the closet but at the mall. Wisdom in portraying the balance God intends for the demonstration of true beauty in his creation is as much applied to clothing selection as to any other area of life.

PUTTING THE PRINCIPLES INTO PRACTICE

1. Study 1 Peter 3:3–4; Job 10:11; Psalm 139:13–14; and Ephesians 4:1. How do you need to adjust your view of clothing selection to be in balance with fashion, figure, and faith?

2. With someone to assist, determine your body's silhouette.

   - Is your body's silhouette a triangle, inverted triangle, rectangle, or an hourglass?
   - Note areas of your silhouette that need to be enhanced or disguised.
   - What lines will be best for you to use to create a well-proportioned figure?
   - Evaluate your existing wardrobe against these principles and consider giving the items that are not good for your silhouette to someone who would benefit from their use.

3. If you are slender, ample, tall (5'9" or above), or short (5'4" or shorter), give special consideration to the guidelines in Table 38.2.

   - Compare the guidelines to your existing wardrobe. Remove any clothing items that do not meet the appropriate recommendations.
   - Make a checklist of these guidelines. Take the checklist with you when shopping to remind you of flattering choices.

4. If you need help making wise clothing choices according to the line and design principles, identify someone who could go shopping with you to help you. Choose someone who shares your view of how fashion, figure, and faith interact. And go shopping!

ABOUT THE AUTHOR

Beth Mackey received her bachelor of science degree in home economics education from Purdue University. She is the oldest of six children and has four children of her own (two girls and two boys) and five grandchildren. Consequently, she has spent over fifty years assisting and managing clothing care in a home. Mrs. Mackey teaches clothing and textiles classes at The Master's College in Santa Clarita, California, where she and her husband, Dr. R. W. Mackey II, reside.

Chapter Thirty-Nine

Merging Quality and Fit to Equal Value

Beth Mackey

Consumers prize *value*, and a major component of value is quality. One expression of quality in a garment is sewing construction. A manufacturer may reduce the cost of producing a garment by lessening the quality of construction. Many people sew their own garments for this very reason: to ensure a well-constructed garment. People who sew garments and understand the construction process should be able to judge the quality of construction in ready-made garments. However, if a seamstress has not been taught proper construction procedures, her sewing knowledge may hinder her when judging clothing according to fit and/or construction. Whether or not you sew, you might be well served by these guidelines, which will help you select well-constructed clothing.

CHARACTERISTICS OF QUALITY CLOTHING CONSTRUCTION

When shopping for clothing, do not be afraid to examine a garment's construction before trying it on. As you are looking over the garment, take note of these areas:

Cut of the Fabric

Lengthwise and crosswise threads are woven together to make fabric. These threads make up the grain of the fabric, in either a lengthwise or a crosswise grain. The fabric is considered *straight of grain* if the threads are perpendicular when they intersect. When garment pieces are cut out of the fabric, the pieces need to be cut so the fabric is *straight of grain*. Fabric will stretch out of shape if it is not cut on grain. This stretching can be readily observed in the hem; as the fabric stretches the hem will sag.

Design of the Fabric

The print or design on the fabric should be going in the proper direction. It should not hang upside down when the garment is on the body. Plaids and horizontal patterns should match at all seams to make a continuous flow of the pattern.

Napped fabric must be cut out so the nap brushes the same direction for the entire garment. For example, the color in corduroy tends to be lighter or darker depending on which way the nap is stroked. If the nap brushes down, it is lighter in color than when brushed up. A color change will be evident when the garment pieces are sewn together if the pieces are not all cut in the same direction.

Buttons and Buttonholes

The buttons should be spaced evenly and sewn on securely with a *thread shank*. The *thread shank* is the thread wrapped around the stitches between the button and the fabric of the garment. The buttonhole will then have room to lie smoothly under the button. Buttonholes should be placed evenly and have enough thread covering the edges of the buttonhole so that the cut fabric does not ravel.

Zippers

Zippers should be centered so the laps are evenly placed over the zipper and do not show any of the zipper's teeth. The laps of the zipper are the folded edges of the fabric that cover the zipper. The stitching around the zipper should be small enough to secure it. The zipper should lie flat without rippling. It should be placed with no more than ¼ inch between the finished edge of the garment and the tip of the zipper. A hook and eye should be placed at the finished edge.

Seams

The seams in the garment should lie flat and be sewn with stitches small enough to hold the seam together. If the seam does not separate when pulled, it is secure. A *chain-stitched* seam is not the best stitch because it can be undone and open very easily. The cut edge of the *seam allowance* should be finished to prevent unraveling. All loose threads should be trimmed.

Seam allowances that are ⅝ inch in width are the most secure seams. If the seam allowances have an *overlock stitch* to finish the edge, the seam allowances may be less than ⅝ inch, but a very secure *straight stitch* should hold the seam together.

Interfacing

Interfacing is a layer of fabric used in collars, cuffs, waistbands, facings, and behind buttons and buttonholes to add body and support. Interfacing can be a woven, nonwoven, or a knit fabric of varying weight or thickness. A quality garment will have an appropriate interfacing weight for the design of the garment and should not be easily detected.

Facing

The *facing* is the fabric extension sewn to a part of the garment to reinforce and finish off the edge of the garment. A facing will be found at the neck edge, at the opening where buttons and buttonholes are placed, or at the back of a waistband, cuff, and collar. Usually facings are made from the same fabric as the garment.

The well-constructed *facing* will be understitched so it does not show from the outside of the garment. *Understitching* is a row of stitching near the stitched seam that catches the *facing* and the seam allowance. This stitching is seen only on the inside of the garment. In addition, the edge that is not sewn to the garment should be finished so it does not unravel.

Lining

The lining should be shorter than the garment at the hem. It should be understitched wherever it is attached to the outer fabric to keep it from rotating to the outside of the garment. In a tailored jacket, the lining should have extra fabric in the back and in the hem. This allows wearing ease with movement of the body and prevents stress on the seams or the hem.

Hems

Ideally the width of a hem allowed in any garment should be generous, although a narrow hem is more favorable for some styles. Garment style and fabric weight will determine the best type and width of the hem. A skirt that is flared is more suited for a narrow hem because it allows the skirt to hang in loose folds. Lightweight fabric in a skirt or dress should have a hem that is two inches wide. A narrow hem is appropriate for a garment made of lightweight knit. The stitching in a hem should not pucker and should be invisible on the outside of the garment.

Cuffs

The optional opening for the cuff is best if it opens toward the back of the sleeve. Two fastening buttons on the cuff are a good choice, allowing adjustment in the tightness of the cuff when buttoned.

Collars

Collars should be equal in length and symmetrical. Understitching prevents the underside of the collar from showing.

Waistband

The waistband on a quality-constructed garment overlaps at least one inch at the zipper. When the waistband is closed around the waist, the top of the zipper will be hidden.

Pockets

Pockets should be reinforced with stitching at the corners or at the openings if they are inserted into side seams. This reinforcement keeps the pocket from pulling on the garment when hands are inserted and removed.

PROPER FIT IN QUALITY CONSTRUCTION

Whether sewing clothes or purchasing them ready-made, good fit is as important as quality construction. A well-constructed garment is the foundation to proper fit. Consider the "Fabulous Fit Guidelines" when evaluating the fit of a garment.

Wrinkles Indicate Improper Fit

Wrinkles in a garment indicate an improper fit. Learn to "read" the wrinkles. Many times an alteration will correct an improper fit.

- Diagonal wrinkles indicate the length or width of the garment is not appropriate (usually too little fabric) for the body area that is just *above* the wrinkles.
- Horizontal wrinkles usually mean that the garment is smaller than the body at that area.
- Horizontal or diagonal wrinkles, which appear more as loose folds, signal that the garment is longer or wider than the body at that area of the fold.
- Vertical wrinkles indicate an incorrect length: The garment is too short for the body.

Fit of a Tailored Jacket

Because a tailored jacket is usually a major wardrobe expense, its proper fit is important.

- The upper back should lie smooth.
- The shoulder-sleeve seam should be smooth with no puckers. The shoulder-sleeve seam should be set right at the end of the shoulder unless the style dictates otherwise.
- The sleeve should allow for ease in movement.
- The hem of the sleeve should come just past the wristbone.
- The jacket, when buttoned, should not show any sign of pulling on the button across the front.

✒ FABULOUS FIT GUIDELINES ✒

- The garment allows for movement and is comfortable. Always sit, bend, and walk in the garment to ensure comfort.

- Hemlines are parallel to the floor.

- Side seams are straight, perpendicular to the floor.

- The collar fits comfortably when buttoned at the neck.

- A scoop neck hugs the chest so when the wearer moves or bends over, there is no gap.

- *Armscye* (pronounced *ahrm-sahy*, the armhole opening in a garment) seams that come just before the end of the shoulder require a little fullness at the cap of the sleeve to allow room for the upper arm muscle. Puckers or tucks should be absent.

- Sleeves have ample girth across the forearm. Long sleeves need room for bending arms.

- A garment with fitted waist should come to the natural waistline, not above or below, or it will be uncomfortable.

- Bust darts point to the end of the bust, not above or below. The underarm bust dart should end 1½ to 2 inches from the bust point. The waist dart should end about ½ inch from the bust point.

- Darts should point to the area of greatest fullness when large body curves are present.

- Pockets should remain closed when the garment is on the body. If they do not lie closed, then the garment is too small.

- Princess styles cannot be altered if the bust does not sit in the curved area allowed, because the fullness for the bust is cut into the fabric.

- Accessories should stay in place when moving; otherwise, the wearer will be constantly adjusting them.

Proper Fit of Men's Suits

The fit of men's clothing will follow the fit of a tailored garment. In most department stores, the salesperson is trained to advise on the fit, but it is always wise to know what to look for to ensure a good choice. When contemplating a purchase, consider the following details:

- Jackets should hang straight from the shoulders. They should not show any indication of bulges from the body or any wrinkles from poor sizing.
- Armholes of the sleeves should be large enough to allow for movement.
- Collars should be smooth and also fit snug at the neck.
- Shirt collars should show ½ inch above the suit collar.

- Lapels should not gap but rather lie flat across the chest.
- Sleeve lengths should be long enough to show ½ inch of the cuffs of dress shirts.
- When the jackets are buttoned, they should not show signs of pulling on the buttons.
- Vents or pleats do not hang open but lie closed when the jackets are buttoned.
- Jackets should be long enough for the height of the wearer. Sizes come in tall, regular, and short. Jackets should cover the seat of the slacks.
- The creases of slacks should be straight on grain and contain adequate fullness.

The Proverbs 31 woman sewed garments of quality for her family (vv. 13, 22). Whether the garments are sewn or purchased, women are encouraged to be diligent in providing quality garments for themselves and their families.

PUTTING THE PRINCIPLES INTO PRACTICE

1. Identify fitting problems you typically have with your clothing:

   - Can these fitting problems be altered?
   - Can you do the alterations yourself?
   - Can you hire someone to do the alterations? If so, what is the cost? Consider any alteration in the overall cost of the garment.

2. Go shopping for the sole purpose of examining ready-made garments against the quality qualifications presented in this chapter.
3. If you make your own clothing, compare what you have sewn with the guidelines for fitting presented in this chapter.

   - Identify areas of garment construction and fitting that need improvement.
   - Set goals of how you can improve in these areas. For example, find someone to teach you proper construction techniques or enroll in a reputable sewing class.

4. Review Proverbs 31:13, 21–22. In what ways do these verses encourage you to improve the selection and care of your family's clothing?
5. Find someone to go shopping with you. Another opinion can be very helpful in evaluating the garment's fit. Enjoy fellowship in the shopping trip.

Chapter Forty

Will It Come Out in the Wash?

Beth Mackey

Clothing care is far more than just throwing soiled laundry into the washer and dryer. Proper clothing care includes: laundering, dry cleaning, ironing, storage of seasonal items, mending, and accessory care. Clothing is an investment. If you launder and care for your clothing properly, your garments will stay looking their best for as long as you need them.

WHY WOULD A CHRISTIAN CARE ABOUT CLOTHING CARE?

According to Genesis 1, God has given the man and woman he created and their descendants dominion over all the earth (Gen. 1:26–28). We, as his creation, are to use and to develop the earth's material goods to sustain ourselves. Our basic needs are food, clothing, and shelter—material goods that need to be maintained. When properly washing and mending clothing, you are taking care of material goods so the clothing, in turn, can serve you and in this process allow you and your family to pursue God-given functions.

Proverbs 20:4 says, "The sluggard does not plow in the autumn; he will seek at harvest and have nothing." The sluggard, who did not plow at the proper time, did not have any harvest. Consider this verse in relation to clothing care. If you are lazy and do not routinely take proper care of your clothing, it will not serve your needs at the proper time. You are called to faithful, intelligent care.

The woman in Proverbs 31 cares for the needs of her household: "She looks well to the ways of her household and does not eat the bread of idleness" (v. 27). This woman is industrious and diligently meets her family's needs. God provides clothing for you (Matt. 6:28–30). You should not desire to be lazy but should care properly for what God has given you. God gives; you and I serve as stewards and maintain.

LAUNDRY BASICS: BEFORE YOU WASH

This is the way we wash our clothes, wash our clothes, wash our clothes,
This is the way we wash our clothes, so early Monday morning.

Get to know your washer and dryer. If the instruction booklet is available (in paper or online), read it. These instructions will help you use the machines to your best advantage. In a sense, the washer and dryer are your helpers. If you understand how they work best, you can give them their respective jobs and know the work will be done well. What our great-grandmothers did by hand, we now do by automation—the washer and dryer can be working while you accomplish other tasks.

There are two types of washing machines, top-loading and front-loading. A top-loading washer has an agitator to move the clothes through the wash water. Front-loading washers rely on the clothes to tumble against each other causing the agitation. There are benefits to both. Researching how each works is helpful when choosing a washer that best suits your needs.

ESTABLISH A LAUNDRY CYCLE

Household and clothing items retain their usefulness when the following schedule is followed:

- Wash sheets weekly unless a person is sick, then more often.
- Blankets should be washed seasonally.
- Change bath towels at least twice a week and hand towels daily.
- Kitchen towels should be changed daily. Attempt to build your supply of towels so that the soiled towels can be laundered weekly.
- Wash shirts, pants, and shorts after each wearing or the second wearing if perspiration or other stains are not present.
- Launder briefs, undershirts, and socks after each wearing; bras after the second wearing unless there are perspiration odors or stains.
- Wash baby laundry after each wearing.

Sorting

Keep a dirty-clothes hamper available to all family members in a convenient location. Usually, this is in a bedroom or a bathroom. The goal is for family members to put dirty clothes in the hamper or to hang clothes that could be worn again before laundering.

Clothing Preparation

Some simple habits can present disastrous results. When my children were small, I liked wearing an apron with pockets as I did my cleaning. When I found small things that were out of place, I put them into a pocket. Like most young families, we were on a tight budget, but we had just been able to buy my husband a nice sport shirt. I decided that my apron could be washed in the load with the shirt, but I forgot to check the apron's pockets, in which a black crayon lurked. The crayon melted onto some of the items in that load, but in keeping with Murphy's Law, most of the melted crayon was on the shirt. To prevent such catastrophes, prepare clothes to be washed:

- Turn knits inside out to prevent snagging.

- Check pockets for items. Tissues can make a large cloud of lint. Lipstick, pen, or crayon could ruin the entire wash load.

- Zip the zippers to prevent stress on the zipper mechanism.

- Snap the snaps, button the buttons, and hook the bra straps to keep them from being pulled during the wash load or catching on other items.

- Sort clothes into three groups by color: whites, colors, and darks. Not everything should be laundered in the same way even in these different piles but will vary according to the type of fabric used to make the garment.

- Wash darker items and lighter items separately. Laundering them together may cause the light items to turn dingy over time.

- Read the *care label* on clothing items. (By federal law all clothing items are required to have a care label on the inside of the garment.)

- Some clothing items need cold water wash, some hot water, and some need to be hand washed.

- Drying temperatures vary as well.

Managing the Color Groups

- *Whites* must be washed separately and in the hottest water the fabric can tolerate (120°F is most efficient at removing soil and dirt). In the whites pile, separate any items that need to be and can be bleached. If no bleaching is necessary, whites and very light pastels can be washed together if they are able to withstand the same water and drying temperature.

- *Colors*—Make sure all of the items in the colors pile can be washed in the same way (according to the care labels). Red (consider dark pinks as red also) items may bleed onto lighter colored items. Make sure reds are washed separately. You do not want to find out, as have many young male college students, that the red sweatshirt may turn the white garments pink when washed together. Even an item with red trim can bleed onto other clothes or run into the other parts of the clothing item. Wash these items separately for a while, at least until they do not bleed any longer. Corduroy should be washed inside out to keep the pile (the fuzzy part of the fabric in corduroy) from matting. Wash in as cool a temperature as possible. Using a cold-water cycle (60–80°F) will help preserve original colors and prevent bleeding of darker colors onto lighter ones.

- *Darks*—Make sure all of the items in the *darks* pile can be washed in the same way (according to the care labels). Wash jeans inside out to keep them from fading. Wash all dark clothing in as cool a temperature as possible.

Stain Removal Pretreatment

The next step before washing is treating any stains. Perspiration and body-oil marks should be pretreated with liquid detergent, dishwashing liquid, or shampoo (colorless, of course). An old toothbrush or complexion or nail brush is helpful in rubbing liquid into fabric and dislodging stains. Treating a stain as soon as it occurs is best. The longer a stain remains in a garment, the more difficult to remove. Pretreat the stain before putting the garment in a hamper. Use a spray-on pretreatment (Shout, RESOLVE, or Mary Ellen's Stain Remover—Formula 1 for whites or Formula 2 for colors).[1] This method works well on polyester fibers with oil-based stains such as cooking oils and animal fats. Detergent can be poured directly onto the stain, working just as well as a pretreatment spray. Pretreat the stain from the wrong side of the stain. Blot the spot with a paper towel or a cloth. Do not rub the spot as it will push the stain more deeply into the fibers. Another way to absorb the ingredient making the spot is to blot or push the spot from the back of the fabric on to an absorbent towel. This pulls the spot from the fibers. If the detergent is powder, make a paste with the powder and water and work it into the stain as you would with the liquid.

Types of Stains

For easy reference, post a copy of Table 40.1, "Stain Removal Guide for Common Stains," in the laundry area. Many laundry products come with pamphlets; articles appear in magazines or websites; laundry products also offer these guidelines. Whenever a stain is treated and then laundered, check to see if it is completely gone before putting the item in the dryer. If necessary, air-dry the item if you cannot tell whether or not the stain is gone. You may need to re-treat or even treat and rewash the clothing before the stain is completely removed.

---

[1] See http://www.maryellenproducts.com/home.php. Soilove is recommended by Mary Hunt and available online or in stores in western states.

Table 40.1
⤳ STAIN REMOVAL GUIDE ⤳
for Common Stains

Stain	Treatment
Baby food Baby formula Cheese sauce Egg Gelatin Ice cream Milk Pudding	These protein stains can be removed by soaking and agitating the item in cold water before washing, thereby rinsing out the stain. Do not wash this type of stain in hot water, which will cook the protein into the fibers of the fabric. Wash with detergent. If a protein stain is old, use an enzyme presoak with the detergent.
Alcoholic beverages Berries Coffee Fruit juice Soft drinks Tea Tomato juice	These are *tannin* stains. *Tannin* is an astringent (it leaves the dry taste in your mouth after you consume the food item). Use detergent and water as warm as the garment will endure. The complete removal of old tannin stains requires chlorine or oxygen bleach that is safe for the fabric. Do not use soaps as they can make the stain more permanent.
Bacon fat Butter Cooking oils Margarine Mayonnaise Salad dressing	For oil-based stains, use a pretreatment spray, then a heavy-duty detergent with hot water. If no pretreatment spray is available, work a runny paste of powdered detergent mixed with water into the fabric. Do not dry the garment in the dryer until the stain is removed. Dryer heat will set the stain. Treatment may need to be repeated.
Chocolate Collar and cuff soil Cosmetics Grass Mustard Lipstick	Pretreat with liquid detergent with enzymes by pouring the detergent into the stain and working it into the fabric. Soak in the detergent with warm water. If mustard does not come out, use a chlorine or oxygen bleach safe for the fabric and the hottest water safe for the fabric.
Blood	Rinse in cold water. Rub with bar soap such as *Ivory* until removed.
Unknown stains	Start treatment by using the least destructive stain removal method for the fabric. An example of this would be applying RESOLVE with OxiClean added to the detergent before laundering.

Candle wax	Using ice cubes, harden the wax. Then scrape off excess with a dull knife. Any wax left in the fibers can be lessened by laying the wax side on paper towels and pressing with a warm iron on the back side of the stain. Proceed with a heavy-duty detergent wash. Colored candles may leave a dye stain that will also need to be treated. As a rule, using white or off-white candles will eliminate problems with dye stain.
Gum Rubber cement Adhesive tape	Use ice cubes to harden the item; then once it is hardened, scrape it off with a dull knife or a fingernail. If this procedure is unsuccessful, a product called Goo Gone, which removes adhesives, can be used, following the directions on the bottle.
Water-soluble paint	Water-soluble paint (usually *tempera*) should come out with washing. It is best to rinse the paint out before it dries. Red tempera paint is more difficult to remove. Chlorine bleach may be necessary.

WASHING

The children's song may say, "This is the way we wash our clothes," but for modern homemakers, exactly what does that mean? Three items are typically used: laundry products, aids, and fabric softeners.

Types of Laundry Products

- *Detergents* are suitable for all types of clothing, from lightly to heavily soiled items. Use a light-duty detergent (such as *Ivory* or *Dreft*) on baby clothes. Pretreat a stain by pouring the detergent on the stain and working it into the soiled area. If the detergent is granular, lightly dampen the area and work the granules into the stain (or make a paste with the granules as described in Table 40.1).

- Detergents contain *enzymes*. They basically "eat" the dirt off the laundry similar to the way stomach enzymes digest food. The enzymes work best in warm water as with body temperature and the stomach. Hot water does not make enzymes work any better and could actually *set in* stains. Using warm rather than hot water will also conserve energy. Detergents actually condition the water. In a sense, they make the water "wetter" and surround the soiling agent, keeping it from redepositing on the fabric until the soil is rinsed away.

- *Soap*, consisting of fats and *alkali* (sodium or potassium hydroxide), has been used for centuries. Soap leaves a *curd*, a sticky yellow residue that deposits in the washer and on fabrics when used in hard water. Because of this reaction, soap is not usually a popular choice.

Types of Laundry Aids

- *Chlorine bleach* in liquid form is widely used. Bleach aids in soil removal, acts as a disinfectant, and whitens fabrics. Directions normally appear on the packaging for the correct amounts to use in the wash load. Diluting bleach in water and then pouring the mixture into the washer after it has begun to agitate is best. If the bleach is added directly to a load of clothes before agitation, it will sit on the fabric and cause color fading or weaken the fabric. Chlorine bleach can be used on cotton and washable synthetics. The use of chlorine bleach on linen can cause the fabric to yellow.

- *Oxygen bleach*, also known as *all-fabric bleach* or *color-safe bleach*, comes in dry and liquid forms. Add it to the agitating water before the clothes are added so it has a chance to dissolve. Check for colorfastness on clothing items before using it in the wash load.

- *Baking soda* may be added to a wash load to help deodorize the clothes. It will also aid in conditioning the water. For a full load, use one cup of baking soda in the wash cycle, not the rinse.

Popular Examples of Brand Names of Laundry Products and Aids

- Heavy-duty detergents: Tide, Wisk, Era, Fab, Cheer, Oxydol
- Light-duty detergents: Woolite, Ivory, Delicare, Dreft
- Liquid chlorine bleach: Clorox, Purex
- Liquid and powdered all-fabric bleaches: Clorox 2, Snowy, Biz, Borateem
- Pretreatment spray and aerosol: RESOLVE, Shout, Soilove, Mary Ellen's Stain Removers, Clorox
- Detergent booster: OxiClean

Most detergents are similar. Some detergents come with an additive or booster included (such as Tide with Bleach). Using a product that is detergent only and then adding a detergent additive (bleach, nonchlorine bleach or booster) as needed allows for more control in the wash cycle and is usually less expensive.

Once stains have been pretreated, the clothes are ready to be laundered according to the sorted loads. Be careful not to overload the washer. Mixing large items with small items into various loads keeps the weight of the wet clothes from putting too much strain on the washing machine.

Fabric Softeners

The best fabric softeners are liquid and are added to the rinse cycle. Use the softener dispenser in the washing machine with equal parts of water to help dilute the softener, thus helping to eliminate fabric softener spots on the clothes. This is not necessarily a problem with front-loading washers since they normally do not have room in the dispensers for adding water to the liquid softener. If a liquid softener is not available, dryer sheets may be added to the dryer to help soften the clothing and to remove static cling.

Fabric softening sheets, if used at all, are designed for synthetic fabrics. They should not be used with towels, including dish towels, sheets, diapers, or cotton underwear. The waxy coating reduces a fabric's absorbency. In fact, if used often, any fabric can acquire a greasy or waxy feel.[2]

Drying Clothes

When machine drying, follow the care labels on the clothes to prevent fabric from shrinking or stretching. Some items that have been washed together should not be dried together. Separate items and dry according to their individual care labels.

If an item should be drip-dried, hang it on a clothesline or over a drying rack. A clothesline can be set up in a laundry area or even with a retractable spool in a small outside area. When line drying jeans, hang them from the bottom of the pant legs, allowing the weight of the waist and pockets to eliminate wrinkles. Hanging dark items to line dry, out of direct sunlight, helps maintain color and freshness.

Do not overload the dryer, which will extend drying time and may cause clothes to be more wrinkled. Remove clothes promptly after drying or even when slightly damp to minimize shrinkage. Avoid overdrying. If clothes are left in the dryer, run a short cycle with a damp towel to help eliminate the wrinkles.

If possible, set the dryer load out on a large work surface to fold and to organize. Realistically, for a large family, folding the clothes right away may not work. However, clothes will be less wrinkled if they are loosely laid out on a large surface rather than stuffed in a laundry basket waiting to be folded. The dryer is empty for the next load to be dried, and the folding can be done as time permits. Cleaning out the dryer filter after each load allows the dryer to work efficiently, reduces time required to dry the load, and prevents the possibility of fire.

Dry Cleaning

Dry cleaning uses a quick-drying chemical solvent instead of water. Moisture and steam are then used to reduce wrinkles. If using a home process, remove the garment from the dry cleaning bag immediately and allow the garment to

---

[2] Cheryl Mendelson, *Home Comforts: The Art and Science of Keeping House* (New York: Scribner, 1999), 331.

air out. A good dry cleaning service will do minor repairs like reinforcing loose buttons or hems. Professional dry cleaning is best for fragile fabrics and the most valuable garments.

Home dry cleaning kits (Dryel, Woolite) provide an inexpensive substitute for professional dry cleaning and can be useful for deodorizing and removing light stains. Read the directions carefully before using this product. When my daughter was in high school, she had purchased a nice wool sweater that required dry cleaning. Using the home dry cleaning product as instructed, she placed the sweater and the sheet with the cleaner on it in the bag provided in the kit. However, I had neglected to tell her to put it into the dryer and not the washing machine. After running it through a wash cycle, she removed it from the washing machine and all we heard was, "Oh, no! Oh, no!" The sweater had shrunk to fit a small child.

Some clothing items can be hand washed or washed in a delicate cycle even though the tag says to dry-clean. These items are made of cotton, rayon, cotton/rayon, or silk. Try this only on items that are not expensive. Delicate wash with mild detergent in cold water often works. Line dry these items. Laundered in this manner, they will require extra pressing.

Hand Washables and Delicates

Launder hand washables in cold water with a mild detergent or a special product such as Woolite. A soap flake such as *Ivory* or a mild dish detergent may also be used. Wool sweaters can be hand washed in a sudsy soap. Woolite is great for this. Soak the sweater for ten to fifteen minutes, then gently squeeze the soapy water through the sweater. Rinse the same way. Place the sweater in the fold of a large bath towel and blot. Gently squeeze out the water. Be careful to lift it all at once without any part of it hanging. This will prevent the sweater from stretching. Dry the sweater on a flat surface, reshape, and air-dry.

IRONING AND PRESSING

Ironing or pressing clothes, even if the items are considered permanent press, gives a finished look that makes a good impression. Read the instruction book that accompanies the iron. Some irons require distilled water. Others may require filtered water. Use the setting that matches the fabric content of the garment. Silk and synthetics need low heat, wool requires medium heat, and high heat is used for cotton and linen. The fabric content is listed on the inside label of the garment.

When ironing a garment, do the small areas first, then the larger areas.

This will keep you from rewrinkling the portion of the garment already ironed. For example, to iron a shirt or blouse, start with the collar and cuffs. Iron the front placket (where the buttons and buttonholes are located), then the body of the shirt last.

Keep a can of spray starch and a spray bottle of water in the work area. To achieve a crisp-looking garment, spray starch works well. On shirts and blouses, even a small amount of spray starch helps the collars to stand up nicely. Use the spray bottle of water to dampen a garment made of cotton or linen. Even if the iron is on the steam setting, the extra spray aids in wrinkle removal.

When removing clothes from the dryer, hang up items that are normally hung even if they need to be ironed. This will help remove some wrinkles. Hang them in a place that will be a "to-be-ironed" reminder.

STORING GARMENTS

Wire hangers will distort the shape of the shoulders in a garment. Use a thick or padded hanger. The heavy plastic hangers help to preserve garment shape as well as keep garments from bunching up in the closet. Knit items should be folded and stored on shelves, in a box, or in drawers since hanging knits will cause them to lose their shape.

Formal wear should be stored in breathable garment bags. Expensive garments that are worn more often should have a cover that hangs just over the shoulders to keep off the dust. Place a clothes brush or a lint roller in the closet for convenience.

Wool items should be stored (when they are out of season) in garment bags. Clean them before storing. This extra care will preserve the garment and protect it from moths. Other off-season garments should be grouped in a closet so that clothing for the present season is easily accessible.

MENDING

"A stitch in time saves nine" is a phrase that reminds you to mend a tear when first noticed. If a garment with an unrepaired tear is laundered, the tear will fray or expand, making it more difficult to repair. As part of the laundry routine, sew on or replace any loose or missing buttons. More than likely, the garment hung in the closet minus a button will not be worn. Also, watch for seams that are coming apart or hems that are loosening. If clothing is repaired after wearing, the garment's care will be simpler and its life possibly increased.

ACCESSORY CARE

Accessories are items that can "set off" an outfit or detract from it. Caring for clothing accessories such as shoes, hats, scarves, and coats, is critical to wardrobe maintenance.

Shoes

- Leather shoes should be polished periodically. Having a shoe brush or cloth in the closet to brush off dust before putting them away keeps them looking nice.
- Tennis shoes can be washed and then dried even in the dryer, although you may need ear plugs because of the loud thumping accompanying the process.
- Allow dress shoes or shoes worn occasionally to be aired out before storing them in a box. Never place socks in shoes after taking shoes off.

Baseball Hats

Baseball hats can be washed in the washing machine if they are inserted into a form that helps hats hold their shape. Wash them in a gentle cycle or hand wash. Air dry the hats after stretching them over the hat form.

Scarves

- Note the fiber content of the scarf when it is purchased. If it is silk, washing it by hand is possible, but pressing it will take extra care. It may also be dry-cleaned. Polyester scarves may be laundered by washing them in the washing machine on a delicate cycle. They should not require pressing.
- Wool scarves normally require professional dry cleaning. A home dry cleaning process may work nicely for these.

Coats

- Dry-clean wool coats before storing at the conclusion of the wearing season.
- Washable coats should be laundered when they are no longer needed for the season.

PUTTING THE PRINCIPLES INTO PRACTICE

1. How can your laundry area be improved to help you work more efficiently?

   - Do you have appropriate laundry products?
   - Are stain treatment supplies available?
   - Make a copy of stain treatment procedures to have in your laundry room.

- Read through your washer and dryer instruction booklet and leave it in a convenient place for easy reference.
- Install a clothesline for line drying or purchase a collapsible clothes drying rack.

2. Take some time to plan and purchase hampers for dirty clothes, putting them in appropriate places for each family member. There are many choices, including decorative and thematic hampers, for a bedroom or bathroom.
3. Plan extra time on your next visit to the grocery store to read labels on laundry products and see what is available for your needs. If you have Internet access, visit the websites listed at the end of the chapter to glean additional information.

✑ REMINDERS ✑

- Compare prices of a brand name with an off-brand detergent, which may clean just as well.
- Look for coupons on detergent websites.
- Become familiar with any at-home stain remedies.

4. Why does the proper care of clothing please God?
5. Visit the following websites for additional laundry tips:

- The website for Tide: Tide.com
- The website for the Soap and Detergent Association: Cleaning101.com

Appendix

Perceptions of Homemaking Study

METHOD OF DATA COLLECTION

The survey instrument used in this study sought to identify the twenty-first-century woman's knowledge of the facts regarding and her ability to perform successfully the life skills commonly associated with the management of the home. Four demographic questions, twenty-seven Likert-type (scaled) questions, and three open-ended questions comprised the survey instrument. The Likert-type (scaled) questions requested that respondents select the number best representing their knowledge of the facts regarding or their ability to perform the skill being measured. The 1–4 scale was arranged in ascending order with one being strongly disagree and four being strongly agree.

The survey was distributed in electronic and paper format. Distribution was international. The posting of the survey instrument on TrueWoman.com and GirlsGoneWise.com accelerated the data collection base. Approximately 50 percent of the respondents were derived from the visitors to these international websites.

Data collection commenced in June 2009. Analysis of the data began in October 2009. SurveyMonkey.com was used to collect the majority of the responses. Paper copies were manually posted into SurveyMonkey.com to allow for consistency in the data analysis.

The demographic and scaled questions were tabulated by SurveyMonkey.com. The open-ended questions were collected by SurveyMonkey.com and interpreted manually. Surveys answered in part or whole numbered 2,256. Respondents skipped some questions in 242 of these; 2,014 completed surveys were analyzed and are reported in this analysis.

SURVEY RESULTS

The data collected from the 2,256 individuals who began the survey follows.

Age of Respondents

15–24	N=254
25–34	N=557
35–44	N=506
45–54	N=539
55–64	N=289
65–74	N=96
75–84	N=14
85–90	N=1
Total	N=__2,256__

Gender of Respondents

Male	N=77
Female	N=2,179
Total	N=__2,256__

Continent of Origin (Birth) of Respondents

Asia	N=53
Europe	N=64
South America	N=28
Africa	N=16
South Pacific	N=26
North America	N=2,069
Total	N=__2,256__

Response to the Question,
"Do You Consider Yourself a Christian?"

Yes	N=2,232
No	N=24
Total	N=__2,256__

LIKERT-TYPE (SCALED) STATEMENT RESPONSES

The data collected from the 2,014 individuals who completed the entire survey follows.

	Strongly Disagree 1	Disagree 2	Agree 3	Strongly Agree 4
1. I understand God's design for the home.	The mean score (average) of 3.64 suggests that the respondents understand God's design for the home.			
2. Establishing a godly home is a command for all believers, regardless of their age, marital status, or occupation.	The mean score (average) of 3.77 suggests that the respondents believe establishing a godly home is a command for all believers, regardless of their ages, marital status, or occupations.			
3. I am able to use my energy effectively.	The mean score (average) of 3.00 suggests that the respondents are able to use their energy effectively.			
4. I am able to establish realistic goals for the care of my home.	The mean score (average) of 3.03 suggests that the respondents are able to establish realistic goals for the care of their homes.			
5. I am able to use money effectively.	The mean score (average) of 3.07 suggests that the respondents are able to use money effectively.			
6. I am able to use my time effectively.	The mean score (average) of 2.86 suggests that the respondents are not able to use their time effectively.			
7. The pattern for homemaking outlined in the Bible is relevant for the 21st century.	The mean score (average) of 3.69 suggests that the respondents believe the pattern for homemaking outlined in the Bible is relevant for the 21st century.			
8. The plan for marriage outlined in the Bible is relevant for the 21st century.	The mean score (average) of 3.82 suggests that the respondents believe the plan for marriage outlined in the Bible is relevant for the 21st century.			
9. The Bible offers relevant parenting advice for the 21st century.	The mean score (average) of 3.82 suggests that the respondents believe the Bible offers relevant parenting advice for the 21st century.			

10. I know the characteristics of the stages of child development.	The mean score (average) of 3.08 suggests that the respondents know the characteristics of the stages of child development.
11. I am aware of the impact of culture on the 21st century Christian family.	The mean score (average) of 3.54 suggests that the respondents are aware of the impact of culture on the 21st-century Christian family.
12. I am capable of setting up a household in the United States.	The mean score (average) of 3.52 suggests that the respondents are capable of setting up a household in the United States.
13. I am capable of setting up a household in a foreign culture.	The mean score (average) of 2.76 suggests that the respondents are not capable of setting up a household in a foreign culture.
14. I have established standard routines for managing a household.	The mean score (average) of 3.10 suggests that the respondents have established standard routines for managing a household.
15. I am capable of making wise consumer decisions.	The mean score (average) of 3.30 suggests that the respondents are capable of making wise consumer decisions.
16. I know how to use technology to increase the quality of my home life.	The mean score (average) of 3.16 suggests that the respondents know how to use technology to increase the quality of their home life.
17. I could establish a home-based business.	The mean score (average) of 2.43 suggests that the respondents could not establish a home-based business.
18. I am aware of the principles of food sanitation.	The mean score (average) of 3.41 suggests that the respondents are aware of the principles of food sanitation.
19. I am able to apply basic nutritional knowledge to my food choices.	The mean score (average) of 3.48 suggests that the respondents are able to apply basic nutritional knowledge to their food choices.
20. I can plan a well-balanced meal.	The mean score (average) of 3.38 suggests that the respondents can plan a well-balanced meal.
21. I can prepare a well-balanced meal without the use of commercially prepared products.	The mean score (average) of 3.38 suggests that the respondents can prepare a well-balanced meal without the use of commercially prepared products.

22. I practice biblical hospitality.	The mean score (average) of 3.12 suggests that the respondents practice biblical hospitality.
23. I can identify basic textiles.	The mean score (average) of 2.97 suggests that the respondents cannot identify basic textiles.
24. God cares about my clothing selections.	The mean score (average) of 3.57 suggests that the respondents believe God cares about their clothing selections.
25. I can perform basic sewing skills (sew on a button, replace a hem, etc.).	The mean score (average) of 3.27 suggests that the respondents can perform basic sewing skills (sew on a button, replace a hem, etc.).
26. I can sew a basic garment.	The mean score (average) of 2.74 suggests that the respondents cannot sew a basic garment.
27. I know basic stain removal procedures.	The mean score (average) of 3.23 suggests that the respondents know basic stain removal procedures.

The cumulative responses (each respondent was able to list three reasons) to the statement, "Feminism has impacted the twenty-first-century **culture** in the following ways" numbered 3,281. These responses revealed the following implications:

1. Feminism has impacted the twenty-first-century culture in the following ways:

a. Moms/women working outside the home
b. Demeaning of the model of biblical womanhood
c. Breakdown of the family
d. Weakened/devalued men
e. Increase in abortion

The cumulative responses (each respondent was able to list three reasons) to the statement "Feminism has impacted the twenty-first-century **evangelical community** in the following ways" totaled 2,696. These responses revealed the following general effects:

2. Feminism has impacted the twenty-first-century evangelical community in the following ways:

a. Women pastors/leaders
b. Lack of biblical submission

  c. Women working outside the home
  d. Lack of understanding of biblical gender roles
  e. Weakened family/increased divorce rate

The cumulative responses (each respondent was able to list four skills) to the statement, "The homemaking skills many Christian women lack are" numbered 4,105. These responses revealed the following general effects:

3. The homemaking skills many Christian women lack are:

  a. Cooking
  b. Sewing
  c. Organization
  d. Time management
  e. Hospitality
  f. Cleaning

If you would like to add your perceptions to the study, you may access the survey at http://www.surveymonkey.com/s/6NKMVCH.

General Index

Page numbers in boldface refer to charts, figures, and tables.

Scripture Index

For additional resources and updates,
visit www.BiblicalWoman.org.